Windows 8.1 Administration: Storage, Security, & Networking

Pocket Consultant

William R. Stanek
Author and Series Editor

PUBLISHED BY
Microsoft Press
A Division of Microsoft Corporation
One Microsoft Way
Redmond, Washington 98052-6399

Library of Congress Control Number: 2013955480
ISBN: 978-0-7356-8261-0

Printed and bound in the United States of America.

Second Printing: April 2014

Microsoft Press books are available through booksellers and distributors world-wide. If you need support related to this book, email Microsoft Press Book Support at mspinput@microsoft.com. Please tell us what you think of this book at http://www.microsoft.com/learning/booksurvey.

Acquisitions Editor: Anne Hamilton
Developmental Editor: Karen Szall
Editorial Production: Online Training Solutions, Inc. (OTSI)
Project Editor: Rosemary Caperton
Technical Reviewer: Rozanne Whalen; Technical Review services provided by Content Master, a member of CM Group, Ltd.
Copyeditor: Denise Bankaitis (OTSI)
Indexer: Krista Wall (OTSI)
Cover: Best & Company Design

Contents

What do you think of this book? We want to hear from you!

Microsoft is interested in hearing your feedback so we can continually improve our
books and learning resources for you. To participate in a brief online survey, please visit:

microsoft.com/learning/booksurvey

What do you think of this book? We want to hear from you!

Microsoft is interested in hearing your feedback so we can continually improve our
books and learning resources for you. To participate in a brief online survey, please visit:

microsoft.com/learning/booksurvey

Acknowledgments

To my readers—thank you for being there with me through many books and many years. It has been an honor and a privilege to be your pocket consultant.

To my wife—for many years, through many books, many millions of words, and many thousands of pages she's been there, providing support and encouragement and making every place we've lived a home.

To my kids—for helping me see the world in new ways, for having exceptional patience and boundless love, and for making every day an adventure.

To Anne, Karen, Martin, Lucinda, Juliana, and many others who've helped out in ways both large and small.

Special thanks to my son Will for not only installing and managing my extensive dev lab for all my books since *Windows 8 Administration Pocket Consultant* but for also performing check reads of all those books.

—WILLIAM R. STANEK

Introduction

Windows 8.1 Administration Pocket Consultant: Storage, Security, & Networking is designed to be a concise and compulsively usable resource for Windows administrators, developers, and programmers, and for anyone else who wants to use the storage, security, and networking features of Windows 8.1. This is the readable resource guide that you'll want on your desk or in your pocket at all times. The book discusses everything you need to perform core tasks. Because the focus is on providing you with the maximum value in a pocket-sized guide, you don't have to wade through hundreds of pages of extraneous information to find what you're looking for. Instead, you'll find exactly what you need to get the job done.

In short, the book is designed to be the one resource you consult whenever you have questions regarding storage, security, and networking in Windows 8.1. To this end, the book concentrates on configuration options, frequently used tasks, documented examples, and options that are representative but not necessarily inclusive. One of the goals is to keep the content so concise that the book remains compact and easy to navigate while ensuring that the book is packed with as much information as possible—making it a valuable resource.

Anyone transitioning to Windows 8.1 from Windows 8 might be surprised at just how much has been updated, because changes both subtle and substantial have been made throughout the operating system. For anyone transitioning from Windows 7 or earlier, the extensive user interface (UI) changes will be among the most substantial revisions to the operating system. Like Windows 8, Windows 8.1 supports a touch UI, in addition to the traditional mouse and keyboard. When you are working with touch-enabled computers, you can manipulate on-screen elements in ways that weren't possible previously. You can do any of the following:

- **Tap** Tap an item by touching it with your finger. A tap or double-tap of elements on the screen generally is the equivalent of a mouse click or double-click.

- **Press and hold** Press your finger down and leave it there for a few seconds. Pressing and holding elements on the screen generally is the equivalent of a right-click.

- **Swipe to select** Slide an item a short distance in the opposite direction compared to how the page scrolls. This selects the item and might also bring up related commands. If press and hold doesn't display commands and options for an item, try using swipe to select instead.

- **Swipe from edge (slide in from edge)** Starting from the edge of the screen, swipe or slide in. Sliding in from the right edge displays the charms. Sliding in from the left edge shows open apps and allows you to switch between them easily. Sliding in from the top or bottom edge shows commands for the active element.

- **Pinch**   Touch an item with two or more fingers, and then move the fingers toward each other. Pinching zooms out.
- **Stretch**   Touch an item with two or more fingers, and then move the fingers away from each other. Stretching zooms in.

You also are able to enter text by using the on-screen keyboard. Although the UI changes are substantial, they aren't the most significant changes to the operating system. The most significant changes are below the surface, affecting the underlying architecture and providing many new features. Some of these features are revolutionary in that they forever change the way we use Windows.

Who is this book for?

The focus of *Windows 8.1 Administration Pocket Consultant: Storage, Security, & Networking* is on the Standard, Professional, and Enterprise editions of Windows 8.1. The book is designed for the following readers:

- Accomplished users who are looking to configure and maintain Windows 8.1
- Current Windows system administrators and support staff
- Administrators upgrading to Windows 8.1 from earlier releases of Windows
- Administrators transferring from other platforms

To pack in as much information as possible, I had to assume that you have basic networking skills and a basic understanding of Windows operating systems. As a result, I don't devote entire chapters to understanding Windows basics, Windows architecture, or Windows networks. I do, however, cover firmware management, boot configuration data, Trusted Platform Module (TPM), BitLocker Drive Encryption, Storage Spaces, Work Folders, and much more. The book also goes into depth on troubleshooting, and I've tried to ensure that each chapter, where appropriate, has troubleshooting guidelines and discussions to accompany the main text. From the start, troubleshooting advice is integrated into the book, instead of being captured in a single, catchall troubleshooting chapter inserted as an afterthought. I hope that after you read these chapters and dig into the details, you'll be able to improve the overall experience of your users and reduce problems.

How is this book organized?

Rome wasn't built in a day, nor was this book intended to be read in a day, in a week, or even in a month. Ideally, you'll read this book at your own pace, a little each day as you work your way through. This book is organized into 10 chapters. The chapters are arranged in a logical order, taking you from boot configuration and startup to drive encryption, storage configuration, data access, and networking optimization.

Ease of reference is an essential part of this hands-on guide. This book has an expanded table of contents and an extensive index for finding answers to problems quickly. Many other quick-reference features have also been added to the book, including quick step-by-step procedures, lists, tables with fast facts, and extensive cross references.

Although designed and written to stand on its own, this book can also be used with *Windows 8.1 Administration Pocket Consultant: Essentials & Configuration* by William R. Stanek (Microsoft Press, 2013). The latter book focuses on deployment, installation, configuration, optimization, maintenance, and much more.

Conventions used in this book

I've used a variety of elements to help keep the text clear and easy to follow. You'll find code listings in monospace type, except when I tell you to actually enter a command. In that case, the command appears in **bold** type, as does any text that the user is supposed to enter. When I introduce and define a new term, I put it in *italics*.

Other conventions include the following:

- **Best Practices** To examine the best technique to use when working with advanced configuration and maintenance concepts
- **Caution** To warn you about potential problems
- **Important** To highlight important concepts and issues
- **More Info** To provide more information on a subject
- **Note** To provide additional details on a particular point that needs emphasis
- **Real World** To provide real-world advice when discussing advanced topics
- **Security Alert** To point out important security issues
- **Tip** To offer helpful hints or additional information

I truly hope you find that *Windows 8.1 Administration Pocket Consultant: Storage, Security, & Networking* provides everything that you need to perform the essential tasks on Windows 8.1 systems as quickly and efficiently as possible. You are welcome to send your thoughts to me at *williamstanek@aol.com*. Thank you.

Other resources

No single magic bullet for learning everything you'll ever need to know about Windows 8.1 exists. Even though some books are offered as all-in-one guides, there's just no way one book can do it all. With this in mind, I hope you use this book as it is intended to be used—as a concise and easy-to-use resource. It covers everything you need to perform essential storage, networking, and security tasks, but it is by no means exhaustive.

Your current knowledge will largely determine your success with this or any other Windows resource or book. As you encounter new topics, take the time to practice what you've learned and read about. Seek out further information as necessary to get the practical hands-on know-how and knowledge you need.

For topics this book doesn't cover, you might want to look to *Windows 8.1 Administration Pocket Consultant: Essentials & Configuration*. I also recommend that you regularly visit the Microsoft website for Windows (*microsoft.com/windows/*) and *support.microsoft.com* to stay current with the latest changes. To help you get the most out of this book, you can visit my corresponding website at *pocket-consultant. com*. This site contains information about Windows 8.1 and updates to the book.

Errata and book support

We've made every effort to ensure the accuracy of this book and its companion content. Any errors that have been reported since this book was published are listed at:

http://aka.ms/Win81APC_SSN/errata

If you find an error that is not already listed, you can report it to us through the same page.

If you need additional support, email Microsoft Press Book Support at:

mspinput@microsoft.com

Please note that product support for Microsoft software is not offered through the addresses above.

We want to hear from you

At Microsoft Press, your satisfaction is our top priority, and your feedback is our most valuable asset. Please tell us what you think of this book at:

http://aka.ms/tellpress

The survey is short, and we read every one of your comments and ideas. Thanks in advance for your input!

Stay in touch

Let's keep the conversation going! We're on Twitter: *http://twitter.com/MicrosoftPress*.

CHAPTER 1

Managing firmware, boot configuration, and startup

A s surprising as it might seem, when a computer fails to start or experiences a Stop error that crashes the operating system, the most basic element involved in starting a computer and loading an operating system—the firmware—is often overlooked as a possible cause. This happens because most people dig in and begin troubleshooting Windows without looking at the firmware. The trouble with this approach is that many computer problems originate in firmware, either because the firmware itself is flawed or because the firmware has been improperly configured. To distinguish between problems in firmware and problems in the operating system, you need to understand how the startup process works and what occurs during each of its phases. You also need to understand firmware itself. Primed with a solid understanding of these subjects, you'll be better prepared to diagnose and resolve related problems.

Navigating and understanding firmware options

The startup process involves firmware, firmware interfaces, and an operating system. During startup, firmware is the first code that runs. Firmware performs basic initialization of the computer and provides the services that enable a computer to start loading an operating system.

Platform firmware is implemented in motherboards and chipsets. All computers —whether tablets, desktops, or laptops—have motherboard chipsets, and there are many different types. Although older motherboard chipsets might not be up-datable, most newer ones have updatable firmware. Chipset firmware is separate and different from the computer's underlying firmware interface.

Windows for the ARM processor architecture, also called Windows On ARM (or WOA), is designed with platform firmware that is also implemented in a motherboard chipset. With WOA, though, the board is a series of silicon layers packaged together in a very small form factor called a System on a Chip (SoC). At the time of this writing, there are two variants of Windows On ARM: Windows RT, which was originally designed for tablets, and Windows Phone operating system, which was originally designed for smartphones. Though Windows RT has nearly the same UI as Windows 8.1, the Windows Phone operating system has a UI that has substantial differences from Windows 8.1.

> **NOTE** WOA presents a special case for firmware, boot configuration, and startup. Although I've tried to integrate some WOA discussion into this chapter, not everything I discuss in this chapter will apply to WOA. Further, it is important to point out that I refer to WOA throughout this chapter rather than discussing either Windows RT or Windows Phone operating system specifically. In the future, Windows Phone operating system might be merged into Windows RT (or a new variant might be created by merging aspects of both).

Firmware interface types and boot data

Every computer has firmware, yet it's the interface between that firmware and the operating system that handles the startup process. The way a firmware interface works and the tasks it performs depend on the type of firmware interface. Currently, the prevalent firmware interfaces are:

- Basic input/output system (BIOS)
- Extensible Firmware Interface (EFI)
- Unified Extensible Firmware Interface (UEFI)

A computer's BIOS, EFI, or UEFI provides the hardware-level interface between hardware components and software. Like chipsets themselves, BIOS, EFI, and UEFI can be updated. Most technical documentation refers to a computer's firmware interface simply as *firmware*. For example, documentation might specify to make "such and such a change in firmware" or to "check firmware." Technically, you make the change in the firmware interface, and the firmware interface makes the change in firmware.

UEFI is both a type of firmware interface and an industry standard. UEFI, as a firmware interface, is modular and does not necessarily serve the same purpose or provide the same functionality as BIOS or EFI. UEFI, as a standard, is designed to provide extensible and testable interfaces. For WOA, UEFI is the lowest layer of the system and, as with other chip architectures, UEFI provides the services necessary to load the operating system. WOA also supports Trusted Platform Module (TPM) for trusted boot and hardware-based drive encryption.

It's also important to understand that BIOS, EFI, and UEFI work in distinctly different ways. BIOS is based on x86, 16-bit, real-mode architecture and was originally designed to get a computer started after the computer was powered on. This is why BIOS performs firmware-to-operating-system interfacing and platform initialization.

Regardless of the firmware interface type, Windows 8.1 uses a pre–operating system boot environment. The boot environment is an extensible abstraction layer that makes it possible for the operating system to work with multiple types of firmware interfaces without requiring the operating system to be specifically written to work with these firmware interfaces. Within the boot environment, startup is controlled by using the parameters in the Boot Configuration Data (BCD) store.

All computers running current Windows operating systems have a BCD store. The BCD store is contained in a file called the BCD registry. The location of this registry depends on the computer's firmware, as follows:

- On BIOS-based operating systems, the BCD registry file is stored in the \Boot\Bcd directory of the active partition.
- On EFI-based operating systems, the BCD registry file is stored on the EFI system partition.

Entries in the BCD store identify the boot manager to use during startup and the specific boot applications available. The default boot manager is Windows Boot Manager. Windows Boot Manager controls the boot experience and enables you to choose which boot application is to run. Boot applications load a specific operating system or operating system version. For example, the boot application for Windows 8.1 is the Windows Boot Loader, which enables you to boot BIOS-based and EFI-based computers in much the same way.

Typically, you can press F8 or F12 during startup of the operating system to access the Advanced Boot Options menu, and then use this menu to select one of several advanced startup modes, including Safe Mode, Enable Boot Logging, and Disable Driver Signature Enforcement. These advanced modes temporarily modify the way the operating system starts to help you diagnose and resolve problems; however, they don't make permanent changes to the boot configuration or to the BCD store.

Boot services, run-time services, and beyond

BIOS manages the preboot data flow between the operating system and attached devices, such as the video adapter, keyboard, mouse, and hard drive. When BIOS initializes a computer, it first determines whether all attached devices are available and functioning, and then it begins to load the operating system.

Over the years, these basic features of BIOS were expanded to encompass the following:

- **Boot services**   Refers to the collection of interfaces and protocols that are present in the boot environment. The services at a minimum provide an operating system loader with access to platform capabilities required to complete the operating system boot. These services are also available to drivers and applications that need access to platform capabilities. Boot services are terminated after the operating system takes control of the computer.
- **Run-time services**   Refers to the interfaces that provide access to underlying platform-specific hardware, such as timers, that might be useful during operating system run time. These services are available during the boot process but also persist after the operating system loader terminates boot services.

- **Advanced Configuration and Power Interface (ACPI)**   Refers to a table-based interface to the system board that enables the operating system to implement operating system–directed power management and system configuration.

- **Services for system management BIOS (SMBIOS)**   Refers to a table-based interface that is required by the Wired for Management Baseline (WMB) specification and used to relate platform-specific management information to the operating system or to an operating system–based management agent.

Generally, computers with BIOS use hard drives that have master boot record (MBR) partitions. To break free of the 16-bit roots of BIOS, Intel developed EFI as a firmware implementation for its 64-bit Itanium-based processors. EFI is based on x64, 64-bit, real-mode architecture. As with BIOS, EFI performs firmware-to-operating-system interfacing, platform initialization, and other functions. With the introduction of EFI, Intel also provided a new table architecture for hard drives, called the GUID partition table (GPT).

MBR is now considered a legacy partitioning scheme, with GPT as the preferred partitioning scheme. A legacy MBR is located at the first logical block on a disk that is not using the GPT disk layout. The first 512 bytes on an MBR disk have the following layout:

- The MBR begins with a 424-byte boot code, which is used to select an MBR partition record and load the first logical block of that partition. The boot code on the MBR is not executed by UEFI.

- The boot code is followed by a 4-byte unique MBR disk signature, which can be used by the operating system to identify the disk and distinguish the disk from other disks on the system. The unique signature is written by the operating system and not used by UEFI.

- A 2-byte separator follows the disk signature. At byte offset 446, there is an array of four MBR partition records, with each record being 16 bytes in length. Block 510 contains 0x55 and block 511 contains 0xAA. Block 512 is reserved.

The four partition records each define the first and last logical blocks that a particular partition uses on a disk:

- Each 16-byte MBR partition record begins with a 1-byte boot indicator. For example, a value of 0x80 identifies a bootable legacy partition. Any other value indicates that this is not a bootable legacy partition. This value is not used by UEFI.

- The boot indicator is followed by a 3-byte address identifying the start of the partition. At byte offset 4, there's a 1-byte value that indicates the operating system type, which is followed by a 3-byte value that identifies the end of the partition. These values are not used by UEFI.

- At byte offset 8, there's a 4-byte value indicating the first logical block of the partition, and this is followed by a 4-byte value indicating the size of the partition in units of logical blocks. Both of these values are used by UEFI.

NOTE If an MBR partition has an operating system type value of 0xEF, firmware must add the UEFI system partition GUID to the handle for the MBR partition. This enables boot applications, operating system loaders, drivers, and other lower-level tools to locate the UEFI system partition, which must physically reside on the disk.

A protective MBR may be located at the first logical block on a disk that is using the GPT disk layout. The protective MBR precedes the GUID Partition Table header and is used to maintain compatibility with tools that do not understand GPT partition structures. The purpose of the protective MBR is to protect the GPT partitions from boot applications, operating system loaders, drivers, and other lower-level tools that don't understand the GPT partitioning scheme. The protective MBR does this by defining a fake partition covering the entire disk. When a disk has a protective MBR, the first 512 bytes on the disk have the following layout:

- The protective MBR begins with a 424-byte boot code, which is not executed by UEFI.
- The boot code is followed by a 4-byte disk signature, which is set to zero and not used by UEFI.
- A 2-byte separator follows the disk signature. This separator is set to zero and not used by UEFI.
- At byte offset 446, there is an array of four MBR partition records, with each record being 16 bytes in length. Only the first partition record—the protective partition record—is used. The other partition records are set to zero.
- Block 510 contains 0x55, and block 511 contains 0xAA. Block 512 is reserved.

The protective partition record reserves the entire space on the disk after the first 512 bytes for the GPT disk layout. The protective partition record begins with a 1-byte boot indicator that is set to 0x00, which indicates a non-bootable partition. The boot indicator is followed by a 3-byte address identifying the start of the partition at 0x000200, which is the first usable block on the disk.

At byte offset 4, there's a 1-byte value set to 0xEE to indicate the operating system type as GPT Protective. This is followed by a 3-byte value that identifies the last usable block on the disk, which is the end of the partition (or 0xFFFFFF if it is not possible to represent this value).

At byte offset 8, there is a 4-byte value set to 0x00000001, which identifies the logical block address of the GPT partition header. This is followed by a 4-byte value indicating size of the disk minus one block (or 0xFFFFFFFF if the size of the disk is too large to be represented).

UEFI

As Intel began developing EFI, Intel developers and others around the world began to recognize the need to break the tie between firmware and processor architecture. This led to the development of UEFI. The UEFI 2.4 specification was finalized in April 2013. The UEFI specifications define a model for the interface between operating systems and platform firmware. The interface consists of data tables that contain platform-related information, in addition to boot and run-time service calls that are available to the operating system and its loader. The interface is independent of the processor architecture. Because UEFI abstracts the processor architecture, UEFI works with computers that have x86, x64, ARM, or an alternative architecture. As with EFI, computers with UEFI generally use hard drives that have GPT partitions. However, UEFI doesn't replace all the functionality in either BIOS or EFI and can, in fact, be wrapped around BIOS or EFI.

REAL WORLD UEFI 2.4 is an incremental enhancement of UEFI 2.31, which was released in April 2011. UEFI 2.4 adds support for NIC iSCSI and FCoE boot capabilities and current boot mode. UEFI 2.4 also has improvements to prevent conflicts with Secure Boot and enables hashes of certificates to be used for revocation and timestamp support. Secure boot and other advanced security features are discussed in Chapter 2, "Using TPM and BitLocker Drive Encryption."

In UEFI, the system abstraction layer (SAL) is the firmware that abstracts platform implementation differences and provides the basic interface to all higher-level software. UEFI defines boot services and run-time services.

UEFI boot services include:

- Event, timer, and task priority services that create, wait for, signal, check, and close events; set timers; and raise or restore the priority of tasks.

- Memory allocation services that allocate or free memory pages, get memory maps, and allocate or free pooled memory.

- Driver model boot services that handle protocol interfaces for devices, open and close protocol streams, and connect or disconnect from controllers.

- Image services that load, start, and unload images.

- Miscellaneous services that set watchdog timers, copy and set memory, install configuration tables, and perform cyclic redundancy checking (CRC) calculations.

UEFI run-time services include:

- Variable services that get, set, and query variables.

- Time services that get and set time and get and set wakeup time.

- Virtual memory services that set virtual address mapping and convert memory pointers.

- Miscellaneous services that reset the computer, return counters, and pass information to the firmware.

UEFI defines architecture-independent models for EFI-loaded images, device paths, device drivers, driver signing, and secure boot. It also defines the following:

- Console support, which enables simple text and graphics output.

- Human Interface Infrastructure support, which describes the basic mechanisms for managing user input and provides definitions for related protocols, functions, and type definitions that can help abstract user input.

- Media support, which enables I/O access to file systems, files, and media devices.
- Peripheral Component Interconnect (PCI), small computer system interface (SCSI), and Internet small computer system interface (iSCSI) bus support, which enables I/O access across a PCI, SCSI, or iSCSI bus, in addition to SCSI or iSCSI boot.
- USB support, which enables I/O access over USB host controllers, USB buses, and USB devices.
- Compression support, which provides algorithms for compressing and decompressing data.
- ACPI table support, which enables installation or removal of an ACPI table.
- EFI byte code virtual machine support, which enables loading and executing EFI device drivers.
- Network protocol support, which defines the Simple Network Protocol (SNP), Preboot Execution Environment (PXE), and Boot Integrity Services (BIS) protocols. SNP provides a packet-level interface to network adapters. PXE is used for network access and network booting. BIS is used to check the digital signature of a data block against a digital certificate for the purpose of checking integrity and authorization. PXE uses BIS to check downloaded network boot images before executing them.
- Managed network protocol support, which defines the Managed Network Service Binding Protocol (MNSBP) and the Managed Network Protocol (MNP). These services enable multiple event-driven drivers and applications to access and use network interfaces simultaneously. MNSBP is used to locate communication devices that are supported by an MNP drive and manage instances of protocol drivers. MNP is used by drivers and applications to perform raw asynchronous network-packet I/O.
- Network addressing protocol support, which defines the following protocols: Address Resolution Protocol Service Binding Protocol (ARPSBP), Address Resolution Protocol (ARP), DHCPv4, DHCPv4 service binding, DHCPv6, and DHCPv6 service binding.
- Miscellaneous network protocol support, which defines the following protocols: virtual LAN configuration, EAP and EAP management, TCPv4, TCPv4 service binding, TCPv6, TCPv6 service binding, IPv4, IPv4 service binding and configuration, IPv6, IPv6 service binding and configuration, IPSec and IPSec2 configuration, FTPv4, FTPv4 service binding, UDPv4, UDPv4 service binding, UDPv6, UDPv6 service binding, Multicast TFTPv4, and Multicast TFTPv6.

NOTE With WOA, ACPI is used for plug and play enumeration of devices (such as touch controllers, displays, and so on) during boot and for power management of devices outside of the SoC. Otherwise, there is no device tree or ability to discover what is connected to a SoC or determine how the SoC is connected.

To be clear, UEFI is not designed to replace either BIOS or EFI. Although UEFI uses a different interface for boot services and run-time services, some platform firmware must perform the functions that BIOS and EFI need for system configuration and setup because UEFI does not do this. For this reason, UEFI is often implemented on top of traditional BIOS and EFI, in which case UEFI takes the place of the initialization entry points into BIOS or EFI.

Navigating startup and power states

When a computer is first started, the firmware interface activates all the hardware required by the computer to initialize and load the operating system, including:

- Motherboard chipsets
- Processors and processor caches
- System memory
- Graphics and audio controllers
- Internal drives
- Internal expansion cards

After the firmware interface completes this process, it transfers control of the computer to the operating system. The firmware interface implementation determines what happens next:

- With BIOS-based computers running current Windows operating systems, Windows Boot Manager and Windows Boot Loader are used to boot into the operating system. Windows Boot Manager initializes the operating system by starting the Windows Boot Loader, which in turn starts the operating system by using information in the BCD store. Through the BCD parameters, you can add options that control the way the operating system starts, the way computer components are used, and the way operating system features are used.

- With Itanium-based computers, Ia64ldr.efi, Diskpart.efi, and Nvrboot.efi are used to boot into the operating system. Ia64ldr.efi handles the task of loading the operating system, whereas Diskpart.efi identifies the boot partitions. Through Nvrboot.efi, you set the parameters that enable startup.

- With other EFI-based computers, Bootmgfw.efi manages the boot process and passes control to the Windows Boot Loader. Through Bcdedit.exe, you set the parameters that enable startup.

- With UEFI, UEFI boot services provide an abstraction layer. Currently, this abstraction layer is wrapped around BIOS or EFI. A computer with BIOS in its underlying architecture uses a BIOS-based approach to booting into the operating system. A computer with EFI in its underlying architecture uses an EFI-based approach to booting into the operating system.

- With WOA, UEFI boot services provide an abstraction layer. Windows Boot Manager initializes the operating system by starting the Windows Boot Loader, which in turn starts the operating system by using information in the BCD store. Information needed to configure the device is stored in tables.

Working with firmware interfaces

When you power on most computers, you can access the firmware interface by pressing the key designated for Setup in the initial display. For example, you might press F2 or Delete during the first few seconds of startup to enter the firmware interface. Firmware interfaces have control options that make it possible for you to adjust the functionality of hardware. You can use these controls to do the following:

- Adjust LCD brightness (on laptop computers).
- Adjust the hard drive noise level.
- Adjust the number of cores the processor is using and their speed.
- Change the boot sequence.
- Change the complementary metal oxide semiconductor (CMOS) date and time.
- Restore the firmware interface to the default configuration.
- Turn on or off modular add-on devices.

Firmware interfaces have the ability to report basic configuration details, including information about the following:

- AC adapter capacity (on laptop computers)
- Battery charge and health (on laptop computers)
- LCD type and native resolution (on laptop computers)
- Firmware version
- Memory
- Processors
- Storage devices
- Video chipsets

Most firmware interfaces allow you to create supervisor, user, and/or general passwords that are not accessible from the operating system. If a supervisor password is set, you need to provide the password before you can modify the firmware configuration. If a user password is set, you need to enter the password during startup before the computer will load the operating system. If you forget these passwords, you might not be able to operate the computer or change firmware settings until you clear the forgotten passwords, which generally also clears any customization you have made to the firmware interface.

A firmware interface update can often resolve problems or add features to the computer's firmware interface. If you are not experiencing problems on a computer and are not aware of any additional features in the firmware interface that are needed, you might not need to update a computer to the latest version of the firmware interface. An additional cautionary note is that if a firmware interface update is not performed properly, it can harm the computer and prevent it from starting.

Examining firmware interfaces

The information and configuration options available in the firmware interface depend on the computer with which you are working, the type of firmware interface, and the version of the firmware interface. Most desktop computers have more configuration options than do laptop computers.

As configured on my laptop computer, the firmware interface provides several menu pages offering information and controls, including Main, Advanced, Security, and Boot. The Main page provides basic information about the computer's configuration, including:

- System time and date.
- System memory size.
- Extended memory size.
- Memory speed, such as 1,333 MHz.
- CPU type, such as Intel Core i5-2430.
- CPU speed, such as 2.40 GHz.
- CPU cache levels for L1 cache, L2 cache, and L3 cache.
- Hard drive type and model, such as WDC WD5000BPVT-75HXZ 500 GB.
- Optical disk type and model, such as PLDS DVD +/- RW DU 8A-(S1) ATAPI.
- System BIOS version, such as A02.
- AC adapter type, such as 65 W.
- Serial tag number.
- Asset tag number.
- Product name.

On the Main page, you can set the system date and time by using the options provided. The Advanced page provides additional configuration information and enables you to manage important settings. On the Advanced page, you can view or set the following:

- Intel Multiple Monitor status as Enabled or Disabled. When this setting is enabled, the computer's integrated graphic card and add-in graphic card might be able to work together in the operating system. When it is disabled, only one graphic card (either the integrated card or a plug-in card) can be used in the operating system.
- Intel SpeedStep status as Enabled or Disabled. When this setting is enabled, the CPU can operate in multiple performance states. When it is disabled, the computer is prevented from adjusting the processor's performance.
- Intel Virtualization status as Enabled or Disabled. When this setting is enabled, a virtual machine monitor can use hardware virtualization capabilities.
- Intel Turbo Boost status as Enabled or Disabled. When this setting is enabled, processor cores can run faster than the base operating frequency if they're operating below temperature, current, and power limits.

- USB PowerShare status as Enabled or Disabled. When this setting is enabled, users can use the USB PowerShare port to charge external devices by using the stored system battery power even if the computer is turned off.
- USB Emulation status as Enabled or Disabled. When this setting is enabled, firmware can handle USB devices during the POST process (which occurs before the operating system starts).
- USB Wake Support status as Enabled or Disabled. When this setting is enabled, USB devices can wake the computer.

The Security page enables you to view and set supervisor, user, and hard drive passwords. The status information tells you the current state for each password, such as:

- Supervisor Password Is: Clear
- User Password Is: Clear
- Hard Disk Password Status: Clear

The following additional configuration options enable you to manage passwords:

- **Set Supervisor Password**   Controls access to the firmware interface
- **Set User Password**   Controls access to the computer
- **Set Hard Disk Password**   Controls access to the computer's hard drive

To set a password, select the option, and then press Enter. When prompted, type the new password, and then type the new password again to confirm it. Press Enter to continue.

On the Boot page, the Boot Priority Order enables you to view and manage the priority order for boot devices. A sample boot priority order listing from a Dell desktop computer is as follows:

1. Hard drive
2. USB hard drive
3. CD/DVD
4. USB CD/DVD
5. USB Floppy
6. Network

When you power on the computer, the computer tries to boot using the device listed first. If that fails, the computer tries the second device, and so on. You can use the Up Arrow and Down Arrow keys to select a device, and then use the plus sign (+) or the hyphen (-) to move the device up or down in the list.

The Exit page enables you to exit the firmware interface and resume startup of the computer. As with most firmware interfaces, you have a few options:

- **Exit Saving Changes**   Exits the firmware interface and saves your changes
- **Exit Discarding Changes**   Exits the firmware interface and discards your changes
- **Discard Changes**   Discards your changes without exiting the firmware interface
- **Save Changes**   Saves your changes without exiting the firmware interface

Regardless of the menu page with which you are working, you have a set of options that are standard in most firmware interfaces:

- Press F1 to get help.
- Press the Up Arrow or Down Arrow key to select an item.
- Press Enter to select the current option on a submenu.
- Press the Left Arrow or Right Arrow key to select a menu page.
- Press + or - to change values.
- Press F9 to apply setup defaults (you must confirm when prompted).
- Press Esc to exit (and then select an option to save or discard changes).
- Press Enter to apply or execute a command.
- Press F10 to save changes and exit the firmware interface. (When prompted to confirm, Yes is selected. Press Enter to save changes and exit. Press the spacebar to select No, and then press Enter to remain in the firmware interface.)

As you can tell, the configuration options here aren't very extensive. In contrast, desktop computers can have a dizzying array of options and suboptions. When you are working with a desktop computer, you'll likely find options that serve similar purposes. However, because few standards and conventions exist among firmware interface manufacturers, the options might have different labels and values.

Power states and power management

To better understand the hardware aspects related to boot issues, let's dig in and take a look at ACPI. A computer's motherboard chipset, firmware, and operating system must support ACPI for the related advanced power state features to work. ACPI-aware components track the power state of the computer. An ACPI-aware operating system can generate a request that the system be switched into a different ACPI mode, and the firmware interface responds by enabling the requested ACPI mode.

As shown in Table 1-1, there are six different power states, ranging from S0 (the system is completely on and fully operational) to S5 (the system is completely off). The states S1, S2, S3, and S4 are referred to as sleep states, in which the system appears off because of low power consumption but retains enough of the hardware context to return to the working state without a system reboot.

Motherboard chipsets support specific power states. For example, one motherboard might support the S0, S1, S4, and S5 states but not the S2 and S3 states. In Windows operating systems, the sleep power transition refers to switching off the system to a sleep or a hibernate mode, and the wake power transition refers to switching on the system from a sleep or a hibernate mode. The sleep and hibernate modes enable users to switch systems off and on much faster than the regular shutdown and startup processes.

Thus, a computer is waking up when the computer is transitioning from the Off state (S5) or any sleep state (S1–S4) to the On state (S0). The computer is turning off (going to sleep) when the computer is transitioning from the On state (S0) to the Off state (S5) or one of the sleep states (S1–S4). A computer cannot enter one sleep state directly from another; it must enter the On state before entering a different sleep state.

TABLE 1-1 Power states for ACPI in firmware and hardware

STATE	TYPE	DESCRIPTION
S0	On state	The system is completely operational, fully powered, and completely retains the context (such as the volatile registers, memory caches, and RAM).
S1	Sleep state	The system consumes less power than the S0 state. All hardware and processor contexts are maintained.
S2	Sleep state	The system consumes less power than the S1 state. The processor loses power, and processor context and contents of the cache are lost.
S3	Sleep state	The system consumes less power than the S2 state. Processor and hardware contexts, cache contents, and chipset context are lost. The system memory is retained.
S4	Hibernate state	The system consumes the least power compared to all other sleep states. The system is almost at the Off state. The context data is written to the hard drive, and no context is retained. The system can restart from the context data stored on the disk.
S5	Off state	The system is in a shutdown state and retains no context. The system requires a full reboot to start.

When you are working with firmware, you can go to the Advanced/Power Management screen or a similar screen to manage ACPI and related settings. Power settings you might find include the following:

- **Restore AC Power Loss or AC Recovery**   Determines the mode of operation if a power loss occurs, for which you'll get settings such as Stay Off, Last State, and Power On. Stay Off (or Power Off) means the system will remain off after power is restored. Last State restores the system to the state it was in before power failed. Power On means the system will turn on after power is restored.

- **Wake On LAN From S4/S5 or Auto Power On**   Determines the action taken when the system power is off and a PCI Power Management wake event occurs. You'll notice settings like Power On or Power Off. You might also notice Enabled or Disabled.

- **ACPI Suspend State or Suspend Mode**   Sets the suspend mode. Typically, you're able to set S1 state or S3 state as the suspend mode.

NOTE In this list, I provide two standard labels for each setting because your computer hardware might not have these exact labels. The firmware variant with which you are working determines the actual labels that are associated with boot, power, and other settings.

Because Intel and AMD also have other technologies to help reduce startup and resume times, you might also find power settings, such as these for Intel:

- Enhanced Intel SpeedStep Technology (EIST), which can be either disabled or enabled
- Intel Quick Resume Technology Driver (QRTD), which can be either disabled or enabled

EIST (also known as SpeedStep) enables the system to dynamically adjust processor voltage and core frequency, which can result in decreased average power consumption and decreased average heat production. When EIST or a similar technology is enabled and in use, you'll find two different processor speeds on the System page in Control Panel. The first speed listed is the specified speed of the processor. The second speed is the current operating speed, which should be less than the first speed. If EIST is off, both processor speeds will be equal. Advanced Settings for Processor Power Management under Power Options can also affect how this technology works. Generally speaking, you should not use this technology with Windows 8.1 (although you might want to use this technology with Windows Vista).

QRTD makes it possible for an Intel Viiv technology-based computer to behave like a consumer electronic device, with instant on/off after an initial boot. Intel QRTD manages this behavior through the Quick Resume mode function of the Intel Viiv chipset. Pressing the power button on the computer or a remote control puts the computer in the Quick Sleep mode, and you can switch the computer to the Quick Resume mode by moving the mouse, pressing an on/off key on the keyboard (if available), or pressing the Sleep button on the remote control. Quick Sleep mode is different from standard sleep mode. In Quick Sleep mode, the computer's video card stops sending data to the display, the sound is muted, and the monitor light-emitting diode (LED) indicates a lowered power state on the monitor, but the power continues to be supplied to vital components on the system, such as the processor, fans, and so on. This technology was originally designed for legacy Windows operating systems and generally should not be used with Windows 8.1. (On older hardware, you might need to disable this feature in firmware to enable Windows 8.1 to properly sleep and resume.)

After you look at the computer's power settings in firmware, you should also review the computer's boot settings in firmware. Often, you can configure the following boot settings:

- **Boot Drive Order**   Determines the boot order for boot devices.
- **Boot To Hard Disk Drive**   Determines whether the computer can boot to hard drives. Can be set to Disabled or Enabled.
- **Boot To Removable Devices**   Determines whether the computer can boot to removable media. Can be set to Disabled or Enabled.

- **Boot To Network**   Determines whether the computer can perform a network boot. Can be set to Disabled or Enabled.

- **USB Boot**   Determines whether the computer can boot to USB flash devices. Can be set to Disabled or Enabled.

On some computers, you might have a list of bootable devices and be able to select which to boot.

As for power settings, your computer might not have the exact labels shown here, but the labels should be similar. You need to optimize these settings for the way you plan to use the computer. When you use BitLocker Drive Encryption, you should enable Boot To Removable Devices, USB Boot, or both to ensure that the computer can detect the USB flash drive with the encryption key during the boot process.

Diagnosing and resolving startup problems

To diagnose and resolve startup problems, you need to understand the sequence of events that occur after you press the power button on a computer. When you press the power button, the following happens:

1. The firmware interface performs system configuration, also known as power-on self test (POST).

2. The firmware interface performs setup of the computer, also known as initialization of the computer.

3. The firmware interface passes control to the operating system loader, also known as the boot manager.

4. The boot manager starts the boot loader. The boot loader uses the firmware interface boot services to complete the operating system boot and load the operating system. Loading the operating system involves:

   a. Loading (but not running) the operating system kernel (typically, Ntoskrnl.exe).

   b. Loading (but not running) the hardware abstraction layer (HAL) (typically, Hal.dll).

   c. Loading the HKEY_LOCAL_MACHINE\SYSTEM registry hive into memory (from %SystemRoot%\System32\Config\System).

   d. Scanning the HKEY_LOCAL_MACHINE\SYSTEM\Services key for device drivers and then loading (but not initializing) the drivers that are configured for the boot class into memory. Drivers are also services (which means both device drivers and system services are prepared).

   e. Enabling memory paging.

5. The boot loader passes control to the operating system kernel.

6. The kernel and the HAL initialize the Windows executive, which in turn processes the configuration information stored in the HKEY_LOCAL_MACHINE\SYSTEM\CurrentControlSet hive, and then starts device drivers and system services.

7. The kernel starts the Session Manager (Smss.exe), which in turn:

   a. Initializes the system environment by creating system environment variables.

   b. Starts the Win32 subsystem (Csrss.exe). Here, Windows switches the display output from text mode to graphics mode.

   c. Starts the Windows Logon Manager (Winlogon.exe), which in turn starts the Services Control Manager (Services.exe) and the Local Security Authority (Lsass.exe) and waits for a user to log on.

   d. Creates additional paging files that are required.

   e. As necessary, performs delayed renaming of in-use files that were updated in the previous session.

8. The Windows Logon Manager waits for a user to log on. The logon user interface and the default credential provider collect the user name and password and pass this information to the Local Security Authority for authentication.

9. The Windows Logon Manager runs Userinit.exe and the File Explorer shell. Userinit.exe initializes the user environment by creating user environment variables, running startup programs, and performing other essential tasks.

This sequence of events is for a cold start of a computer from power on through logon. The sequence of events varies if the computer is resuming from sleep, standby, or hibernation. The sequence of events also varies if you are starting an operating system other than Windows or a Windows operating system other than Windows Vista or later.

> **REAL WORLD** With WOA, the sequence of events is similar but slightly different. Here, UEFI provides the services necessary for loading the operating system. Windows Boot Manager initializes the operating system by starting the Windows Boot Loader, which in turn starts the operating system by using information in the BCD store. The boot loader passes control to the operating system kernel. The kernel and the HAL initialize the Windows executive. Information needed to configure WOA is stored in tables so the operating system can read the table and configure WOA. In order to load device drivers and continue boot, the Windows executive initializes the simple peripheral buses (a series of low-power serial buses) and then the device drivers that support connections to those buses. The kernel can then start the Session Manager, which in turn brings up the rest of the system.

Sometimes you can identify the source of a startup problem by pinpointing where the startup process breaks. Table 1-2 lists the various startup phases and provides a possible cause of problems in each phase. The phase numbers are meant only to aid in the subsequent discussion.

TABLE 1-2 Troubleshooting startup

PHASE	PHASE TITLE	POSSIBLE CAUSE OF PROBLEM
1	System configuration, power-on self-test	Hardware failure or missing device
2	Setup, initial startup	Firmware configuration, the disk subsystem, or the file system
3	Operating system loader, boot manager	BCD data, improper operating system selection for loading, or invalid boot loader
4	Kernel, HAL, Windows executive	Driver or service configuration or service dependencies
5	Session Manager	Graphics display mode, system environment, or component configuration

Troubleshooting startup phase 1

When you turn on a computer from a cold state, system configuration (power-on self test) occurs first. During this phase, the firmware performs initial checks of hardware, verifies that required devices are present, and reads the system configuration settings from nonvolatile memory on the motherboard. Although nonvolatile memory could be Electronically Erasable Programmable Read-Only Memory (EE-PROM), flash, or battery-backed RAM, it is more typically flash memory that remains even after you shut down and unplug the computer.

After the motherboard firmware performs its tests and reads its settings, add-on devices that have their own firmware, such as video cards and host controller cards, perform their tests and load their settings. If startup fails in this phase, the computer likely has a hardware failure. A required device, such as a keyboard, mouse, or hard drive, could also be missing. In most cases, the firmware interface displays an error message that indicates the problem. If video isn't working, the firmware interface might indicate the problem by emitting a series of beeps.

You can resolve a problem with a keyboard, mouse, or display by checking the device's connection to the computer. If another device is causing a problem, you might be able to resolve the problem by changing the device configuration in the firmware interface, or you might need to replace the device.

Troubleshooting startup phase 2

After system configuration is complete, the computer enters the setup, or initial startup, phase. Firmware interface settings determine the devices the computer uses to start the operating system. The boot order and the boot enabled or disabled state of each device affects startup. As discussed previously, the computer tries to boot by using the device listed first. If that fails, the computer tries the second boot device, and so on. If none of the configured devices are bootable, you'll get an error similar to the following:

```
Non-system disk or disk error
Replace and press any key when ready to continue
```

Here, you'll want to check the boot order and be sure it is set correctly. If you are trying to boot from DVD media, check that the media is present and that DVD booting is enabled. If you are trying to boot from a hard drive, make sure booting from a hard drive is enabled and listed prior to any USB or other removable media you've inserted. If you've recently installed a hard drive, power off and unplug the computer, and then verify that all cables are connected correctly and that any jumpers are configured correctly.

Because configuring boot options in firmware isn't necessarily intuitive, I'll provide examples from a cross-section of computers by various vendors. On an HP notebook computer, the boot settings are found on the Boot Options and Boot Order submenus on the System Configuration page. The Boot Options submenu has these options:

- **F10 And F12 Delay (sec)**   Sets the amount of time for the user to press F10 or F12 at startup. On this notebook, F10 and F12 access boot options and advanced boot options, respectively.
- **DVD Boot**   Enables or disables DVD boot during startup.
- **Floppy Boot**   Enables or disables the floppy boot during startup.
- **Internal Network Adapter Boot**   Enables or disables networking booting during startup.

Use the Up Arrow and Down Arrow keys to select an option, and then press Enter to view and set the option.

On the Boot Order submenu, the boot order is listed as the following:

1. USB Floppy
2. ATAPI CD/DVD ROM Drive
3. Notebook Hard Drive
4. USB Diskette On Key
5. USB Hard Drive
6. Network Adapter (only if Internal Network Adapter Boot is enabled)

Here, you use the Up Arrow and Down Arrow keys to select a device, and then press F5 or F6 to move the device up or down in the list. It is important to note that this computer (like many newer computers) distinguishes between USB flash keys (referred to as *USB diskettes on keys*) and USB drives (referred to as *USB hard drives*). Computer users won't really perceive a difference between the two.

On a Dell Inspiron laptop, you manage boot settings on the Boot page. The boot order is listed as:

1. Hard drive
2. USB hard drive
3. CD/DVD
4. USB CD/DVD
5. USB Floppy
6. Network

You use the Up Arrow and Down Arrow keys to navigate the boot priority list. Press Enter to select a priority level for editing and then to select the device that should have that priority. Select Disabled to temporarily disable that boot priority level.

More desktop computers are being shipped with hardware redundant array of independent disks (RAID) controller cards. On a Dell computer I have, the SATA Operation option of the Drives submenu is used to enable or disable the hardware RAID controller card. Typically, RAID controller cards for desktop computers support RAID 0 and RAID 1. RAID 0 offers no data protection and just stretches a logical disk volume across multiple physical disks. RAID 1 offers data protection by mirroring the disks. When disks are mirrored, two physical disks appear as one disk, and each disk has identical copies of any data.

> **REAL WORLD**   A computer with a hardware RAID controller might not boot if one of the drives required for RAID operations is removed from the computer without first disabling the hardware RAID. If the remaining drive is bootable, disable RAID in BIOS, and then restart the computer to enable booting of the operating system.

Troubleshooting startup phase 3

After setup, the firmware interface passes control to the boot manager. The boot manager in turn starts the boot loader.

On computers using BIOS, the computer reads information from the master book record (MBR), which usually is the first sector of data on the disk. The MBR contains boot instructions and a partition table that identifies disk partitions. The active partition, also known as the boot partition, also has boot code in its first sector of data. The data provides information about the file system on the partition and enables the firmware to locate and start the Bootmgr stub program in the root directory of the boot partition. Bootmgr switches the process into 32-bit or 64-bit protected mode from real mode and loads the 32-bit or 64-bit Windows Boot Manager (found within the stub file itself), as appropriate. Windows Boot Manager locates and starts the Windows Boot Loader (Winload).

Problems can occur if the active boot partition does not exist or if any boot sector data is missing or corrupt. Errors you might get include:

```
Error loading operating system
```

and

```
Invalid partition table
```

In many cases, you can restore proper operations by using the Startup Repair tool.

In contrast, computers using EFI have a built-in boot manager. When you install Windows, Windows adds an entry to the EFI boot manager called Windows Boot Manager, which points to the boot manager's executable file on the EFI system partition (\Efi\Microsoft\Boot\Bootmgfw.efi). The boot manager then passes control to the Windows Boot Loader.

Problems can occur if you install a different operating system or change the EFI boot manager settings. In many cases, you'll be able to restore proper operations by using the Startup Repair tool or by changing EFI boot manager settings.

Troubleshooting startup phase 4

The boot loader uses the firmware interface boot services to complete operating system boot. The boot loader loads the operating system kernel (Ntoskrnl.exe), and then loads the hardware abstraction layer (HAL), Hal.dll. Next, the boot loader loads the HKEY_LOCAL_MACHINE\SYSTEM registry hive into memory (from %SystemRoot%\System32\Config\System), and then it scans the HKEY_LOCAL_MACHINE\SYSTEM\Services key for device drivers. The boot loader scans this registry hive to find drivers that are configured for the boot class and loads them into memory.

After the boot loader passes control to the operating system kernel, the kernel and the HAL initialize the Windows executive, which in turn processes the configuration information stored in the HKEY_LOCAL_MACHINE\SYSTEM\CurrentControlSet hive and then starts device drivers and system services. Drivers and services are started according to their start-type value. This value is set on the Start subkey under HKEY_LOCAL_MACHINE\SYSTEM\CurrentControlSet\Services*Name*, where *Name* is the name of the device or service. Valid values are 0 (identifies a boot driver), 1 (identifies a system driver), 2 (identifies an auto-load driver or service), 3 (identifies a load-on-demand driver or service), 4 (identifies a disabled and not-started driver or service), and 5 (identifies a delayed-start service). Drivers are started in the following order: boot, system, auto load, load on demand, and delayed start.

Most problems in this phase have to do with invalid driver and service configurations. Some drivers and services are dependent on other components and services. If dependent components or services are not available or are not configured properly, this also could cause startup problems.

During startup, subkeys of HKEY_LOCAL_MACHINE\SYSTEM are used to configure devices and services. The Select subkey has several values used in this regard:

- The Current value is a pointer to the ControlSet subkey containing the current configuration definitions for all devices and services.
- The Default value is a pointer to the ControlSet subkey containing the configuration definition the computer uses at the next startup, if no error occurs and you don't use an alternate configuration.

- The Failed value is a pointer to the ControlSet subkey containing a configuration definition that failed to load Windows.

- The LastKnownGood value is a pointer to the ControlSet subkey containing the configuration definition that was used for the last successful logon.

During normal startup, the computer uses the Default control set. Generally, if no error has occurred during startup or you haven't selected the last known good configuration, the Default, Current, and LastKnownGood values all point to the same ControlSet subkey, such as ControlSet001. If startup fails and you access the last known good configuration by using the Advanced Boot options, the Failed entry is updated to point to the configuration definition that failed to load. If startup succeeds and you haven't accessed the last known good configuration, the value of LastKnownGood is updated to point to the current configuration definition.

Troubleshooting startup phase 5

During the final phase of startup, the kernel starts the Session Manager (Smss.exe). The Session Manager initializes the system environment by creating system environment variables and starting the Win32 subsystem (Csrss.exe). This is the point at which Windows switches from the text presentation mode used initially to a graphics presentation mode. Generally, if the display adapter is broken or not properly seated, the computer won't display in either text or graphics mode, but if the display adapter is configured improperly, you'll often notice this when the computer switches to graphics mode.

The display is only one of several components that might first present problems during this late phase of startup. If startup fails during this phase, you can identify problem components by using boot logging. If the computer has a Stop error in this phase, use the information provided by the Stop message to help you identify the problem component.

The Session Manager starts the Windows Logon Manager (Winlogon.exe), which in turn starts the Services Control Manager (Services.exe) and the Local Security Authority (Lsass.exe) and waits for a user to log on. When a user logs on, the Windows Logon Manager runs Userinit.exe and the File Explorer shell. Userinit.exe initializes the user environment by creating user environment variables, running startup programs, and performing other essential tasks. The File Explorer shell provides the desktop, taskbar, and menu system.

If you encounter startup problems during or after logon, the problem is likely due to a misconfigured service or startup application. As part of troubleshooting, you can temporarily disable services and startup applications, as discussed in the section "Managing system boot configuration," later in this chapter.

Managing startup and boot configuration

During startup of the operating system, you can press F8 or F12 to access the Advanced Boot Options menu, and then use this menu to select one of several advanced startup modes. These advanced modes don't make permanent changes to the boot configuration or to the BCD store. Tools you can use to modify the boot configuration and manage the BCD store include the Startup And Recovery dialog box, the System Configuration utility, and the BCD Editor. The sections that follow discuss how these tools are used.

Setting startup and recovery options

The Startup And Recovery dialog box controls the basic options for the operating system during startup. You can use these options to set the default operating system, how long to display the list of available operating systems, and how long to display recovery options when needed. Whether or not you boot a computer to different operating systems, you'll want to optimize these settings to reduce the wait time during startup and, in this way, speed up the startup process.

You can configure options in the Startup And Recovery dialog box by completing the following steps:

1. In Control Panel, tap or click System And Security, and then tap or click System to display the System window.

2. In the left pane of the System window, tap or click Advanced System Settings to display the System Properties dialog box.

3. On the Advanced tab of the System Properties dialog box, under Startup And Recovery, tap or click Settings. This displays the Startup And Recovery dialog box, shown in Figure 1-1.

4. On a computer with multiple operating systems, use the Default Operating System list to specify the operating system that you want to start by default.

5. Set the timeout interval for the operating system list by selecting the Time To Display List Of Operating Systems check box and specifying the interval in seconds. To speed up the startup process, you could use a value of 5 seconds.

6. Set the timeout interval for the recovery options list by selecting the Time To Display Recovery Options When Needed check box and specifying the interval in seconds. Again, to speed up the startup process, use a value of 5 seconds.

7. Under System Failure, select Write An Event To The System Log if you want to record events related to system failure. If you want the computer to automatically restart after a failure, select Automatically Restart.

8. Tap or click OK to save your settings.

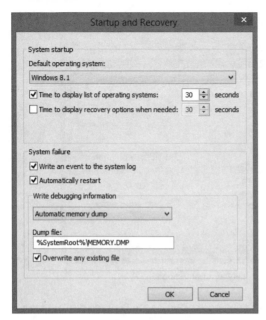

FIGURE 1-1 Configure system startup options.

Managing system boot configuration

The System Configuration utility (Msconfig.exe) enables you to fine-tune the way a computer starts. Typically, you use this utility during troubleshooting and diagnostics. For example, as part of troubleshooting, you can configure the computer to use a diagnostic startup in which only basic devices and services are loaded.

In Control Panel, the System Configuration utility is available under System And Security/Administrative Tools. You can also start the System Configuration utility by pressing the Windows key, typing **msconfig.exe** (which typically is entered automatically into the Apps Search box), and then pressing Enter. As shown in Figure 1-2, this utility has a series of tabs with options.

The General tab options enable you to configure the way startup works and are the starting point for troubleshooting and diagnostics. By using these options, you can choose to perform a normal startup, diagnostic startup, or selective startup. After you restart the computer and resolve any problems, open the System Configuration utility again, select Normal Startup on the General tab, and then tap or click OK.

The Boot tab options enable you to control the way that individual startup-related processes work. You can configure the computer to start in one of various Safe Boot modes and set additional options, such as No GUI Boot. If, after troubleshooting, you find that you want to keep these settings, select the Make All Boot Settings Permanent check box to save the settings to the boot configuration startup entry.

FIGURE 1-2 Use the System Configuration utility for troubleshooting.

Tapping or clicking the Advanced Options button on the Boot tab displays the BOOT Advanced Options dialog box, shown in Figure 1-3. In addition to locking PCI and enabling debugging, you can use the advanced options to do the following:

- Specify the number of processors the operating system should use, regardless of whether the processors are discrete socketed CPUs or cores on a single CPU. You should use this option when you suspect a problem with additional processors that are available and you want to identify the problem as being related to multiprocessor configurations or parallelism. Consider the following scenario: A computer is shipped with a single CPU that has four processor cores. A custom application used in-house for inventory management performs very poorly while running on this computer, but very well on computers with single processors. You configure the computer to boot with only one processor and find that the application's performance actually improves. You re-enable all the processors and let the software development team know that the application behaves as if it has not been properly optimized for parallelism.

- Specify the maximum amount of memory the operating system should use. Use this option when you suspect a problem with additional memory you've installed in a computer. Consider the following scenario: A computer is shipped with 8 gigabytes (GB) of RAM, and you installed another 8 GB of RAM. Later, you find that you cannot start Windows 8.1. You could eliminate the new RAM as the potential cause by limiting the computer to 8,192 megabytes (MB) of memory.

FIGURE 1-3 Use advanced boot options to help troubleshoot specific types of problems.

If you suspect that services installed on a computer are causing startup problems, you can quickly determine this by choosing a diagnostic or selective startup on the General tab. After you've identified that services are indeed causing startup problems, you can temporarily disable services by using the Services tab options and then rebooting to determine if the problem goes away. If the problem no longer appears, you might have pinpointed it. You can then permanently disable the service or check with the service vendor to find out if an updated executable file is available. You disable a service by clearing the related check box on the Services tab.

Similarly, if you suspect applications that run at startup are causing problems, you can quickly determine this by tapping or clicking Open Task Manager on the Startup tab. You disable a startup application by selecting it on the Startup tab and then tapping or clicking Disable. If the problem no longer appears, you might have pinpointed the cause of it. You can then permanently disable the startup application or check with the software vendor to find out if an updated version is available.

Keep in mind that if you use the System Configuration utility for troubleshooting and diagnostics, you should later remove your selective startup options. After you restart the computer and resolve any problems, open the System Configuration utility again, restore the original settings, and then tap or click OK.

Using the BCD Editor

The BCD store contains multiple entries. On a BIOS-based computer, you'll find the following entries:

- One Windows Boot Manager entry. There is only one boot manager, so only one boot manager entry is visible.

- One or more Windows Boot Loader application entries, with one for each instance of Windows Vista or later installed on the computer. If you've installed Windows Server 2008 or later, you'll also find entries for each installation.

Windows Boot Manager is a boot loader application. There are also other boot loader applications, including:

- Operating system loader, identified as Osloader
- Windows Boot Sector Application, identified as Bootsector
- Firmware Boot Manager, identified as Fwbootmgr
- Windows Resume Loader, identified as Resume

You can view and manage the BCD store by using the BCD Editor (Bcdedit.exe). The BCD Editor is a command-line utility. You can use the BCD Editor to view the entries in the BCD store by following these steps:

1. Enter **cmd.exe** in the Apps Search box. One way to do this is to press the Windows key, and then enter **cmd.exe**.

2. Press and hold or right-click the command prompt, and then tap or click Run As Administrator.

3. Enter **bcdedit** at the command prompt.

Table 1-3 summarizes commands you can use when you are working with the BCD store. These commands make it possible for you to do the following:

- Create, import, export, and identify the entire BCD store
- Create, delete, and copy individual entries in the BCD store
- Set or delete entry option values in the BCD store
- Control the boot sequence and the boot manager
- Configure and control Emergency Management Services (EMS)
- Configure and control boot debugging, in addition to hypervisor debugging

TABLE 1-3 Commands for the BCD Editor

COMMAND	DESCRIPTION
/bootdebug	Enables or disables boot debugging for a boot application.
/bootems	Enables or disables EMS for a boot application.
/bootsequence	Sets the one-time boot sequence for the boot manager.
/copy	Makes copies of entries in the store.
/create	Creates new entries in the store.
/createstore	Creates a new (empty) boot configuration data store.
/dbgsettings	Sets the global debugger parameters.
/debug	Enables or disables kernel debugging for an operating system entry.
/default	Sets the default entry that the boot manager will use.

COMMAND	DESCRIPTION
/delete	Deletes entries from the store.
/deletevalue	Deletes entry options from the store.
/displayorder	Sets the order in which the boot manager displays the multiboot menu.
/ems	Enables or disables EMS for an operating system entry.
/emssettings	Sets the global EMS parameters.
/enum	Lists entries in the store.
/export	Exports the contents of the system store to a file. This file can be used later to restore the state of the system store.
/hypervisorsettings	Sets the hypervisor parameters.
/import	Restores the state of the system store by using a backup file created with the /export command.
/mirror	Creates a mirror of entries in the store.
/set	Sets entry option values in the store.
/store	Sets the BCD store to use. If not specified, the system store is used.
/sysstore	Sets the system store device. This only affects EFI systems.
/timeout	Sets the boot manager timeout value.
/toolsdisplayorder	Sets the order in which the boot manager displays the tools menu.
/v	Sets output to verbose mode.

Managing the BCD store

The BCD Editor is an advanced command-line tool for viewing and manipulating the configuration of the pre–operating system boot environment. Although I discuss tasks related to modifying the BCD data store in the sections that follow, you should attempt to modify the BCD store only if you are an experienced IT pro. As a safeguard, you should make a full backup of the computer prior to making any changes to the BCD store. Why? If you make a mistake, your computer might end up in a nonbootable state, and you would then need to initiate recovery.

Viewing BCD entries

Computers can have system and nonsystem BCD stores. The system BCD store contains the operating system boot entries and related boot settings. Whenever you work with the BCD Editor, you work with the system BCD store.

On a computer with only one operating system, the BCD entries for your computer will look similar to those in Listing 1-1. As the listing shows, the BCD store for this computer has two entries: one for the Windows Boot Manager, and one for the Windows Boot Loader. Here, the Windows Boot Manager calls the boot loader, and the boot loader uses Winload.exe to boot Windows 8.1.

LISTING 1-1 Entries in the BCD Store on a single-boot computer

```
Windows Boot Manager
--------------------
identifier              {bootmgr}
device                  partition=\Device\HarddiskVolume1
description             Windows Boot Manager
locale                  en-US
inherit                 {globalsettings}
integrityservices       Enable
default                 {current}
resumeobject     {16b857b4-9e02-11e0-9c17-b7d085eb0682}
displayorder            {current}
                        {16b857ad-9e02-11e0-9c17-b7d085eb0682}
toolsdisplayorder       {memdiag}
timeout                 30
custom:26000025         Yes

Windows Boot Loader
-------------------
identifier              {current}
device                  partition=C:
path                    \Windows\system32\winload.exe
description              Windows 8.1
locale                  en-US
inherit                 {bootloadersettings}
recoverysequence        {16b857b6-9e02-11e0-9c17-b7d085eb0682}
integrityservices       Enable
recoveryenabled         Yes
allowedinmemorysettings 0x15000075
osdevice                partition=C:
systemroot              \Windows
resumeobject                    {16b857b4-9e02-11e0-9c17-b7d085eb0682}
nx                      OptIn
bootmenupolicy          Standard
```

BCD entries for Windows Boot Manager and Windows Boot Loader have similar properties. These properties include those summarized in Table 1-4.

TABLE 1-4 BCD entry properties

PROPERTY	DESCRIPTION
Description	Shows descriptive information to help identify the type of entry.
Device	Shows the physical device path. For a partition on a physical disk, you'll find an entry such as partition=C:.
FileDevice	Shows the path to a file device, such as partition=C:.
FilePath	Shows the file path to a necessary file, such as \Hiberfil.sys.
Identifier	Shows a descriptor for the entry. This can be a boot loader application type, such as Bootmgr or Ntldr, a reference to the current operating system entry, or the globally unique identifier (GUID) of a specific object. Well-known identifiers are listed in Table 1-5, later in this chapter.
Inherit	Shows the list of entries to be inherited.
Locale	Shows the computer's locale setting, such as en-US. The locale setting determines the language shown in the user interface (UI). The \Boot folder contains locale subfolders for each locale supported, and each of these subfolders has language-specific UI details for the Windows Boot Manager and the Windows Memory Diagnostic utility (Memdiag.exe).
Osdevice	Shows the path to the operating system device, such as partition=C:.
Path	Shows the actual file path to the boot loader application, such as \Windows\System32\Winload.exe.

When you are working with the BCD store and the BCD Editor, you'll find references to well-known identifiers, summarized in Table 1-5, in addition to GUIDs. When a GUID is used, it has the following format, where each *N* represents a hexadecimal value:

`{NNNNNNNN-NNNN-NNNN-NNNN-NNNNNNNNNNNN}`

such as:

`{16b857ad-9e02-11e0-9c17-b7d085eb0682}`

The dashes that separate the parts of the GUID must be entered in the positions shown. Both well-known identifiers and GUIDs are enclosed in braces.

TABLE 1-5 Well-known identifiers

IDENTIFIER	DESCRIPTION
{badmemory}	Contains the global RAM defect list that can be inherited by any boot application entry.
{bootloadersettings}	Contains the collection of global settings that should be inherited by all Windows Boot Loader application entries.
{bootmgr}	Indicates the Windows Boot Manager entry.
{current}	Represents a virtual identifier that corresponds to the operating system boot entry for the operating system that is currently running.
{dbgsettings}	Contains the global debugger settings that can be inherited by any boot application entry.
{default}	Represents a virtual identifier that corresponds to the boot manager default application entry.
{emssettings}	Contains the global EMS settings that can be inherited by any boot application entry.
{fwbootmgr}	Indicates the firmware boot manager entry. This entry is used on EFI systems.
{globalsettings}	Contains the collection of global settings that should be inherited by all boot application entries.
{hypervisorsettings}	Contains the hypervisor settings that can be inherited by any operating system loader entry.
{memdiag}	Indicates the memory diagnostic application entry.
{ntldr}	Indicates the Windows Legacy OS Loader (Ntldr) that can be used to start Windows operating systems earlier than Windows Vista. Used when you've installed a legacy operating system.
{ramdiskoptions}	Contains the additional options required by the boot manager for RAM disk devices.
{resumeloadersettings}	Contains the collection of global settings that should be inherited by all Windows resume-from-hibernation application entries.

When a computer has additional instances of Windows installed, the BCD store has additional entries for each additional operating system. For example, the BCD store might have one entry for the Windows Boot Manager and one Windows Boot Loader entry for each operating system.

Although the Windows Boot Manager and Windows Boot Loader are the primary types of entries that control startup, the BCD store also includes information about boot settings and boot utilities. The Windows Boot Loader entry can have parameters that track the status of boot settings, such as whether No Execute (NX) policy is set to Opt In or Opt Out. The Windows Boot Loader entry also can provide information about available boot utilities, such as the Windows Memory Diagnostic utility.

To view the actual value of the GUIDs needed to manipulate entries in the BCD store, enter **bcdedit /v** at an elevated command prompt.

Creating and identifying the BCD store

By using the BCD Editor, you can create a nonsystem BCD store by using the following command:

```
bcdedit /createstore StorePath
```

StorePath is the folder path to the location where you want to create the nonsystem store, such as:

```
bcdedit /createstore c:\non-sys\bcd
```

On an EFI system, you can temporarily set the system store device by using the /sysstore command. Use the following syntax:

```
bcdedit /sysstore StoreDevice
```

StoreDevice is the actual system store device identifier, such as:

```
bcdedit /sysstore c:
```

The device must be a system partition. Note that this setting does not persist across reboots and is used only in cases in which it is not clear which system store device should be used.

Importing and exporting the BCD store

The BCD Editor provides separate commands for importing and exporting the BCD store. You can use the /export command to export a copy of the system BCD store's contents to a specified folder. Use the following command syntax:

```
bcdedit /export StorePath
```

StorePath is the actual folder path to which you want to export a copy of the system store, such as:

```
bcdedit /export c:\backup\bcd
```

To restore an exported copy of the system store, you can use the /import command. Use the following command syntax:

```
bcdedit /import ImportPath
```

ImportPath is the actual folder path from which you want to import a copy of the system store, such as:

```
bcdedit /import c:\backup\bcd
```

On an EFI system, you can add /clean to the /import command to specify that all existing firmware boot entries should be deleted. Here is an example:

```
bcdedit /import c:\backup\bcd /clean
```

Creating and deleting BCD entries

The BCD Editor provides separate commands for creating, copying, and deleting entries in the BCD store. You can use the /create command to create identifier, application, and inherit entries in the BCD store.

As shown previously in Table 1-5, the BCD Editor recognizes many well-known identifiers, including {dbgsettings}, which is used to create a debugger settings entry; {ntldr}, used to create a Windows Legacy OS entry; and {ramdiskoptions}, used to create a RAM disk additional options entry. To create identifier entries, you use the following syntax:

```
bcdedit /create Identifier /d "Description"
```

Identifier is a well-known identifier for the entry you want to create, such as:

```
bcdedit /create {ntldr} /d "Legacy Windows OS Loader"
```

You can also create entries for specific boot loader applications, including:

- **Bootsector**   Identifies a real-mode boot sector application; used to set the boot sector for a real-mode application
- **Osloader**   Identifies an operating system loader application; used to load Windows Vista or later
- **Resume**   Identifies a Windows Resume Loader application; used to resume the operating system from hibernation
- **Startup**   Identifies a real-mode application

Use the following command syntax:

```
bcdedit /create /application AppType /d "Description"
```

AppType is one of the previously listed application types, such as:

```
bcdedit /create /application osloader /d "Windows 8.1"
```

You can delete entries in the system store by using the /delete command and the following syntax:

```
bcdedit /delete Identifier
```

If you are trying to delete a well-known identifier, you must use the /f command to force deletion, such as:

```
bcdedit /delete {ntldr} /f
```

By default, when the /delete command is used, the /cleanup option is implied, which means that the BCD Editor cleans up any other references to the entry being deleted. This ensures that the data store doesn't have invalid references to the identifier you removed. Because entries are also removed from the display order, this could result in a different default operating system being set. If you want to delete the entry and clean up all other references except the display order entry, you can use the /nocleanup command.

Setting BCD entry values

After you create an entry, you need to set additional entry option values as necessary. The basic syntax for setting values is:

```
bcdedit /set Identifier Option Value
```

Identifier is the identifier of the entry to be modified, *Option* is the option you want to set, and *Value* is the option value, such as:

```
bcdedit /set {current} device partition=d:
```

To delete options and their values, use the /deletevalue command with the following syntax:

```
bcdedit /deletevalue Identifier Option
```

Identifier is the identifier of the entry to be modified, and *Option* is the option you want to delete, such as:

```
bcdedit /deletevalue {current} badmemorylist
```

When you are working with options, Boolean values can be entered in several different ways. For True, you can use 1, On, Yes, or True. For False, you can use 0, Off, No, or False.

To view the BCD entries for all boot utilities and the values for settings, enter **bcdedit /enum all /v** at an elevated command prompt. This command enumerates all BCD entries regardless of their current state and lists them in verbose mode. Each additional entry has a specific purpose and lists values that you can set, including the following:

- **Resume From Hibernate**   The Resume From Hibernate entry shows the current configuration for the resume feature. The pre–operating system boot utility that controls resume is Winresume.exe, which in this example is stored in the C:\Windows\System32 folder. The hibernation data, as specified in the FilePath parameter, is stored in the Hiberfil.sys file in the root folder on the OSDevice (C: in this example). Because the resume feature works differently if the computer has Physical Address Extension (PAE) and debugging enabled, these options are tracked by the PAE and DebugOptionEnabled parameters.

- **Windows Memory Tester**   The Windows Memory Tester entry shows the current configuration for the Windows Memory Diagnostic utility. Memtest is the pre–operating system boot utility that controls memory diagnostics. Because the Windows Memory Diagnostic utility is designed to detect bad memory by default, the BadMemoryAccess parameter is set to Yes by default. You can turn this feature off by entering **bcdedit /set {memdiag} badmemoryaccess NO**. With memory diagnostics, you can configure the number of passes by using Passcount and the test mix as Basic or Extended by using Testmix. Here is an example: bcdedit /set {memdiag} passcount 2 textmix basic.

- **Windows Legacy OS Loader** The Windows Legacy OS Loader entry shows the current configuration for the loading of earlier versions of Windows. The Device parameter sets the default partition to use, such as C:, and the Path parameter sets the default path to the loader utility, such as Ntldr.

- **EMS Settings** The EMS Settings entry shows the configuration used when booting with EMS. Individual Windows Boot Loader entries control whether EMS is enabled. If EMS is provided by the BIOS and you want to use the BIOS settings, you can enter **bcdedit /emssettings bios**. With EMS, you can set an EMS port and an EMS baud rate. Here is an example: bcdedit /emssettings EMSPORT:2 EMSBAUDRATE:115200. You can enable or disable EMS for a boot application by using /bootems, following the identity of the boot application with the state you want, such as On or Off.

- **Debugger Settings** The Debugger Settings entry shows the configuration used when booting with the debugger turned on. Individual Windows Boot Loader entries control whether the debugger is enabled. You can view the hypervisor debugging settings by entering **bcdedit /dbgsettings**. When debug booting is turned on, DebugType sets the type of debugger as SERIAL, 1394, or USB. With SERIAL debugging, DebugPort specifies the serial port being used as the debugger port, and BaudRate specifies the baud rate to be used for debugging. With 1394 debugging, you can use Channel to set the debugging channel. With USB debugging, you can use TargetName to set the USB target name to be used for debugging. With any debug type, you can use the /Noumex flag to specify that user-mode exceptions should be ignored. Here are examples of setting the debugging mode: bcdedit /dbgsettings SERIAL DEBUGPORT:1 BAUDRATE:115200, bcdedit /dbgsettings 1394 CHANNEL:23, bcdedit /dbgsettings USB TARGETNAME:DEBUGGING.

- **Hypervisor Settings** The Hypervisor Settings entry shows the configuration used when working with the hypervisor with the debugger turned on. Individual Windows Boot Loader entries control whether the debugger is enabled. You can view the hypervisor debugging settings by entering **bcdedit /hypervisorsettings**. When hypervisor debug booting is turned on, HypervisorDebugType sets the type of debugger, HypervisorDebugPort specifies the serial port being used as the debugger port, and Hypervisor-BaudRate specifies the baud rate to be used for debugging. These parameters work the same as with Debugger Settings. Here is an example: bcdedit /hypervisorsettings SERIAL DEBUGPORT:1 BAUDRATE:115200. You can also use FireWire for hypervisor debugging. When you do, you must separate the word *channel* from the value with a colon, as shown in this example: bcdedit /hypervisorsettings 1394 CHANNEL:23.

Table 1-6 summarizes key options that apply to entries for boot applications (Bootapp). Because Windows Boot Manager, Windows Memory Diagnostic, Windows OS Loader, and Windows Resume Loader are boot applications, these options also apply to them.

TABLE 1-6 Key options for boot application entries

OPTION	VALUE DESCRIPTION
BadMemoryAccess	When true, enables an application to use the memory on the bad memory list. When false, applications are prevented from using memory on the bad memory list.
BadMemoryList	An integer list that defines the list of Page Frame Numbers of faulty memory in the system.
BaudRate	Sets an integer value that defines the baud rate for the serial debugger.
BootDebug	Sets a Boolean value that enables or disables the boot debugger.
BootEMS	Sets a Boolean value that enables or disables EMS.
Channel	Sets an integer value that defines the channel for the 1394 debugger.
ConfigAccessPolicy	Sets the access policy as either DEFAULT or DISALLOWMMCONFIG.
DebugAddress	Sets an integer value that defines the address of a serial port for the debugger.
DebugPort	Sets an integer value that defines the serial port number for the serial debugger.
DebugStart	Can be set to ACTIVE, AUTOENABLE, or DISABLE.
DebugType	Can be set to SERIAL, 1394, or USB.
EMSBaudRate	Defines the baud rate for EMS.
EMSPort	Defines the serial port number for EMS.
FirstMegaBytePolicy	Sets the first megabyte policy as USENONE, USEALL, or USEPRIVATE.
GraphicsModeDisabled	Sets a Boolean value that enables or disables graphics mode.
GraphicsResolution	Defines the graphics resolution, such as 1024 × 768 or 800 × 600.
Locale	Sets the locale of the boot application.

OPTION	VALUE DESCRIPTION
Noumex	When Noumex is set to TRUE, user-mode exceptions are ignored. When Noumex is set to FALSE, user-mode exceptions are not ignored.
NoVESA	Sets a Boolean value that enables or disables the use of Video Electronics Standards Association (VESA) display modes.
RecoveryEnabled	Sets a Boolean value that enables or disables the use of a recovery sequence.
RecoverySequence	Defines the recovery sequence to use.
TargetName	Defines the target name for the USB debugger as a string.
TestSigning	Sets a Boolean value that enables or disables use of prerelease test-code signing certificates.
TruncateMemory	Sets a physical memory address at or above which all memory is disregarded.

Table 1-7 summarizes key options that apply to entries for Windows OS Loader (Osloader) applications.

TABLE 1-7 Key options for Windows OS Loader applications

OPTION	VALUE DESCRIPTION
AdvancedOptions	Sets a Boolean value that enables or disables advanced options.
BootLog	Sets a Boolean value that enables or disables the boot initialization log.
BootStatusPolicy	Sets the boot status policy. Can be DisplayAllFailures, IgnoreAllFailures, IgnoreShutdownFailures, or Ignore-BootFailures.
ClusterMode Addressing	Sets the maximum number of processors to include in a single Advanced Programmable Interrupt Controller (APIC) cluster.
ConfigFlags	Sets processor-specific configuration flags.
DbgTransport	Sets the file name for a private debugger transport.
Debug	Sets a Boolean value that enables or disables kernel debugging.
DriverLoad FailurePolicy	Sets the driver load failure policy. Can be Fatal or UseErrorControl.

OPTION	VALUE DESCRIPTION
Ems	Sets a Boolean value that enables or disables kernel EMS.
Hal	Sets the file name for a private HAL.
HalBreakPoint	Sets a Boolean value that enables or disables the special HAL breakpoint.
HypervisorLaunchType	Configures the hypervisor launch type. Can be Off or Auto.
IncreaseUserVA	Sets an integer value (in megabytes) that increases the amount of virtual address space that the user-mode processes can use.
Kernel	Sets the file name for a private kernel.
LastKnownGood	Sets a Boolean value that enables or disables booting to the last known good configuration.
MaxProc	Sets a Boolean value that enables or disables the display of the maximum number of processors in the system.
Msi	Sets the message signaled interrupt (MSI). Can be Default or ForceDisable.
NoCrashAuto Reboot	Sets a Boolean value that enables or disables automatic restart on crash.
NoLowMem	Sets a Boolean value that enables or disables the use of low memory.
NumProc	Sets the number of processors to use on startup.
Nx	Controls no-execute protection. Can be OptIn, OptOut, AlwaysOn, or AlwaysOff.
OneCPU	Sets a Boolean value that forces or does not force only the boot CPU to be used.
OptionsEdit	Sets a Boolean value that enables or disables the options editor.
OSDevice	Defines the device that contains the system root.
Pae	Controls PAE. Can be Default, ForceEnable, or ForceDisable.
PerfMem	Sets the size (in megabytes) of the buffer to allocate for performance data logging.
RemoveMemory	Sets an integer value (in megabytes) that removes memory from the total available memory that the operating system can use.

OPTION	VALUE DESCRIPTION
RestrictAPICCluster	Sets the largest APIC cluster number to be used by the system.
ResumeObject	Sets the identifier for the resume object that is associated with this operating system object.
SafeBoot	Sets the computer to use a Safe Boot mode. Can be Minimal, Network, or DsRepair.
SafeBoot AlternateShell	Sets a Boolean value that enables or disables the use of the alternate shell when booted into safe mode.
Sos	Sets a Boolean value that enables or disables the display of additional boot information.
SystemRoot	Defines the path to the system root.
UseFirmwarePCISettings	Sets a Boolean value that enables or disables use of BIOS-configured PCI resources.
UsePhysical Destination	Sets a Boolean value that forces or does not force the use of the physical APIC.
Vga	Sets a Boolean value that forces or does not force the use of the VGA display driver.
WinPE	Sets a Boolean value that enables or disables booting to Windows Preinstallation Environment (Windows PE).

Changing Data Execution Prevention and Physical Address Extension options

Data Execution Prevention (DEP) is a memory-protection technology. Windows 8 and Windows 8.1 are the first versions of Windows that require a processor that supports DEP. Windows 8 and Windows 8.1 will not install on computers that aren't DEP-enabled.

When DEP is enabled, the computer's processor marks all memory locations in an application as nonexecutable unless the location explicitly contains executable code. If code is executed from a memory page marked as nonexecutable, the processor can raise an exception and prevent the code from executing. This behavior prevents malicious application code, such as virus code, from inserting itself into most areas of memory.

For computers with processors that support the non-execute (NX) page-protection feature, you can configure the operating system to opt in to NX protection by setting the nx parameter to OptIn, or opt out of NX protection by setting the nx parameter to OptOut. Here is an example:

```
bcdedit /set {current} nx optout
```

When you configure NX protection to OptIn, DEP is turned on only for essential Windows programs and services. This is the default. When you configure NX protection to OptOut, all programs and services—not just standard Windows programs and services—use DEP. Programs that shouldn't use DEP must be specifically opted out. You can also configure NX protection to be always on or always off by using AlwaysOn or AlwaysOff, such as:

```
bcdedit /set {current} nx alwayson
```

NOTE You opt out of programs by using advanced system settings. In Control Panel, select System And Security, select System, and then select Advanced System Settings. This opens the System Properties dialog box to the Advanced tab. Select Settings on the Performance panel of the Advanced tab. On the Data Execution Prevention tab in the Performance Options dialog box, select Turn On DEP For All Programs Except Those I Select. Finally, click Add to specify a program that shouldn't use DEP.

Processors that support and opt in to NX protection must be running in PAE mode. You can configure PAE by setting the PAE parameter to Default, ForceEnable, or ForceDisable. When you set the PAE state to Default, the operating system uses its default configuration for PAE. When you set the PAE state to ForceEnable, the operating system uses PAE. When you set the PAE state to ForceDisable, the operating system will not use PAE. Here is an example:

```
bcdedit /set {current} pae default
```

Changing the operating system display order

You can change the display order of boot managers associated with a particular installation of Windows by using the /displayorder command. The syntax is:

```
bcdedit /displayorder id1 id2 … idn
```

id1 is the operating system identifier of the first operating system in the display order, *id2* is the identifier of the second, and so on. You could change the display order of the operating systems identified in these BCD entries:

```
Windows Boot Loader
-------------------
identifier              {16b857b4-9e02-11e0-9c17-b7d085eb0682}

Windows Boot Loader
-------------------
identifier              {14504de-e96b-11cd-a51b-89ace9305d5e}

Windows Boot Loader
-------------------
identifier              {8b78e48f-02d0-11dd-af92-a72494804a8a}
```

by using the following command:

```
bcdedit /displayorder {8b78e48f-02d0-11dd-af92-a72494804a8a}
{16b857b4-9e02-11e0-9c17-b7d085eb0682}
{14504de-e96b-11cd-a51b-89ace9305d5e}
```

You can set a particular operating system as the first entry by using /addfirst with /displayorder, as in:

```
bcdedit /displayorder {16b857b4-9e02-11e0-9c17-b7d085eb0682} /addfirst
```

You can set a particular operating system as the last entry by using /addlast with /displayorder, as in:

```
bcdedit /displayorder {8b78e48f-02d0-11dd-af92-a72494804a8a} /addlast
```

Changing the default operating system entry

You can change the default operating system entry by using the /default command. The syntax for this command is:

```
bcdedit /default id
```

id is the operating system ID in the boot loader entry. You could set the operating system identified in this BCD entry as the default:

```
Windows Boot Loader
-------------------
identifier              {16b857b4-9e02-11e0-9c17-b7d085eb0682}
```

by using the following command:

```
bcdedit /default {16b857b4-9e02-11e0-9c17-b7d085eb0682}
```

If you want to use a legacy operating system, such as Windows XP, as the default, use the identifier for the Windows Legacy OS Loader. The related BCD entry looks like this:

```
Windows Legacy OS Loader
------------------------
identifier                    {466f5a88-0af2-4f76-9038-095b170dc21c}
device                partition=C:
path                  \ntldr
description           Early Microsoft Windows Operating System
```

Following this, you could set Ntldr as the default by entering:

```
bcdedit /default {466f5a88-0af2-4f76-9038-095b170dc21c}
```

Changing the default timeout

You can change the timeout value associated with the default operating system by using the /timeout command. Set the /timeout command to the wait time you want to use (in seconds) as follows:

```
bcdedit /timeout 30
```

To boot automatically to the default operating system, set the timeout to 0 seconds.

Changing the boot sequence temporarily

Occasionally, you might want to boot to a particular operating system one time and then revert to the default boot order. To do this, you can use the /bootsequence command. Follow the command with the identifier of the operating system to which you want to boot after restarting the computer, such as:

```
bcdedit /bootsequence {16b857b4-9e02-11e0-9c17-b7d085eb0682}
```

When you restart the computer, the computer will set the specified operating system as the default for that restart only. Then, when you restart the computer again, the computer will use the original default boot order.

Using TPM and BitLocker Drive Encryption

M any of the security features built into the Windows 8.1 operating system are designed to protect a computer from attacks by individuals accessing the computer over a network or from the Internet. But what about when individuals have direct physical access to a computer or your data? In these instances, Windows security safeguards don't apply. If someone can start a computer—even if it's to another operating system he has installed—he could gain access to any data stored on the computer, perhaps even your organization's most sensitive data. In addition, with the increased use of USB flash drives, users often take their data with them, and if they lose the USB flash drive, the data typically has no protection, meaning that anyone who finds the flash drive could read and access the data.

To protect computers and data in these instances, Windows 8.1 includes Measured Boot, BitLocker Drive Encryption, BitLocker To Go, and the Trusted Platform Module (TPM) Services architecture. Together these features help protect computers and data stored on USB flash drives. BitLocker Drive Encryption is a full-volume encryption technology. BitLocker To Go is a virtual-volume encryption technology for USB flash drives. TPM is a feature you can use with BitLocker Drive Encryption to enhance security.

Creating trusted platforms

A computer running Windows 8.1 must be equipped with a compatible TPM in addition to compatible firmware to take advantage of TPM Services. Windows 8.1 supports TPM version 1.2 or later and requires firmware that is compliant with the Trusted Computing Group (TCG). Firmware that is TCG-compliant supports the Static Root of Trust Measurement as defined by the TCG. For some configurations of TPM and BitLocker Drive Encryption, you also need to be sure that the firmware supports reading USB flash drives at startup.

TPM: the essentials

Windows 8.1 includes the Encrypting File System (EFS) for encrypting files and folders. By using EFS, users can protect sensitive data so that it can be accessed only with their public key certificate. Encryption certificates are stored as part of the data in a user's profile. If users have access to their profiles and the encryption keys they contain, they can access their encrypted files.

Although EFS offers excellent data protection, it doesn't safeguard a computer from attack by someone who has direct physical access. In a situation in which a user loses a computer, a computer is stolen, or an attacker is logging on to a computer, EFS might not protect the data because the attacker might be able to gain access to the computer before it boots. She could then access the computer from another operating system and change the computer's configuration. She might then be able to hack into a logon account on the original operating system and log on as the user, or configure the computer so that she can log on as a local administrator. Either way, the attacker could eventually gain full access to a computer and its data.

To seal a computer from physical attack and wrap it in an additional layer of protection, Windows 8.1 includes the TPM Services architecture. TPM Services protect a computer by using a dedicated hardware component called a TPM. A TPM is a microchip that is usually installed on the motherboard of a computer, where it communicates with the rest of the system by using a hardware bus. Computers running Windows 8.1 can use a TPM to provide enhanced protection for data, to ensure early validation of the boot file's integrity, and to guarantee that a disk has not been tampered with while the operating system was offline.

A TPM has the ability to create cryptographic keys and encrypt them so that they can be decrypted only by the TPM. This process, referred to as *wrapping* or *binding,* protects the key from disclosure. A TPM has a master "wrapping" key called the storage root key (SRK). The SRK is stored within the TPM to ensure that the private portion of the key is secure.

Computers that have a TPM can create a key that has been not only wrapped but sealed. The process of sealing the key ensures that the key is tied to specific platform measurements and can be unwrapped only when those platform measurements have the same values they had when the key was created. This is what gives TPM-equipped computers increased resistance to attack.

Because the TPM stores private portions of key pairs separately from memory controlled by the operating system, keys can be sealed to the TPM to provide absolute assurances about the state of a system and its trustworthiness. TPM keys are unsealed only when the integrity of the system is intact. Further, because the TPM uses its own internal firmware and logic circuits for processing instructions, it does not rely on the operating system and is not subject to external software vulnerabilities.

The TPM can also be used to seal and unseal data that is generated outside the TPM, and this is where the true power of the TPM lies. In Windows 8.1, the feature that accesses the TPM and uses it to seal a computer is called BitLocker Drive Encryption. Although BitLocker Drive Encryption can be used in both TPM and non-TPM configurations, the most secure method is to use TPM.

When you use BitLocker Drive Encryption and a TPM to seal the boot manager and boot files of a computer, the boot manager and boot files can be unsealed only if they are unchanged from the time when they were last sealed. This means that you can use the TPM to validate a computer's boot files in the pre–operating system environment. When you seal a hard disk by using TPM, the hard disk can be unsealed only if the data on the disk is unchanged since it was last sealed. This guarantees that a disk has not been tampered with while the operating system was offline.

When you use BitLocker Drive Encryption but do not use a TPM to seal the boot manager and boot files of a computer, TPM cannot be used to validate a computer's boot files in the pre–operating system environment. This means that in this instance, there is no way to guarantee the integrity of the boot manager and boot files of a computer.

TPM: management and policies

Windows 8.1 provides several tools for working with a TPM, including the following:

- **Trusted Platform Module Management**   A console for configuring and managing a TPM. You can access this tool by typing **tpm.msc** in the Apps Search box, and then pressing Enter.
- **Manage The TPM Security Hardware**   A wizard for creating the required TPM owner password. You can access this tool by typing **tpminit** in the Apps Search box, and then pressing Enter.

REAL WORLD   Access to the Trusted Platform Module Management console can be restricted in Group Policy. If you are unable to open the console, check whether a Group Policy Object (GPO) being processed includes Management Console restrictions under Windows Components\Microsoft Management Console.

To perform TPM management tasks on a local computer, you must be a member of the local computer's Administrators group or be logged on as the local computer administrator. When you are working with Trusted Platform Module Management, you can determine the exact state of the TPM. If you try to start Trusted Platform Module Management without turning on TPM, you'll get an error stating this. You'll also get an error if you try to run the Initialize The TPM Security Hardware Wizard without turning on TPM.

You will be able to perform management tasks with the TPM tools only when you've turned on TPM in firmware. When you are working with the Trusted Platform Module Management console, shown in Figure 2-1, you should note the TPM status and the TPM manufacturer information. The TPM status indicates the exact state of the TPM (see Table 2-1). The TPM manufacturer information shows whether the TPM supports specification version 1.2 or 2.0. Support for TPM version 1.2 or later is required.

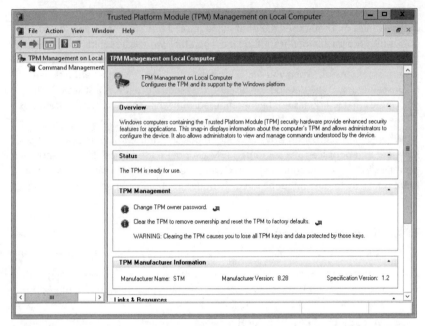

FIGURE 2-1 Use the Trusted Platform Module Management console to initialize and manage TPM.

TABLE 2-1 Understanding TPM states

TPM STATES	DESCRIPTION
The TPM is on and ownership has not been taken.	The TPM is turned on in firmware but hasn't been initialized yet.
The TPM is on and ownership has been taken.	The TPM is turned on in firmware and has been initialized.
The TPM is off and ownership has not been taken.	The TPM is turned off in software and hasn't been initialized yet either.
The TPM is off and ownership has been taken.	The TPM has been initialized but is turned off in software.

NOTE Although earlier releases of Windows showed the exact TPM state, Windows 8.1 typically shows either a status of "The TPM is ready for use" or "The TPM is not ready for use." If the TPM is ready for use, the TPM is on and ownership has been taken.

By default, Windows 8.1 and Windows Server 2012 R2 store full TPM owner authorization information in the registry of the local computer. This significant change enables administrators of the local computer to perform TPM management tasks without having to provide the TPM owner password.

The Configure The Level Of TPM Owner Authorization Information Available To The Operating System policy controls the level of authorization information stored in the registry. This policy is found in the Administrative Templates policies for Computer Configuration under System\Trusted Platform Module Services. This policy has three enabled settings:

- **Full** The full TPM owner authorization, the TPM administrative delegation blob, and the TPM user delegation blob are stored in the registry. This setting enables a TPM to be used without requiring remote or external storage of the TPM owner authorization. Note that TPM-based applications designed for earlier versions of Windows or that rely on TPM anti-hammering logic might not support full TPM owner authorization in the registry.

- **Delegated** Only the TPM administrative delegation blob and the TPM user delegation blob are stored in the registry. This level is appropriate for TPM-based applications that rely on TPM anti-hammering logic. When you use this setting, Microsoft recommends that you remotely or externally store the TPM owner authorization.

- **None** No TPM owner authorization information is stored in the registry. Use this setting for compatibility with earlier releases of Windows and for applications that require external or remote storage of the TPM owner authorization. When this setting is used, remote or external storage of the TPM owner authorization is required, just as it was in earlier releases of Windows.

CAUTION   If you change the policy setting from Full to Delegated or vice versa, the full TPM owner authorization value is regenerated and any copies of the original TPM value will be invalid.

When this policy is set to Delegated or None, you'll be prompted for the TPM owner password before you are able to perform most TPM administration tasks (see Figure 2-2).

With earlier releases of Windows, Microsoft recommended remotely storing the TPM owner authorization in Active Directory Domain Services (AD DS) for domain-joined computers, which could be accomplished by enabling the Turn On TPM Backup To Active Directory Domain Services policy, extending schema for the directory, and setting appropriate access controls.

Enabling backup to Active Directory changes the default way TPM owner information is stored. Specifically, when Turn On TPM Backup To Active Directory Domain Services is enabled and Configure The Level Of TPM Owner Authorization Information Available To The Operating System is disabled or not configured, only the TPM administrative delegation blob and the TPM user delegation blob are stored in the registry. Here, to store the full TPM owner information, you must use the enabled setting of Full (or disable Active Directory backup of the TPM owner authorization).

FIGURE 2-2 Supply the TPM owner password, if prompted for one.

Related policies under System\Trusted Platform Module Services include:

- Ignore The Default List Of Blocked TPM Commands
- Ignore The Local List Of Blocked TPM Commands
- Standard User Lockout Duration
- Standard User Individual Lockout Threshold
- Standard User Total Lockout Threshold

These policies control the way command block lists are used and when lockout is triggered after multiple failed authorization attempts. An administrator can fully reset all lockout-related parameters in the Trusted Platform Module Management console. On the Action menu, tap or click Reset TPM Lockout. When the full TPM owner authorization is stored in the registry, you don't need to provide the TPM owner password. Otherwise, follow the prompts to provide the owner password or select the file containing the TPM owner password.

Enabling TPM

The TPM Services architecture in Windows 8.1 provides the basic features required to configure and deploy TPM-equipped computers. This architecture can be extended with a feature called BitLocker Drive Encryption, which is discussed in the section "BitLocker Drive Encryption: the essentials" later in this chapter.

Before you can use TPM, you must enable TPM in firmware. In some cases, computers that have TPM might ship with it already enabled. In most cases, however, you'll find that TPM is not enabled by default.

With one of my computers, I needed to do the following:

1. Start the computer, and then press F2 during startup to access the firmware. In the firmware, I accessed the Advanced screen and then the Peripheral Configuration screen.

2. On the Peripheral Configuration screen, Trusted Platform Module was listed as an option. After scrolling down to highlight this option, I pressed Enter to display an options menu. From the menu, I chose Enable, and then pressed Enter.

3. To save the changes to the setting and exit the firmware, I pressed F10. When prompted to confirm that I wanted to exit, I pressed Y, and the computer then rebooted.

With a different computer, I needed to do the following:

1. Start the computer, and then press F2 during startup to access the firmware. In the firmware, I accessed the Security menu and then the TPM Security screen (see Figure 2-3).

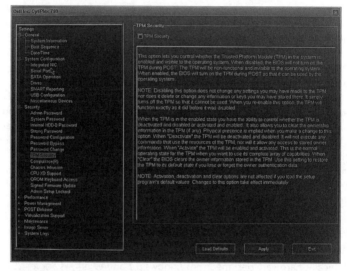

FIGURE 2-3 Enable the TPM in firmware, as necessary.

2. On the TPM Security screen, I needed to select the TPM Security check box, and tap or click Apply.

3. A prompt reminded me that I needed to turn off and then restart the computer for TPM security to be fully enabled.

4. When I exited firmware, the computer rebooted.

Next, you need to initialize and prepare the TPM for first use in software. As part of this process, you take ownership of the TPM, which sets the owner password on the TPM. After TPM is enabled, you can manage the TPM configuration.

Initializing and preparing a TPM for first use

Initializing a TPM configures it for use on a computer so that you can use the TPM to secure volumes on the computer's hard drives. The initialization process involves turning on the TPM and then setting ownership of the TPM. By setting ownership of the TPM, you assign a password that helps ensure that only the authorized TPM owner can access and manage the TPM. The TPM password is required to turn off the TPM if you no longer want to use it, and to clear the TPM before the computer is recycled. In an Active Directory domain, you can configure Group Policy to save TPM passwords.

By using an administrator account, you can initialize the TPM and create the owner password by completing the following steps:

1. Start the Trusted Platform Module Management console. On the Action menu, tap or click Prepare The TPM to start the Manage The TPM Security Hardware Wizard (tpminit).

   NOTE If the Initialize The TPM Security Hardware Wizard detects firmware that does not meet Windows requirements for a TPM or a TPM is not found, you will not be able to continue and should check that the TPM has been turned on in firmware.

   REAL WORLD If a TPM was previously initialized and then cleared, you are prompted to restart the computer and follow on-screen instructions during startup to reset the TPM in firmware. The wizard should start again when you next log on; however, on my systems, this did not occur. Instead, when I clicked Restart, I needed to enter firmware by pressing F2 during startup. I then needed to disable TPM, save the changes, and exit firmware. This triggered an automatic reset. After this, I needed to enter firmware by pressing F2, which let me enable TPM, save changes, and then exit firmware. This triggered another automatic reset. When the operating system loaded, I logged on and then needed to restart the Initialize The TPM Security Hardware Wizard.

2. When the wizard finishes its initial tasks, you'll get a prompt similar to the one shown in Figure 2-4. Tap or click Restart to restart the computer.

3. Typically, hardware designed for Windows 8.1 and Windows Server 2012 R2 can automatically complete the initialization process. On other hardware, you'll need physical access to the computer to respond to the manufacturer's firmware confirmation prompt. Figure 2-5 shows an example. Here, you must press F10 to enable and activate the TPM and allow a user to take ownership of the TPM.

4. When Windows starts and you log on, the Manage The TPM Security Hardware Wizard continues running. Windows will take ownership of the TPM. Setting ownership on the TPM prepares it for use with the operating system.

FIGURE 2-4 After the wizard prepares Windows to use TPM, you'll need to restart the computer so that the TPM hardware can be initialized in firmware.

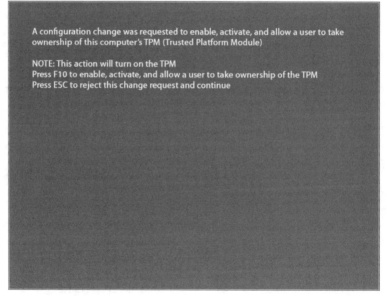

FIGURE 2-5 Confirm the configuration change when prompted.

5. After ownership is set, TPM is ready for use and you'll receive confirmation of this, as shown in Figure 2-6.

FIGURE 2-6 TPM ownership is set, and the TPM is ready for use.

6. Before tapping or clicking Close, you might want to save the TPM owner password. Tap or click Remember My TPM Owner Password. In the Save As dialog box, select a location to save the password backup file, and then tap or click Save.

7. In the TPM Management console, the status should be listed as "The TPM is ready for use."

NOTE By default, the password backup file is saved as *ComputerName*.tpm. Ideally, you should save the TPM ownership password to removable media, such as a USB flash drive, and store the media in a secure location. In a domain where the TPM Backup To Active Directory Domain Services policy is applied, you won't have the option to save the TPM password. Here, the password is saved to Active Directory automatically.

MORE INFO The password backup file is an unencrypted XML file that can be opened in any text editor to confirm the name of the computer to which the password belongs. In the following example, the password was created for ENGPC85:

```
<?xml version="1.0" encoding="UTF-8"?><tpmOwnerData
version="1.0" softwareAuthor="Microsoft Windows[Version 6.3]"
creationDate="2014-04-24T17:19:43-08:00"creationUser="ENGPC85\
Administrator" machineName="ENGPC85">        <tpmInfo
manufacturerId="1398033696"/>        <ownerAuth>cBHECAgNV8Z2EBJbER
TSD87HJKL=</ownerAuth></tpmOwnerData>
```

Turning an initialized TPM on or off

Computers that have TPM might ship with TPM turned on. If you decide not to use TPM, you should take ownership of the TPM, and then turn off the TPM. This ensures that the operating system owns the TPM but that the TPM is in an inactive state. If you want to reconfigure or recycle a computer, you should clear the TPM. Clearing the TPM invalidates any stored keys, and data encrypted by these keys can no longer be accessed.

By using an administrator account, you can turn off TPM by completing the following steps:

1. Start the Trusted Platform Module Management console.

2. On the Action menu, tap or click Turn TPM Off.

3. When the full TPM owner authorization is stored in the registry, you don't need to provide the TPM owner password. Otherwise, follow the prompts to provide the owner password or select the file containing the TPM owner password.

After you follow the previous procedure to turn off the TPM in software, you can turn on the TPM in software at any time by following the steps in the "Initializing and preparing a TPM for first use" section.

Clearing the TPM

Clearing the TPM erases information stored on the TPM and cancels the related ownership of the TPM. You should clear the TPM when a TPM-equipped computer is to be recycled. Clearing the TPM invalidates any stored keys, and data encrypted by these keys can no longer be accessed.

After clearing the TPM, you should take ownership of the TPM. This will write new information to the TPM. You might then want to turn off the TPM so it isn't available for use.

By using an administrator account, you can clear the TPM, take ownership, and then turn off TPM by completing the following steps:

1. Start the Trusted Platform Module Management console. On the Action menu, tap or click Clear TPM. This starts the Manage the TPM Security Hardware Wizard.

    CAUTION Clearing the TPM resets it to factory defaults. As a result, you lose all keys and data protected by those keys. You do not need the TPM owner password to clear the TPM.

2. Read the warning on the Clear The TPM Security Hardware page, shown in Figure 2-7, and then tap or click Restart. Tap or click Cancel to exit without clearing the TPM.

FIGURE 2-7 Tap or click Restart to confirm that you want to clear the TPM.

3. Typically, hardware designed for Windows 8.1 and Windows Server 2012 R2 can automatically complete the re-initialization process. On other hardware, you'll need physical access to the computer to respond to the manufacturer's firmware confirmation prompt. Figure 2-8 shows an example. Here, you must press F12 to clear, enable, and activate the TPM, or press ESC to cancel and continue loading the operating system.

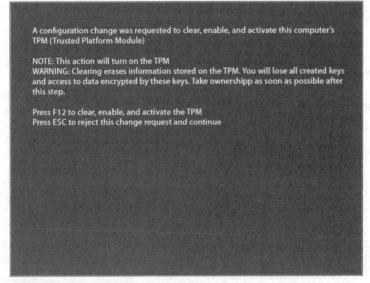

FIGURE 2-8 Confirm the configuration change when prompted.

4. Follow steps 4–7 in the "Initializing and preparing a TPM for first use" section.

Changing the TPM owner password

You can change the TPM password at any time. The key reason to do this is if you suspect that the TPM owner password has been compromised. Your company's security policy also might require TPM owner password changes in certain situations.

To change the TPM owner password, complete the following steps:

1. Start the Trusted Platform Module Management console. On the Action menu, tap or click Change Owner Password. This starts the Manage The TPM Security Hardware Wizard.

2. When the full TPM owner authorization is stored in the registry, you don't need to provide the TPM owner password. Otherwise, follow the prompts to provide the owner password or select the file containing the TPM owner password.

3. On the Create The TPM Owner Password page, shown in Figure 2-9, you can elect to create the password automatically or manually.

FIGURE 2-9 Create the new TPM owner password.

4. If you want the wizard to create the password for you, select Automatically Create The Password (Recommended). The new TPM owner password is displayed. Tap or click Change Password.

5. If you want to create the password, select Manually Create The Password. Enter and confirm a password of at least eight characters, and then tap or click Change Password.

6. Before tapping or clicking Close, you might want to save the TPM owner password. Tap or click Remember My TPM Owner Password. In the Save As dialog box, select a location to save the password backup file, and then tap or click Save.

BitLocker Drive Encryption: the essentials

BitLocker is built into all editions of Windows 8.1 and added as a feature for all editions of Windows Server. Although BitLocker Drive Encryption and BitLocker To Go are often referred to simply as BitLocker, they are separate but similar features. BitLocker Drive Encryption is designed to protect the data on the internal hard drives of lost, stolen, or inappropriately decommissioned computers and is a volume-level encryption technology. BitLocker To Go is designed to protect the data on removable data drives, such as external hard drives and USB flash drives, and is a virtual-volume encryption technology. Standard BitLocker encrypts by wrapping the entire volume or only the used portion of the volume in protected encryption. BitLocker To Go, on the other hand, creates a virtual volume on a USB flash drive. This virtual volume is encrypted by using an encryption key stored on the USB flash drive.

Understanding BitLocker Drive Encryption

On a computer without BitLocker Drive Encryption, a user with direct physical access to the computer has a variety of ways he could gain full control and then access the computer's data, whether that data is encrypted with EFS or not. For example, a user could use a boot disk to boot the computer and reset the administrator password. A user could also install and then boot to a different operating system and then use this operating system to unlock the other installation.

BitLocker Drive Encryption prevents all access to a computer's drives except by authorized personnel by wrapping entire drives or only the used portion of drives in tamper-proof encryption. If an unauthorized user tries to access a BitLocker-encrypted drive, the encryption prevents the user from viewing or manipulating the protected data in any way. This dramatically reduces the risk of an unauthorized person gaining access to confidential data through offline attacks.

> **IMPORTANT** BitLocker Drive Encryption is meant to be used when a computer is not in a physically secure location and requires additional protection. However, the encryption processes can reduce disk throughput, which in turn can affect a computer's overall performance.

BitLocker Drive Encryption can use a TPM to validate the integrity of a computer's boot manager and boot files at startup and to guarantee that a computer's hard disk has not been tampered with while the operating system was offline. BitLocker Drive Encryption also stores measurements of core operating system files in the TPM.

Every time the computer is started, Windows validates the boot files, the operating system files, and any encrypted volumes to ensure that they have not been modified while the operating system was offline. If the files have been modified, Windows alerts the user and refuses to release the key required to access Windows. The computer then goes into Recovery mode, prompting the user to provide a recovery key before it permits access to the boot volume. The Recovery mode is also used if a BitLocker-encrypted disk drive is transferred to another system.

BitLocker Drive Encryption can be used in both TPM and non-TPM computers. If a computer has a TPM, BitLocker Drive Encryption uses the TPM to provide enhanced protection for that computer's data and to ensure early boot file integrity. These features together help prevent unauthorized viewing and accessing of data by encrypting the entire Windows volume and by safeguarding the boot files from tampering. If a computer doesn't have a TPM or its TPM isn't compatible with Windows, BitLocker Drive Encryption can be used to encrypt entire volumes, and in this way protect the volumes from tampering. This configuration, however, doesn't offer the added security of early boot file integrity validation.

On computers with a compatible TPM that is initialized, BitLocker Drive Encryption typically uses one of the following TPM modes:

- **TPM-Only**   In this mode, only TPM is used for validation. When the computer boots, TPM is used to validate the boot files, the operating system files, and any encrypted volumes. Because the user doesn't need to provide an additional startup key, this mode is transparent to the user, and the user logon experience is unchanged. However, if the TPM is missing or the integrity of files or volumes has changed, BitLocker enters Recovery mode and requires the user to provide a recovery key or password to regain access to the boot volume.

- **TPM and PIN**   In this mode, both TPM and a user-entered numeric key are used for validation. When the computer boots, TPM is used to validate the boot files, the operating system files, and any encrypted volumes. The user must enter a PIN when prompted to continue startup. If the user doesn't have the PIN or is unable to provide the correct PIN, BitLocker enters Recovery mode instead of booting to the operating system. As before, BitLocker also enters Recovery mode if the TPM is missing or the integrity of boot files or encrypted volumes has changed.

- **TPM and Startup Key**   In this mode, both TPM and a startup key are used for validation. When the computer boots, TPM is used to validate the boot files, the operating system files, and any encrypted volumes. The user must have a USB flash drive with a startup key to log on to the computer. If the user doesn't have the startup key or is unable to provide the correct startup key, BitLocker enters Recovery mode. As before, BitLocker also enters Recovery mode if the TPM is missing or the integrity of boot files or encrypted volumes has changed.

- **TPM and Smart Card Certificate**   In this mode, both TPM and a smart card certificate are used for validation. When the computer boots, TPM is used to validate the boot files, the operating system files, and any encrypted volumes. The user must have a smart card with a valid certificate to log on to the computer. If the user doesn't have a smart card with a valid certificate and is unable to provide one, BitLocker enters Recovery mode. As before, BitLocker also enters Recovery mode if the TPM is missing or the integrity of boot files or encrypted volumes has changed.

With Windows 8.1 and Windows Server 2012 R2, network unlock enables the system volume on a computer with TPM to be automatically unlocked on startup, if the computer is joined and connected to the domain. When it is not joined and connected to the domain, other means of validation can be used, such as a startup PIN.

On computers without a TPM or on computers that have incompatible TPMs, Windows 8.1 and Windows Server 2012 R2 can be configured to use an unlock password for the operating system drive. To configure this, you must enable the Configure Use Of Passwords For Operating System Drives policy in the Administrative Templates policies for Computer Configuration under Windows Components\ BitLocker Drive Encryption. The unlock password can be configured with minimum length and complexity requirements. The default minimum password length is eight characters, meaning the password must be at least eight characters. Complexity requirements can be:

- Always validated by using the Require Password Complexity setting.
- Validated if possible by using the Allow Password Complexity setting.
- Not validated by using the Do Now Allow Password Complexity setting.

The unlock password is validated when you enable BitLocker Drive Encryption and set the password, and whenever the password is changed by a user. With required complexity, you can only set a password (and enable encryption) when the computer can connect to a domain controller and validate the complexity of the password. With allowed complexity, the computer will attempt to validate the complexity of the password when you set it but will allow you to continue and enable encryption if no domain controllers are available.

On computers without a TPM or on computers that have incompatible TPMs, BitLocker Drive Encryption also can use Startup Key Only or Smart Card Certificate Only mode. Startup Key Only mode requires a USB flash drive containing a startup key. The user inserts the USB flash drive in the computer before turning it on. The key stored on the flash drive unlocks the computer.

Smart Card Certificate Only mode requires a smart card with a valid certificate. The user validates the smart card certificate after turning on the computer. The certificate unlocks the computer.

It's also important to point out that standard users can reset the BitLocker PIN and password on operating system drives, fixed data drives, and removable data drives. If you don't want standard users to be able to perform these tasks, enable the Disallow Standard Users From Changing The PIN Or Password policy. This Computer Configuration policy is found under Windows Components\BitLocker Drive Encryption\Operating System Drives.

Several important changes have been made to BitLocker Drive Encryption since the technology was first implemented. Specifically, you can do the following:

- Encrypt FAT volumes and NTFS volumes. When you encrypt FAT volumes, you have the option of specifying whether encrypted volumes can be unlocked and viewed. This option is configured through Group Policy and is enabled when you turn on BitLocker. In the Administrative Templates policies for Computer Configuration under Windows Components\BitLocker Drive Encryption, there are separate policies for earlier versions of Windows that allow FAT-formatted fixed drives and FAT-formatted removable drives to be unlocked and viewed.

- Allow a data-recovery agent to be used with BitLocker Drive Encryption. This option is configured through Group Policy. The data-recovery agent allows an encrypted volume to be unlocked and recovered by using a recovery agent's personal certificate or a 48-digit recovery password. You can optionally save the recovery information in Active Directory. In the Administrative Templates policies for Computer Configuration, there are separate policies for operating system volumes, other fixed drives, and removable drives.

- Deny write access to removable data drives not protected with BitLocker. This option is configured through Group Policy. If you enable this option, users have read-only access to unencrypted removable data drives and read/write access to encrypted removable data drives.

In a domain, domain administrators are the default data-recovery agents. A homegroup or workgroup has no default data-recovery agent, but you can designate one. Any user you want to designate as a data-recovery agent needs a personal encryption certificate. You can generate a certificate by using the Cipher utility and then use the certificate to assign the data-recovery agent in Local Security Policy under Public Key Policies\BitLocker Drive Encryption.

Earlier releases of Windows support AES encryption with a diffuser. Windows 8 and Windows 8.1 move away from this to support standard AES with 128-bit encryption by default or 256-bit encryption (if you enable the Choose Drive Encryption Method And Cipher Strength policy to set the cipher strength to 256-bit encryption). The cipher strength must be set prior to turning on BitLocker. Changing the cipher strength has no effect if the drive is already encrypted or encryption is in progress.

Hardware encryption, secure boot, and network unlock

Most BitLocker-related settings are controlled with the Administrative Templates policies for Computer Configuration under Windows Components\BitLocker Drive Encryption. Windows 8.1 supports disk drives with hardware encryption (referred to as *encrypted hard drives*). Encryption in hardware is faster and moves the processing burden from the computer's processor to the hardware processor on the hard drive. By default, if a computer has hardware encryption, Windows 8.1 will use it with BitLocker.

In Group Policy, you can precisely control whether to permit software-based encryption when hardware encryption is not available and whether to restrict encryption to those algorithms and cipher strengths supported by hardware. Do this by enabling the Configure Use Of Hardware-Based Encryption For Fixed Data Drives policy and configuring the related options. When the policy is enabled, you must specifically allow software-based encryption when hardware-based encryption isn't available.

> **MORE INFO** The Choose Drive Encryption Method And Cipher Strength policy doesn't apply to hardware-based encryption. You can set the encryption methods you want for hardware-based policy under Fixed Data Drives in the Configure Use Of Hardware-Based Encryption For Fixed Data Drives policy. With hardware-based encryption, the encryption algorithm is set when the drive is partitioned.

Next, you might want to configure policy to control the permitted encryption types. Windows 8.1 allows users to encrypt full volumes or used space only. Encrypting full volumes takes longer, but it's more secure because the entire volume is protected. Encrypting used space protects only the portion of the drive used to store data. By default, either option can be used. If you want to allow only one type or the other, enable and configure related Enforce Drive Encryption Type policy for BitLocker. There are separate Enforce Drive Encryption Type policies for the operating system, fixed data drives, and removable data drives.

REAL WORLD In high-security environments, you will want to encrypt entire volumes. At the time of this writing, and unless fixed with a future update or service pack, deleted files appear as free space when you encrypt used space only. As a result, until the files are wiped or overwritten, information in the files could be recovered with certain tools.

Operating system drives are handled as special cases. Windows 8.1 enables you to pre-provision BitLocker so that you can turn on encryption prior to installation. Windows 8.1 also can be configured to do the following:

- Require additional authentication at startup. If you enable and configure the related policy, Require Additional Authentication At Startup, user input is required, even if the platform lacks a pre-boot input capability. To enable a USB keyboard to be used on such a platform in the pre-boot environment, you should set the Enable Use Of BitLocker Authentication Requiring Preboot Keyboard Input On Slates policy to Enabled.

- Allow secure boot for integrity validation. Secure boot is used by default to verify Boot Configuration Data (BCD) settings according to the TPM validation profile settings (also referred to as Secure Boot policy). When you use secure boot, the settings of the Use Enhanced Boot Configuration Data Validation Profile policy are ignored (unless you specifically disable secure boot support by setting Allow Secure Boot For Integrity Validation to Disabled).

You set TPM validation profile settings by platform. For BIOS-based firmware, you use the Configure TPM Platform Validation Profile For BIOS-Based Firmware Configurations policy. For firmware based on Unified Extensible Firmware Interface (UEFI), you use the Configure TPM Platform Validation Profile For Native UEFI Firmware Configurations policy. When you enable these policies, you specify exactly which platform configuration registers to validate during boot (see Figure 2-10).

For BIOS-based firmware, Microsoft recommends validating Platform Configuration Registers (PCRs) 0, 2, 4, 8, 9, 10, and 11. For UEFI firmware, Microsoft recommends validating PCRs 0, 2, 4, 7, and 11. In both instances, PCR 11 validation is required for BitLocker protection to be enforced. PCR 7 validation is required to support secure boot with UEFI (and you'll need to enable this by selecting the related option).

FIGURE 2-10 Specify the PCRs to validate.

IMPORTANT Like Windows 8, Windows 8.1 is designed to be run on computers with UEFI. As discussed in Chapter 1, "Managing firmware, boot configuration, and startup," UEFI doesn't replace all the functionality in either BIOS or EFI and can, in fact, be wrapped around BIOS or EFI. When a computer has UEFI and is running Windows 8.1, UEFI is the first link in the chain of trust for secure boot. UEFI 2.3.1 and later are able to run internal integrity checks that verify the firmware's digital signature before running it. If the firmware's digital signature has been modified or replaced (as an example, by a firmware rootkit), the firmware will not load.

With Secure Boot, firmware also verifies the digital signature on the Windows boot loader as part of initialization. If a rootkit is installed and the Windows boot loader has been modified, the computer will be prevented from starting. After the Secure Boot, the boot loader verifies the digital signature of the operating system kernel as part of Trusted Boot. Also as part of Trusted Boot, the kernel in turn verifies all remaining boot components, including boot drivers and startup files. Finally, Measured Boot allows third-party software running on a remote server to also verify the security of every startup component.

When you protect a computer with BitLocker, you can require additional authentication at startup. Typically, this means a user is required to have a startup key on a USB flash drive, a startup PIN, or both. The Network Unlock feature provides this additional layer of protection without requiring the startup key, startup PIN, or both by automatically unlocking the operating system drive when a computer is started, if the following conditions are met:

- The BitLocker-protected computer has an enabled TPM.
- The computer is on a trusted, wired network.
- The computer is joined to and connected to a domain.
- A Network Unlock server with an appropriate Network Unlock certificate is available.

Because the computer must be joined to and connected to the domain for network unlock to work, user authentication is still required when a computer is not connected to the domain. When connected to the domain, the client computer connects to a Network Unlock server to unlock the system drive. Typically, the Network Unlock server is a domain controller configured to use and distribute Network Unlock certificates to clients. The Network Unlock certificates in turn are used to create the network unlock keys.

You can configure a domain controller to distribute this certificate to clients. To do this, create an X.509 certificate for the server, for example by using Certmsg.mc, then use the BitLocker Driver Encryption Network Unlock Certificate setting to add this certificate to a GPO applied to the domain controller. You'll find this Computer Configuration setting under Windows Settings\Security Settings\Public Key Policies.

Finally, Windows 8.1 also enables you to provision BitLocker during operating system deployment. You can do this from the Windows PreInstallation Environment (Windows PE). It's important to point out that Windows PowerShell includes a DISM module that you can import. Because this module doesn't support wildcards when searching for feature names, you can use the Get-WindowsOptionalFeature cmdlet to list feature names, as shown in this example:

```
get-windowsoptionalfeature -online | ft
```

To completely install BitLocker and related management tools, use the following command:

```
enable-windowsoptionalfeature -online -featurename bitlocker,bitlocker-
utilities, bitlocker-networkunlock -all
```

Deploying BitLocker Drive Encryption

Deploying BitLocker Drive Encryption in an enterprise changes the way administrators and users work with computers. A computer with BitLocker Drive Encryption usually requires user intervention to boot to the operating system—a user must enter a PIN, insert a USB flash drive containing a startup key, or use a smart card with a valid certificate. Because of this requirement, after you deploy BitLocker Drive Encryption, you can no longer be assured that you can perform remote administration that requires a computer to be restarted without having physical access to the computer—someone might need to be available to enter the required PIN, insert the USB flash drive with the startup key, or use a smart card with a valid certificate.

To work around this issue, you can configure network unlock on your trusted, wired networks. Before you use BitLocker Drive Encryption, you should perform a thorough evaluation of your organization's computers. You need to develop plans and procedures for the following:

- Evaluating the various BitLocker authentication methods and applying them as appropriate
- Determining whether computers support TPM, and thus whether you must use TPM or non-TPM BitLocker configurations
- Storing, using, and periodically changing encryption keys, recovery passwords, and other validation mechanisms used with BitLocker

You need to develop procedures for tasks such as these:

- Performing daily operations with BitLocker-encrypted drives
- Providing administrative support for BitLocker-encrypted drives
- Recovering computers with BitLocker-encrypted drives

These procedures need to take into account the way BitLocker encryption works and the requirements to have PINs, startup keys, smart cards, and recovery keys available whenever you work with BitLocker-encrypted computers. After you evaluate your organization's computers and develop basic plans and procedures, you need to develop a configuration plan for implementing BitLocker Drive Encryption.

Several implementations of BitLocker Drive Encryption are available. Although computers running Windows 8.1 and Windows Server 2012 R2 can work with any of the available versions, earlier versions of Windows can't necessarily work with the latest version of BitLocker. For example, you might need to configure Group Policy to allow access from earlier versions of Windows.

To turn on BitLocker Drive Encryption on the drive containing the Windows operating system, the drive must have at least two partitions:

- The first partition is for BitLocker Drive Encryption. This partition, designated as the active partition, holds the files required to start the operating system and is not encrypted.
- The second is the primary partition for the operating system and your data. This partition is encrypted when you turn on BitLocker.

With implementations of BitLocker prior to Windows 7, you need to create the partitions in a certain way to ensure compatibility. This is no longer the case in Windows 7 and later. When you install Windows 7 and later, an additional partition is created automatically during setup. By default, this additional partition is used by the Windows Recovery Environment (Windows RE). However, if you enable BitLocker on the system volume, Windows usually moves Windows RE to the system volume and then uses the additional partition for BitLocker.

Using BitLocker on a hard disk is easy. On a computer with a compatible TPM, you must initialize the TPM as discussed in the "Initializing and preparing a TPM for first use" section earlier in this chapter, and then you need to enable BitLocker. On a computer without a compatible TPM, you need to enable BitLocker only on your hard disk.

You can use local Group Policy and Active Directory–based Group Policy to help manage and maintain TPM and BitLocker configurations. Group Policy settings for TPM Services are found in Administrative Templates policies for Computer Configuration under System\Trusted Platform Module Services. Group Policy settings for BitLocker are found in Administrative Templates policies for Computer Configuration under Windows Components\BitLocker Drive Encryption. There are separate subfolders for fixed data drives, operating system drives, and removable data drives.

Policies you might want to configure include the following:

- Trusted Platform Module Services policies
  - Configure The Level of TPM Owner Authorization Information Available To The Operating System
  - Configure The List Of Blocked TPM Commands
  - Ignore The Default List Of Blocked TPM Commands
  - Ignore The Local List Of Blocked TPM Commands
  - Standard User Individual Lockout Threshold
  - Standard User Lockout Duration
  - Standard User Total Lockout Threshold
  - Turn On TPM Backup To Active Directory Domain Services
- BitLocker Drive Encryption policies
  - Choose Default Folder For Recovery Password
  - Choose Drive Encryption Method And Cipher Strength
  - Prevent Memory Overwrite On Restart
  - Provide The Unique Identifiers For Your Organization
  - Validate Smart Card Certificate Usage Rule Compliance
- Fixed Drive policies
  - Allow Access To BitLocker-Protected Fixed Data Drives From Earlier Versions Of Windows
  - Choose How BitLocker-Protected Fixed Drives Can Be Recovered
  - Configure Use Of Hardware-Based Encryption For Fixed Data Drives
  - Configure Use Of Passwords For Fixed Data Drives
  - Configure Use Of Smart Cards On Fixed Data Drives
  - Deny Write Access To Fixed Drives Not Protected By BitLocker
  - Enforce Drive Encryption Type On Fixed Data Drives
- Operating System Drive policies
  - Allow Enhanced PINs For Startup
  - Allow Network Unlock At Startup

- Allow Secure Boot For Integrity Validation
- Choose How BitLocker-Protected Operating System Drives Can Be Recovered
- Configure Minimum PIN Length For Startup
- Configure TPM Platform Validation Profile For BIOS-Based Firmware Configurations
- Configure TPM Platform Validation Profile For Native UEFI Firmware Configurations
- Configure TPM Platform Validation Profile (Windows Vista, Windows 7, Windows Server 2008, Windows Server 2008 R2)
- Configure Use Of Passwords For Operating System Drives
- Disallow Standard Users From Changing The PIN Or Password
- Enforce Drive Encryption Type On Operating System Drives
- Enable User Of BitLocker Authentication Requiring Preboot Keyboard Input On Slates
- Require Additional Authentication At Startup
- Reset Platform Validation Data After BitLocker Recovery
- Removable Data Drive policies
  - Allow Access To BitLocker-Protected Removable Data Drives From Earlier Versions Of Windows
  - Choose How BitLocker-Protected Removable Drives Can Be Recovered
  - Configure Use Of Hardware-Based Encryption For Removable Data Drives
  - Configure Use Of Passwords For Removable Data Drives
  - Configure Use Of Smart Cards On Removable Data Drives
  - Control Use Of BitLocker On Removable Drives
  - Deny Write Access To Removable Drives Not Protected By BitLocker
  - Enforce Drive Encryption Type On Removable Data Drives

Active Directory includes TPM and BitLocker recovery extensions for Computer objects. For TPM, the extensions define a single property of the Computer object, called ms-TPM-OwnerInformation. When the TPM is initialized or when the owner password is changed, the hash of the TPM ownership password can be stored as a value of the ms-TPM-OwnerInformation attribute on the related Computer object. For BitLocker, these extensions define Recovery objects as child objects of Computer objects and are used to store recovery passwords and associate them with specific BitLocker-encrypted volumes.

By default, Windows 8.1 stores the full TPM owner authorization, the TPM administrative delegation blob, and the TPM user delegation in the registry. Because of this change, you no longer have to save this information separately to Active Directory for backup and recovery purposes. For more information, see the "TPM: management and policies" section earlier in this chapter.

To ensure that BitLocker recovery information is always available, you can configure Group Policy to save recovery information in Active Directory as follows:

- With Choose How BitLocker-Protected Fixed Drives Can Be Recovered, enable the policy and accept the default options to allow data recovery agents and save the recovery information in Active Directory.

- With Choose How BitLocker-Protected Operating System Drives Can Be Recovered, enable the policy and accept the default options to allow data recovery agents and save the recovery information in Active Directory.

- With Choose How BitLocker-Protected Removable Drives Can Be Recovered, enable the policy and accept the default options to allow data recovery agents, and then save the recovery information in Active Directory.

REAL WORLD For Federal Information Processing Standard (FIPS) compliance, you cannot create or save BitLocker recovery passwords. Instead, you need to configure Windows to create recovery keys. The FIPS setting is located in the Security Policy Editor at Local Policies\Security Options\System Cryptography: Use FIPS Compliant Algorithms For Encryption, Hashing, And Signing.

To configure BitLocker to use recovery keys, enable the security option System Cryptography: Use FIPS Compliant Algorithms For Encryption, Hashing, And Signing in local Group Policy or Active Directory–based Group Policy as appropriate. With this setting enabled, users can only generate recovery keys.

Managing BitLocker Drive Encryption

You can configure and enable BitLocker Drive Encryption on both system volumes and data volumes. When you encrypt system volumes, you must unlock the computer at startup, typically by using a TPM and network unlock when connected to the domain in addition to a TPM, a startup key, a startup PIN, or any required or optional combination of these. To enforce the strictest and highest security possible, use all three authentication methods.

In the current implementation of BitLocker, you do not have to encrypt a computer's system volume prior to encrypting a computer's data volumes. When you use encrypted data volumes, the operating system mounts BitLocker data volumes as it would any other volume, but it requires either a password or a smart card with a valid certificate to unlock the drive.

The encryption key for a protected data volume is created and stored independently from the system volume and all other protected data volumes. To allow the operating system to mount encrypted volumes, the key chain protecting the data volume is stored in an encrypted state on the operating system volume. If the operating system enters Recovery mode, the data volumes are not unlocked until the operating system is out of Recovery mode.

Setting up BitLocker Drive Encryption requires these steps:

1. Partitioning a computer's hard disks appropriately and installing the operating system (if you are configuring a new computer). Windows Setup partitions the drives for you automatically. However, the volume where BitLocker data is stored must always be the active, system volume.

2. Initializing and configuring a computer's TPM (if applicable).

3. Turning on the BitLocker Drive Encryption feature (as necessary).

4. Checking firmware to ensure that the computer is set to start first from the disk containing the active, system partition and the boot partition, not from a USB or CD/DVD drive (applicable only when you encrypt system volumes).

5. Turning on and configuring BitLocker Drive Encryption.

NOTE When you are using a Microsoft account on a non–domain-joined computer, you have an additional save option. You can save the recovery key to the Windows Live SkyDrive. The user's SkyDrive account will then contain a BitLocker folder with a separate file for each saved recovery key.

After you've turned on and configured BitLocker encryption, you can use several techniques to maintain the environment and perform recovery.

Preparing for BitLocker Drive Encryption

As discussed previously, BitLocker Drive Encryption can be used in a TPM or a non-TPM configuration. Either configuration requires some preliminary work before you can turn on and configure BitLocker Drive Encryption.

With Windows 8.1 Pro and Enterprise editions, BitLocker should be installed by default. If it's not, you can install the BitLocker Drive Encryption feature by using the Add Features Wizard. You need to restart the computer to complete the installation process.

You can determine the readiness status of a computer by accessing the BitLocker Drive Encryption console. In Control Panel, tap or click System And Security, and then tap or click BitLocker Drive Encryption. If the system isn't properly configured, you'll receive an error message. Note the following:

- If you get an error message related to TPM on a computer with a compatible TPM, refer to the "Enabling TPM" section earlier in this chapter to learn more about TPM states and enabling TPM in firmware.

- If you get an error message related to TPM on a computer with an incompatible TPM or no TPM, you need to change the computer's Group Policy settings so that you can turn on BitLocker Drive Encryption without a TPM.

You can configure policy settings for BitLocker encryption in local Group Policy or in Active Directory–based Group Policy. In local policy, you apply the settings to the computer's local GPO. For domain policy, you apply the settings to a Group Policy object processed by the computer. While you are working with domain policy, you can also specify requirements for computers with a TPM.

To configure the way BitLocker can be used with or without a TPM, follow these steps:

1. Open the appropriate GPO for editing in the Group Policy Management Editor.

2. In the Administrative Templates policies for Computer Configuration under Windows Components\BitLocker Drive Encryption\Operating System Drives, double-tap or double-click the Require Additional Authentication At Startup setting.

   IMPORTANT There are several versions of this policy and they are specific to the operating system. Configure the version or versions of this policy that are appropriate for your working environment and the computers to which the policy will be applied. The options for each related policy are slightly different because the TPM features supported are slightly different for each operating system.

3. In the Require Additional Authentication At Startup dialog box, define the policy setting by selecting Enabled.

4. Do one of the following:

   - If you want to allow BitLocker to be used without a compatible TPM, select the Allow BitLocker Without A Compatible TPM check box. This changes the policy setting so that you can use BitLocker encryption with a password or startup key on a computer without a TPM.

   - If you want to require BitLocker to be used with a TPM, clear the Allow BitLocker Without A Compatible TPM check box. This changes the policy setting so that you can use BitLocker encryption on a computer with a TPM by using a startup PIN, a startup key, or both.

5. On a computer with a compatible TPM, several authentication methods can be used at startup to provide added protection for encrypted data. These authentication methods can be allowed or required. Use Table 2-2 to help you configure how TPM is used with these authentication methods. The methods available depend on the operating system–specific version of the policy with which you are working.

TABLE 2-2 Common options for using TPM with BitLocker

WHEN THE COMPUTER STARTS	SETTING FOR			
	CONFIGURE TPM STARTUP	CONFIGURE TPM STARTUP PIN	CONFIGURE TPM STARTUP KEY	CONFIGURE TPM STARTUP KEY AND PIN
Allow TPM to be used at startup	Allow TPM	Do Not Allow	Do Not Allow	Do Not Allow
Require TPM to be used at startup	Require TPM	Do Not Allow	Do Not Allow	Do Not Allow

	SETTING FOR			
WHEN THE COMPUTER STARTS	CONFIGURE TPM STARTUP	CONFIGURE TPM STARTUP PIN	CONFIGURE TPM STARTUP KEY	CONFIGURE TPM STARTUP KEY AND PIN
Use TPM only with a startup key	Allow or Require TPM	Allow or Require Startup PIN with TPM	Do Not Allow	Do Not Allow
Use TPM only with a startup PIN	Allow or Require TPM	Do Not Allow	Allow or Require Startup Key with TPM	Do Not Allow
Use TPM only with a startup key and PIN	Allow or Require TPM	Do Not Allow	Do Not Allow	Allow or Require Startup Key and PIN with TPM
Allow TPM with any other authentication method	Allow or Require TPM	Allow Startup PIN with TPM	Allow Startup Key with TPM	Allow Startup Key and PIN with TPM

6. Tap or click OK to save your settings. This policy is enforced the next time Group Policy is applied.

7. Close the Group Policy Management Editor. To apply Group Policy immediately to the computer you are logged on to, enter **gpupdate.exe /force** in the Apps Search box, and then press Enter.

Computers that have a startup key or a startup PIN also have a recovery password or certificate. The recovery password or certificate is required in the event that any of the following occur:

- Changes are made to the system startup information
- The encrypted drive must be moved to another computer
- The user is unable to provide the appropriate startup key or PIN

The recovery password or certificate should be managed and stored separately from the startup key or startup PIN. Although users are given the startup key or startup PIN, administrators should be the only ones with the recovery password or certificate. As an administrator, you need the recovery password or certificate to unlock the encrypted data on the volume if BitLocker enters a locked state. Generally, unless you use a common data-recovery agent, the recovery password or certificate is unique to this particular BitLocker encryption. This means you cannot use it to recover encrypted data from any other BitLocker-encrypted volume—even from other BitLocker-encrypted volumes on the same computer. To increase security, you should store startup keys and recovery data apart from the computer.

When BitLocker is installed, the BitLocker Drive Encryption console is available in Control Panel. Your configuration options for BitLocker depend on whether the computer has a TPM and on how you've configured Group Policy.

Enabling BitLocker on nonsystem volumes

Encrypting a nonsystem volume protects the data stored on the volume. Any volume formatted with FAT, FAT32, exFAT, or NTFS can be encrypted with BitLocker. The length of time it takes to encrypt a drive depends on the amount of data to encrypt, the processing power of the computer, and the level of activity on the computer.

Before you enable BitLocker, you should configure the appropriate Fixed Data Drive policies and settings in Group Policy, and then wait for Group Policy to be refreshed. If you don't do this and you enable BitLocker, you might need to turn BitLocker off, and then turn BitLocker back on because certain state and management flags are set when you turn on BitLocker.

If you dual-boot a computer or move drives between computers, the Allow Access To BitLocker-Protected Fixed Data Drives From Earlier Versions Of Windows setting in Group Policy can ensure that you have access to the volume on other operating systems and computers. Unlocked drives are read-only. To ensure that you can recover an encrypted volume, you should allow data-recovery agents and store recovery information in Active Directory.

To enable BitLocker encryption on a nonsystem volume, follow these steps:

1. In File Explorer, press and hold or right-click the data volume, and then tap or click Turn On BitLocker. BitLocker then verifies that your computer meets its requirements and then initializes the drive.

    NOTE If BitLocker is already enabled, the Manage BitLocker option is displayed instead of Turn On BitLocker.

2. On the Choose How You Want To Unlock This Drive page, shown in Figure 2-11, choose one or more of the following options, and then tap or click Next:

    - **Use A Password To Unlock The Drive**   Select this option if you want the user to be prompted for a password to unlock the drive. Passwords allow a drive to be unlocked in any location and to be shared with other people.

    - **Use My Smart Card To Unlock The Drive**   Select this option if you want the user to use a smart card and enter the smart card PIN to unlock the drive. Because this feature requires a smart card reader, it's typically used to unlock a drive in the workplace and not for drives that might be used outside the workplace.

    NOTE When you tap or click Next, the wizard generates a recovery key. You can use the key to unlock the drive if BitLocker detects a condition that prevents it from unlocking the drive during boot. Note that you should save the key on removable media or on a network share. You can't store the key on the encrypted volume or the root directory of a fixed drive.

FIGURE 2-11 Choose an option for unlocking a drive.

3. On the How Do You Want To Back Up Your Recovery Key? page, choose a save location for the recovery key, preferably a USB flash drive or other removable media.

4. You can now optionally save the recovery key to another folder, print the recovery key, or both. For each option, tap or click the option, and then follow the wizard's steps to set the location for saving or printing the recovery key. When you have finished, tap or click Next.

5. If allowed in Group Policy, you can elect to encrypt used disk space only or the entire drive, and then tap or click Next. Encrypting the used disk space only is faster than encrypting an entire volume. It's also the recommended option for newer computers and drives (except in high-security environments).

6. On the Are You Ready To Encrypt This Drive? page, tap or click Start Encrypting. The amount of time the encryption process takes depends on the amount of data being encrypted and other factors.

Because the encryption process can be paused and resumed, you can shut down the computer before the drive is completely encrypted, and the encryption of the drive will resume when you restart the computer. The encryption state is also maintained in the event of a power loss.

Enabling BitLocker on USB flash drives

Encrypting USB flash drives protects the data stored on the volume. Any USB flash drive formatted with FAT, FAT32, exFAT, or NTFS can be encrypted with BitLocker. The length of time it takes to encrypt a drive depends on the size of the drive, the processing power of the computer, and the level of activity on the computer.

Before you enable BitLocker, you should configure the appropriate Removable Data Drives policies and settings in Group Policy and then wait for Group Policy to be refreshed. If you don't do this and you enable BitLocker, you might need to turn BitLocker off and then turn BitLocker back on because certain state and management flags are set when you turn on BitLocker.

To be sure that you can recover an encrypted volume, you should allow data-recovery agents and store recovery information in Active Directory. If you use a flash drive with earlier versions of Windows, the Allow Access To BitLocker-Protected Removable Data Drives From Earlier Versions Of Windows policy can ensure that you have access to the USB flash drive on other operating systems and computers. Unlocked drives are read-only.

To enable BitLocker encryption on a USB flash drive, follow these steps:

1. Insert the USB flash drive. In File Explorer, press and hold or right-click the USB flash drive, and then tap or click Turn On BitLocker. BitLocker then verifies that your computer meets its requirements and then initializes the drive.

2. On the Choose How You Want To Unlock This Drive page, choose one or more of the following options, and then tap or click Next:

   - **Use A Password To Unlock This Drive**   Select this option if you want the user to be prompted for a password to unlock the drive. Passwords allow a drive to be unlocked in any location and to be shared with other people.

   - **Use My Smart Card To Unlock The Drive**   Select this option if you want the user to use a smart card and enter the smart card PIN to unlock the drive. Because this feature requires a smart card reader, it's typically used to unlock a drive in the workplace and not for drives that might be used outside the workplace.

3. On the How Do You Want To Back Up Your Recovery Key? page, tap or click Save The Recovery Key To A File.

4. In the Save BitLocker Recovery Key As dialog box, choose a save location, and then tap or click Save.

5. You can now print the recovery key if you want to. When you have finished, tap or click Next.

6. If allowed in Group Policy, you can elect to encrypt used disk space only or the entire drive, and then tap or click Next. Encrypting the used disk space only is faster than encrypting an entire volume. It's also the recommended option for newer computers and drives (except in high-security environments).

7. On the Are You Ready To Encrypt This Drive? page, tap or click Start Encrypting. Be sure to pause encryption before removing the drive and then resume to complete the encryption. Do not otherwise remove the USB flash drive until the encryption process is complete. The amount of time the encryption process takes depends on the amount of data to encrypt and other factors.

The encryption process does the following:

1. It adds an Autorun.inf file, the BitLocker To Go reader, and a Read Me.txt file to the USB flash drive.

2. It creates a virtual volume with the encrypted contents of the drive.

3. It encrypts the virtual volume to protect it. USB flash drive encryption takes approximately 6 to 10 minutes per gigabyte to complete. The encryption process can be paused and resumed, as long as you don't remove the drive.

When you insert an encrypted drive into a USB slot on a computer running Windows 8.1, a notification on the secure desktop is displayed, as shown in Figure 2-12. If the notification disappears before you can tap or click it, just remove and then reinsert the encrypted drive.

Unlock drive H:
This drive is BitLocker protected.

FIGURE 2-12 Tap or click the notification.

Tap or click the notification to display the BitLocker dialog box shown in Figure 2-13. This dialog box is also displayed on the secure desktop.

When you are prompted, enter the password. Optionally, tap or click More Options to expand the dialog box so that you can select Automatically Unlock On This Computer to save the password in an encrypted file on the computer's system volume. Finally, tap or click Unlock to unlock the drive so that you can use it.

FIGURE 2-13 Unlock the encrypted drive.

If you forget or lose the password for the drive but have the recovery key, tap or click More Options, and then tap or click Enter Recovery Key. Enter the 48-digit recovery key, and then tap or click Unlock. This key is stored in the XML-formatted recovery key file as plain text.

Enabling BitLocker on system volumes

Before you can encrypt a system volume, you must remove all bootable media from a computer's CD/DVD drives, in addition to all USB flash drives. You can then enable BitLocker encryption on the system volume by completing the following steps:

1. In File Explorer, press and hold or right-click the system volume, and then tap or click Turn On BitLocker. Windows checks the computer and the drive to ensure that BitLocker can be enabled. Tap or click Next.

    NOTE If BitLocker is already enabled, the Manage BitLocker option is displayed instead of Turn On BitLocker. As part of the setup, Windows prepares the required BitLocker partition, if necessary. If Windows RE is in this partition, Windows moves Windows RE to the system volume and then uses this additional partition for BitLocker.

    NOTE If the computer doesn't have a TPM, the Allow BitLocker Without A Compatible TPM option must be enabled for operating system volumes in the Require Additional Authentication At Startup policy.

2. As Figure 2-14 shows, you can now configure BitLocker startup preferences. Continue as discussed in the separate procedures that follow. If the computer doesn't have a TPM, your options will be different. You'll be able to create a password to unlock the drive, or you can insert a USB flash drive and store the startup key on the flash drive.

FIGURE 2-14 Configure BitLocker startup preferences.

When a computer has a TPM, you can use BitLocker to provide basic integrity checks of the volume without requiring any additional keys. In this configuration, BitLocker protects the system volume by encrypting it. This configuration does the following:

- Grants access to the volume to users who can log on to the operating system
- Prevents those who have physical access to the computer from booting to an alternative operating system to gain access to the data on the volume
- Allows the computer to be used with or without a TPM for additional boot security
- Does not require a password or a smart card with a PIN

To use BitLocker without any additional keys, follow these steps:

1. On the Choose How To Unlock Your Drive At Startup page, tap or click Let BitLocker Automatically Unlock My Drive.

2. On the How Do You Want To Back Up Your Recovery Key? page, tap or click Save To A File.

3. In the Save BitLocker Recovery Key As dialog box, choose the location of your USB flash drive or an appropriate network share, and then tap or click Save. Do not use a USB flash drive that is BitLocker-encrypted.

4. You can now optionally save the recovery key to another location, print the recovery key, or both. Tap or click an option, and then follow the wizard steps to set the location for saving or printing the recovery key. When you have finished, tap or click Next.

5. If allowed in Group Policy, you can elect to encrypt used disk space only or the entire drive, and then tap or click Next. Encrypting the used disk space only is faster than encrypting an entire volume. It's also the recommended option for newer computers and drives (except in high-security environments).

6. On the Encrypt The Drive page, tap or click Start Encrypting. The amount of time the encryption process takes depends on the amount of data to encrypt and other factors.

To enhance security, you can require additional authentication at startup. This configuration does the following:

- Grants access to the volume only to users who can provide a valid key
- Prevents those who have physical access to the computer from booting to an alternative operating system to gain access to the data on the volume
- Allows the computer to be used with or without a TPM for additional boot security
- Requires a password or a smart card with a PIN
- Optionally uses network unlock to unlock the volume when the computer is joined to and connected to the domain

You can enable BitLocker encryption for use with a startup key by following these steps:

1. Insert a USB flash drive in the computer (if one is not already there). Do not use a USB flash drive that is BitLocker-encrypted.

2. On the Choose How To Unlock Your Drive At Startup page, tap or click the Insert A USB Flash Drive option.

3. On the Back Up Your Startup Key page, tap or click the USB flash drive, and then tap or click Save.

4. Next, you need to save the recovery key. Because you should not store the recovery key and the startup key on the same medium, remove the USB flash drive and insert a second USB flash drive.

   NOTE The startup key is different from the recovery key. If you create a startup key, this key is required to start the computer. The recovery key is required to unlock the computer if BitLocker enters Recovery mode, which might happen if BitLocker suspects the computer has been tampered with while the computer was offline.

5. On the How Do You Want To Back Up Your Recovery Key? page, tap or click Save To A File.

6. In the Save BitLocker Recovery Key As dialog box, choose the location of your USB flash drive, and then tap or click Save. Do not remove the USB drive with the recovery key.

7. You can now optionally save the recovery key to a network folder, print the recovery key, or both. Tap or click an option, and then follow the wizard's steps to set the location for saving or printing the recovery key. When you have finished, tap or click Next.

8. If allowed in Group Policy, you can elect to encrypt used disk space only or the entire drive, and then tap or click Next. Encrypting the used disk space only is faster than encrypting an entire volume. It's also the recommended option for newer computers and drives (except in high-security environments).

9. On the Encrypt The Volume page, confirm that Run BitLocker System Check is selected, and then tap or click Continue.

10. Confirm that you want to restart the computer by tapping or clicking Restart Now. The computer restarts, and BitLocker ensures that the computer is BitLocker-compatible and ready for encryption. If the computer is not ready for encryption, you will get an error and need to resolve the error status before you can complete this procedure. If the computer is ready for encryption, the Encryption In Progress status bar is displayed. You can monitor the status of the disk volume encryption by pointing to the BitLocker Drive Encryption icon in the notification area. By double-tapping or double-clicking this icon, you can open the Encrypting dialog box and monitor the encryption process more closely. You also have the option to pause the encryption process. Volume encryption takes approximately 1 minute per gigabyte to complete.

    By completing this procedure, you have encrypted the operating system volume and created a recovery key unique to that volume. The next time you turn on your computer, either the USB flash drive with the startup key must be plugged into a USB port on the computer or the computer must be connected to the domain network and using network unlock. If the USB flash drive is required for startup and you do not have the USB flash drive containing your startup key, you will need to use Recovery mode and supply the recovery key to gain access to the data.

You can enable BitLocker encryption for use with a startup PIN by following these steps:

1. On the Choose How To Unlock Your Drive At Startup page, select the Enter A PIN option.

2. On the Enter A PIN page, enter and confirm the PIN. The PIN can be any number you choose and must be 4 to 20 digits in length. The PIN is stored on the computer.

3. Insert a USB flash drive on which you want to save the recovery key, and then tap or click Set PIN. Do not use a USB flash drive that is BitLocker-encrypted.

4. Continue with steps 5-9 in the previous procedure.

When the encryption process is complete, you have encrypted the entire volume and created a recovery key unique to this volume. If you created a PIN or a startup key, you are required to use the PIN or startup key to start the computer (or the computer must be connected to the domain network and using network unlock). Otherwise, you will observe no change to the computer unless the TPM changes or cannot be accessed, or if someone tries to modify the disk while the operating system is offline. In this case, the computer enters Recovery mode, and you need to enter the recovery key to unlock the computer.

Managing and troubleshooting BitLocker

You can determine whether a system volume, data volume, or inserted removable drive uses BitLocker by tapping or clicking System And Security in Control Panel, and then double-tapping or double-clicking BitLocker Drive Encryption. You'll find the status of BitLocker on each volume, as shown in Figure 2-15.

The BitLocker Drive Encryption service must be started for BitLocker to work properly. Usually, this service is configured for manual startup and runs under the LocalSystem account.

To use smart cards with BitLocker, the Smart Card service must be started. Typically, this service is configured for manual startup and runs under the LocalService account.

After you create a startup key or PIN and a recovery key for a computer, you can create duplicates of the startup key, startup PIN, or recovery key as necessary for backup or replacement purposes by using the options on the BitLocker Drive Encryption page in Control Panel.

> **NOTE** With fixed data and operating system drives, another way to access this page is to press and hold or right-click the volume in File Explorer, and then tap or click Manage BitLocker. If BitLocker is turned off, the Turn On BitLocker option is displayed instead.

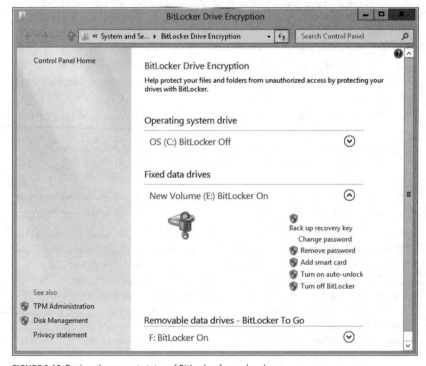

FIGURE 2-15 Review the current status of BitLocker for each volume.

The management options provided depend on the type of volume with which you are working and the encryption settings you choose. The available options include the following:

- **Back Up Recovery Key**   Enables you to save or print the recovery key. Tap or click this option, and then follow the prompts.

- **Change Password**   Allows you to change the encryption password. Tap or click this option, enter the old password, and then enter and confirm the new password. Tap or click Change Password.

- **Remove Password**   Tap or click this option to remove the encryption password requirement for unlocking the drive. You can do this only if another unlocking method is configured first.

- **Add Smart Card**   Enables you to add a smart card for unlocking the drive. Tap or click this option, and then follow the prompts.

- **Remove Smart Card**   Tap or click this option to remove the smart card requirement for unlocking the drive.

- **Change Smart Card**   Enables you to change the smart card used to unlock the drive. Tap or click this option, and then follow the prompts.

- **Turn On Auto-Unlock**   Tap or click this option to turn on automatic unlocking of the drive.

- **Turn Off Auto-Unlock**   Tap or click this option to turn off automatic unlocking of the drive.

- **Turn Off BitLocker**   Tap or click this option to turn off BitLocker and decrypt the drive.

Recovering data protected by BitLocker Drive Encryption

If you've configured BitLocker Drive Encryption and the computer enters Recovery mode, you need to unlock the computer. To unlock the computer by using a recovery key stored on a USB flash drive, follow these steps:

1. Turn on the computer. If the computer is locked, the computer opens the BitLocker Drive Encryption Recovery console.

2. When you are prompted, insert the USB flash drive that contains the recovery key, and then press Enter.

3. The computer will unlock and reboot automatically. You do not need to enter the recovery key manually.

If you saved the recovery key file in a folder on another computer or on removable media, you can use another computer to open and validate the recovery key file. To locate the correct file, find Password ID on the recovery console displayed on the locked computer and write down this number. The file containing the recovery key uses this Password ID as the file name. Open the file and locate the recovery key.

To unlock the computer by typing the recovery key, follow these steps:

1. Turn on the computer. If the computer is locked, the BitLocker Drive Encryption Recovery console opens.

2. Type the recovery key, and then press Enter. The computer will unlock and reboot automatically.

A computer can become locked if a user tries to enter the recovery key but is repeatedly unsuccessful. In the recovery console, you can press Esc twice to exit the recovery prompt and turn off the computer. A computer might also become locked if an error related to TPM occurs or boot data is modified. In this case, the computer halts very early in the boot process, before the operating system starts. At this point, the locked computer might not be able to accept standard keyboard numbers. If that is the case, you must use the function keys to enter the recovery password. Here, the function keys F1–F9 represent the digits 1 through 9, and the F10 function key represents 0.

Disabling or turning off BitLocker Drive Encryption

When you need to make changes to TPM or make other changes to the system, you might first need to temporarily turn off BitLocker encryption on the system volume. You cannot temporarily turn off BitLocker encryption on data volumes; you can only decrypt data volumes.

To temporarily turn off BitLocker encryption on the system volume, follow these steps:

1. In Control Panel, tap or click System And Security, and then double-tap or double-click BitLocker Drive Encryption.

2. For the system volume, tap or click Turn Off BitLocker Drive Encryption.

3. In the What Level Of Decryption Do You Want? dialog box, tap or click Disable BitLocker Drive Encryption.

   By completing this procedure, you have temporarily disabled BitLocker on the operating system volume.

To turn off BitLocker Drive Encryption and decrypt a data volume, follow these steps:

1. In Control Panel, tap or click System And Security, and then double-tap or double-click BitLocker Drive Encryption.

2. For the appropriate volume, tap or click Turn Off BitLocker Drive Encryption.

3. In the What Level Of Decryption Do You Want? dialog box, tap or click Decrypt The Volume.

To turn off BitLocker Drive Encryption and decrypt a USB flash drive, follow these steps:

1. In Control Panel, tap or click System And Security, and then double-tap or double-click BitLocker Drive Encryption.

2. For the appropriate volume, tap or click Turn Off BitLocker Drive Encryption.

3. In the What Level Of Decryption Do You Want? dialog box, tap or click Decrypt The Volume.

CHAPTER 3

Managing disk drives and file systems

M ost computers have several types of drives, including internal hard drives and removable media drives. An internal hard drive is typically the primary storage device. In most cases, the first hard drive installed is designated Disk 0. If additional hard drives are installed, they are designated Disk 1, Disk 2, and so on. This chapter discusses tools and techniques for managing hard drives and file systems. You'll learn how to partition and format disks and how to convert disks from one disk type to another. You'll also learn about features of Windows 8.1 that affect how drives are used, including Windows ReadyBoost, Windows ReadyDrive, and Windows SuperFetch.

Disk management essentials

Windows 8.1 enables you to designate a physical hard drive as a basic disk or a dynamic disk.

- **Basic disks**   The disk type used most often in the past, a basic disk can be divided into one or more partitions on Windows 8.1. A partition is a logi-cal section of a disk that operates as if it were a physically separate disk. To use a partition, you must format it to use a particular file system and assign it a drive designator. The formatted partition is then referred to as a basic volume, and you can access it as a local disk on the computer. Windows 8.1 supports both primary and extended partitions on basic disks. A primary partition is used to start the operating system. You access a primary partition directly by its drive designator. You cannot subdivide a primary partition. An extended partition, on the other hand, is accessed indirectly. After you create an extended partition, you must divide it into one or more logical drives. You can then access the logical drives independently of each other.

- **Dynamic disks**   Dynamic disks enable you to perform most common disk maintenance tasks without having to restart the computer. Like a basic disk, a dynamic disk can be divided; however, dynamic disks are divided into volumes rather than partitions. A volume is very similar to a partition. The most commonly used type of volume is a simple volume. A simple volume is a volume on a single disk that can be used to start the operating system and for general data storage. Other types of volumes can also be used, includ-ing those that enable you to extend a single volume across several disks (a spanned volume). As with a partition or a logical drive, you must format a volume on a dynamic disk and assign it a drive designator before you can use it. The formatted volume is referred to as a *dynamic volume*, and you can access it as a local disk on the computer. When a dynamic volume combines space from multiple physical drives, it still appears as a single local disk and is accessed by a single drive designator.

You can change storage types from basic to dynamic and from dynamic to basic. When you convert a basic disk to a dynamic disk, partitions are changed to volumes of the appropriate type automatically and data is not lost. Converting a dynamic disk to a basic disk isn't so easy. You need to delete the volumes on the dynamic disk before you can change the disk type to a basic disk. Deleting the volumes destroys the information they contain, and the only way to get it back is to restore the data from a backup.

All computers running Windows 8.1 use Unified Extensible Firmware Interface (UEFI), which can be wrapped around BIOS or Extensible Firmware Interface (EFI). In addition to a disk type, all disks have a partition style, which is either master boot record (MBR) or GUID partition table (GPT). Although both 32-bit and 64-bit edi-tions of Windows 8.1 support MBR and GPT partitions, the GPT partition style is not recognized by early releases of Windows.

The MBR contains a partition table that describes where the partitions are located on the disk. In this partition style, the first sector on a hard disk contains the MBR and a binary code file called the *master boot code,* which is used to boot the system. This sector is not partitioned and is hidden from view to protect the system.

With the MBR partitioning style, disks support volumes of up to 4 terabytes (TB) and use one of two types of partitions—primary or extended. Each MBR drive can have up to four primary partitions or three primary partitions and one extended partition. Primary partitions are drive sections that you can access directly for file storage. You make a primary partition accessible to users by creating a file system on it. Unlike primary partitions, extended partitions cannot be accessed directly. Instead, you can configure extended partitions with one or more logical drives that are used to store files. Being able to divide extended partitions into logical drives enables you to divide a physical drive into more than four sections.

GPT was originally developed for high-performance Itanium-based computers. GPT is recommended for disks larger than 2 TB on x86 and x64. The key difference between the GPT partition style and the MBR partition style is how partition data is stored. With GPT, critical partition data is stored in the individual partitions, and redundant primary and backup partition tables are used for improved structural integrity.

Although underlying differences exist between the GPT and MBR partitioning styles, most disk-related tasks are performed in the same way. This means that after you set up and configure your drives it usually doesn't matter whether the disk is using MBR or GPT. That said, keep the following in mind:

- Basic MBR disks can have up to four primary partitions—or three primary partitions and one extended partition, with one or more logical drives in the extended partition—and dynamic MBR disks can have an unlimited number of volumes.

- GPT disks support partitions of up to 18 exabytes (EB) in size and up to 128 partitions. Computers using GPT disks for boot have two required partitions and one or more optional OEM or data partitions. The required partitions are the EFI system partition and the Microsoft Reserved partition. Although the optional partitions that you encounter depend on the system configuration, the optional partition type encountered most often is the primary partition. Primary partitions are used to store user data on GPT disks.

- On a BIOS-based computer, you can use MBR for booting or for data disks and GPT only for data disks. On an EFI-based computer, you can have both GPT and MBR disks, but you must have at least one GPT disk that contains the ESP, MSR, and either a primary partition or a simple volume that contains the operating system for booting.

Windows 8.1 supports FAT, FAT32, exFAT, NTFS, and ReFS. With FAT, the number of bits used with the file allocation table determines the variant you are working with and the maximum volume size. FAT16, also known just as FAT, defines its file allocation tables by using 16 bits. Volumes that are 4 gigabytes (GB) or less in size are formatted with FAT16. There's also a 32-bit version of FAT, known as FAT32. FAT32 defines its file allocation tables by using 32 bits, and you can create FAT32 volumes that are 32 GB or less by using the Windows format tools. Although Windows can mount larger FAT32 volumes created with third-party tools, you should use NTFS for volumes larger than 32 GB.

In a significant change from earlier releases of Windows, NTFS and exFAT are the preferred formats for large internal and external hard disks. Extended FAT, or exFAT, is an enhanced version of FAT. Technically, exFAT could have been called FAT64 (and is called that by some). The exFAT file system defines its file allocation tables by using 64 bits, which enables exFAT to overcome the 4-GB file size limit and the 32-GB volume size limit of FAT32 file systems. The exFAT format supports allocation unit sizes of up to 128 KB for volumes up to 256 TB. The exFAT format is designed so that it can be used with and easily moved between any compliant operating system or device. This gives exFAT an advantage over FAT.

With exFAT, you can have more than 1,024 files in a single directory, and exFAT supports access control lists and transactions. Additionally, exFAT uses a cluster bitmap for fast allocation and a per-file contiguous bit for fast file access, improving overall performance. Improved contiguous on-disk layout enhances performances for media tasks, such as recording and playing back digital media.

Resilient File System (ReFS) can be thought of as the next generation of NTFS. As such, ReFS remains compatible with core NTFS features while cutting noncore features to focus on reliability. Thus, ReFS does not support disk quotas, Encrypting File System (EFS), compression, file screening, or storage reporting but does include built-in reliability features, including a data integrity scanner that eliminates the need to use the Check Disk utility to analyze and repair ReFS volumes.

Windows 8.1 provides several tools for working with a computer's disks. The first and most often overlooked tool is the This PC console. Other tools include Disk Management, FSUtil, and DiskPart. Partitions and volumes on MBR and GPT disks can be formatted by using exFAT and NTFS. When you create partitions or volumes in Disk Management, you have the opportunity to format the disk and assign it a drive letter or a mount point as part of the volume creation process. Although Disk Management lets you format the partitions and volumes on MBR disks by using exFAT and NTFS, only NTFS can be used to format partitions and volumes on GPT disks. If you want to format GPT disks by using FAT or FAT32, you must use either the Format or DiskPart command at the command prompt.

You can change partition table styles from MBR to GPT or from GPT to MBR. Changing partition table styles is useful when you want to move disks between BIOS-based and EFI-based computers or when you receive new disks that are formatted for the wrong partition table style. You can convert partition table styles only on empty disks, however. This means that the disks must be either new or newly formatted. You could, of course, empty a disk by removing its partitions or volumes.

As discussed in the section "Hardware encryption, secure boot, and network unlock" in Chapter 2, "Using TPM and BitLocker Drive Encryption," Windows 8.1 adds support for hard drives with hardware encryption (referred to as *encrypted hard drives*). Encrypted hard drives have built-in processors that shift the encryption-decryption activities from the operating system to the hardware, freeing up operating system resources. Windows 8.1 will use hardware encryption with BitLocker when available.

Windows 8.1 supports both Standard Format and Advanced Format hard drives. Standard Format drives have 512 bytes per physical sector and are also referred to as *512b drives*. Advanced Format drives have 4,096 bytes per physical sector and are referred to as *512e drives*. 512e represents a significant shift for the hard drive industry, and it allows for large, multiterabyte drives.

> **REAL WORLD** Disks perform physical media updates in the granularity of their physical sector size. 512b drives work with data 512 bytes at a time; 512e drives work with data 4,096 bytes at a time. At an administrator command prompt, you can use FSUtil to determine bytes per physical sector by entering:
>
> ```
> Fsutil fsinfo ntfsinfo DriveDesignator
> ```
>
> *DriveDesignator* is the designator of the drive to check, such as
>
> ```
> Fsutil fsinfo ntfsinfo c:
> ```
>
> Having a larger physical sector size is what makes it possible for drive capacities to jump well beyond previous physical capacity limits. When there is only a 512-byte write, hard disks must perform additional work to complete the sector write. For best performance, applications must be updated to read and write data properly in this new level of granularity (4,096 bytes).

Using the This PC console

To access the This PC console, on the Start screen, tap or click File Explorer. In File Explorer, tap or click the location path selection button, and then tap or click This PC.

> **NOTE** In File Explorer, the Address Path shows the absolute or relative path that you are currently accessing and provides options for working with this path. From left to right, it has four interface elements: a Location Indicator icon, a Location Path Selection list button, Location Path entries, and a Previous Locations button.

You can use the This PC console to quickly determine the available storage devices on a computer. Whenever you are working with the This PC window, shown in Figure 3-1, the Computer option on the menu bar has the following location, network, and system options:

- **Properties** Displays the Properties dialog box for the currently selected item
- **Open** Opens the currently selected item in the same File Explorer window
- **Rename** Enables you to rename the currently selected item
- **Access Media** Enables you to connect or disconnect from a media server
- **Map Network Drive** Enables you to map or disconnect a network drive
- **Add A Network Location** Enables you to create a shortcut to a website, FTP site, a storage space, or other network locations
- **Open Control Panel** Opens the Control Panel view in the current window
- **Uninstall Or Change A Program** Opens the Programs And Features page in Control Panel
- **System Properties** Opens the System page in Control Panel
- **Manage** Opens Computer Management in a new window

FIGURE 3-1 The This PC console provides easy access to a computer's storage devices.

The This PC console provides the following details:

- **Hard disk drives** Local disks available on the computer are listed under Devices And Drives. Press and hold or right-click a disk to display available management options, including Open, which opens the disk in File Explorer. To view important disk tools, tap or click the Drive Tools Manage option on the menu bar.

- **Devices with removable storage** Removable storage devices on the computer also are listed, including CD, DVD, USB flash drives, and floppy disk drives. Press and hold or right-click a device to display available management options, including Eject, which is convenient for ejecting current media so that new media can be inserted.

  TIP USB flash drives, eSATA, and FireWire/USB-attached external hard drives are being used more and more in place of floppy disks and other types of removable media. If a computer has a USB, eSATA, or FireWire port, you can easily connect or disconnect a drive. Before you disconnect a USB, eSATA, or FireWire drive, you should ensure that it is in a safe state. The Eject option provides one way to do this. Tap or click the disk designator in File Explorer or any related view to display the Drive option on the menu bar. Tap or click Drive, and then tap or click Eject. As long as the drive is not in use, you should be able to safely disconnect the drive.

- **Network Location** Lists any mapped network drives. A network drive provides access to a shared folder or a disk on another computer. In the This PC window, start the Map Network Drive Wizard by tapping or clicking Computer on the menu bar, tapping or clicking Map Network Drive, and then tapping or clicking Map Network Drive. To disconnect a network drive, press and hold or right-click the network location, and then tap or click Disconnect.

Using Disk Management

When you want to configure drives, the tool of choice is Disk Management. Disk Management provides the tools you need to manage disks, partitions, volumes, logical drives, and their related file systems. Disk Management is a Microsoft Management Console (MMC) snap-in that can be accessed through a preconfigured console included with Windows or added to any custom console you've created. By using Disk Management, you can perform the following tasks:

- Determine the capacity, free space, status, and other properties of disks
- Create partitions and logical drives on basic disks
- Create volumes on dynamic disks
- Extend volumes to increase their size
- Format volumes and specify the file system to use
- Assign drive letters and paths to volumes
- Convert basic disks to dynamic disks, and vice versa

Disk Management is included in the Computer Management console. You can start Computer Management at a prompt by entering **compmgmt.msc**. Alternatively, enter **compmgmt.msc** in the Apps Search box.

When you start Computer Management, you are automatically connected to the local computer. To examine drives on another computer, press and hold or right-click the Computer Management entry in the console tree, and then tap or click Connect To Another Computer on the shortcut menu. You can now choose the system whose drives you want to examine. From the command line, you can connect to another computer when starting Computer Management by entering **compmgmt.msc /computer=*ComputerName***, where *ComputerName* is the name of the remote computer to which you want to connect.

In the default configuration, shown in Figure 3-2, Disk Management displays the Volume List view in its upper panel and the Graphical view in its lower panel. Although only two views can be shown at any one time, three views are available:

- **Volume List view** Provides a detailed summary of the drives on the computer. Tapping or clicking a column label, such as Layout or Status, sorts the disk information based on that column.
- **Graphical view** Provides a graphical overview of the physical and logical drives available. Summary information for the physical disk devices includes the disk number and device type, such as basic, removable, or DVD; the disk capacity; and the status of the disk device, such as online or offline. Additional details are also provided for each logical disk on the physical disk, including the drive letter and text label for the associated partition or volume; the file system type, such as exFAT or NTFS; the size of the drive section; and the local disk status, such as healthy or unhealthy.

- **Disk List view**   Provides summary information about physical drives. This information includes the disk number and device type, such as basic, removable, or DVD; the disk capacity; the size of unallocated space on the disk (if any); the status of the disk device, such as online or offline; and the device interface type, such as integrated device electronics (IDE) or Advanced Technology Attachment (ATA).

FIGURE 3-2 Use Disk Management to manage disk configurations.

You can change the view for the top or bottom pane by using options on the View menu. To change the top view, tap or click View, choose Top, and then select the view you want to use. To change the bottom view, tap or click View, choose Bottom, and then select the view you want to use.

As you can tell, the available views provide overviews of available disks. To get more detailed information on a local disk, press and hold or right-click it in the Volume List view, and then tap or click Properties. You'll get a dialog box much like the one shown in Figure 3-3. This is the same dialog box that you can access from File Explorer (by pressing and holding or right-clicking the top-level icon for the drive, and then tapping or clicking Properties). If it is available, you can use the Customize tab to select a view template to determine what folders look like in File Explorer's Contents pane.

FIGURE 3-3 Examine detailed information for a drive in the Properties dialog box.

Using FSUtil and DiskPart

Windows 8.1 provides several command-line tools for working with disks, including the following:

- **FSUtil** Meant to be used by support professionals who need to manage disks at a fairly low level. By using FSUtil, you can examine and work with metadata and other information related to disks, including update sequence number (USN) change journals, reparse points, and hard links. You can also obtain detailed sector and cluster information, such as the number of free or reserved sectors on a disk. To view a list of commands available in FSUtil, enter **fsutil** at an elevated command prompt. To learn more about a specific command, enter **fsutil** *CommandName* **help**.

- **DiskPart** A text-mode command interpreter that you can use to manage disks, partitions, and volumes from the command prompt. Not only can DiskPart perform many of the same operations as Disk Management, but it can also be used with scripts to automate disk management processes. You start DiskPart by entering **diskpart** at an elevated command prompt. You will then be at the DISKPART> prompt. If you type **help** and then press Enter, you will get a list of available commands and a description of their usage.

NOTE Unlike Disk Management, which provides a friendly interface and is fairly easy to use, FSUtil and DiskPart are complex tools meant for advanced administrators. Their use is covered in detail in *Windows Command-Line Administrator's Pocket Consultant, Second Edition* by William R. Stanek (Microsoft Press, 2008). You'll find a detailed example of using DiskPart in the "Marking a partition as active" section, later in this chapter.

Improving disk performance

Windows 8.1 has several features that affect how disks are used. These include:

- **Windows ReadyBoost** Boosts system performance by using USB flash drives as additional sources for caching
- **Windows ReadyDrive** Boosts system performance on mobile computers equipped with hybrid drives
- **Windows SuperFetch** Boosts system performance by using a modified memory management algorithm

Each of these features is discussed in the sections that follow.

Understanding and using Windows ReadyBoost

A computer's hard drives aren't used just for reading and writing application data and user documents. The operating system makes extensive use of a computer's hard drives for paging files and for the system cache. Because reading from and writing to a disk is significantly slower than reading from and writing to physical memory (RAM), these operations can cause a bottleneck that degrades performance. Windows 8.1 includes Windows ReadyBoost as a way to reduce the impact related to reading and writing the system cache.

With Windows ReadyBoost, USB flash drives with sufficiently fast memory are used to extend the disk-caching capabilities of the computer's main memory. By using flash drives for caching, Windows 8.1 can make random reads faster by caching data on the USB flash drive instead of a disk drive. Because this caching is applied to all disk content, not just the page file or system dynamic-link libraries (DLLs), the computer's overall performance is boosted because flash devices can be read up to 10 times faster than physical disk drives.

USB flash drives that can be used with Windows ReadyBoost include USB 2.0 or later flash drives, Secure Digital (SD) cards, and CompactFlash cards. These drives must have sufficiently fast flash memory and be at least 256 MB or larger in size. To enhance performance, I recommend purchasing USB flash drives with high-speed memory. If the flash drive has both slow and fast flash memory, only the fast flash memory portion will be used for boosting performance. From 230 MB to 15,196 MB of flash memory can be reserved on a USB flash drive for Windows ReadyBoost. A recommended amount of memory to use is from one to three times the available system memory. However, keep in mind that as of the time of this writing, the most you can reserve is 15,196 MB.

Memory on USB flash drives is primarily used for random I/O because most flash devices are slower than a disk drive for sequential I/O. Windows ReadyBoost maximizes performance by automatically passing large, sequential read requests to the computer's disk drive for servicing. To make it possible for a USB flash drive to be removed at any time, all data writes are made to the hard disk before being copied to the flash device. This means all data stored on the flash drive is duplicated on the hard disk, and there is no potential for data loss when removing the flash drive. Additionally, because the flash device's memory might contain sensitive information, Windows ReadyBoost encrypts the data so that it can be used only with the computer on which it was originally written.

Enabling and configuring Windows ReadyBoost

With Windows ReadyBoost, USB flash drives with sufficiently fast flash memory can be used as additional sources of system cache. When you insert a USB flash drive into a USB 2.0 or later port, Windows 8.1 analyzes the speed of the flash memory on the device. If the flash memory performs at a sufficiently high speed, the computer's physical memory can be extended to the USB flash drive. In most cases, you'll want the flash memory to be at least as fast as the computer's bus speed.

> **TIP** Windows can incorrectly flag a device as failing to meet the performance requirements. If a device fails the initial performance test, you can retest the device by using the ReadyBoost tab. In File Explorer, press and hold or right-click the device, and then tap or click Properties. In the Properties dialog box, tap or click the ReadyBoost tab, and then tap or click Test Again.

The following steps show how you can enable and configure how Windows ReadyBoost works the first time you use a USB flash drive with a computer:

1. Insert a USB flash drive into a USB 2.0 or later port. The AutoPlay dialog box should be displayed automatically (unless you've changed the AutoPlay defaults in Control Panel).

2. When you tap or click Speed Up My System–Windows ReadyBoost, the device's Properties dialog box opens to the ReadyBoost tab, shown in Figure 3-4. Do one of the following, and then tap or click OK:

   - If you want the device to automatically reserve the maximum amount of space for Windows ReadyBoost, select Dedicate This Device To Ready-Boost. Choosing this setting prevents a user from writing files to the device. It just configures Windows ReadyBoost to use as much space as can be reserved.

   - If you want to use less space than the maximum possible, select Use This Device, and then use the Space To Reserve For System Speed slider or combo box to set the amount of space to use with Windows ReadyBoost. If you reserve less than the total amount of space available, the free space can be used for files and data.

FIGURE 3-4 Configure Windows ReadyBoost settings.

Windows 8.1 extends the computer's physical memory to the device. The default configuration enables Windows ReadyBoost to reserve all available space on the device for boosting system speed.

REAL WORLD To use a USB flash drive with Windows ReadyBoost, the drive must have at least 2.5 megabits per second (Mbps) throughput for 4-kilobyte (KB) random reads and 1.75 Mbps throughput for 512-KB random writes. Although you can enable Windows ReadyBoost on a device you've encrypted with BitLocker To Go, keep in mind that encryption and decryption processes can affect read/write performance. If you use BitLocker To Go and Windows ReadyBoost, I recommend that you also automatically unlock the device when the device is inserted. Otherwise, the user has to validate the device prior to getting the performance benefits of Windows ReadyBoost.

To use Windows ReadyBoost with a USB flash drive that you have already inserted or that you previously declined to use with Windows ReadyBoost, follow these steps:

1. Open File Explorer or another Explorer view, such as This PC.

2. Press and hold or right-click the USB flash drive in the list, and then tap or click Properties.

3. On the ReadyBoost tab, configure the options as discussed in step 2 of the previous procedure. Tap or click OK.

For USB flash drives that do not support Windows ReadyBoost, you cannot enable the drive. You can safely remove a USB flash drive that uses the entire drive for Windows ReadyBoost at any time without losing data or negatively impacting the system. However, when the drive is removed, system performance returns to its usual level—the performance level experienced without the device. To safely remove a device containing both reserved Windows ReadyBoost space and data files, follow these steps:

1. Open File Explorer or another Explorer view, such as This PC.

2. Press and hold or right-click the device, and then tap or click Eject. If you've opened files on the device or opened the device for viewing in File Explorer, you might need to close files and File Explorer windows before you can eject the device.

Understanding and using Windows ReadyDrive

Windows ReadyDrive improves performance on mobile computers equipped with hybrid drives. A hybrid drive is a drive that uses both flash RAM and a physical drive for storage. Because flash RAM is much faster than a physical disk, mobile computers running Windows 8.1 write data and changes to data to the flash memory first and periodically sync these writes and changes to the physical disk. This approach reduces the spinning of the physical drive and thus saves battery power.

The flash RAM on hybrid drives can be used to provide faster startup and resume from sleep or hibernation. In this case, the information needed for starting or resuming the operating system is written to the flash RAM prior to shutting down, entering sleep, or going into hibernation. When you start or wake the computer, this information is read from the flash RAM.

You do not need to enable Windows ReadyDrive because it's enabled for use automatically on mobile computers with hybrid drives.

Understanding and using Windows SuperFetch

Windows 8.1 improves performance and responsiveness by changing the way user processes and background processes are used. In early releases of Windows, user processes and background processes had the same memory-use prioritization: user processes and background processes are both loaded into memory as they are used. Because there is no prioritization, there is often contention for memory, and performance lags also often occur because background processes remain resident in memory after they run. Therefore, data for user processes must be loaded into memory when it is requested. Windows 8.1 corrects this issue by ensuring that background processes are unloaded after they run and when data for user processes is reloading into memory.

In early releases of Windows, user processes and background processes have the same I/O priority, which often results in conflicts and poor read/write performance. Windows 8.1 corrects this by implementing high-priority I/O and low-priority I/O queues. High-priority I/O is used by user processes for read and write operations to physical drives. Low-priority I/O is used by background process read and write operations to physical drives.

> **NOTE** With Windows 8.1, many services and routine housekeeping tasks run as background processes. For example, on Windows 8.1, Disk Defragmenter is scheduled to run automatically to periodically defragment disks. When Disk Defragmenter runs, it runs as a background process and uses low-priority I/O.

The key feature that makes memory and I/O prioritization work is Windows SuperFetch. Windows SuperFetch improves system performance by using a modified memory-management algorithm. Unlike the memory-management algorithm in early versions of Windows, SuperFetch optimizes memory usage based on the way the current user is using the computer. SuperFetch does this by performing the following tasks:

- **Differentiating between user applications and background services running on the computer** SuperFetch makes the computer more responsive to user requests by prioritizing the current user's processes over background tasks. Because user processes always have priority over background tasks, background tasks do not take up all the processor time and the system remains responsive to user requests.

- **Optimizing memory for users after running background tasks** Housekeeping tasks on Windows 8.1 make better use of process idle time than they did on earlier versions of Windows. More system and maintenance tasks, such as Disk Defragmenter and Disk Backup, run during idle time. When the computer is idle, background processes run as they typically would. However, when background processes end, SuperFetch repopulates memory to the state that it was in prior to running the background processes. This ensures that memory is optimized for user processes and that the computer is responsive to user requests.

- **Tracking the most frequently used applications and anticipating user needs** SuperFetch keeps track of which applications users run most frequently and also tracks when those applications are typically used. SuperFetch then uses the tracking information to preload the application and ready it for use when it expects that the user will need the application. This ensures faster startup for applications and faster user switching over time.

- **Taking advantage of the low-priority I/O designation** SuperFetch takes advantage of the high-priority I/O and low-priority I/O queues in Windows 8.1 to improve read/write times for user processes and improve a computer's overall responsiveness. When multiple processes are competing for I/O, high-priority processes always get more I/O time than do low-priority processes. As a result, user processes and applications have better performance, and there is less contention for I/O time when both user processes and background processes are running.

All versions of Windows 8.1 support SuperFetch. As an administrator, you should understand how SuperFetch works and the way it is configured. Some basic characteristics of SuperFetch follow:

- Runs as a service named SuperFetch. This service runs automatically at startup and logs on using the LocalSystem account.

- Uses the Svchost.exe executable, running in a network-restricted mode. This means SuperFetch can access only the local computer and doesn't have access to any networks to which the computer might be connected.

- Depends on the Filter Manager component for proper operations. Filter Manager provides file information and file-system information needed by SuperFetch, and it is installed automatically with the operating system.
- Writes prefetch data to the %SystemRoot%\Prefetch folder. The prefetch data is used to quickly start applications. Within the Prefetch folder, you'll also find several database files used to track application usage history and speed up application performance. Application faults are also tracked in a database history file.

NOTE The Prefetch folder is self-maintaining. There's no need to delete it or empty its contents.

When you make major changes to the operating system, install service packs or updates, or install or reconfigure applications, users might occasionally experience slow startup. The extent to which this occurs depends on how extensive the changes are and how much memory-usage information SuperFetch has to rebuild. Occasionally, such as when you install a new service pack, several restarts are required over time to normalize the startup speed.

Working with basic and dynamic disks

Not that long ago, all Windows-based computers shipped with their hard disks configured as basic disks. Now, because people want larger or more robust disks, computer manufacturers have responded by shipping more computers with their hard disks configured as dynamic disks. Instead of having a single 500-GB drive, a new computer might have a spanned disk with 1,000 GB, where two 500-GB physical drives act as a single logical disk. In this scenario, disk spanning is used to make multiple disks appear to be a single disk. One way to implement this on Windows 8.1 is to use dynamic disks.

As more and more computers are shipped with dynamic disks, you might wonder whether your computers that use basic disks should be converted to dynamic disks. In some cases, the need for standardization might prompt your decision. For example, for better manageability, you might want all desktops in a particular department to have the same configuration. In other cases, IT management might direct the change because the conversion from basic disks to dynamic disks can be considered an upgrade process. (That is, you are moving computers from an older disk type to a newer disk type.) However, before you decide to move from one disk type to another, you should understand what is involved, what features are supported, and what features are not supported.

A basic disk is a physical disk that has one or more basic volumes that can be configured as primary partitions, plus an optional extended partition consisting of logical drives. A primary partition is a drive section that you can access directly for file storage. Each physical drive can have up to four primary partitions. You make a primary partition accessible to users by creating a file system on it. In place of one of the four permitted primary partitions, you can create an extended partition (meaning that the basic disk could have up to three primary partitions and one extended partition). Unlike with primary partitions, you can't access extended partitions directly. Instead, you can configure extended partitions with one or more logical drives that are used to store files. Being able to divide extended partitions into logical drives enables you to divide a physical drive into more than four sections. For example, you could create logical drives F, G, and H in a single extended partition.

A dynamic disk is a physical disk that has one or more dynamic volumes. Unlike a basic disk, a dynamic disk can have an unlimited number of volumes—any one of which can be extended or used as a system volume.

A key advantage of dynamic disks used to be their ability to combine physical disks by using the spanning, striping, or mirroring features of Windows. However, Windows 8.1 also allows you to span, stripe, or mirror basic disks. When you span or stripe drives, you create a single volume that extends from one disk to other disks by using all or part of each disk in the set. The difference between spanning and striping is how data is written. Windows 8.1 recognizes spanned disks in the same way it would a single partition, and write operations to the spanned disk are made to the entire partition randomly. With striping, Windows 8.1 writes a portion of the data to each of the underlying disks that make up the volume. In most cases, striping gives you faster read/write access to data because data is read from and written to multiple disks. With mirroring, two drives are combined to create a single fault-tolerant volume. If any one volume fails, the other volume in the set is still available, and the volume can be recovered.

CAUTION Technically, disk striping is a redundant array of independent disks (RAID) level 0 (RAID-0), and disk mirroring is RAID level 1 (RAID-1). Although disk mirroring is fault-tolerant, neither disk striping nor spanning provides fault tolerance, and the failure of any disk in the set causes the volume to fail.

Now, because you can span, stripe, and mirror drives by using the basic disk type, the key features that distinguish dynamic disks from basic disks are enhanced error correction and detection and the ability to modify disks without having to restart the computer. Other features available on a disk depend on the disk formatting, such as whether you are using exFAT or NTFS.

When you format a disk with a file system, the file system structures the disk by using clusters, which are logical groupings of sectors. With 512b drives, FAT, FAT32, exFAT, and NTFS use a fixed sector size of 512 bytes but allow the cluster size to be variable. For example, the cluster size might be 4,096 bytes, so if there are 512 bytes per sector, each cluster is made up of eight sectors.

Table 3-1 provides a summary of the default cluster sizes for FAT16, FAT32, exFAT, and NTFS. You have the option of specifying the cluster size when you create a file system on a disk, or you can accept the default cluster-size setting. Either way, the cluster sizes available depend on the type of file system you are using.

REAL WORLD Four FAT file systems are used by Windows platforms: FAT12, FAT16, FAT32, and exFAT. The difference between FAT12, FAT16, and FAT32 is the number of bits used for entries in their file allocation tables, namely 12, 16, or 32 bits. From a user's perspective, the main difference in these file systems is the theoretical maximum volume size, which is 16 MB for a FAT12 volume, 4 GB for FAT16, and 2 TB for FAT32. When the term FAT is used without an appended number, it generally refers to both FAT16 and FAT32. Extended FAT, or exFAT, is an enhanced version of FAT32. Although exFAT retains the ease-of-use advantages of FAT32, it overcomes the 4-GB file size limit and the 32-GB volume size limit of FAT32 file systems. The exFAT format also supports allocation unit sizes of up to 32,768 KB. The exFAT format is designed so that it can be used with and easily moved between any compliant operating system or device. This gives exFAT an advantage over FAT32.

TABLE 3-1 Default cluster sizes for FAT16, FAT32, exFAT, and NTFS

VOLUME SIZE	CLUSTER SIZE			
	FAT16	FAT32	EXFAT	NTFS
7 MB to 16 MB	512 bytes (as FAT12)	Not supported	4 KB	512 bytes
17 MB to 32 MB	512 bytes	Not supported	4 KB	512 bytes
33 MB to 64 MB	1 KB	512 bytes	4 KB	512 bytes
65 MB to 128 MB	2 KB	1 KB	4 KB	512 bytes
129 MB to 256 MB	4 KB	2 KB	4 KB	512 bytes
257 MB to 512 MB	8 KB	4 KB	32 KB	512 bytes
513 MB to 1,024 MB	16 KB	4 KB	32 KB	1 KB
1,025 MB to 2 GB	32 KB	4 KB	32 KB	4 KB
2 GB to 4 GB	64 KB	4 KB	32 KB	4 KB
4 GB to 8 GB	Not supported	4 KB	32 KB	4 KB
8 GB to 16 GB	Not supported	8 KB	32 KB	4 KB
16 GB to 32 GB	Not supported	16 KB	32 KB	4 KB
32 GB to 2 TB	Not supported	*	128 KB	4 KB
2 TB to 16 TB	Not supported	*	128 KB	4 KB
16 TB to 32 TB	Not supported	*	128 KB	8 KB
32 TB to 64 TB	Not supported	*	128 KB	16 KB
64 TB to 128 TB	Not supported	*	128 KB	32 KB
128 TB to 256 TB	Not supported	*	128 KB	64 KB

If you are using the Windows formatting tools, you are limited to 32 GB. Larger volumes can be created by using third-party tools.

The important thing to know about clusters is that they are the smallest unit in which disk space is allocated. Each cluster can hold one file at most. So, if you create a 1-KB file and the cluster size is 4 KB, there will be 3 KB of empty space in the cluster that isn't available to other files. That's just the way it is. If a single cluster isn't big enough to hold an entire file, the remaining file data goes into the next available cluster and then the next, until the file is completely stored. For FAT, for example, the first cluster used by the file has a pointer to the second cluster, and the second cluster has a pointer to the next, and so on until you get to the final cluster used by the file, which has an end-of-file (EOF) marker.

The disk I/O subsystem manages the physical structure of disks. Windows manages the logical disk structure at the file system level. The logical structure of a disk relates to the basic or dynamic volumes you create on a disk and the file systems with which those volumes are formatted. You can format both basic volumes and dynamic volumes by using FAT or NTFS. Each file system type has a different structure, and there are advantages and disadvantages of each.

Although you can use both basic and dynamic disks on the same computer, the disks that make up a volume must use the same disk type. Converting from basic to dynamic and vice versa is covered in the "Converting a basic disk to a dynamic disk or vice versa" section, later in this chapter. Remember that although you can convert the disk type from basic to dynamic and preserve the data on the disk, you must delete any existing partitioning on a dynamic disk before you can convert from dynamic to basic. Deleting the partitioning destroys any data on the associated disks. Finally, dynamic disks cannot be created on any removable-media drives or on any disk on a portable computer. Laptops, Tablet PCs, and other types of portable computers can have only basic disks.

CAUTION Be careful when working with laptops. Some laptop configurations might make Disk Management think that you can convert a basic disk to a dynamic disk. This can occur on computers that do not support Advanced Power Management (APM) or Advanced Configuration and Power Interface (ACPI). Although support for dynamic disks might seem to be enabled, this is an error, and trying to convert a basic disk to a dynamic disk on one of these laptops could corrupt the entire disk.

NOTE External hard drives attached via FireWire, USB, or eSATA can in some cases be converted to dynamic disks. Microsoft Knowledge Base article 299598, "How To: Convert an IEEE 1394 Disk Drive to a Dynamic Disk Drive," details how this can be done. However, this article doesn't provide enough cautions. The external hard drive must be used only with a single computer. If you think you will need to move the drive to another computer in the future, you shouldn't convert it to a dynamic disk. Further, before attempting to convert any external hard drive attached via FireWire or USB, you should back up the data. If possible, perform the conversion on an identical but nonessential drive in a development or testing environment and then test the drive operation.

Preparing basic and dynamic disks

When it comes to using basic and dynamic disks, you perform several related tasks, such as initializing new disks, setting a drive as active, or changing the drive type. Before performing these tasks, however, you should understand what the active, boot, system, and other drive designations mean.

Understanding drive designations

Basic disks can have both primary and extended partitions. A primary partition can be used to start the operating system. Although you cannot subdivide a primary partition, you divide extended partitions into one or more logical drives and then access the logical drives independently of each other.

Dynamic disks are divided into volumes, with the simple volume being the most common volume type. A simple volume is a volume on a single disk, which can be used to start the operating system. Dynamic volumes, on the other hand, combine space from multiple physical drives.

Whether working with basic or dynamic disks, you should pay particular attention to five special types of drive sections on MBR disks:

- **Active**   The active partition or volume is the drive section from which a computer starts. If the computer uses multiple operating systems, the active drive section must contain the startup files for the operating system you want to start and it must be a primary partition on a basic disk or a simple volume on a dynamic disk. The active partition is not typically marked as such in Disk Management. In most cases, it is the primary partition or the first simple volume on Disk 0. However, if you change the default configuration, you will find an Active label.

  CAUTION   With removable media disks, you might observe an Active status, which shouldn't be confused with the Active label associated with an active partition. Specifically, USB and FireWire card readers that use CompactFlash or other types of cards are displayed as having an Active status when media is inserted and the related drive is online. It's also important to note that in some cases, a removable media drive might be listed as Disk 0. In this case, you need to look for the active partition on the first physical hard disk according to its disk number. For example, if the computer has Disk 0, Disk 1, and Disk 2, and the first physical disk in sequence is Disk 1, the active partition is most likely on the first primary partition or simple volume on Disk 1.

- **System**   The system partition or volume contains the hardware-specific (bootstrap) files needed to load the operating system. The system partition or volume can be mirrored but can't be part of a striped or spanned volume. The system partition is labeled as such in the Status column in Disk Management's Volume List and Graphical views.

- **Boot**   The boot partition or volume contains the operating system and its support files. The boot partition or volume can be mirrored but can't be part of a striped or spanned volume. On most systems, system and boot are the same partition or volume. Although it seems that the boot and system partitions are named backward, this convention has been used since the earliest days of Windows and has not changed. Like the active partition, the boot partition is not typically marked as such in Disk Management. In most cases, it is the primary partition or the first simple volume on Disk 0. However, if the operating system is installed on a different partition or volume, you might find a Boot label.

- **Page file**   A page file partition or volume contains a paging file used by the operating system. Because a computer can page memory to multiple disks, according to the way virtual memory is configured, a computer can have multiple page file partitions or volumes. However, depending on the service packs configured, the computer might only report the primary volume being used as a paging file.

- **Crash dump**   The crash dump partition or volume is the one to which the computer attempts to write dump files in the event of a system crash. Dump files can be used to diagnose the causes of system failure. By default, dump files are written to the %SystemRoot% folder, but they can be located on any partition or volume.

Each computer has one active, one system, one boot, and one crash dump partition or volume, and these partitions or volumes can be combined. The page file designation is the only drive designation that you might observe on multiple partitions or volumes.

Installing and initializing new physical disks

Windows 8.1 makes it much easier to add new physical disks to a computer. After you install the disks following the disk manufacturer's instructions, you need to log on and start Disk Management. If the new disks have already been initialized, meaning they already have disk signatures enabling them to be read and written to, they should be brought online automatically if you choose Rescan Disks from the Action menu. If you are working with new disks that have not been initialized, meaning they don't have disk signatures, Disk Management will start the Initialize And Convert Disk Wizard as soon as Disk Management starts and detects the new disks.

You can use the Initialize And Convert Disk Wizard to initialize the disks by completing the following steps:

1. Tap or click Next to exit the Welcome page. On the Select Disks To Initialize page, the disks you added are selected for initialization automatically, but if you don't want to initialize a particular disk, you can clear the related option.

2. Tap or click Next to display the Select Disks To Convert page. This page lists the new disks, in addition to any nonsystem or boot disks that can be converted to dynamic disks. The new disks aren't selected by default. If you want to convert the disks, select them, and then tap or click Next.

3. The final page shows you the options you've selected and the actions that will be performed on each disk. If the options are correct, tap or click Finish. The wizard then performs the designated actions. If you've elected to initialize a disk, the wizard writes a disk signature to the disk. If you've elected to convert a disk, the wizard converts the disk to a dynamic disk after writing the disk signature.

If you don't want to use the wizard, you can close it and use Disk Management instead to view and work with the disk. In the Disk List view, the disk is marked with a red icon that has an exclamation point, and the disk's status is listed as Not Initialized. Press and hold or right-click the disk's icon, and then tap or click Initialize Disk. Confirm the selection (or add to the selection if more than one disk is available for initializing), and then tap or click OK to start the initialization of the disk. Conversion to a dynamic disk would proceed as discussed in the section "Converting a basic disk to a dynamic disk or vice versa," later in this chapter.

Changing a disk's partition table style

You can change partition table styles from MBR to GPT or from GPT to MBR. Changing partition table styles is useful when you want to move disks between computers that have different processor architectures or you receive new disks that are formatted for the wrong partition table style. You can convert partition table styles only on empty disks, however. This means the disks must be either new or newly formatted. You could, of course, empty a disk by removing its partitions or volumes.

You can use both Disk Management and DiskPart to change the partition table style. To use Disk Management to change the partition style of an empty disk, start Computer Management from the Administrative Tools in Control Panel or enter **compmgmt.msc** in the Apps Search box, and then press Enter. In Computer Management, expand the Storage node, and then select Disk Management. All available disks are displayed. Press and hold or right-click the disk to convert in the left pane of the Graphical view, and then tap or click Convert To GPT Disk or Convert To MBR Disk, as appropriate.

To use DiskPart to change the partition style of an empty disk, invoke DiskPart by entering **diskpart** at an elevated command prompt, and then select the disk you want to convert. For example, if you want to convert Disk 2, enter **select disk 2**. After you select the disk, you can convert it from MBR to GPT by entering **convert gpt**. To convert a disk from GPT to MBR, enter **convert mbr**.

Marking a partition as active

You don't typically need to change a partition's designation. If you are using only Windows 8.1 or if you are multibooting to Windows 8.1 and any other version of Windows, you do not have to change the active partition. With MBR disks, the active partition is typically the primary partition or the first simple volume on Disk 0. If you install Windows 8.1 on drive C and another version of Windows on a different partition, such as drive D, you don't need to change the active partition to boot Windows 8.1 or the other operating system. However, if you want to boot an operating system that is not based on Windows, you usually have to mark its operating system partition as active and then reboot to use that operating system.

NOTE Only primary partitions can be marked as active. You can't mark logical drives as active and you can't mark volumes as active. When you upgrade a basic disk containing the active partition to a dynamic disk, this partition becomes a simple volume that's active automatically.

To mark a partition as active, complete the following steps:

1. Start Disk Management by entering **diskmgmt.msc** at a prompt or in the Apps Search box.

2. Press and hold or right-click the primary partition you want to mark as active, and then tap or click Mark Partition As Active.

CAUTION If you mark a partition or volume as active, Disk Management might not let you change the designation. As a result, if you restart the computer, the operating system might fail to load. The only workaround I've found is to use DiskPart to make the appropriate changes either before rebooting or before using the Startup Repair tool following a failed start.

Listing 3-1 shows a sample DiskPart session for setting the active partition. As you can tell, when you first start DiskPart, it shows the DiskPart program name and the version you are using, in addition to the name of the computer. You then select the disk with which you want to work and list its partitions. In this example, you select Disk 0, list its partitions, and then select Partition 1. After you've selected a disk and a partition on that disk, you can work with that partition. Just type the Active command at this point, and press Enter to set the partition as active. When you have finished, quit DiskPart by using the Exit command.

NOTE This example uses Disk 0. On your system, Disk 0 might not be the one with which you want to work. You can use the List Disk command to list the available disks and then use the information provided to determine the disk with which to work.

LISTING 3-1 Using DiskPart to set the active partition

```
C:>diskpart
Microsoft DiskPart version 6.3.9431
Copyright (C) 1999-2013 Microsoft Corporation.
On computer: ENGPC85

DISKPART> select disk 0

Disk 0 is now the selected disk.

DISKPART> list partition

  Partition ###  Type              Size     Offset
  -------------  ----------------  -------  ---------
  Partition 1    Primary           932 GB   1024 KB

DISKPART> select partition 1
```

```
Partition 1 is now the selected partition.

DISKPART> active

DiskPart marked the current partition as active.

DISKPART> exit
```

Converting a basic disk to a dynamic disk or vice versa

The easiest way to convert a basic disk to a dynamic disk or vice versa is to use Disk Management. When you upgrade to a dynamic disk, partitions are automatically changed to volumes of the appropriate type. Any primary partitions become simple volumes. Any logical drives in an extended partition become simple volumes. Any unused (free) space in an extended partition is marked as Unallocated. You can't change these volumes back to partitions. Instead, you must delete the volumes on the dynamic disk and then change the disk back to a basic disk. Deleting the volumes destroys all the information on the disk.

Before you convert a basic disk to a dynamic disk, you should be sure that you don't need to boot the computer to a previous version of Windows. You should also be sure that the disk has 1 MB of free space at the end of the disk. Although Disk Management reserves this free space when creating partitions and volumes, disk management tools on other operating systems might not; as a result, the conversion will fail. It's also important to note the following restrictions:

- You can't convert removable media to dynamic disks. You can configure removable media drives only as basic drives with primary partitions.
- You can convert disks' non-system and non-boot partitions that are part of spanned or striped volumes. These volumes become dynamic volumes of the same type; however, you must convert all drives in the set together.

To convert a basic disk to a dynamic disk, complete the following steps:

1. In Disk Management, either in the Disk List view or in the left pane of the Graphical view, press and hold or right-click a basic disk that you want to convert, and then tap or click Convert To Dynamic Disk.

2. In the Convert To Dynamic Disk dialog box, select the check boxes for the disks you want to convert, as shown in Figure 3-5.

FIGURE 3-5 Select the basic disk to convert.

3. If the disk you are converting has no formatted volumes, tapping or clicking OK converts the disk, and you do not need to perform the remaining steps. If the disk you are converting has formatted volumes, tapping or clicking OK displays the Disks To Convert dialog box. Follow the remaining steps to complete the conversion.

4. The Disks To Convert dialog box shows the disks you're converting so that you can confirm the conversion. Notice the value in the Will Convert column, which should be Yes so long as the disk meets the conversion criteria, and then tap or click Details to view the volumes on the selected drive. When you are ready to continue, tap or click OK to close the Convert Details dialog box.

5. To begin the conversion, tap or click Convert. Disk Management warns you that after you convert the disk, you won't be able to boot previous versions of Windows from volumes on the selected disks. Tap or click Yes to continue.

6. Next, you are warned that file systems on the disks to be converted will be dismounted, meaning they will be taken offline and be inaccessible temporarily. Tap or click Yes to continue. If a selected drive contains the boot partition, the system partition, or a partition in use, Disk Management will need to restart the computer, and you will get another prompt.

To convert a dynamic disk to a basic disk, complete the following steps:

1. Before you can change a dynamic disk to a basic disk, you must delete all dynamic volumes on the disk. Because this destroys all the data on the volumes, you should back up the volumes, and then verify the backups before making the change.

2. When you are ready to start the conversion process, start Disk Management. In Disk Management, press and hold or right-click the disk you want to convert, and then tap or click Convert To Basic Disk. This changes the dynamic disk to a basic disk, and you can then create new partitions and logical drives on the disk.

Working with disks, partitions, and volumes

Before you can store data on a physical disk, you must prepare the disk by setting a disk type, partitioning its space, assigning a drive designator, and formatting its partitions or volumes.

After partitioning a disk, you must assign each partition or volume a drive designator. The drive designator can be a letter or a path. You use drive letters to access file systems in various partitions on physical drives. Generally speaking, the drive letters A through Z are available. However, the drive letter A is usually assigned to a system's floppy drive. If the system has a second floppy drive or another removable-media drive, the letter B is usually assigned to it (or unassigned otherwise). The drive letter C is usually assigned to the first partition or volume created on Disk 0. The drive letter D is usually assigned to the first CD-ROM or DVD-ROM drive. Thus, on most systems, the drive letters E through Z are available. If you need additional volumes, you can create them by using drive paths.

A drive path is set as a folder location on an existing local disk. For example, you could mount additional drives as C:\Docs1, C:\Docs2, and C:\Docs3. Drive paths can be used with basic and dynamic disks. The only restriction for drive paths is that you mount them on empty folders that are on NTFS-formatted local disks.

Formatting a partition or a volume sets the file system that will be used and creates the necessary file structures. In general, you can format a partition or a volume as FAT, FAT32, exFAT or NTFS. There are restrictions and requirements for the use of each, however.

FAT, also referred to as FAT16, is a 16-bit file system designed to be used with volume sizes of up to 4 GB. FAT uses a boot sector that stores information about the disk type, the starting and ending sectors, and the active partition. FAT gets its name from the file allocation table it uses to track the cluster locations of files and folders. There is a primary table and a duplicate table. The duplicate is used to restore the primary table if it becomes corrupted. FAT also has the capability to mark clusters (sections of disk containing data) as unused, in use, bad, or reserved. This helps to make FAT a fairly robust file system. FAT is best with volumes of 2 GB or less, and it has a maximum file size of 2 GB. FAT can also be used with floppy disks and removable disks.

FAT32 is a 32-bit version of FAT16, with some additional features and capabilities. Like FAT16, FAT32 uses a primary and a duplicate file allocation table. FAT32 can also mark clusters as unused, in use, bad, or reserved, and it too can be used with removable disks. FAT32 has a minimum volume size of 33 MB, a maximum volume size of 32 GB, and a maximum file size of 4 GB.

ExFAT is an enhanced, 64-bit version of FAT. To retain the speed and other advantages of FAT, use exFAT for volumes larger than 32 GB. Windows 8.1 supports exFAT on both internal and external volumes.

NOTE The 4-GB maximum file size limitation for FAT32 is specific to Windows. With FAT32, some other operating systems can create larger volumes.

NTFS is very different from FAT. Instead of using a file allocation table, NTFS uses a relational database to store information about files and folders. This database is called the master file table (MFT); it stores a record of each file and folder on a volume, and additional information that helps to maintain the volume. Overall, the MFT makes NTFS much more reliable and recoverable than FAT16 or FAT32. NTFS can recover from disk errors more readily than can FAT16 and FAT32, and NTFS generally has fewer disk problems.

Some, but not all, of this resiliency is built into exFAT, which uses transactions to improve reliability and recoverability. Both NTFS and exFAT have a maximum volume size of 256 TB with standard format disks and a maximum file size that is limited only by the volume size.

Although you can't use NTFS or exFAT with floppy disks, you can use NTFS and exFAT with removable disks. Additionally, unlike FAT16 and FAT32, which have limited security features (namely that you can mark a file only as read-only, hidden, or system), exFAT supports basic access controls. Only NTFS has advanced security that lets you use permissions to set specific file and folder access, however, and only NTFS supports other advanced features like compression, encryption, and disk quotas.

> **NOTE** Several versions of NTFS have been implemented. Because most current computers have NTFS 5 or later, I focus on NTFS 5 and later in this book. Also, if you upgrade a system with an early version of Windows, you are given the opportunity to convert existing NTFS volumes to the latest version during installation. In most cases, you should do this because it ensures support for the latest NTFS features. If you're curious about the actual NTFS version for a volume, enter the following at an elevated administrator prompt:
>
> **fsutil fsinfo ntfsinfo c:**
>
> c: is the designator of the drive with which you want to work. If the internal NTFS version is listed as 3.1, you're actually working with NTFS 5.1.

Partitioning disks and preparing them for use

Disk Management is the primary tool that you use to partition disks and prepare them for use. By using Disk Management, you can partition disks, assign drive designators, and format partitions and volumes. Disk Management's command-line counterparts include DiskPart for partitioning and drive-designator assignment and Format for formatting.

Creating partitions, logical drives, and simple volumes

Windows 8.1 simplifies the Disk Management user interface by using one set of dialog boxes and wizards for both partitions and volumes. The first three volumes on a basic drive are created automatically as primary partitions. If you try to create a fourth volume on a basic drive, the remaining free space on the drive is converted automatically to an extended partition with a logical drive of the size you designate. You designate the size by using the new volume feature it created in the extended partition. Any subsequent volumes are created in the extended partition and logical drives automatically.

> **NOTE** As discussed previously, an MBR drive can have four primary partitions. However, if you create a fourth primary partition, you are unable to further divide the drive, and this is why Windows 8.1 automatically creates an extended partition. The extended partition enables you to create multiple logical drives within the partition.

In Disk Management, you create partitions, logical drives, and simple volumes by completing the following steps:

1. In Disk Management's Graphical view, press and hold or right-click an unallocated or free area, and then tap or click New Simple Volume. This starts the New Simple Volume Wizard. Read the Welcome page, and then tap or click Next.

2. The Specify Volume Size page, shown in Figure 3-6, specifies the minimum and maximum size for the volume in megabytes and lets you size the volume within these limits. Size the partition in megabytes by using the Simple Volume Size box, and then tap or click Next.

FIGURE 3-6 Set the size of the volume.

3. On the Assign Drive Letter Or Path page, shown in Figure 3-7, specify whether you want to assign a drive letter or path, and then tap or click Next. The available options are as follows:

- **Assign The Following Drive Letter** Select an available drive letter in the selection list provided. By default, Windows 8.1 selects the lowest available drive letter and excludes reserved drive letters, in addition to those assigned to local disks or network drives.

- **Mount In The Following Empty NTFS Folder** Choose this option to mount the partition in an empty NTFS folder. You must then enter the path to an existing folder or tap or click Browse to search for or create a folder to use.

- **Do Not Assign A Drive Letter Or Drive Path** Choose this option if you want to create the partition without assigning a drive letter or path. Later, if you want the partition to be available for storage, you can assign a drive letter or path at that time.

NOTE Volumes don't have to be assigned a drive letter or a path. A volume with no designators is considered to be unmounted and is for the most part unusable. An unmounted volume can be mounted by assigning a drive letter or a path at a later date. See the section "Assigning, changing, or removing drive letters and paths," later in this chapter.

FIGURE 3-7 Assign the drive designator or choose to wait until later.

4. Use the Format Partition page, shown in Figure 3-8, to determine whether and how the volume should be formatted. If you want to format the volume, choose Format This Volume With The Following Settings, and then configure the following options:

- **File System** Sets the file system type as FAT, FAT32, exFAT, or NTFS. NTFS is selected by default in most cases. If you create a file system as FAT or FAT32, you can later convert it to NTFS by using the Convert utility; however, you can't convert NTFS partitions to FAT or FAT32.

- **Allocation Unit Size** Sets the cluster size for the file system. This is the basic unit in which disk space is allocated. The default allocation unit size is based on the selected file system and the size of the volume and, by default, is set dynamically prior to formatting. To override this feature, you can set the allocation unit size to a specific value. If you use many small files, you might want to use a smaller cluster size, such as 512 or 1,024 bytes. With these settings, small files use less disk space.

- **Volume Label** Sets a text label for the partition. This label is the partition's volume name and by default is set to New Volume. You can change the volume label at any time by pressing and holding or right-clicking the volume in File Explorer, choosing Properties, and entering a new value in the Label box provided on the General tab.

- **Perform A Quick Format** Tells Windows 8.1 to format without checking the partition for errors. With large partitions, this option can save you a few minutes. However, it's usually better to check for errors, which enables Disk Management to mark bad sectors on the disk and lock them out.

- **Enable File And Folder Compression** Turns on compression for the disk. Built-in compression is available only for NTFS. Under NTFS, compression is transparent to users and compressed files can be accessed just like regular files. If you select this option, files and directories on this drive are compressed automatically. For more information on compressing drives, files, and directories, see the section "Compressing drives and data" in Chapter 4, "Configuring and maintaining storage."

FIGURE 3-8 Set the formatting options for the partition.

5. Tap or click Next, confirm your options, and then tap or click Finish.

Creating spanned and striped volumes

With spanning and striping, you create a single volume that extends across multiple disks. When working with spanning and striping, keep the following in mind:

- A spanned volume uses free space on multiple disks of the same type. If you have unallocated space on two or more disks of the same type, you can combine this space to create a spanned volume. A spanned volume has no fault tolerance and has average read/write performance. Files are written to the entire spanned volume randomly. If any one of the disks fails, the entire volume fails, and all data is lost.

- A striped volume uses free space on multiple disks and stripes the data as it is written. Striping gives you faster read/write access to data because data is read from and written to multiple disks. For example, with a three-disk striped volume, data from a file will be written to Disk 1, then to Disk 2, and then to Disk 3 in 64-KB blocks. Like a spanned volume, a striped volume has no fault tolerance, so if any one of the disks fails, the entire volume fails, and all data is lost. This approach also is referred to as *RAID 0*.

- A striped with parity volume uses three or more volumes, each on a separate drive, to create a striped set with parity error checking. In the case of failure, data can be recovered. This approach, also referred to as *RAID 5*, gives fault tolerance with less overhead than mirroring and better read performance than disk mirroring.

NOTE If you have only one disk available, you will not be able to create a spanned or striped volume. Also note that simple and spanned volumes can be extended to increase their volume size. RAID 0 and RAID 5 volumes, however, cannot be extended. When you create a RAID 0 or RAID 5 volume, you should be very certain that the volume size is what you want to use. Otherwise, you might have to delete and then re-create the striped volume. Additionally, the boot and system volumes shouldn't be part of a RAID 0 or RAID 5 set. Don't use RAID 0 or RAID 5 with these volumes.

MORE INFO To allow for fault tolerance, RAID 5 writes parity checksums with the blocks of data. If any of the drives in the striped set fails, you can use the parity information to recover the data. If two disks fail, however, the parity information isn't sufficient to recover the data, and you'll need to rebuild the striped set from backup.

In Disk Management, you create spanned or striped volumes on disks by completing the following steps:

1. In Disk Management's Graphical view, press and hold or right-click an unallocated area, and then tap or click New Spanned Volume, New Striped Volume, or New RAID-5 Volume, as appropriate. Read the Welcome page, and then tap or click Next. Keep in mind that although Windows 8.1 supports spanning and striping on basic disks, some basic disks cannot be spanned or striped.

2. On the Select Disks page, select the disks that will be part of the volume and specify the size of the volume segments on those disks. The disks must be the same disk type, either basic or dynamic. Tap or click Next.

   Available disks are shown in the Available list. Select a disk in this list, and then tap or click Add to add the disk to the Selected list. If you make a mistake, you can remove a disk from the Selected list by selecting the disk, and then tapping or clicking Remove.

   Specify the space that you want to use on each disk by selecting each disk in the Selected list, and then by using Select The Amount Of Space In MB to specify the amount of space to use. Keep in mind that the Maximum box shows you the largest area of free space available on the selected disk, and the Total Volume Size box shows the total disk space currently allocated to the volume.

   TIP There's a quick way to use the same amount of space on all selected disks. To do this, highlight each disk by pressing Shift and then tapping or clicking the first disk and the last disk in the Selected list. Now, when you set the amount of space to use, you'll set the amount for all selected disks.

3. Follow steps 3–5 in the previous section, "Creating partitions, logical drives, and simple volumes."

Shrinking or extending volumes

Windows 8.1 doesn't use Ntldr and Boot.ini to load the operating system. Instead, Windows 8.1 has a preboot environment in which Windows Boot Manager is used to control startup and load the boot application you've selected. The Windows Boot Manager also frees the Windows operating system from its reliance on MS-DOS, enabling you to use drives in ways you couldn't before. Windows 8.1 enables you to extend and shrink both basic and dynamic disks. You can use Disk Management or DiskPart to extend and shrink volumes. You cannot shrink or extend striped volumes.

In extending a volume, you convert areas of unallocated space and add them to the existing volume. For spanned volumes on dynamic disks, the space can come from any available dynamic disk, not only those on which the volume was originally created. This enables you to combine areas of free space on multiple dynamic disks and use those areas to increase the size of an existing volume.

> **CAUTION** Before you try to extend a volume, you should know about several limitations. First, simple and spanned volumes can be extended only if they are formatted and the file system is NTFS. You can't extend striped volumes. You can't extend volumes that aren't formatted or that are formatted with FAT, FAT32, or exFAT. Additionally, you can't extend a system or boot volume, regardless of its configuration.

You can shrink a basic volume, simple volume, or spanned volume by completing the following steps:

1. In Disk Management, press and hold or right-click the volume that you want to shrink, and then tap or click Shrink Volume. This option is available only if the volume meets the previously discussed criteria.

2. In the Shrink dialog box, shown in Figure 3-9, enter the amount of space by which to shrink the disk. The Shrink dialog box provides the following information:

    - **Total Size Before Shrink In MB** Lists the total capacity of the volume in megabytes. This is the formatted size of the volume.

    - **Size Of Available Shrink Space In MB** Lists the maximum amount by which you can shrink the volume. This doesn't represent the total amount of free space on the volume; rather, it represents the amount of space that can be removed, not including any data reserved for the master file table, volume snapshots, page files, and temporary files.

    - **Enter The Amount of Space To Shrink In MB** Lists the total amount of space that will be removed from the volume. The initial value defaults to the maximum amount of space that can be removed from the volume. For optimal drive performance, you should ensure that the volume has at least 10 percent of free space after the shrink operation.

    - **Total Size After Shrink In MB** Lists what the total capacity of the volume in megabytes will be after you shrink the volume. This is the new formatted size of the volume.

3. Tap or click Shrink.

FIGURE 3-9 Specify the amount of space by which to shrink a volume.

You can extend a basic volume, simple volume, or a spanned volume by completing the following steps:

1. In Disk Management, press and hold or right-click the volume that you want to extend, and then tap or click Extend Volume. This option is available only if the volume meets the previously discussed criteria and free space is available on one or more of the system's disks.

2. In the Extend Volume Wizard, read the introductory message, and then tap or click Next.

3. On the Select Disks page, select the disk or disks from which you want to allocate free space. Any disks currently being used by the volume will automatically be selected. By default, all remaining free space on those disks will be selected for use.

4. You can specify the additional space that you want to use on other disks by performing the following tasks:

   ■ In the Available list, tap or click the disk, and then tap or click Add to add the disk to the Selected list.

   ■ Select each disk in the Selected list, and then use Select The Amount Of Space In MB to specify the amount of unallocated space to use on the selected disk.

5. Tap or click Next, confirm your options, and then tap or click Finish.

Formatting partitions and volumes

When you format a partition or a volume, you create a file system that can be used to store data and that permanently deletes any existing data in the associated section of the physical disk. This is high-level formatting that creates the file system structure rather than low-level formatting that initializes a drive for use. (New drives are initialized when you connect them, if they haven't already been prepared by the manufacturer.) To format a partition or a volume, press and hold or right-click the volume in Disk Management, and then tap or click Format. This opens the Format dialog box, shown in Figure 3-10. If you compare Figure 3-10 with Figure 3-8, you'll find that the available options are essentially the same.

FIGURE 3-10 Use the Format dialog box to format a partition or a volume by specifying its file system type and volume label.

After selecting the appropriate options, tap or click OK. Because formatting a partition destroys any existing data, Disk Management gives you one last chance to stop the procedure. Tap or click OK to start formatting the partition. Disk Management then changes the status of the drive to reflect the formatting and, unless you are using the Perform A Quick Format option, the percentage of completion. When formatting is complete, the drive status will change to indicate that formatting is complete.

Assigning, changing, or removing drive letters and paths

Each primary partition, logical drive, or volume on a computer can be assigned one drive letter and one or more drive paths if the drive paths are mounted on empty NTFS folders. After it is assigned, the drive letter or path remains the same each time you start the computer. Except on partitions or volumes that are designated as system or boot, you can change the drive letter or path assignment at any time. You can also remove a drive letter or path assignment, except on partitions or volumes that are designated as system or boot.

To manage a partition's or a volume's drive letters or paths, go to Disk Management. In either the Volume List view or the Graphical view, press and hold or right-click the partition or volume you want to configure, and then tap or click Change Drive Letter And Paths. This opens the dialog box shown in Figure 3-11. You can now perform the following actions:

- **Add a drive path** Tap or click Add, select Mount In The Following Empty NTFS Folder, and then enter the path to an existing folder. You can also tap or click Browse to search for or create a folder.

- **Remove a drive path** Select the drive path to remove, tap or click Remove, and then tap or click Yes.

- **Assign a drive letter** Tap or click Add, select Assign The Following Drive Letter, and then choose an available letter to assign to the drive.

- **Change the drive letter**   Select the current drive letter, and then tap or click Change. Select Assign The Following Drive Letter, and then choose a different letter to assign to the drive.
- **Remove a drive letter**   Select the current drive letter, tap or click Remove, and then tap or click Yes.

FIGURE 3-11 Use this dialog box to add, change, or remove drive letter and path assignments.

NOTE   If you try to change the letter of a drive that's in use, Windows 8.1 displays a warning. You need to exit programs that are using the drive and try again or enable Disk Management to force the change by tapping or clicking Yes when prompted.

REAL WORLD   If the drive letter you want to use isn't available, it means that it is in use or reserved for another purpose. Sometimes, you can resolve this problem by swapping drive letters. For example, if drive D is being used by the DVD-RW drive and drive E is a local disk, you might want to swap these letters so that D is used by the local disk and E is used by the DVD-RW drive. To do this, you must remove the drive letter assigned to the DVD-RW drive and free drive letter D for use. Next, set the drive letter assignment for the local disk to D. This frees up E, which you can assign to the DVD-RW drive. Keep in mind that changing the letter of a drive can have unintended consequences. For example, the path to an application might be stored in the registry with the drive letter. This path would no longer be valid if you change the drive letter. Shortcuts to files or programs on the drive would also be affected by the drive letter change and would need to be modified or re-created.

Assigning, changing, or deleting a volume label

A volume label is a text descriptor for a partition or a volume. The volume label is displayed when the drive is accessed in various Windows 8.1 utilities, such as File Explorer, and is designed to provide additional descriptive information about the contents of a drive.

NOTE   With FAT and FAT32, the volume label can be up to 11 characters in length and can include spaces. With NTFS, the volume label can be up to 32 characters in length. FAT and FAT32 don't allow you to use some special characters, including * / \ [ ] : ; | = , . + " ? < >, that NTFS does allow.

You can assign, change, or delete a volume label by using either Computer Management or the This PC console. In Computer Management, you can assign, change, or delete a label by completing the following steps:

1. Open Computer Management. Expand the Storage node, and then select the Disk Management node.

2. In the Volume List view, press and hold or right-click the drive icon, and then tap or click Properties.

3. On the General tab of the Properties dialog box, use the label box to enter a new label for the volume or to delete the existing label. Tap or click OK.

In the This PC console, you can assign, change, or delete a label by completing these steps:

1. To access the This PC console, tap or click File Explorer on the Start screen. In File Explorer, tap or click the location path selection button, and then tap or click This PC.

2. Press and hold or right-click the drive icon, and then tap or click Properties.

3. On the General tab of the Properties dialog box, use the label box to enter a new label or to delete the existing label. Tap or click OK.

Deleting partitions, volumes, and logical drives

To change the configuration of an existing drive that's fully allocated, you might need to delete existing partitions, logical drives, or volumes. Because this deletion is irreversible, you should always back up and verify any important files and folders before deleting a partition, a logical drive, or a volume. If a computer has spanned or striped volumes, be careful when deleting volumes. Deleting any volume in a set erases the entire volume set, meaning the entire volume and all its data are lost.

CAUTION Deleting a partition, a logical drive, or a volume is a drastic step that cannot be reversed. It removes the associated file system, and all data in the file system is lost.

NOTE To protect the integrity of the system, you can't delete the system or boot partition. However, Windows 8.1 lets you delete the active partition or volume if it is not designated as boot or system. Always check to be sure that the partition or volume you are deleting doesn't contain important data or files.

You can delete a primary partition, a volume, or a logical drive by completing the following steps:

1. In Disk Management, press and hold or right-click the partition, volume, or drive you want to delete, and then tap or click Explore. Using File Explorer, move all the data to another volume or verify an existing backup to ensure that the data was properly saved.

2. In Disk Management, press and hold or right-click the partition, volume, or drive again, and then tap or click Delete Partition, Delete Volume, or Delete Logical Drive, as appropriate.

3. Tap or click Yes to confirm that you want to delete the selected item.

Deleting an extended partition is a slightly different operation from deleting a primary partition or a logical drive. To delete an extended partition, you must first delete all the logical drives on the partition by following the steps in the preceding procedure. You can then select the extended partition area itself and delete it.

Converting a volume to NTFS

Windows 8.1 provides a command-line utility for converting FAT or FAT32 volumes to NTFS. This utility, named Convert (Convert.exe), is located in the %SystemRoot%\System32 folder. When you convert a volume by using this tool, the file and directory structure is preserved and no data is lost.

> **CAUTION** Windows 8.1 doesn't provide a utility for converting NTFS to FAT or FAT32. The only way to go from NTFS to FAT or FAT32 is to delete the partition by following the steps outlined in the previous section, and then re-create the partition as a FAT or FAT32 volume. Deleting a partition deletes its data. Note also that Convert doesn't convert exFAT volumes to NTFS.

If you want to convert a drive, use the following syntax at an elevated command prompt:

```
convert volume /FS:NTFS
```

volume is the drive letter followed by a colon (:), a drive path, or a volume name. For example, if you want to convert drive D to NTFS, you would use the following command:

```
convert D: /FS:NTFS
```

The complete syntax for the Convert command is

```
Convert volume /FS:NTFS [/V] [/X] [/CvtArea:filename] [/NoSecurity]
```

These options and switches are used as follows:

- **volume** Sets the volume to work with and must include the full drive designator (the drive letter followed by a colon). You also can specify a mount point or volume name.
- **/FS:NTFS** Converts the designated volume to NTFS. This is the only file system option.
- **/V** Sets verbose mode, which provides more detail in the output.
- **/X** Forces the volume to dismount before the conversion (if necessary).
- **/CvtArea:filename** Specifies a contiguous file in the root directory to be the placeholder for the NTFS system files stored on the MFT. If you omit a file name, Convert uses the default configuration and reserves 12.5 percent of the partition or volume size. This helps to prevent fragmentation of the MFT.
- **/NoSecurity** Sets the NTFS security settings on all files and folders so that the Everyone group can access them. This effectively makes the entire file system accessible to anyone who can access the system locally or remotely.

Before starting the conversion, the Convert command checks whether the drive has enough free space to perform the conversion. Generally, Convert needs a block of free space that's equal to roughly 25 percent of the total space used on the drive. For example, if the drive stores 100 GB of data, Convert needs about 25 GB of free space. If there isn't enough free space, Convert cancels the operation and tells you that you need to free up some space. On the other hand, if there is enough free space, Convert initiates the conversion. Be patient. The conversion process takes several minutes (longer for large drives). Don't access files or applications on the drive while the conversion is in progress.

NOTE Before using the Convert command, double-check whether the partition is being used as the active boot partition or a system partition containing the operating system. With MBR disks, you can convert the active boot partition to NTFS. Doing so requires that the system gain exclusive access to this partition, which can be obtained only during startup. Thus, if you try to convert the active boot partition to NTFS, Windows 8.1 displays a prompt asking if you want to schedule the drive to be converted the next time the system starts. If you tap or click Yes, you can restart the system to begin the conversion process. Often, several restarts of a system are required to completely convert the active boot partition. Don't panic. Let the system proceed with the conversion.

REAL WORLD You can improve performance on the volume by using the /CvtArea option so that space for the MFT is reserved. This option helps prevent fragmentation of the MFT. How? Over time, the MFT might grow larger than the space allocated to it. The operating system must then expand the MFT into other areas of the disk. Although the Windows 8.1 Disk Defragmenter utility can defragment the MFT, it cannot move the first section of the MFT, and it is very unlikely that there will be space after the MFT because the space will be filled by file data.

To help prevent fragmentation in some cases, you might want to reserve more space than the default (12.5 percent of the partition or volume size). For example, you might want to increase the size of the MFT if the volume will have many small or average-size files rather than a few large files. To specify the amount of space to reserve, you can use FSUtil to create a placeholder file equal in size to that of the MFT you want to create. You can then convert the volume to NTFS and specify the name of the placeholder file to use with the /CvtArea option.

Here, I use FSUtil to create a 1.5-GB (1,500,000,000 bytes) placeholder file named Temp.txt:

```
fsutil file createnew c:\temp.txt 1500000000
```

To use this placeholder file for the MFT when converting drive C to NTFS, you would enter the following command:

```
convert c: /fs:ntfs /cvtarea:temp.txt
```

Notice that the placeholder file is created on the partition or volume that is being converted. During the conversion process, the file is overwritten with NTFS metadata and any unused space in the file is reserved for future use by the MFT.

Recovering a failed simple, spanned, or striped volume

Basic partitions and simple volumes are fairly easy to troubleshoot and recover because only one disk is involved. Spanned or striped volumes, on the other hand, might have multiple disks. If disks don't have striping with parity, the failure of any one disk makes the entire volume unusable. The drive status might show that the drive is Missing, Failed, Online (Errors), Offline, or Unreadable.

You might encounter the Missing (and sometimes Offline) status if drives have been disconnected or turned off. If the drives are part of an external storage device, check the storage device to ensure that it is connected properly and has power. Reconnecting the storage device or turning on the power should make the drives accessible. You then must start Disk Management and rescan the missing drive. Press and hold or right-click the missing drive, and then tap or click Rescan Disks. When Disk Management finishes, press and hold or right-click the drive, and then tap or click Reactivate.

You might get the Failed, Online (Errors), and Unreadable status notifications if a drive has I/O problems. As before, try rescanning the drive, and then try to reactivate it. If the drive doesn't come back to the Healthy state, you might need to replace it.

> **TIP** Sometimes you might need to reboot the computer to get a disk back online. If this still doesn't resolve the problem, check for problems with the drive, its controller, and the cables. Also, make sure that the drive has power and is connected properly.

Regenerating a striped set with parity

With RAID 5, you can recover the striped set with parity if a single drive fails. You'll know that a striped set with parity drive has failed because the set's status changes to Failed Redundancy and the individual volume's status changes to Missing, Offline, or Online (Errors).

You can repair RAID-5 disks, but you must rebuild the set by using disks with the same partition style—either MBR or GPT. You need to get all drives in the RAID-5 set online. The set's status should read Failed Redundancy. The corrective action you take depends on the failed volume's status:

- If the status is Missing or Offline, make sure that the drive has power and is connected properly. Then open Disk Management, press and hold or right-click the failed volume, and select Reactivate Volume. The drive's status should change to Regenerating and then to Healthy. If the drive's status doesn't return to Healthy, press and hold or right-click the volume and select Regenerate Parity.

- If the status is Online (Errors), press and hold or right-click the failed volume and select Reactivate Volume. The drive's status should change to Regenerating and then to Healthy. If the drive's status doesn't return to Healthy, press and hold or right-click the volume and select Regenerate Parity.

- If one of the drives shows as Unreadable, you might need to rescan the drives on the system by choosing Rescan Disks from the Action menu of Disk Management. If the drive status doesn't change, you might need to reboot the computer.

- If one of the drives still won't come back online, you will need to repair the failed region of the RAID-5 set. Press and hold or right-click the failed volume, and then select Remove Volume. You now need to select an unallocated space on a separate dynamic disk for the RAID-5 set. This space must be at least as large as the region to repair, and it can't be on a drive that the RAID-5 set is already using. If you don't have enough space, the Repair Volume command is unavailable, and you need to free up space by deleting other volumes or by replacing the failed drive.

BEST PRACTICES If possible, you should back up the data before you perform this procedure to ensure that if you have problems, you can recover your data.

Using disk mirroring

With disk mirroring, you use identically sized volumes on two different drives to create a redundant data set. The drives are written with identical sets of information, and if one of the drives fails, you can still obtain the data from the other drive.

Although disk mirroring offers fault tolerance, the major drawback to disk mirroring is that it effectively cuts the amount of storage space in half. For example, to mirror a 500-GB drive, you need another 500-GB drive. That means you use 1,000 GB of space to store 500 GB of information.

Creating mirrored volumes

You create a mirror set by following these steps:

1. In the Disk Management Graphical view, press and hold or right-click an area marked Unallocated on a disk, and then tap or click New Mirrored Volume. This starts the New Mirrored Volume Wizard. Read the Welcome page, and then tap or click Next.

2. Create the volume as described in the section "Creating spanned and striped volumes," earlier in the chapter. The key difference is that you must create two volumes of identical size, and these volumes must be on separate drives. You won't be able to continue past the Selected Disks window until you select the two disks with which you want to work.

3. As with other RAID techniques, mirroring is transparent to users. Users view the mirrored set as a single drive that they can access and use like any other drive.

NOTE The status of a normal mirror is Healthy. During the creation of a mirror, you'll get a status of Resynching, which tells you that Disk Management is creating the mirror.

Rather than create a new mirrored volume, you can use an existing volume to create a mirrored set. To do this, the volume you want to mirror must be a basic partition or simple volume, and you must have an area of unallocated space on a second drive of equal or larger size than the existing volume.

In Disk Management, you can mirror an existing volume by following these steps:

1. Press and hold or right-click the basic partition or simple volume you want to mirror, and then tap or click Add Mirror. This displays the Add Mirror dialog box.

2. In the Disks list, select a location for the mirror, and then tap or click Add Mirror. Windows 8.1 begins the mirror creation process. In Disk Management, you'll get a status of Resynching on both volumes. The disk on which the mirrored volume is being created has a warning icon.

Breaking a mirrored set

You might want to or need to break a mirrored set. For example, if you no longer want to mirror your drives, you can break a mirror, which enables you to use the disk space for other purposes. If one of the mirrored drives in a set fails, disk operations can continue, but at some point you'll need to fix the mirror, and to do this you must break the mirror and then reestablish it. Although breaking a mirror doesn't delete the data in the set, you should always back up the data before you perform this procedure. This ensures that if you have problems, you can recover your data.

In Disk Management, you can break a mirrored set by following these steps:

1. Press and hold or right-click one of the volumes in the mirrored set, and then tap or click Break Mirrored Volume.

2. Confirm that you want to break the mirror by tapping or clicking Yes. If the volume is in use, you'll receive another warning dialog box. Tap or click Yes to confirm that it's okay to continue.

   Windows 8.1 then breaks the mirror, creating two independent volumes. (You don't need to break a mirror before you remove mirroring; Windows breaks the mirrored set as part of the removal process.)

Removing a mirrored set

In Disk Management, you can remove one of the volumes from a mirrored set. When you do this, all data on the mirror you remove is deleted, and the space it used is marked as Unallocated.

To remove a mirror, follow these steps:

1. In Disk Management, press and hold or right-click one of the volumes in the mirrored set, and then tap or click Remove Mirror. This displays the Remove Mirror dialog box.

2. In the Remove Mirror dialog box, select the disk from which to remove the mirror.

3. Confirm the action when prompted. All data on the removed mirror is deleted.

Moving a dynamic disk to a new system

An important advantage of dynamic disks over basic disks is that you can easily move dynamic disks from one computer to another. For example, after setting up a computer, if you decide that you don't really need an additional hard disk, you can move it to another computer where it can be better used. Before moving disks, you should complete the following steps:

1. Open Disk Management on the computer where the dynamic disks are currently installed and check their status. The status should be Healthy. If it isn't, you should fix any problems before moving the disks.

    CAUTION Drives with BitLocker Drive Encryption cannot be moved by using this technique. Windows 8.1 Enterprise and Ultimate editions include BitLocker Drive Encryption, which wraps drives in a protected seal so that any offline tampering is detected and results in the disk being unavailable until an administrator unlocks it. For more information about BitLocker Drive Encryption, see Chapter 2.

2. Check the hard disk subsystems on the original computer and on the computer to which you want to transfer the disk. Both computers should have identical hard disk subsystems. If they don't, the Plug and Play ID on the system disk from the original computer won't match what the destination computer is expecting. As a result, the destination computer won't be able to load the right drivers, and boot might fail.

3. Check whether any dynamic disks that you want to move are part of a spanned, extended, or striped set. If they are, you should make a note of which disks are part of which set and plan on moving all disks in a set together. If you move only part of a disk set, be aware of the consequences. For spanned, extended, or striped volumes, moving only part of the set makes the related volumes unusable on the current computer and on the computer to which you are planning to move the disks.

When you are ready to move the disks, complete the following steps:

1. On the original computer, start Computer Management. Then, in the left pane, select Device Manager. In the Device list, expand Disk Drives. This shows a list of all the physical disk drives on the computer. In turn, press and hold or right-click each disk that you want to move, and then tap or click Uninstall. If you are unsure which disks to uninstall, press and hold or right-click each disk in turn, and then tap or click Properties. In the Properties dialog box, tap or click the Volumes tab, and then tap or click Populate. This shows you the volumes on the selected disk.

2. Next, select the Disk Management node in Computer Management on the original computer. Press and hold or right-click each disk that you want to move, and then tap or click Remove Disk.

3. After you perform these procedures, you can move the dynamic disks. If the disks are hot-swappable and this feature is supported on both computers, remove the disks from the original computer and then install them on the destination computer. Otherwise, turn off both computers, remove the drives from the original computer, and then install them on the destination computer. When you have finished, restart the computers.

4. On the destination computer, open Disk Management, and then tap or click Rescan Disks on the Action menu. When Disk Management finishes scanning the disks, press and hold or right-click any disk marked Foreign, and then tap or click Import. You should now be able to access the disks and their volumes on the destination computer.

NOTE The volumes on the dynamic disks should retain the drive letters that they had on the original computer. If a drive letter is already used on the destination computer, a volume receives the next available drive letter. If a dynamic volume previously did not have a drive letter, it does not receive a drive letter when it is moved to another computer. Additionally, if automounting is disabled, the volumes aren't automatically mounted, and you must manually mount volumes and assign drive letters.

Using storage spaces

Storage technologies are in transition from traditional approaches to standards-based approaches. As a result, storage spaces are replacing software RAID as the preferred approach for spanning disks and achieving data redundancy. Storage spaces make it possible for you to group drives together in a storage pool that can be used to allocate storage.

Getting started with storage spaces

To use storage spaces, a computer must have one or more extra hard drives in addition to the hard drive on which Windows is installed. The drives can be internal drives, external drives, or allocated from network-attached storage.

With storage spaces, the physical layout of disks is abstracted. Here, a "disk" can be a logical reference to a virtual disk in network-attached storage or an actual physical disk. This means a disk just becomes a unit of storage and volumes can be created to allocate space within disks for file systems.

Taking this concept a few steps further, you can pool available space on disks so that units of storage (virtual disks) can be allocated from this pool on an as-needed basis. These units of storage, in turn, are apportioned with volumes to allocate space and create usable file systems.

Technically, the pooled storage is referred to as a *storage pool* and the virtual disks created within the pool are referred to as *storages spaces*. Given a set of "disks," you can create a single storage pool by allocating all the disks to the pool, or create multiple storage pools by allocating disks separately to each pool.

Creating redundant data sets

You manage storage spaces by using the Storage Spaces console, which can be accessed in Control Panel. In Control Panel, select System And Security, and then select Storage Spaces. By default, when you access Storage Spaces, you have view-only access to the available storage. To manage storage, you must select Change Settings, which requires administrator privileges on the computer.

Figure 3-12 shows a computer with an allocated storage space called Primary Storage. Here, the storage space has 4 TB of available capacity but is using only 4.75 GB of that capacity. Storage is allocated by using two simple volumes: a G: volume with 2 TB of storage and an H: volume with 2 TB of storage.

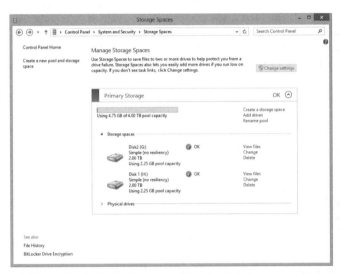

FIGURE 3-12 Use the Storage Spaces console to allocate and manage storage.

You can use Storage Spaces to create many types of volumes, including:

- **Simple volumes** Creates a simple volume by writing one copy of your data to one or more drives. With simple volumes there is no redundancy and no associated overhead. As an example, you can create a single volume that spans two 1-TB drives, making 2 TB of storage available. However, because there is no resiliency, a failure of any drive in a simple volume causes the entire volume to fail.

- **Two-way mirrors** Creates a mirrored set by writing two copies of a computer's data, helping to protect against a single drive failure. Two-way mirrors require at least two drives. With two-way mirrors there is a one-half (50 percent) overhead for redundancy. As an example, you could allocate two 1-TB drives as a two-way mirror, giving you 1 TB of mirrored storage.

- **Three-way mirrors** Creates a mirrored set by writing three copies of a computer's data and by using disk striping with mirroring, helping to protect against two simultaneous drive failures. Three-way mirrors require at least five drives. With three-way mirrors there is a two-thirds (66.66 percent) overhead for redundancy. As an example, you could allocate six 2-TB drives as a three-way mirror, giving you 4 TB of mirrored storage.

- **Parity volumes** Creates a volume that uses disk striping with parity, helping to provide fault tolerance with less overhead than mirroring. With parity volumes there is a one-third (33.33 percent) overhead for redundancy. As an example, you could allocate three 2-TB drives as a parity volume, giving you 4 TB of protected storage.

When a computer has extra hard drives in addition to the hard drive on which Windows is installed, you can allocate one or more of the additional drives to a storage pool. However, keep in mind that if you use a formatted drive with a storage pool, Windows permanently deletes all the files on that drive.

Working with storage pools

Working with storage pools is a multistep process:

1. You create a storage pool to pool available space on one or more disks.
2. You allocate space from this pool to create one or more virtual disks.
3. You create one or more volumes on each virtual disk to allocate storage for file systems.

The sections that follow examine procedures related to each of these steps. Also discussed are procedures for managing existing storage pools.

Creating a storage pool and allocating storage

You must create a storage pool before you can allocate storage. When you create a storage pool, you allocate one or more drives to the storage pool and then create a storage space within the storage pool. This initial storage space can use all or part of the available capacity in the storage pool. If there is unused capacity in the pool, that unused capacity can be allocated to the same storage space or another storage space later. Keep in mind that if you use a formatted drive with a storage pool, Windows permanently deletes all the files on that drive.

To create a storage pool and allocate storage, complete the following steps:

1. In Control Panel, select System And Security, and then select Storage Spaces.
2. Select Create A New Pool And Storage Space. On the Create A Storage Pool page, shown in Figure 3-13, additional drives that are available to the computer but have not yet been assigned are listed as available drives.

FIGURE 3-13 Select one or more drives to be part of the storage pool.

3. Select the drives that should be allocated to the storage pool. If you are unsure whether a drive has files that shouldn't be permanently deleted, select
View Files and then review the available files to confirm whether you should
allocate the drive to the storage space. If you selected a drive that shouldn't
be formatted for use with the storage pool, be sure to clear the selection
before continuing.

IMPORTANT   If you open a window to view a drive, you must close this window
before continuing (in addition to any other windows where you might be viewing the drive's contents). Failure to do this might prevent Windows from gaining
exclusive access to the drive, which in turn will cause storage space creation to fail.

4. When you select Create Pool, Windows will prepare the drives and allocate
them to the storage pool.

5. Next, you are prompted to create the associated storage space (see Figure
3-14). Configure the storage space by using the following options:

- **Name**   Sets a text label for the storage space. This label is used as the
volume name.

- **Drive Letter**   Selects an available drive letter for the storage space, such
as F.

- **File System**   Sets the file system type, such as NTFS or ReFS.

- **Resiliency Type**   Sets the type of storage space to create as Simple,
Two-way Mirror, Three-way Mirror, or Parity.

IMPORTANT   When you create a storage space, you can modify the name, drive
letter and storage space size at any time. However, after the resiliency type is set,
you cannot change it without deleting and then recreating the storage space.

FIGURE 3-14 Configure the storage space for use.

6. Use the Size options to specify the maximum size of the storage space. Keep the following in mind:

   ■ Before you allocate space, note the total pool capacity and the available pool capacity. Rather than allocate all available pool capacity to a single storage space, you can allocate part of the available storage to one storage space and part of the available storage to other storage spaces.

   ■ When you specify a maximum size for the storage space, note the size including overhead for any resiliency. This is the maximum total size of the storage space. For example, if you are creating a two-way mirror and enter 930 GB as the maximum size, the size including resiliency is 1.81 TB.

   ■ Because you can add drives to a pool at any time, you can allocate more space than is currently available. For example, if you have three 1-TB drives, you could allocate 6 TB to the storage pool. When the computer runs low on capacity in the pool, you would then need to add more drives.

7. Before you create the storage space, you should close any open windows where the drive is selected or displayed.

8. When you select Create Storage Space, Windows will format and create the storage space in the selected storage pool.

If there is a problem creating the storage space, Windows will display a warning and automatically try creating the pool again. In the example shown in Figure 3-15, Windows was able to allocate one of the selected drives to the storage pool but was not able to allocate the second drive. Because of this, Windows displayed a "Waiting to retry" warning. After waiting at least 90 seconds, you can determine whether Windows was able to successfully allocate space by selecting the Refresh button. Alternatively, you can close and then open the Storage Spaces console.

FIGURE 3-15 Windows displays a warning if there is a problem allocating storage.

If Windows isn't able to complete the storage space configuration successfully within 30 minutes, you might want to remove the drives from the storage space and then try to create the storage space again. To remove a drive, complete the following steps:

1. On the Storage Spaces page in Control Panel, select the Remove option for the drive you want to remove.

2. On the Remove A Drive page, select View Files and then review the available files to confirm that you are removing the correct storage space. If you selected the wrong storage space, select the Back button and then select the correct storage space before continuing.

3. On the Remove A Drive page, select Remove Drive.

Adding drives to a storage space

You can add extra drives to a storage space at any time by completing the following steps:

1. In Control Panel, select System And Security, and then select Storage Spaces.

2. Select Change Settings. On the management panel for the storage space you want to configure, select Add Drives.

3. Select the drive or drives that should be allocated to the storage pool. Keep in mind that if you use a formatted drive with a storage pool, Windows permanently deletes all the files on that drive.

4. When you select Add Drives, Windows will prepare the drive or drives and allocate them to the storage pool. If there is a problem adding drives, Windows will display a warning and automatically try to add the drives again.

Changing the storage configuration

You can change the configuration of a storage space at any time by completing the following steps:

1. In Control Panel, select System And Security, and then select Storage Spaces.

2. Select Change Settings. On the management panel for the storage space you want to configure, select Change for the storage space you want to configure.

3. As necessary, use the options provided to modify the name of the storage space, the associated drive letter, and the size of the storage space.

4. Select Change Storage Space. If there is a problem modifying the storage space, Windows will display a warning and automatically try to modify the storage space again later. Because Windows needs exclusive access to the storage space to change the configuration, Windows will close any open windows using the drive in addition to any open connections to the drive.

Deleting a storage space

If you no longer need a storage space, you can delete it. Deleting a storage space permanently removes all the files that it contains.

To delete a storage space, complete the following steps:

1. In Control Panel, select System And Security, and then select Storage Spaces.

2. Select Change Settings. On the Storage Spaces panel, each allocated storage space is listed. Select the Delete option for the storage space you want to remove.

3. On the Delete A Storage Space page, shown in Figure 3-16, select View Files and then review the available files to confirm that you are removing the correct storage space. If you selected the wrong storage space, select the Back button, and then select the correct storage space before continuing.

FIGURE 3-16 Delete a storage space when it is no longer needed.

4. On the Delete A Storage Space page, select Delete Storage Space.

Deleting a storage pool

Before you can delete a storage pool, you must delete any associated storage spaces as discussed in the "Deleting a storage space" section earlier in the chapter. Deleting a storage pool permanently removes all the files that it contains and causes any drives currently allocated to the pool to be reformatted.

To delete a storage pool, complete the following steps:

1. In Control Panel, select System And Security, and then select Storage Spaces.

2. Select Change Settings. Select the Delete Pool option for the storage pool you want to remove. This option is only available if the pool doesn't have any currently allocated storage spaces.

3. On the Delete A Storage Pool page, select Delete Storage Pool.

Troubleshooting storage spaces

Typical problems creating storage spaces and allocating storage were discussed previously. Other problems you might experience with storage spaces relate to drive failures and a loss of resiliency. When a storage space uses two-way mirroring, three-way mirroring, or parity, you can recover resiliency by reconnecting a disconnected drive or replacing a failed drive. When a storage space uses a simple volume and drives were disconnected, you can recover the volume by reconnecting the drives.

Selecting the notification icon for Action Center displays the related notifications. If there is a problem with storage spaces, Action Center updates the related notification panel in the desktop notification area with a message stating "Check Storage Spaces for issues," as shown in Figure 3-17. Selecting the notification icon and then selecting the link provided opens the Storage Spaces console in Control Panel.

FIGURE 3-17 View Action Center notifications to start troubleshooting storage space problems.

As shown in Figure 3-18, the Storage Spaces console provides warnings that show exactly what is wrong. In this example, a storage space using two-way mirroring has reduced resiliency because one of the drives is missing, failed, or disconnected.

FIGURE 3-18 Check the Storage Spaces console for errors.

When storage spaces use external drives, a missing drive might be a common problem you encounter. In this case, users can continue to work and redundancy will be restored when you reconnect the drive. On the other hand, if a drive failed, you'll need to complete the following steps to restore redundancy:

1. Physically remove the failed drive. If the drive is connected internally, you'll need to shut down and unplug the computer before you can remove the drive. Otherwise, just disconnect an externally connected drive.

2. Physically add or connect a replacement drive. Next, add the drive to the storage space by doing the following:

   a. On the Storage Spaces page in Control Panel, select Change Settings. On the management panel for the storage space you want to configure, select Add Drives.

   b. Select the drive that should be allocated to the storage pool. Keep in mind that if you use a formatted drive with a storage pool, Windows permanently deletes all the files on that drive.

   c. When you select Add Drives, Windows will prepare the drive and allocate it to the storage pool.

3. At this point, the failed drive should be listed as "Retired." Remove the failed drive from the storage space by selecting the related Remove option and then confirming that you want to remove the drive by selecting Remove Drive.

Windows restores redundancy by copying data as necessary to the new disk. During this process, the status of the storage space is typically listed as "Repairing." You'll also notice a value depicting how much of the repair task is completed. When this value reaches 100 percent, the repair is complete.

CHAPTER 4

Configuring and maintaining storage

- Working with removable storage devices **131**
- Working with data discs **133**
- Managing disk compression and file encryption **137**
- Troubleshooting common disk problems **144**

In the previous chapter, I showed you how to manage disk drives and file systems. In this chapter, I discuss techniques you can use to work with other types of storage, including removable storage devices and data discs. I also discuss techniques for managing disk compression, implementing file encryption, and troubleshooting common disk problems.

Working with removable storage devices

Removable storage devices can be formatted with NTFS, FAT, FAT32, and exFAT. You connect external storage devices to a computer instead of installing them inside the computer. This makes external storage devices easier and faster to install than most internal hard drives. Most external storage devices have a USB, FireWire, or eSATA interface. When working with USB and FireWire, the transfer speed and overall performance of the device from a user's perspective depend primarily on the version supported.

Currently, several versions of USB and FireWire are used. USB 2.0 is the industry standard while the world transitions to USB 3.0. USB 2.0 devices can be rated as either full speed (up to 12 megabits per second [Mbps]) or high speed (up to 480 Mbps). Although high-speed USB 2.0 supports data transfers at a maximum rate of 480 Mbps, sustained data transfer rates usually are from 10 to 30 Mbps. The actual sustainable transfer rate depends on many factors, including the type of device, the data that you are transferring, and the speed of the computer. Each USB controller on a computer has a fixed amount of bandwidth that all devices attached to the controller must share. The data transfer rates will be significantly slower if a computer's USB port is an earlier version than the device you are using. For example, if you connect a USB 2.0 device to a USB 1.0 port, or vice versa, the device operates at the significantly reduced USB 1.0 transfer speed.

USB 1.0, 1.1, and 2.0 ports all look alike; however, most USB 3.0 ports I've seen have a special coloring to differentiate them. Still, the best way to determine which type of USB ports a computer has is to refer to the documentation that came with the computer. Newer monitors have USB 2.0 ports to which you can also connect devices. When you have USB devices connected to a monitor, the monitor acts like a USB hub device. As occurs with any USB hub device, all devices attached to the hub share the same bandwidth, and the total available bandwidth is determined by the speed of the USB input to which the hub is connected on a computer.

FireWire (IEEE 1394) is a high-performance connection standard that uses a peer-to-peer architecture in which peripherals negotiate bus conflicts to determine which device can best control a data transfer. Several versions of FireWire are currently used. FireWire 400 (IEEE 1394a) has maximum sustained transfer rates of up to 400 Mbps. IEEE 1394b supports 400 Mbps (S400), 800 Mbps (S800), and 1,600 Mbps (S1600). As with USB devices, if you connect an IEEE 1394b device to an IEEE 1394a port or vice versa, the device operates at the significantly reduced FireWire 400 transfer speed.

As with USB ports, the sustained transfer rate for IEEE 1394a and IEEE 1394b ports will be considerably less than the maximum rate possible. IEEE 1394a and IEEE 1394b ports and cables have different shapes, making it easier to tell the difference between them—if you know what you're looking for. With that said, FireWire 400 ports and cables look exactly like early versions of FireWire that were implemented prior to the finalization of the IEEE 1394a and IEEE 1394b specifications. FireWire cables and ports that have four pins and four connectors lack bus power. FireWire 400 cables and ports have six pins and six connectors. FireWire 800 and FireWire 1600 cables and ports have nine pins and nine connectors.

Network-ready devices might connect directly to your network via Ethernet cable. Many of these devices are now rated at 1 gigabit per second (Gbps), which is the same as saying 1,000 Mbps. Devices rated at 10 Gbps are also becoming increasingly available.

Before you purchase an external device for a computer, you should consider what interfaces your computer supports and the interfaces the device uses. In some cases, you might be able to get a device with a dual interface that supports USB 2.0 and FireWire 400, or a triple interface that supports USB 2.0, FireWire 400, and FireWire 800. A device with dual or triple interfaces will give you more options.

In the This PC console or Disk Management, you can work with removable disks by pressing and holding or right-clicking a disk, and then using the following commands:

- Tap or click Open to examine the disk's contents in File Explorer.
- Tap or click Format to format removable disks as discussed in the "Formatting partitions and volumes" section in Chapter 3, "Managing disk drives and file systems." Removable disks generally are formatted with a single partition.
- Tap or click Properties to view or set properties. On the General tab of the Properties dialog box, you can set the volume label as discussed in the "Assigning, changing, or deleting a volume label" section in Chapter 3.

When you work with removable disks, you can customize disk and folder views. To do this, press and hold or right-click the disk or folder, and then tap or click the Customize tab. You can then specify the default folder type to control the default details displayed. For example, you can set the default folder type as Documents or Pictures And Videos. You can also set folder pictures and folder icons.

Removable disks support network file and folder sharing. You configure sharing on removable disks in the same way that you configure standard file sharing. You can assign share permissions, configure caching options for offline file use, and limit the number of simultaneous users. You can share an entire removable disk, in addition to individual folders stored on the removable disk. You can also create multiple share instances.

Removable disk sharing differs from standard NTFS sharing in that there isn't necessarily an underlying security architecture. With exFAT, FAT, or FAT32, folders and files that are stored do not have any security permissions or features other than the basic read-only or hidden attribute flags that you can set.

Working with data discs

CD and DVD disc images are often stored as ISO files, as are Blu-ray discs. Windows 8.1 has built-in capabilities to recognize ISO images and burn them to CD or DVD. Windows 8.1 also has built-in disc burning features that you can use to create data discs. Before you burn data discs, you should familiarize yourself with the disc types and disc file system options that are available.

Disc burning: the essentials

By default, when you insert a blank disc, Windows 8.1 shows a Burn button on the File Explorer toolbar. Tapping or clicking this button starts the Burn A Disc Wizard, which you can use to create a data disc. Keep in mind that computer disc players are different from players for homes or cars. Typically, your computer disc player is designed to read commercially produced discs, in addition to computer-burned discs in specific formats, but a home or car disc player won't necessarily be able to recognize a disc you create on a computer.

Most disc burners support multiple disc types. Windows 8.1 natively supports burning data CDs to CD-R, CD+R, and CD-RW and burning data DVDs to DVD-R, DVD-RW, DVD+R, DVD+RW, and DVD-RAM. DVDs can be single-sided and single-layered or single-sided and dual-layered. Windows 8.1 also natively supports Blu-ray. If a computer has a Blu-ray burner, you might also be able to burn Blu-ray discs.

Windows 8.1 supports two approaches to burning discs:

- Disc mastering
- Live file system

Most Windows-based programs create data discs by using a mastered approach, and discs are written in an appropriate file system format automatically. With a mastered approach, you select a collection of files that you want to copy to a disc, and then burn all the files at once. When you are burning large collections of files, this is a convenient approach, with the added bonus of compatibility with any computer or device that supports the type of data disc you are using.

When you burn files to data discs by using mastering, you burn files in a session. In many disc burning programs, you have the option of leaving a session open in order to add files later, and then you close the session when you are done adding files. By closing the session, you finalize the disc and enable it to be read on other computers and devices. Otherwise, while a session is open, the disc can be read only on a compatible computer.

In contrast, a data disc with a live file system works like any other type of removable storage, such as a USB flash drive or a removable disk drive. You can add files to the disc without having to burn them by just copying and pasting files or by dragging and dropping files. If the disc is re-recordable, you can remove files by selecting them and deleting them. If you eject the disc, you can insert it into your CD/DVD drive later and continue to use it like removable storage.

Data discs with a live file system are formatted by using the Universal Disc Format (UDF) rather than the standard CD File System (CDFS). Generally, only computers can read UDF-formatted data discs. Windows 8.1 supports burning data discs in several UDF versions, including UDF 1.5, UDF 2.0, UDF 2.01 (the default), and UDF 2.5. Although all of these formats will work with current versions of Windows, you'll typically want to use UDF 2.01 or UDF 2.5 to ensure optimal performance. If you must specify the UDF version, such as for compatibility with an operating system not based on Windows, you can do so by pressing and holding or right-clicking the disc in the This PC window and then selecting Format. In the Format dialog box, you'll then be able to specify the UDF version to use.

Mounting ISO images

You mount an ISO image to create a virtual disk that you can work with much like a physical disc. For example, if you mount an ISO image for an application, you can use the mounted ISO image to install the application.

To mount an ISO image as a virtual disk, do one of the following:

- In File Explorer, press and hold or right-click the .iso file that you want to mount, and then tap or click Mount.
- In File Explorer, tap or click the .iso file that you want to use to create a data disk. Next, press and hold or right-click the .iso file that you want to mount, and then tap or click Mount.

Burning ISO images to disc

You burn an ISO image to create a physical disc. You can then use the disc with disc drives in other computers. To burn an ISO image, complete the following steps:

1. Insert a blank disc into your disc burner. If the AutoPlay dialog box is displayed, tap or click the Close button.
2. In File Explorer, press and hold or right-click the .iso file that you want to use to create a data disc, and then tap or click Burn Disc Image.

3. In the Windows Disc Image Burner dialog box, shown in Figure 4-1, use the Disc Burner list to select the disc burner, and then tap or click Burn.

FIGURE 4-1 Burn ISO images to disc.

Burning mastered discs

You can burn a mastered disc by completing the following steps:

1. Insert a blank disc into your disc burner. Do one of the following:
   - In the AutoPlay dialog box, tap when prompted and then select Burn Files To Disc–File Explorer.
   - If the AutoPlay dialog box is not displayed, open the This PC window. In the Computer window, press and hold or right-click the disc burner, and then tap or click Open AutoPlay. In the AutoPlay dialog box, select Burn Files To Disc–File Explorer.

2. In the Burn A Disc Wizard, shown in Figure 4-2, enter a disc title. To create a mastered disc, select With A CD/DVD Player. When you tap or click Next, the data disc is opened in File Explorer. The main pane displays an empty burn list. Don't close this window.

3. In File Explorer, drag files to the burn list or select and copy files to the burn list. Files in the burn list are copied from their original location and written as temporary files to a temporary folder. This temporary folder is created in the user's personal profile. Copies of these files are created to be sure that all the files are in one place and that you have appropriate permissions to access the files before trying to burn the disc.

4. When you are ready to continue, press and hold or right-click an empty area in the Files Ready To Be Written To The Disc panel, and then tap or click Burn To Disc. In the Burn To Disc Wizard, the disc title is set by using the title you provided previously, and the recording speed is set to the maximum speed supported by the disc drive.

5. When you tap or click Next, Windows 8.1 adds the files you selected to a disc image and then writes the files to your data disc. When finished burning the disc, Windows 8.1 automatically ejects the disc by default. Also by default, the temporary files are deleted, and you can then tap or click Finish to exit the Burn To Disc Wizard. If you want to burn the same files to another disc, select the Yes, Burn These Files To Another Disc check box before tapping or clicking Finish.

FIGURE 4-2 Prepare to burn data to a disc.

If an error occurs while burning, you'll get an error message. You'll have the option of trying again with a different disc, deleting the temporary files that have not burned, or saving all the temporary files and trying to burn them later. If you try again, make sure you select a slower burn speed. Although your disc drive might be able to burn at a high speed, the disc itself might not be rated for burning at the speed you selected.

Generally, if you get a burn error, only a portion of your files will have been written to the disc. If the burn session is still open, you can try to burn to the disc again. Occasionally, you might find that you have to use a new blank disc.

Burning discs with live file systems

You can burn a data disc with a live file system by completing the following steps:

1. Insert a blank disc into your disc burner. If the Burn A Disc Wizard doesn't start automatically, open the This PC window. In the This PC window, double-tap or double-click the disc burner. Or if the AutoPlay dialog box is displayed instead, select Burn Files To Disc–File Explorer.

2. In the Burn A Disc Wizard, enter a disc title. To create a UDF disc with a live file system, select Like A USB Flash Drive. When you tap or click Next, Windows creates a live file system on the disc and then opens the data disc in File Explorer.

3. The Files Ready To Be Written To The Disc pane displays an empty burn list. Don't close this window.

4. Because you are working with a live disc, there is no burn list. You can now add files to and remove files from the disc as you would with any other disc device. With re-recordable discs, when files are deleted, they are removed and the space is freed for other files. With standard recordable discs, the files are marked as deleted but actually still exist on the disc. Because of this, the space used by the deleted files is still allocated and cannot be used by other files.

5. While the disc is inserted, Windows 8.1 maintains an open burn session for the disc. If you eject the live data disc, Windows 8.1 closes the burn session so that you can use the disc with other computers. From then on, whenever you insert the disc, you can add or remove files by using File Explorer. Windows will open another burn session only if you modify the disc's contents. As before, you can close the session by ejecting the disc. You can also close a burn session by pressing and holding or right-clicking the disc drive in the This PC window and then tapping or clicking Close Session.

Changing the default burning options

You can change a computer's default burning options by completing the following steps:

1. Open the This PC window. In the This PC window, press and hold or right-click the disc drive, and then tap or click Properties.

2. On the Recording tab, use the Disc Burning list to set the default burner on a computer with multiple disc burners.

3. Use the options provided to specify where temporary files are stored.

4. If you don't want mastered discs to be ejected automatically after they are burned, clear the related check box.

5. By default, Windows closes discs with live file systems when you eject them. To confirm or modify this behavior, tap or click Global Settings. In the Global Settings dialog box, specify whether and when sessions are closed by using the options provided, and then tap or click OK.

6. Tap or click OK to save your settings.

Managing disk compression and file encryption

In Windows 8.1, when you format a drive for NTFS, you can enable disk compression or file encryption. You use compression to reduce the disk space that files require, and you use encryption to add an extra layer of protection to your data. Disk compression and file encryption are mutually exclusive. You can use one feature or the other, and neither feature is affected by BitLocker Drive Encryption, which encrypts disks at the volume level and protects a computer from external tampering prior to startup of the operating system.

Compressing drives and data

With compression, all files and directories stored on a drive are automatically compressed when they're created. Because this compression is transparent to users, compressed data can be accessed just like regular data. The difference is that you can store more information on a compressed drive than you can on an uncompressed drive. Note that File Explorer shows the names of compressed resources in blue.

Compressing drives

To compress a drive and all its contents, follow these steps:

1. In File Explorer or Disk Management, press and hold or right-click the drive that you want to compress, and then tap or click Properties.

2. Select Compress This Drive To Save Disk Space, and then tap or click OK.

Compressing directories and files

If you decide not to compress a drive, Windows 8.1 lets you selectively compress directories and files. To compress a file or directory, follow these steps:

1. In File Explorer, press and hold or right-click the file or directory that you want to compress, and then tap or click Properties.

2. On the General tab of the Properties dialog box, tap or click Advanced. In the Advanced Attributes dialog box, select the Compress Contents To Save Disk Space check box, as shown in Figure 4-3. Tap or click OK twice.

For an individual file, Windows 8.1 marks the file as compressed and then compresses it. For a directory, Windows 8.1 marks the directory as compressed and then compresses all the files in it. If the directory contains subfolders, Windows 8.1 displays a dialog box that enables you to compress all the subfolders associated with the directory. Just select Apply Changes To This Folder, Subfolders And Files, and then tap or click OK. After you compress a directory, any new files added or copied to the directory are compressed automatically.

FIGURE 4-3 Compress the selected file or directory.

> **NOTE** If you move an uncompressed file from a different drive to a compressed folder, the file is compressed. However, if you move an uncompressed file to a compressed folder on the same NTFS drive, the file isn't compressed. Note also that you can't encrypt compressed files.

Expanding compressed drives

File Explorer shows the names of compressed files and folders in blue. You can remove compression from a drive by following these steps:

1. In File Explorer or Disk Management, press and hold or right-click the drive that contains the data you want to expand, and then tap or click Properties.

2. Clear the Compress This Drive To Save Disk Space check box, and then tap or click OK.

> **TIP** Windows always checks the available disk space before expanding compressed data. You should, too. If less free space is available than used space, you might not be able to complete the expansion. For example, if a compressed drive uses 150 GB of space and has 70 GB of free space available, you won't have enough free space to expand the drive. Generally, you need about 1.5 to 2 times as much free space as you have compressed data.

Expanding compressed directories and files

If you decide later that you want to expand a compressed file or directory, reverse the process by following these steps:

1. In File Explorer, press and hold or right-click the file or directory, and then tap or click Properties.

2. On the General tab of the Properties dialog box, tap or click Advanced. Clear the Compress Contents To Save Disk Space check box. Tap or click OK twice.

With files, Windows 8.1 removes compression and expands the file. With directories, Windows 8.1 expands all the files within the directory. If the directory
contains subfolders, you have the opportunity to remove compression from the
subfolders. To do this, select Apply Changes To This Folder, Subfolders And Files
when prompted, and then tap or click OK.

> **TIP** Windows 8.1 also provides command-line utilities for compressing and uncom-
> pressing your data. The compression utility is called Compact (Compact.exe). The
> uncompression utility is called Expand (Expand.exe).

Encrypting drives and data

NTFS has many advantages over other file systems that you can use with Windows 8.1.
One of the major advantages is the capability to automatically encrypt and decrypt
data by using the Encrypting File System (EFS). When you encrypt data, you add an
extra layer of protection to sensitive data—and this extra layer acts as a security
blanket blocking all other users from reading the contents of the encrypted files.
Indeed, one of the great benefits of encryption is that only the designated user can
access the data. This benefit is also a disadvantage in that the user must remove
encryption before authorized users can access the data.

> **NOTE** As discussed previously, you can't compress encrypted files. The encryption
> and compression features of NTFS are mutually exclusive. You can use one feature or
> the other, but not both.

Understanding encryption and EFS

File encryption is supported on a per-folder or per-file basis. Any file placed in a
folder marked for encryption is automatically encrypted. Files in encrypted format
can be read only by the person who encrypted the file. Before other users can read
an encrypted file, the user must decrypt the file.

Every encrypted file has a unique encryption key. This means that an encrypted
file can be copied, moved, and renamed just like any other file—and in most cases,
these actions don't affect the encryption of the data. (For details, see the "Working
with encrypted files and folders" section later in this chapter.) The user who encrypts
the file always has access to the file if the user's public-key certificate is available on
the computer that he or she is using. For this user, the encryption and decryption
process is handled automatically and is transparent.

EFS is the process that handles encryption and decryption. The default setup for EFS
allows users to encrypt files without needing special permission. Files are encrypted by
using a public/private key that EFS automatically generates on a per-user basis.

Encryption certificates are stored as part of the data in user profiles. If a user
works with multiple computers and wants to use encryption, an administrator needs
to configure a roaming profile for that user. A roaming profile ensures that the user's
profile data and public-key certificates are accessible from other computers. Without this, users won't be able to access their encrypted files on another computer.

Although they are separate features, both BitLocker Drive Encryption and EFS have a built-in data recovery system to guard against data loss. This recovery system ensures that encrypted data can be recovered in the event that a user's public key certificate is lost or deleted. The most common scenario for this is when a user leaves the company and the associated user account is deleted. A manager might have been able to log on to the user's account, check files, and save important files to other folders, but if the user account has been deleted, encrypted volumes and files will be accessible only if the encryption is removed or if the files are moved to a FAT or FAT32 volume (where EFS encryption isn't supported and BitLocker encryption is not enabled).

To access encrypted files after the user account has been deleted, you need to use a recovery agent. Recovery agents have access to the file encryption key necessary to unlock data in encrypted files. To protect sensitive data, however, recovery agents don't have access to a user's private key or any private key information.

Windows 8.1 will encrypt volumes without designated BitLocker recovery agents, but Windows 8.1 won't encrypt files without designated EFS recovery agents. EFS recovery agents are designated automatically, and the necessary recovery certificates are also generated automatically. This ensures that encrypted files can always be recovered.

Recovery agents are configured at two levels:

- **Domain** The recovery agent for a domain is configured automatically when the first domain controller is installed. By default, the recovery agent is the domain administrator. Through Group Policy, domain administrators can designate additional recovery agents. Domain administrators can also delegate recovery agent privileges to designated security administrators.

- **Local computer** When a computer is part of a workgroup or in a stand-alone configuration, the recovery agent is the administrator of the local computer by default. Additional recovery agents can be designated. Further, if you want local recovery agents in a domain environment rather than domain-level recovery agents, you must delete the recovery policy from the Group Policy for the domain.

You can delete recovery agents if you don't want to use them. However, if you delete all recovery agents for EFS, files can no longer be encrypted by using EFS. One or more recovery agents must be configured for EFS to function.

Encrypting directories and files

With NTFS volumes, Windows 8.1 lets you select files and folders for encryption. When you encrypt files, the file data is converted to an encrypted format that can be read only by the person who encrypted the file. Users can encrypt files only if they have the proper access permissions. When you encrypt folders, the folder is marked as encrypted, but only the files within it are actually encrypted. All files that are created in or added to a folder marked as encrypted are encrypted automatically. Note that File Explorer shows the names of encrypted resources in green.

To encrypt a file or directory, follow these steps:

1. In File Explorer, press and hold or right-click the file or directory that you want to encrypt, and then tap or click Properties.

2. On the General tab of the Properties dialog box, tap or click Advanced, and then select the Encrypt Contents To Secure Data check box. Tap or click OK twice.

NOTE You can't encrypt compressed files, system files, or read-only files. If you try to encrypt compressed files, the files are automatically uncompressed and then encrypted. If you try to encrypt system files, you'll get an error.

For an individual file, Windows 8.1 marks the file as encrypted and then encrypts it. For a directory, Windows 8.1 marks the directory as encrypted and then encrypts all the files in it. If the directory contains subfolders, Windows 8.1 displays a dialog box that enables you to encrypt all the subfolders associated with the directory. Just select Apply Changes To This Folder, Subfolders And Files, and then tap or click OK twice.

NOTE On NTFS volumes, files remain encrypted even when they are moved, copied, and renamed. If you copy or move an encrypted file to a FAT, FAT32, or exFAT drive, the file is automatically decrypted before it is copied or moved. This means that you must have proper permissions to copy or move the file.

Working with encrypted files and folders

Previously, I said that you can copy, move, and rename encrypted files and folders just like any other files. This is true, but I qualified this by saying "in most cases." When you work with encrypted files, you'll have few problems so long as you work with NTFS volumes on the same computer. When you work with other file systems or other computers, you might run into problems. Two of the most common scenarios are these:

- **Copying between volumes on the same computer** When you copy or move an encrypted file or folder from one NTFS volume to another NTFS volume on the same computer, the files remain encrypted. However, if you copy or move encrypted files to a FAT, FAT32, or exFAT volume, the files are decrypted before transfer and then transferred as standard files and therefore end up in their destinations as unencrypted files. FAT, FAT32, and exFAT don't support encryption.

- **Copying between volumes on different computers** When you copy or move an encrypted file or folder from one NTFS volume to another NTFS volume on a different computer, the files remain encrypted so long as the destination computer allows you to encrypt files and the remote computer is trusted for delegation. Otherwise, the files are decrypted and then transferred as standard files. The same is true when you copy or move encrypted files to a FAT, FAT32, or exFAT volume on another computer. FAT, FAT32, and exFAT don't support encryption.

After you transfer a sensitive file that has been encrypted, you might want to confirm that the encryption is still applied. Press and hold or right-click the file, and then tap or click Properties. On the General tab of the Properties dialog box, tap or click Advanced. The Encrypt Contents To Secure Data option should be selected.

Configuring recovery policy

In domains, EFS and BitLocker recovery policies are configured automatically for domain controllers and member computers. By default, domain administrators are the designated EFS and BitLocker recovery agents for all computers in domains. In workgroups or homegroups, the local administrator is the designated EFS recovery agent for a stand-alone workstation. BitLocker has no default recovery agent for homegroups or workgroups.

Through the Group Policy console, you can view, assign, and delete recovery agents by following these steps:

1. Open a Group Policy Object for editing in the Group Policy Management Editor.

2. Open the Encrypted Data Recovery Agents node in Group Policy. To do this, expand Computer Configuration\Windows Settings\Security Settings\Public Key Policies, and then select either Encrypting File System or BitLocker Drive Encryption, as appropriate for the type of recovery agent with which you want to work.

3. The right pane lists the recovery certificates currently assigned. Recovery certificates are listed according to who issued them, to whom they are issued, expiration date, purpose, and other properties.

4. To designate an additional recovery agent, press and hold or right-click the Encrypting File System or BitLocker Drive Encryption node, and then tap or click Add Data Recovery Agent. This starts the Add Recovery Agent Wizard, which you can use to select a previously generated certificate that has been assigned to a user and then mark it as a designated recovery certificate. Tap or click Next.

5. On the Select Recovery Agents page, tap or click Browse Directory. In the Find Users, Contacts, And Groups dialog box, select the user with which you want to work.

   NOTE Before you can designate additional recovery agents, you must set up a root certificate authority (CA) in the domain. Then you must use the Certificates snap-in to generate a personal certificate that uses the EFS Recovery Agent template. The root CA must then approve the certificate request so that the certificate can be used.

6. To delete a recovery agent, select the recovery agent's certificate in the right pane, and then press Delete. When prompted to confirm the action, tap or click Yes to permanently and irrevocably delete the certificate. With EFS, if the recovery policy is empty (meaning that it has no other designated recovery agents), EFS will be turned off so that files can no longer be encrypted; existing EFS-encrypted resources won't have a recovery agent.

Sharing decrypted files

By default, encrypted files can be viewed only by the file owner. If you want other users to be able to access an encrypted file, you must decrypt the file or grant the users special access to the file. If user certificates have been assigned, you can grant access to a file by completing the following procedure:

1. In File Explorer, press and hold or right-click the file or folder, and then select Properties.

2. On the General tab of the Properties dialog box, tap or click Advanced, and then tap or click Details in the Advanced Attributes dialog box.

   The User Access To dialog box appears. Users who have access to the encrypted file are listed by name.

3. To allow another user to access the file, tap or click Add.

4. If a user certificate is available for the user to whom you are granting access, select the user's name in the list provided, and then tap or click OK. Otherwise, tap or click Find User to locate the certificate for the user.

Decrypting files and directories

File Explorer shows the names of encrypted resources in green. If you decide later that you want to decrypt a file or directory, reverse the process by following these steps:

1. In File Explorer, press and hold or right-click the file or directory, and then select Properties.

2. On the General tab of the related Properties dialog box, tap or click Advanced. Clear the Encrypt Contents To Secure Data check box. Tap or click OK twice.

With files, Windows 8.1 decrypts the file and restores it to its original format. With directories, Windows 8.1 decrypts the files within the directory. If the directory contains subfolders, you have the opportunity to remove encryption from the subfolders. To do this, select Apply Changes To This Folder, Subfolders And Files when prompted, and then tap or click OK.

> **TIP** Windows 8.1 also provides a command-line utility called Cipher (Cipher.exe) for encrypting and decrypting your data. Entering **cipher** at the command prompt without additional parameters shows you the encryption status of all folders in the current directory.

Troubleshooting common disk problems

Windows 8.1 makes extensive use of disk drives during startup and normal operations. You can often dramatically improve operating system and application performance by optimizing a computer's disk drives. You should focus on disk space usage, disk errors, and disk fragmentation. You might also want to compress data to reduce the space used by data files, freeing up space for additional files.

NOTE Disk maintenance tools, such as Disk Cleanup, Check Disk, and Disk Defragmenter, take advantage of resource prioritization features in Windows 8.1, as discussed in the "Understanding and using Windows SuperFetch" section in Chapter 3. The changes enable these tools to run in the background to take advantage of system idle time while running. As a result, users get a consistently good performance level even when background maintenance tasks are running.

You should closely monitor disk space usage on all system drives. As drives begin to fill up, their performance and the performance of the operating system as a whole can be reduced, particularly if the system runs low on space for storing virtual memory or temporary files. One way to reduce disk space usage is to use the Disk Cleanup tool to remove unnecessary files and compress old files. To do this, complete the following steps:

1. In the Everywhere Search box, open Disk Cleanup by entering **cleanmgr** and then pressing Enter, or by tapping or clicking the related option on the Apps screen.

2. If the computer has multiple hard disk drives, the Drive Selection dialog box is displayed. Use the Drives drop-down list to choose the drive you want to clean up, and then tap or click OK.

   Disk Cleanup then examines the selected drive, looking for temporary user files that can be deleted and user files that are candidates for deletion. The more files on the drive, the longer the search process takes.

   When Disk Cleanup finishes its initial run, you can add temporary system files that can be deleted and system files that are candidates for deletion by tapping or clicking Clean Up System Files, selecting a system drive to examine, and then tapping or clicking OK. You will then receive a report on files that you can clean up.

3. Use the check boxes provided in the Files To Delete list to choose files that you want to remove. Then tap or click OK. When prompted to confirm the action, tap or click Yes.

To eliminate the need to remind users to run Disk Cleanup, you can schedule Disk Cleanup to run regularly by completing the following steps:

1. Open Computer Management. You are connected to the local computer by default. If you want to view tasks on a remote computer, press and hold or right-click the Computer Management entry in the console tree (left pane), and then tap or click Connect To Another Computer. In the Select Computer dialog box, enter the name of the computer that you want to access, and then tap or click OK.

2. Select and then press and hold or right-click the Task Scheduler node, and then tap or click Create Task. This starts the Create Task Wizard.

3. Configure the task. On the Actions tab, select New. In the New Action dialog box, select Start A Program, and then enter **%WinDir%\System32\cleanmgr.exe** in the Program/Script text box.

By using Disk Management, you can determine the status of disks and the volumes they contain. Disk status is displayed below the physical disk number in the Graphical view and in the Status column in the Disk List view. Volume status is displayed as part of the volume information in Graphical view and in the Status column in Volume List view.

Table 4-1 lists status messages you might receive for disks. You'll find a diagnosis and suggested corrective action in the Resolution column.

TABLE 4-1 Understanding and resolving disk status issues

STATUS	DESCRIPTION	RESOLUTION
Online	The standard disk status. This means the disk is accessible and doesn't have problems.	The drive doesn't have any known problems. You don't need to take any corrective action.
Online (Errors)	I/O errors have been detected on the disk.	You can try to correct temporary errors by pressing and holding or right-clicking the disk, and then tapping or clicking Reactivate Disk. If this doesn't work, the disk might have physical damage, or you might need to run a thorough check of the disk.
Offline	The disk isn't accessible and might be corrupted or temporarily unavailable. If the disk status changes to Missing, the disk can no longer be located or identified on the system.	Check for problems with the drive, its controller, and its cables. Make sure that the drive has power and is connected properly. Use the Reactivate Disk command to bring the disk back online (if possible).
Foreign	The disk has been moved to your computer but hasn't been imported for use. A failed drive brought back online might sometimes be listed as Foreign.	Press and hold or right-click the disk, and then tap or click Import Foreign Disks to add the disk to the system.

STATUS	DESCRIPTION	RESOLUTION
Unreadable	The disk isn't accessible currently, which can occur when disks are being rescanned.	With FireWire/USB card readers, you might encounter this status if the card is unformatted or improperly formatted. You might also encounter this status after the card is removed from the reader. Otherwise, if the drives aren't being scanned, the drive might be corrupted or have I/O errors. Press and hold or right-click the disk, and then tap or click Rescan Disk (the command is also on the Action menu) to try to correct the problem. You might also want to reboot the system.
Unrecognized	The disk is of an unknown type and can't be used on the system. A drive from a system not based on Windows might display this status.	If the disk is from another operating system, don't do anything. You can't use the drive on the computer, so try a different drive.
Not Initialized	The disk doesn't have a valid signature. A drive from a system not based on Windows might display this status.	If the disk is from another operating system, don't do anything. You can't use the drive on the computer, so try a different drive. To prepare the disk for use on Windows 8.1, press and hold or right-click the disk, and then tap or click Initialize Disk.
No Media	No media has been inserted into the DVD or removable drive, or the media has been removed. Only DVD and removable disk types display this status.	Insert a DVD or a removable disk to bring the disk online. With FireWire/USB card readers, this status is usually but not always displayed when the card is removed.

Table 4-2 lists status messages you might receive for volumes. You'll find a diagnosis and suggested corrective action in the Resolution column.

TABLE 4-2 Understanding and resolving volume status issues

STATUS	DESCRIPTION	RESOLUTION
Data Incomplete	Spanned volumes on a foreign disk are incomplete. You must have forgotten to add the other disks from the spanned volume set.	Add the disks that contain the rest of the spanned volume and then import all the disks at one time.
Data Not Redundant	Fault-tolerant volumes on a foreign disk are incomplete. You must have forgotten to add the other disk from a mirror set.	Add the remaining disk, and then import the disks at one time.
Failed	An error disk status. The disk is inaccessible or damaged.	Ensure that the related disk is online, and, as necessary, press and hold or right-click the disk, and then tap or click Reactivate Disk. Press and hold or right-click the volume, and then tap or click Reactivate Volume. You might need to check the disk for a faulty connection.
Failed Redundancy	Fault-tolerant disks are out of sync.	You can try to put the disks back in sync by pressing and holding or right-clicking the failed volume and selecting Reactivate Volume.
Formatting	A temporary status that indicates the volume is being formatted.	The progress of the formatting is indicated as the percent complete, unless the Perform A Quick Format option was selected.
Healthy	The usual volume status.	The volume doesn't have any known problems. You don't need to take any corrective action.

STATUS	DESCRIPTION	RESOLUTION
Healthy (At Risk)	Windows had problems reading from or writing to the physical disk on which the volume is located. This status appears when Windows encounters errors.	Press and hold or right-click the disk, and then tap or click Reactivate Disk. If the disk continues to have this status or has this status periodically, the disk might be failing and you should back up all data on the disk.
Healthy (Unknown Partition)	Windows does not recognize the partition. This can occur because the partition is from a different operating system or is a manufacturer-created partition used to store system files.	No corrective action is necessary.
Initializing	A temporary status that indicates the disk is being initialized.	The drive status should change after a few seconds.
Resynching	A temporary status that indicates that a mirror set is being resynchronized.	Progress is indicated as the percent complete. The volume should return to Healthy status.
Stale Data	Data on foreign disks that are fault tolerant are out of sync.	Rescan the disks or restart the computer, and then check the status. A new status should be displayed, such as Failed Redundancy.
Unknown	The volume cannot be accessed. It might have a corrupted boot sector.	The volume might have a boot sector virus. Check it with an up-to-date antivirus program. If no virus is found, boot from the Windows 8.1 media and use the Recovery Console's Fixmbr command to fix the master boot record.

Repairing disk errors and inconsistencies

Windows 8.1 includes feature enhancements that reduce the amount of manual maintenance you must perform on disk drives. The following enhancements have the most impact on the way you work with disks:

- Transactional NTFS
- Self-healing NTFS

Transactional NTFS enables file operations on an NTFS volume to be performed transactionally. This means programs can use a transaction to group together sets of file and registry operations so that all of them succeed or none of them succeed. While a transaction is active, changes are not visible outside the transaction. Changes are committed and written fully to disk only when a transaction is completed successfully. If a transaction fails or is incomplete, the program rolls back the transactional work to restore the file system to the state it was in prior to the transaction.

Transactions that span multiple volumes are coordinated by the Kernel Transaction Manager (KTM). The KTM supports independent recovery of volumes if a transaction fails. The local resource manager for a volume maintains a separate transaction log and is responsible for maintaining threads for transactions separate from threads that perform the file work.

Traditionally, you have had to use the Check Disk tool to fix errors and inconsistencies in NTFS volumes on a disk. Because this process can disrupt the availability of Windows-based systems, Windows 8.1 uses self-healing NTFS to protect file systems without having to use separate maintenance tools to fix problems. Because much of the self-healing process is enabled and performed automatically, you might need to perform volume maintenance manually only when you are notified by the operating system that a problem cannot be corrected automatically. If such an error occurs, Windows 8.1 notifies you about the problem and provides possible solutions.

Self-healing NTFS has many advantages over Check Disk, including the following:

- Check Disk must have exclusive access to volumes, which means system and boot volumes can be checked only when the operating system starts up. On the other hand, with self-healing NTFS, the file system is always available and does not need to be corrected offline (in most cases).

- Self-healing NTFS attempts to preserve as much data as possible if corruption occurs and reduces failed file system mounting that previously could occur if a volume was known to have errors or inconsistencies. During restart, self-healing NTFS repairs the volume immediately so that it can be mounted.

- Self-healing NTFS reports changes made to the volume during repair through existing Chkdsk.exe mechanisms, directory notifications, and update sequence number (USN) journal entries. This feature also makes it possible for authorized users and administrators to monitor repair operations through Verification, Waiting For Repair Completion, and Progress Status messages.

- Self-healing NTFS can recover a volume if the boot sector is readable but does not identify an NTFS volume. In this case, you must run an offline tool that repairs the boot sector and then allow self-healing NTFS to initiate recovery.

Although self-healing NTFS is a terrific enhancement, at times you might want to (or might have to) manually check the integrity of a disk. In these cases, you can use Check Disk (Chkdsk.exe) to check for and, optionally, repair problems found on FAT, FAT32, exFAT, and NTFS volumes. Although Check Disk can check for and correct many types of errors, the utility primarily looks for inconsistencies in the file system and its related metadata. Beyond this, the usefulness of Check Disk is rather limited.

Checking for disk errors

As part of automated maintenance, Windows 8.1 performs a proactive scan of your computer's NTFS volumes. As with other automated maintenance, Windows scans disks by using Check Disk at 2:00 A.M. if the computer is running on AC power and the operating system is idle. Otherwise, Windows scans disks the next time the computer is running on AC power and the operating system is idle. To change this schedule, you need to modify the run time for automated maintenance by opening Action Center, expanding the Maintenance panel, selecting Change Maintenance Settings, and then selecting a new run schedule.

Although automated maintenance triggers the disk scan, the process of calling and managing Check Disk is handled by a separate task. In Task Scheduler, you'll find the ProactiveScan task in the scheduler library under Microsoft\Windows\ Chkdsk, and you can get detailed run details by reviewing the information provided on the task's History tab.

You can periodically use the Check Disk tool to also check the integrity of disks. Check Disk examines disks and can correct many types of common errors on FAT16, FAT32, exFAT, and NTFS drives.

One of the ways Check Disk locates errors is by comparing the volume bitmap with the disk sectors assigned to files in the file system. Check Disk can't repair corrupted data within files that appear to be structurally intact, however. You can run Check Disk from the command line or through the GUI.

> **IMPORTANT** Because ReFS has a built-in data scrubber that provides proactive error identification, isolation, and correction, Windows automatically repairs and corrects data integrity issues on ReFS volumes. You can, however, run Check Disk on ReFS volumes if you'd like.

With Windows 8.1, Check Disk performs enhanced scan and repair automatically, instead of the legacy scan and repair available with earlier releases of Windows. Here, when you use Check Disk with NTFS volumes, Check Disk performs an online scan and analysis of the disk for errors. Check Disk writes information about any detected corruptions in the $corrupt system file. If the volume is in use, detected corruptions can be repaired by taking the volume offline temporarily. However, unmounting the volume for the repair invalidates all open file handles. With the boot/ system volume, the repairs are performed the next time you start the computer.

Storing the corruption information and then repairing while the volume is dismounted enables Windows to rapidly repair volumes. It also enables you to keep using the disk while a scan is being performed. Typically, offline repair will only take a few seconds, compared to what otherwise would have been hours for very large volumes using the legacy scan and repair technique.

FAT, FAT32, and exFAT (FAT volumes) do not support the enhanced Check Disk features offered in Windows 8.1. When you use Check Disk with FAT volumes, Windows 8.1 uses the legacy scan and repair process. This means the scan and repair process typically requires taking the volume offline and preventing it from being used.

Running Check Disk from the command line

You can run Check Disk from an elevated command prompt or within other tools. At the elevated command prompt, you can test the integrity of drive C by entering the following command:

```
chkdsk /scan C:
```

Check Disk then performs an analysis of the disk and returns a status message regarding any problems it encounters. Unless you specify further options, Check Disk won't repair problems, however. To repair errors on drive C, use this command:

```
chkdsk /spotfix C:
```

Fixing the volume requires exclusive access to the volume. The way this works depends on the type of volume:

- For non-system volumes, you'll get a prompt asking whether you would like to force a dismount of the volume for the repair. In this case, you can enter **Y** to proceed or **N** to cancel the dismount. If you cancel the dismount, you'll get the prompt asking whether you would like to schedule the volume for the repair the next time the computer is started. In this case, you can enter **Y** to schedule the repair or **N** to cancel the repair.

- For system volumes, you'll get a prompt asking whether you would like to schedule the volume for the repair the next time the computer is started. In this case, you can enter **Y** to schedule the repair or **N** to cancel the repair.

You can't run Check Disk with both the /scan and /spotfix options. The reason for this is that the scan and repair tasks are now independent of each other.

The complete syntax for Check Disk is as follows:

```
CHKDSK [volume[[path]filename]] [/F] [/V] [/R] [/X] [/I] [/C] [/B]
[/L[:size]] [/scan] [/forceofflinefix] [/perf] [/spotfix]  [/sdcleanup]
[/offlinescanandfix]
```

The options and switches for Check Disk are used as follows:

- ***volume***   Sets the volume with which to work
- ***path/filename***   Specifies files to check for fragmentation (FAT volumes only)
- **/B**   Re-evaluates bad clusters on the volume (NTFS only; implies /R)
- **/C**   Skips checking of cycles within the folder structure (NTFS only)
- **/F**   Fixes errors on the disk by using the offline (legacy) scan and fix behavior

- **/I**   Performs a minimum check of index entries (NTFS only)
- **/L:*size***   Sets the log file size (NTFS only)
- **/R**   Locates bad sectors and recovers readable information (implies /F)
- **/V**   Displays the full path and name of every file on the disk (FAT volumes); displays cleanup messages if any (NTFS)
- **/X**   Forces the volume to dismount first if necessary (implies /F)

On NTFS volumes, these options can be used to manage the enhanced Check Disk capabilities of Windows 8.1:

- **/forceofflinefix**   Must be used with /scan. Bypasses all online repair and queues errors for offline repair.
- **/scan**   Performs an online scan of the volume, the default. Errors detected during the scan are added to the $corrupt system file.
- **/perf**   Performs the scan as fast as possible by using more system resources.
- **/spotfix**   Enables certain types of errors to be repaired online (the default).
- **/sdcleanup**   Cleans up unneeded security descriptor data. Implies /F (with legacy scan and repair).
- **/offlinescanandfix**   Performs an offline scan and fix of the volume.

Running Check Disk interactively

You can also run Check Disk interactively by using Computer Management. You can check disk drives on the local computer by following these steps:

1. In Computer Management, select the Storage node and then the Disk Management node. In the Volume List or Graphical view, press and hold or right-click a drive, and then tap or click Properties.

2. On the Tools tab, tap or click Check. This displays the Error Checking dialog box, shown in Figure 4-4. For NTFS volumes, you'll have a Scan Drive option. For FAT volumes, you'll have a Scan And Repair Drive option.

FIGURE 4-4 Check Disk is available by tapping or clicking Check on the Tools tab in the Properties dialog box. Use it to check a disk for errors and repair them.

3. Click Scan Drive or Scan And Repair Drive, as appropriate, to start the scan. If no errors are found, Windows will confirm this. If errors are found, you'll be prompted with additional options. As with checking disks at a prompt, the way this works depends on whether you are working with a system or non-system volume and whether the volume is formatted with NTFS or FAT.

Defragmenting disks

Any time you add files to or remove files from a drive, the data on the drive can become fragmented. When a drive is fragmented, large files can't be written to a single continuous area on the disk. As a result, the operating system must write the file to several smaller areas on the disk, which means more time is required to read the file from the disk. To reduce fragmentation, Windows 8.1 automatically defragments disks as part of automated maintenance. As with error checking, the process of calling and managing disk optimization is handled by a separate task. In Task Scheduler, you'll find the Scheduled Defrag task in the scheduler library under Microsoft\Windows\Defrag, and you can get detailed run details by reviewing the information provided on the task's History tab.

Windows 8.1 uses the Optimize Drives utility to analyze and optimize drives. Automatic analysis and optimization of disks can occur while the disks are online if the computer is on AC power and the operating system is running but otherwise idle. By default, disk optimization is a weekly task rather than a daily task—and there's a good reason for this. Typically, you need to optimize your computer's disks only periodically, and optimization once a week should be sufficient in most cases. Note, however, that although non-system disks can be rapidly analyzed and optimized, it can take significantly longer to optimize system disks online. As a result, very large system volumes might not get fully analyzed and optimized on some computers, especially if the computer is powered off during schedule maintenance and then actively used while plugged into AC power.

With manual optimization, Optimize Drives performs an online analysis of a computer's volumes and then reports the percentage of fragmentation. You can then elect to defragment the volumes. Because system, boot, and other volumes can be defragmented online, Windows does not need to take volumes offline before optimizing them.

You can manually optimize FAT, FAT32, exFAT, NTFS, and ReFS volumes by following these steps:

1. In Computer Management, select the Storage node and then the Disk Management node. Press and hold or right-click a drive, and then tap or click Properties.

2. On the Tools tab, tap or click Optimize. In the Optimize Drives dialog box, tap or click the drive you want to check, and then tap or click Analyze. Optimize Drives analyzes the disk to determine whether the disk needs to be defragmented. If so, it recommends that you optimize the drive.

3. The Current Status column shows the status of each drive and the percentage of fragmentation when last checked. You can optimize a drive by tapping or clicking it, and then tapping or clicking Optimize.

NOTE Depending on the size of the disk, defragmentation can take several hours. You can tap or click Stop at any time to stop defragmentation.

Although you previously could set a specific run day and time, Windows now handles the run schedule as part of automated maintenance. By default, analysis (and optimization, if necessary) occur approximately once a week, and you can control the approximate start time by changing the automated maintenance start time. Windows also will notify you if three consecutive runs are missed. All internal drives and certain external drives are optimized automatically as part of the regular schedule, as are new drives that you connect to the computer.

You can configure and manage automated defragmentation by following these steps:

1. In Computer Management, select the Storage node and then the Disk Management node. Press and hold or right-click a drive, and then tap or click Properties.

2. On the Tools tab, tap or click Optimize. This displays the Optimize Drives dialog box, shown in Figure 4-5.

FIGURE 4-5 Windows optimizes drives to maintain read-write performance levels for disk drives.

3. If you want to change how optimization works, tap or click Change Settings. This displays the dialog box shown in Figure 4-6. To cancel automated defragmentation, clear Run On A Schedule. To enable automated defragmentation, select Run On A Schedule.

4. The default run frequency is set as shown. In the Frequency list, you can choose Daily, Weekly, or Monthly as the run schedule. If you don't want to be notified about missed runs, clear the Notify Me check box.

5. If you want to manage which disks are defragmented, tap or click Choose and then select the volumes to defragment. By default, all disks installed within or connected to the computer are defragmented, and any new disks are also defragmented automatically. Select the check boxes for disks that should be defragmented automatically and clear the check boxes for disks that should not be defragmented automatically. Tap or click OK to save your settings.

6. Tap or click OK, and then tap or click Close.

FIGURE 4-6 Specify the run schedule for automated defragmentation.

NOTE Windows automatically performs cyclic pickup defragmentation. With this feature, when a scheduled defragmentation pass is stopped and rerun, the computer automatically picks up the next unfinished volume in line to be defragmented.

Resynchronizing and repairing a mirrored set

Windows 8.1 automatically synchronizes mirrored volumes on drives. However, data on mirrored drives can become out of sync. For example, if one of the drives goes offline, data is written only to the drive that's online.

You can resynchronize and repair mirrored sets, but you must rebuild the set by using disks with the same partition style—either MBR or GPT. You need to get both drives in the mirrored set online. Because a disk in the set has failed, the mirrored set's status should read Failed Redundancy. The corrective action you take depends on the failed volume's status:

- If the status is Missing or Offline, make sure that the drive has power and is connected properly. Then start Disk Management, press and hold or right-click the failed volume, and then tap or click Reactivate Volume. The drive status should change to Regenerating and then to Healthy. If the volume doesn't return to Healthy status, press and hold or right-click the volume, and then tap or click Resynchronize Mirror.

- If the status is Online (Errors), press and hold or right-click the failed volume, and then tap or click Reactivate Volume. The drive status should change to Regenerating and then to Healthy. If the volume doesn't return to Healthy status, press and hold or right-click the volume, and then tap or click Resynchronize Mirror.

- If one of the drives shows a status of Unreadable, you might need to rescan the drives on the system by choosing Rescan Disks from Disk Management's Action menu. If the drive status doesn't change, you might need to reboot the computer.

- If one of the drives still won't come back online, press and hold or right-click the failed volume, and then tap or click Remove Mirror. Next, press and hold or right-click the remaining volume in the original mirror, and then tap or click Add Mirror. You now need to mirror the volume on an unallocated area of a different drive. If you don't have unallocated space on another drive, you need to create space by deleting other volumes or replacing the failed drive.

Repairing a mirrored system volume to enable boot

The failure of a mirrored drive might prevent your system from booting. Typically, this happens when you're mirroring the system or boot volume, or both, and the primary mirror drive has failed.

When you mirror a system volume, the operating system should add an entry to the system's boot manager that enables you to boot to the secondary mirror. Resolving a primary mirror failure is much easier with this entry in the boot manager file than without it because all you need to do is select the entry to boot to the secondary mirror. If you mirror the boot volume and a secondary mirror entry is not created for you (as verified when you enter **bcdedit** at an elevated command prompt), you can modify the boot entries in the boot manager to create one by using the BCD Editor (Bcdedit.exe).

If a system fails to boot to the primary system volume, restart the system and select the Boot Mirror – Secondary Plex option for the operating system you want to start. The system should start as usual. After you successfully boot the system to the secondary drive, you can schedule the maintenance necessary to rebuild the mirror if you want to. You'll need to follow these steps:

1. Shut down the system, replace the failed volume or add a hard disk drive, and then restart the system.

2. Break the mirror set, as discussed in the "Breaking a mirrored set" section in Chapter 3, and then re-create the mirror on the drive you replaced, which is usually Drive 0. Press and hold or right-click the remaining volume that was part of the original mirror, and then tap or click Add Mirror. This displays the Add Mirror dialog box.

3. In the Disks list, select a location for the mirror, and then tap or click Add Mirror. Windows 8.1 begins the mirror creation process. In Disk Management, you'll receive a status of Resynching on both volumes. The disk on which the mirrored volume is being created has a warning icon.

4. If you want the primary mirror to be on the drive that you added or replaced (the original system volume), use Disk Management to break the mirror again. Make sure that the primary drive in the original mirror set has the drive letter that was previously assigned to the complete mirror. If it doesn't, assign the appropriate drive letter.

5. Press and hold or right-click the drive that you added or replaced, and then tap or click Add Mirror. Now re-create the mirror.

6. Check the boot configuration and be sure that the drive that you added or replaced is used during startup. You might need to modify the boot configuration to ensure this.

CHAPTER 5

Configuring user and computer policies

G roup Policy is a set of rules that you can apply to help manage users and computers. In Windows 8.1, Group Policy includes both managed settings, referred to as *policy settings,* and unmanaged settings, referred to as *policy preferences.* Policy settings enable you to control the configuration of the operating system and its components. Policy preferences enable you to configure, deploy, and manage operating system and application settings. The key difference between policy settings and policy preferences is enforcement. Group Policy strictly enforces policy settings, but does not strictly enforce policy preferences.

Group Policy essentials

You use policy settings to control the configuration of the operating system and also to disable options and controls in the user interface for settings that Group Policy is managing. Most policy settings are stored in policy-related branches of the registry. The operating system and compliant applications check these branches to determine whether—and how—various aspects of the operating system are controlled.

Two types of Group Policy are available: local Group Policy and Active Directory–based Group Policy. Local Group Policy is used to manage settings only for local machines. Active Directory–based Group Policy is used to manage the settings of computers throughout sites, domains, and organizational units (OUs). Group Policy simplifies administration by giving administrators centralized control over the privileges, permissions, and capabilities of users and computers. Careful management of policies is essential to proper operations. Policy settings are divided into two broad categories: those that apply to computers and those that apply to users. Computer policies are generally applied during system startup, and user policies are generally applied during logon.

During startup and logon, policies are applied in an exact sequence, which is often important to keep in mind when troubleshooting system behavior. When multiple policies are in place, they are applied in the following order:

1. Local policies
2. Site policies
3. Domain policies
4. OU policies
5. Child OU policies

By default, if policy settings conflict, settings applied later take precedence and overwrite previous policy settings. For example, OU policies take precedence over domain policies. As you might expect, there are exceptions to the precedence rule that enable administrators to block, oversee, and disable policies.

The Group Policy client service isolates Group Policy notification and processing from the Windows logon process, which reduces the resources used for background processing of policy, increases overall performance, and enables delivery and application of new Group Policy files as part of the update process without requiring a restart. By using Network Location Awareness, the Group Policy client can determine the computer state, the network state, and the available network bandwidth for slow-link detection. As a result, the Group Policy client has a better understanding of the operational environment and can better determine which policies should be applied and when they should be applied.

Group Policy event messages are written to a computer's system log. In addition, when you are troubleshooting, you have several options. You can use the detailed event messages in the operational log, which you can access in Event Viewer under Applications And Services Logs\Microsoft\Windows\GroupPolicy\Operational. You also can use Gpupdate.exe to verify that the most current settings have been applied. Although you typically run this command-line tool on the computer you are diagnosing, Windows Server 2012 R2 enables you to schedule Gpupdate.exe to refresh Group Policy on remote computers. For more information, see Chapter 6, "Automating administrative tasks, policies, and procedures," in *Windows Server 2012 R2 Pocket Consultant: Essentials & Configuration* by William R. Stanek (Microsoft Press, 2014).

Accessing and using local group policies

Local Group Policy applies to any user or administrator who logs on to a computer that is a member of a workgroup, in addition to any user or administrator who logs on locally to a computer that is a member of a domain.

As with Windows 7, a computer running Windows 8.1 can have one or more local policy objects associated with it. Local Group Policy is managed through the local Group Policy Object (GPO). The local GPO is stored on individual computers in the %SystemRoot%\System32\GroupPolicy folder. Additional user-specific and group-specific local GPOs are stored in the %SystemRoot%\System32\GroupPolicyUsers folder.

When using computers in a stand-alone configuration rather than a domain configuration, you might find multiple local GPOs useful. You can implement one local GPO for administrators and another local GPO for non-administrators and then you would no longer have to explicitly disable or remove settings that interfere with your ability to manage a computer before performing administrator tasks. In a domain configuration, however, you might not want to use multiple local GPOs. In domains, most computers and users already have multiple GPOs applied to them, and adding multiple local GPOs to this already varied mix can make it confusing to manage Group Policy.

Windows 8.1 has three layers of local GPOs:

- **Local Group Policy**   Local Group Policy is the only local GPO that allows both computer configuration and user configuration settings to be applied to all users of the computer.

- **Administrators and Non-Administrators local Group Policy**   Administrators and Non-Administrators local Group Policy contains only user configuration settings. This policy is applied based on whether the user account being used is a member of the local Administrators group.

- **User-specific local Group Policy**   User-specific local Group Policy contains only user configuration settings. This policy is applied to individual users and groups.

These layers of local GPOs are processed in the following order: local Group Policy, Administrators and Non-Administrators local Group Policy, user-specific local Group Policy.

Because the available User Configuration settings are the same among all local GPOs, a setting in one GPO might conflict with a setting in another GPO. Windows 8.1 resolves conflicts in settings by overwriting any previous setting with the last read and most current setting. The final setting is the one Windows 8.1 uses. When Windows 8.1 resolves conflicts, only the enabled or disabled state of settings matters. A setting of Not Configured does not affect the state of the setting from a previous policy application. To simplify domain administration, you can disable processing of local GPOs on computers running Windows 8.1 by enabling the Turn Off Local Group Policy Objects Processing policy setting in a domain GPO. In Group Policy, this setting is located under the Administrative Templates policies for Computer Configuration under \System\Group Policy.

NOTE   If enabled, local GPOs are always processed. However, they have the least precedence, which means their settings can be superseded by site, domain, and OU settings.

The only local policy object that exists on a computer by default is the local GPO. You can create and manage other local policy objects by using the Group Policy Object Editor. Because local Group Policy is a subset of Group Policy, there are several things you can't do locally that you can do in a domain setting. First, you can't manage any policy preferences. Second, you can manage only a subset of policy settings. Beyond these fundamental differences, local Group Policy and Active Directory–based Group Policy are managed in much the same way.

To work with local GPOs, you must use an administrator account. The quickest way to access the top-level local GPO on a local computer is to enter the following command in the Search box or at a command prompt:

```
gpedit.msc /gpcomputer: "%ComputerName%"
```

This command starts the Group Policy Management Editor in a Microsoft Management Console (MMC) with its target set to the local computer.

You can also manage the top-level local GPO on a computer by following these steps:

1. Open the MMC. One way to do this is by pressing the Windows key, typing **mmc.exe**, and then pressing Enter.

2. In the MMC, tap or click File, and then tap or click Add/Remove Snap-In.

3. In the Add Or Remove Snap-Ins dialog box, tap or click Group Policy Object Editor, and then tap or click Add.

4. In the Select Group Policy Object dialog box, tap or click Finish (because the local computer is the default object). Tap or click OK.

As shown in Figure 5-1, you can now manage local Group Policy settings by using the options provided. Because local Group Policy does not have policy preferences, you will not find separate Policies and Preferences nodes under Computer Configuration and User Configuration.

FIGURE 5-1 Access the top-level local GPO.

You can create and manage other local policy objects as necessary. To create or access other local GPOs, follow these steps:

1. In the MMC, tap or click File, and then tap or click Add/Remove Snap-In.

2. In the Add Or Remove Snap-Ins dialog box, tap or click Group Policy Object Editor, and then tap or click Add.

3. In the Select Group Policy Object dialog box, tap or click Browse. In the Browse For A Group Policy Object dialog box, tap or click the Users tab.

4. On the Users tab, shown in Figure 5-2, the entries in the Group Policy Object Exists column specify whether a particular local policy object has been created. Do one of the following:

   - Select Administrators to create or access the Administrators local GPO. You select Administrators instead of the Administrator user to ensure that the policy is applied to all local administrators.

   - Select Non-Administrators to create or access the Non-Administrators local GPO.

   - Select the local user whose user-specific local GPO you want to create or access.

FIGURE 5-2 Access additional local GPOs.

5. Tap or click OK. Tap or click Finish, and then tap or click OK again. If the selected object doesn't already exist, it will be created. Otherwise, you'll open the object for review and editing.

Accessing and using site, domain, and OU policies

With Active Directory, each site, domain, and OU can have one or more group policies. When you want to work with Active Directory–based Group Policy, you use the Group Policy Management Console (GPMC) to access and work with GPOs. To work with GPOs, you must use an administrator account.

On a computer running a server edition of Windows, the GPMC is available as part of the standard installation. On a computer running a desktop edition of Windows, the GPMC is included in the Remote Server Administration Tools (RSAT). You can download the RSAT for Windows 8.1 by visiting the Microsoft Download Center (*http://download.microsoft.com/*).

After you install the GPMC as part of the RSAT, you can run the GPMC from Server Manager. In Server Manager, tap or click Tools, and then tap or click Group Policy Management.

As shown in Figure 5-3, the left pane of the GPMC has two upper-level nodes by default: Group Policy Management (the console root) and Forest (a node representing the forest to which you are currently connected, which is named after the forest root domain for that forest). When you expand the Forest node, you find the following nodes:

- **Domains** Provides access to the policy settings for domains in the forest being administered. You are connected to your logon domain by default; and you can add connections to other domains. If you expand a domain, you can access the Default Domain Policy GPO, the Domain Controllers OU (and the related Default Domain Controllers Policy GPO), and GPOs defined in the domain.

- **Sites** Provides access to the policy settings for sites in the related forest. Sites are hidden by default.

- **Group Policy Modeling** Provides access to the Group Policy Modeling Wizard, which helps you plan policy deployment and simulate settings for testing purposes. Any saved policy models are also available.

- **Group Policy Results** Provides access to the Group Policy Results Wizard. For each domain to which you are connected, all the related GPOs and OUs are available to work with in one location.

GPOs found in domain, site, and OU containers in the GPMC are actually GPO links and not GPOs themselves. The actual GPOs are found in the Group Policy Objects container of the selected domain. Notice also that the icons for GPO links have a small arrow at the bottom left, similar to shortcut icons. You can open a GPO for editing by pressing and holding or right-clicking it and then selecting Edit.

FIGURE 5-3 Access GPOs for domains, sites, and OUs.

After you've selected a policy for editing or created a new policy, use the Group Policy Management Editor to work with the GPOs. As Figure 5-4 shows, the Group Policy Management Editor has two main nodes:

- **Computer Configuration**   Enables you to set policies that should be applied to computers, regardless of who logs on
- **User Configuration**   Enables you to set policies that should be applied to users, regardless of which computer they log on to

NOTE   Keep in mind that user configuration options set through local policy objects apply only to computers on which the options are configured. If you want the options to apply to all computers that the user might use, you must use domain, site, or OU policies.

FIGURE 5-4 Group Policy options depend on the type of policy you're creating and the add-ons installed.

You will find separate Policies and Preferences nodes under Computer Configuration and User Configuration. When you are working with policy settings, you use the Policies node. The options available under a Policies node depend on the add-ons installed and which type of policy you're creating. You'll usually find that both nodes have the following subnodes:

- **Software Settings**   Sets policies for software settings and software installation. When you install software, subnodes might be added to Software Settings.
- **Windows Settings**   Sets policies for folder redirection, scripts, and security.
- **Administrative Templates**   Sets policies for the operating system, Windows components, and programs. These policies, examined later in this chapter, apply specifically to users and computers.

Configuring policies

To manage users and computers, you need to configure the administrative template policies. These policies provide easy access to registry-based policy settings that control the operating system, Windows components, and programs. Although earlier versions of Windows that support Group Policy use administrative template

(ADM) files with a proprietary markup language to store registry-based policy settings, Windows 8.1 uses a standards-based XML file format called ADMX. Unlike ADM files, which are stored in the GPO to which they relate, ADMX files are stored in a central repository. In domains, central storage of ADMX files makes it easier to work with and manage the files.

Viewing policies and templates

As shown in Figure 5-5, you can view the currently configured templates in the Group Policy Management Editor's Administrative Templates node, which contains policies that can be configured for local systems, OUs, domains, and sites. Different sets of templates are found under Computer Configuration and User Configuration. You can add templates containing new policies manually through the Group Policy Management Console and when you install new Windows components.

Any changes you make to policies available through the administrative templates are saved in the registry. Computer configurations are saved in HKEY_LOCAL_MACHINE, and user configurations are saved in HKEY_USER. Browsing the Administrative Templates node in the Group Policy Management Editor is the best way to become familiar with available administrative template policies. As you browse the templates, you'll find that policies are in one of three states:

- **Not Configured**   The policy isn't used, and its settings do not affect the existing configuration on the computer.
- **Enabled**   The policy is active, and its settings are saved in the registry.
- **Disabled**   The enabled behavior of the policy is not on. The policy might have a specific disabled behavior that is contrary to its enabled setting. This setting is saved in the registry.

FIGURE 5-5 Set user and computer policies through administrative templates.

Enabling, disabling, and configuring policies

In the Group Policy Management Editor, you'll find administrative templates in two nodes: Computer Configuration and User Configuration. In most cases, the policies in these areas don't overlap or conflict with each other. If there is a conflict, however, computer policies have precedence, which means that the computer policy is enforced. Later in this chapter, you'll find details on commonly used policies and how to employ them.

Before you can work with policies, you must access the Group Policy Management Editor for the site, domain, or OU with which you want to work. To access a GPO for a domain or OU, follow these steps:

1. In the GPMC, expand the entry for the forest with which you want to work, and then expand the related Domains node.

2. Expand the node for the domain with which you want to work, and then expand the related Group Policy Objects node.

3. Press and hold or right-click the GPO with which you want to work, and then select Edit. This opens the GPO for editing in the Group Policy Management Editor.

After you've opened a GPO in the Group Policy Management Editor, you can enable, disable, and configure policies by completing the following steps:

1. Under the Computer Configuration or User Configuration node (whichever applies to the type of policy you want to set), access the Administrative Templates folder.

2. In the left pane, tap or click the subfolder containing the policies with which you want to work. The related policies are displayed in the right pane.

3. Double-tap or double-click a policy (or press and hold or right-click a policy and select Edit) to display a properties dialog box.

4. Use the following options to change the state of the policy:

   - **Not Configured**   The policy is not configured.
   - **Enabled**   The policy is enabled.
   - **Disabled**   The policy is disabled.

5. If you enable the policy, set any additional parameters specified on the Setting tab, and then tap or click Apply.

6. Use the Previous Setting or Next Setting button to manage other policies in the current folder. Configure the policies as described in steps 3–5.

7. Tap or click OK when you have finished managing policies.

Adding or removing templates

You can add or remove template folders in the Group Policy Management Editor. To do this, complete the following steps:

1. Access the Group Policy Management Editor for the site, domain, or OU with which you want to work.

2. In the Computer Configuration or User Configuration node, press and hold or right-click the Administrative Templates folder, and then tap or click Add/Remove Templates. This displays the Add/Remove Templates dialog box.

3. To add a template, tap or click Add. Then, in the Policy Templates dialog box, select the template you want to add, and then tap or click Open.

4. To remove a template, select the template, and then tap or click Remove.

5. When you have finished adding and removing templates, tap or click Close.

Working with file and data management policies

Every system administrator needs to be familiar with file and data management policies, which affect the amount of data a user can store on systems, how offline files are used, and whether the System Restore feature is enabled.

Configuring disk quota policies

Policies that control disk quotas are applied at the system level. You access these policies by using the Administrative Templates policies for Computer Configuration under System\Disk Quotas. The available policies are summarized in Table 5-1.

TABLE 5-1 Disk quota policies

POLICY NAME	DESCRIPTION
Apply Policy To Removable Media	Determines whether to extend quota policies to NTFS volumes on removable media. If you do not enable this policy, quota limits apply only to fixed media drives.
Enable Disk Quotas	Turns disk quotas on or off for all NTFS volumes on the computer and prevents users from changing the setting.
Enforce Disk Quota Limit	Specifies whether quota limits are enforced. If quotas are enforced, users are denied disk space if they exceed the quota. This setting overrides settings on the Quota tab for the NTFS volume.
Log Event When Quota Limit Is Exceeded	Determines whether an event is logged when users reach their limit and prevents users from changing their logging options.
Log Event When Quota Warning Level Is Exceeded	Determines whether an event is logged when users reach the warning level.
Specify Default Quota Limit And Warning Level	Sets a default quota limit and warning level for all users. This setting overrides other settings and affects only new users of a volume.

Whenever you work with quota limits, you'll want to use a standard set of policies on all systems. Typically, you won't need to enable all the policies. Instead, you can selectively enable policies and then use the standard NTFS features to control quotas on various volumes. If you want to enable quota limits, use the following technique:

1. Access Group Policy for the system, site, domain, or OU with which you want to work. Next, access the Disk Quotas node by using the Administrative Templates policies for Computer Configuration under System\Disk Quotas.

2. Double-tap or double-click Enable Disk Quotas. Select Enabled, and then tap or click OK.

3. Double-tap or double-click Enforce Disk Quota Limit. If you want to enforce disk quotas on all NTFS volumes residing on this computer, select Enabled. Otherwise, select Disabled, and then set specific limits on a per-volume basis, as discussed in Chapter 8, "Maintaining data access and availability." Tap or click OK.

4. Double-tap or double-click Specify Default Quota Limit And Warning Level. The Specify Default Quota Limit And Warning Level dialog box, shown in Figure 5-6, appears. Select Enabled.

FIGURE 5-6 Use the Specify Default Quota Limit And Warning Level dialog box to establish disk quota values.

5. Drag the Options scroll bar down. Under Default Quota Limit, set a default limit that is applied to new users when they first write to the quota-enabled volume. The limit does not apply to current users and does not affect current limits. On a corporate network share, such as a share used by all members of a team, a good limit is between 1 GB and 5 GB. Of course, this depends on the size of the data files with which users routinely work. Graphic designers and data engineers, for example, might need much more disk space.

6. Drag the Options scroll bar down to set a warning level. A good warning level is about 90 percent of the default quota limit, meaning that if you set the default quota limit to 10 GB, you should set the warning level to 9 GB. Tap or click OK.

7. Double-tap or double-click Log Event When Quota Limit Is Exceeded. Select Enabled so that limit events are recorded in the application log. Tap or click OK.

8. Double-tap or double-click Log Event When Quota Warning Level Is Exceeded. Select Enabled so that warning events are recorded in the application log. Tap or click OK.

9. Double-tap or double-click Apply Policy To Removable Media. Select Disabled so that the quota limits apply only to fixed media volumes on the computer. Tap or click OK.

Configuring System Restore policies

System Restore is designed to save the state of system volumes and enable users to restore a system in the event of a problem. It is a helpful feature for the average user, but it can use a tremendous amount of disk space. By using the System Protection settings in Control Panel, you can turn System Restore off for individual drives or for all drives on a computer.

In the Group Policy console, you'll find the System Restore policies under the Administrative Templates policies for Computer Configuration under System\System Restore. Through System Restore policies, you can override and disable management of this feature. The following policies are available:

- **Turn Off System Restore** If you enable this policy, System Restore is turned off and can't be managed by using the System utility or the System Restore Wizard. If you disable this policy, System Restore is enforced and cannot be turned off.

- **Turn Off Configuration** If you enable this policy, you prevent configuration of the System Restore feature. Users can't access the Settings dialog box but can still turn off System Restore. If you disable this policy, users can access the Settings dialog box but can't manipulate it, and they can still turn off System Restore.

To configure System Restore policies, follow these steps:

1. Access Group Policy for the system, site, domain, or OU with which you want to work. Next, access the System Restore node by using the Administrative Templates policies for Computer Configuration under System\System Restore.

2. To enable or disable System Restore, double-tap or double-click Turn Off System Restore. Select either Enabled or Disabled, and then tap or click OK.

3. To enable or disable configuration of System Restore, double-tap or double-click Turn Off Configuration. Select either Enabled or Disabled, and then tap or click OK.

Configuring Offline File policies

Offline file policies are set at both the computer and the user level, and you'll find identically named policies at each level. If you work with identically named policies at both levels, keep in mind that computer policies override user policies and that these policies can be applied at different times.

The primary policies you'll want to use are summarized in Table 5-2. As the table shows, most offline policies affect access, synchronization, caching, and encryption. You'll find Offline File policies under Administrative Templates for Computer Configuration in Network\Offline Files and under Administrative Templates policies for User Configuration in Network\Offline Files.

TABLE 5-2 Offline file policies

POLICY TYPE	POLICY NAME	DESCRIPTION
Computer	Allow Or Disallow Use Of The Offline Files Feature	Forces enabling or disabling of the offline files feature and prevents overriding by users. Enables administrative control of offline file settings for a system.
Computer	Configure Background Sync	Controls when background synchronization occurs while on slow links. Enabled: background synchronization occurs periodically to synchronize files in shared folders between the client and server. Disabled: default behavior for background synchronization is used.
Computer	Configure Slow-Link Mode	Controls how slow links are used. Enabled: slow-link values for each shared folder used with offline files are configured. Disabled: offline files will not use slow-link mode.
Computer	Enable File Screens	Controls the types of files that can be saved to offline folders. Enabled: users cannot create files with screened extensions. Disabled: users can create any type of file in offline folders.
Computer	Enable File Synchronization On Costed Networks	Controls whether background sync occurs on slow networks that could incur extra data charges. Enabled: sync can occur when the user's network is roaming or near or over plan limit. Disabled: sync won't run in the background.

POLICY TYPE	POLICY NAME	DESCRIPTION
Computer	Enable Transparent Caching	Controls caching of network files over slow links. Enabled: optimizes caching on the client to reduce the number of transmissions over slow links. Disabled: transparent caching is not used.
Computer	Encrypt The Offline Files Cache	Determines whether offline files are encrypted to improve security.
Computer	Files Not Cached	Enables you to specify file extensions of file types that should not be cached.
Computer	Limit Disk Space Used By Offline Files	Limits the amount of disk space that can be used to store offline files.
Computer	Turn On Economical Application Of Administratively Assigned Offline Files	Determines how administratively assigned files and folders are synced at logon. Enabled: only new files and folders are synced at logon. Disabled: all files and folders are synced at logon.
Computer/User	Remove "Make Available Offline" Command	Prevents users from making files available offline.
Computer/User	Remove "Work Offline" Command	Removes Work Offline option from File Explorer to prevent users from manually changing offline or online mode.
Computer/User	Specify Administratively Assigned Offline Files	Uses a Universal Naming Convention (UNC) path to specify files and folders that are always available offline.

You can administratively control which files and folders are available for offline use. Typically, you'll want to do this on file servers or other systems sharing resources on the network. You can use several techniques to administratively control which resources are available offline. Follow these steps to set offline file configuration policies:

1. Access Group Policy for the system, site, domain, or OU with which you want to work. Most offline file policies can be configured for either computer or user policy (with user policy having precedence by default) by using the Offline Files node. You can access the policies for offline files by using either the Administrative Templates policies for Computer Configuration under Network\Offline Files or the Administrative Templates policies for User Configuration under Network\Offline Files, unless specifically noted otherwise.

2. To assign resources that are automatically available offline, double-tap or double-click Specify Administratively Assigned Offline Files. Select Enabled, and then tap or click Show. In the Show Contents dialog box, specify resources according to their UNC path, such as \\CorpServer23\Data. Figure 5-7 shows a list of resources that have been added to the Show Contents dialog box. Tap or click OK until all open dialog boxes are closed.

FIGURE 5-7 Use the Show Contents dialog box to specify resources according to their UNC path.

CAUTION You should carefully consider which resources are automatically made available offline. The more resources you assign through this technique, the more network traffic is generated to maintain offline file caches.

3. To prevent users from making files and folders available offline, double-tap or double-click Remove "Make Available Offline" Command. Select Enabled, and then tap or click OK. After this policy is enforced, users are unable to specify files for use offline.

4. To restrict the types of files that can be created in offline folders, double-tap or double-click Enable File Screens. Select Enabled. In the Extensions box, enter a semicolon-separated list of file extensions to exclude, and then tap or click OK. Be sure to precede each file extension with an asterisk and a period, such as ***.vbs** or ***.js**. After this policy is enforced, users are unable to create files with the specified extensions in offline folders.

5. For Windows 8 and later, you might want to double-tap or double-click Remove "Work Offline" Command, and then select Enabled. After you select this option, users cannot manually change whether Offline Files is in online or offline mode. They can, however, continue to use Offline Files as appropriate.

Offline files are synchronized automatically, with background synchronization used whenever a computer is connected to a slow network. For Windows 8 and later, a slow network is any network with a latency of more than 35 milliseconds. Otherwise, a slow link generally is any network with a latency of more than 80 milliseconds.

You can prevent a computer from entering the slow-link mode and using background synchronization by disabling the Configure Slow-Link Mode policy. If you enable the Configure Slow-Link Mode policy, you can specify slow-link triggers based on network throughput and latency.

To modify the way slow links work, follow these steps:

1. Access Group Policy for the system, site, domain, or OU with which you want to work. Next, access the Offline Files node by using the Administrative Templates policies for Computer Configuration under Network\Offline Files.

2. To modify the triggers for slow links, double-tap or double-click Configure Slow-Link Mode. Select Enabled, and then tap or click Show. In the Show Contents dialog box, you use Value Name to specify resources to manage and Value to specify throughput and latency settings. Keep the following in mind:

   - In Value Name, you can specify values for individual servers according to their UNC path. For example, enter **\\corpserver172*** to control slow-link triggers for all shares on CorpServer172, or **\\corpserver85\data*** for all files and folders on the Data share for CorpServer85.

   - In Value Name, you can specify values for all servers affected by the current policy by entering a value of *****.

   - In Value, you can specify a throughput trigger in bits per second, a latency trigger in milliseconds or a combined throughput and latency trigger. For example, enter **Throughput=1024** to apply slow-link mode when network throughput is less than 1,024 bits per second (bps), enter **Latency=60** to apply slow-link mode when network latency is greater than 60 milliseconds, or enter **Throughput=1024, Latency=60** to define both triggers.

   Figure 5-8 shows a list of resources that have been added to the Show Contents dialog box. Tap or click OK until all open dialog boxes are closed.

   CAUTION You should carefully consider which resources are automatically made available offline. The more resources you assign through this technique, the more network traffic is generated to maintain offline file caches.

FIGURE 5-8 Specify resources and triggers for slow-link mode.

3. By default, Windows syncs in the background while operating in slow-link mode. This sync occurs approximately every six hours. To fine tune background syncing, double-tap or double-click Configure Background Sync. Select Enabled, configure settings as appropriate, and then tap or click OK. When configuring background sync, keep the following in mind:

   - Sync Interval and Sync Variance are used together to define the refresh interval. By default, the Sync Interval is 360 minutes with up to a 60-minute Sync Variance to avoid overloading the network and servers with numerous client requests at the same time.

   - Use Maximum Allowed Time Without A Sync to help ensure that all network folders are refreshed periodically. The value is set in minutes. Thus, if you wanted to ensure that network folders were refreshed at least once a day, you'd enter a value of **1440.**

   - Use Blockout Start Time and Blockout Duration to prohibit refresh during specific times of the day. Blockout Start Time is set using 24-hour–clock time, and Blockout Duration is set in minutes. Thus, if you wanted to ensure that network folders weren't refreshed from 2 P.M. to 6 P.M. daily, you'd enter a start time of **1400** and a duration of **240**.

4. With Windows 8 and later, you can use Enable File Synchronization On Costed Networks to control whether background sync is enabled on cellular and other networks that might charge fees when roaming or near or over data plan usage. By default, syncing on costed networks is disabled. To enable syncing on costed networks, double-tap or double-click Enable File Synchronization On Costed Networks, select Enabled, and then tap or click OK.

Configuring policy for Work Folders

Computers that are members of a workplace can access internal network resources, such as internal websites and business applications. Work Folders make it possible for users to synchronize their corporate data to their devices and vice versa. Those devices can be joined to the corporate domain or a workplace. To deploy Work Folders, an administrator adds the File And Storage Services\Work Folders role to a server, and then configures Work Folders by using Server Manager. Devices access Work Folders via a remote web gateway running on Internet Information Services (IIS).

You can use policy settings to control whether users can change settings when setting up Work Folders on a domain-joined computer. You can also configure policy settings for Work Folders that control the server to which users can connect remotely and access Work Folders. You do this in one of two ways:

- By specifying the exact URL of the file server hosting the Work Folders for the user, such as *https://server18.cpandl.com*
- By specifying the URL used within your organization for Work Folders discovery, such as *https://workfolders.cpandl.com*

With Work Folders, clients use secure encrypted communications as long as the file servers hosting the Work Folders have valid SSL certificates. When a device initiates an SSL connection, the server sends the certificate to the client. The client evaluates the certificate and continues only if the certificate is valid and can be trusted. If you configure a connection to an exact URL, the client can connect directly to the specified sever and synchronize data in Work Folders. The server's certificate must have a common name (CN) or a subject alternative name (SAN) that matches the host header in the request. For example, if the client makes a request to *https://server18.cpandl.com*, the CN or SAN must be server18.cpandl.com.

The discovery process is different. Any server configured with Work Folders acts as a discovery server by default. If you configure a discovery URL, a client connects to one of several servers and the email address of the user is used to discover which specific server hosts the Work Folders for the client. The client is then connected to this server. Each discovery server will need to have a certificate with multiple subject alternative names, which includes the server name and the discovery name. For example, if a client makes a request to *https://workfolders.cpandl.com* and connects to FileServer23.cpandl.com, the server's certificate must have a CN or SAN of fileserver23.cpandl.com and a SAN of workfolders.cpandl.com.

If you want to configure Work Folders in Group Policy, use the following technique:

1. Access Group Policy for the system, site, domain, or OU with which you want to work. Next, access the Work Folders node by using the Administrative Templates policies for User Configuration under Windows Components\Work Folders.

2. Double-tap or double-click Specify Work Folders Settings, and then select Enabled.

3. In the Work Folders URL text box, enter the URL of the file server that hosts the Work Folders for the user or the URL used within your organization for Work Folders discovery.

4. If you want to prevent users from changing settings when setting up Work Folders, select Force Automatic Setup.

5. Tap or click OK.

Working with access and connectivity policies

Access and connectivity policies control network connections, dial-up connections, and Remote Assistance configurations. These policies affect a system's connectivity to the network, and remote access to the system.

Configuring network policies

Many network policies are available. Network policies that control Internet Connection Sharing, Internet Connection Firewall, Windows Firewall, and Network Bridge are configured at the computer level. Network policies that control LAN connections, TCP/IP configuration, and remote access are configured at the user level. The primary policies that you'll want to use are summarized in Table 5-3. You'll find network policies under the Administrative Templates policies for Computer Configuration under Network\Network Connections and the Administrative Templates policies for User Configuration under Network\Network Connections.

TABLE 5-3 Network policies

POLICY TYPE	POLICY NAME	DESCRIPTION
Computer	Prohibit Installation And Configuration Of Network Bridge On Your DNS Domain Network	Determines whether users can install and configure network bridges. This policy applies only to the domain in which it is assigned.
Computer	Require Domain Users To Elevate When Setting A Network's Location	Determines whether the elevation prompt is displayed prior to setting a network's location.
Computer	Route All Traffic Through The Internal Network	Used with DirectAccess. Determines whether remote computers access the Internet via the internal corporate network or via their own Internet connection.
User	Ability To Change Properties Of An All User Remote Access Connection	Determines whether users can view and modify the properties of remote access connections available to all users of the computer.
User	Prohibit Deletion Of Remote Access Connections	Determines whether users can delete remote access connections.

As shown in Table 5-3, network policies for computers are designed to restrict actions on an organization's network. When you enforce these restrictions, users are prohibited from using features such as Internet Connection Sharing in the applicable domain. This is designed to protect the security of corporate networks, but it doesn't prevent users with laptops, for example, from taking their computers home and using these features on their own networks. To enable or disable these restrictions, follow these steps:

1. Access Group Policy for the resource with which you want to work. Next, access the Network Connections node by using the Administrative Templates policies for Computer Configuration under Network\Network Connections.

2. Double-tap or double-click the policy that you want to configure. Select Enabled or Disabled, and then tap or click OK.

User policies for network connections usually prevent access to certain configuration features, such as the advanced TCP/IP property settings. To configure these policies, follow these steps:

1. Access Group Policy for the resource with which you want to work. Next, access the Administrative Templates policies for User Configuration under Network\Network Connections.

2. Double-tap or double-click the policy that you want to configure. Select Enabled or Disabled, and then tap or click OK.

Configuring Remote Assistance policies

Remote Assistance policies can be used to prevent or permit use of remote assistance on computers. Typically, when you set Remote Assistance policies, you'll want to prevent unsolicited offers for remote assistance while permitting requested offers. You can also force a specific expiration for invitations through policy rather than by setting this time limit through the System Properties dialog box of each computer. To improve security, you can use strong invitation encryption. This enhancement, however, limits who can answer Remote Assistance invitations to only those running Windows Vista or later releases of Windows.

To configure policy in this manner, follow these steps:

1. Access Group Policy for the computer with which you want to work. Next, access the Administrative Templates policies for Computer Configuration under System\Remote Assistance.

2. Double-tap or double-click Configure Solicited Remote Assistance. Select Enabled. When enabled, this policy makes it possible for authorized users to solicit remote assistance.

3. You can now specify the level of access for assistants. The Permit Remote Control Of This Computer selection list has two options:

   - **Allow Helpers To Remotely Control The Computer** Permits viewing and remote control of the computer

   - **Allow Helpers To Only View This Computer** Permits only viewing; assistants cannot take control to make changes

4. Next, as shown in Figure 5-9, use the Maximum Ticket Time (Value) and Maximum Ticket Time (Units) options to set the maximum time limit for remote assistance invitations. The default maximum time limit is 1 hour. Tap or click OK.

FIGURE 5-9 Set a time expiration limit for Remote Assistance invitations.

REAL WORLD The method for sending email invitations can be set to Mailto or Simple MAPI. Mailto is a browser-based mail submission technique in which the invitation's recipient connects through an Internet link. Simple MAPI uses Messaging Application Programming Interface (MAPI) for sending the email invitation as an attachment to an email message. If computers can establish a connection with each other over port 80 and you're using a standard email program such as Microsoft Outlook or Windows Mail, you'll probably want to use Mailto.

5. Double-tap or double-click Configure Offer Remote Assistance. In the Configure Offer Remote Assistance dialog box, select Disabled. Disabling this policy prevents unsolicited assistance offers. Tap or click OK.

6. If you want to use strong invitation encryption and limit connections so they can come only from computers running current releases of Windows, double-tap or double-click Allow Only Windows Vista Or Later Connections. In the Allow Only Windows Vista Or Later Connections dialog box, select Enabled. Tap or click OK.

To prevent remote assistance and remote control, follow these steps:

1. Access Group Policy for the computer with which you want to work. Next, access the Administrative Templates policies for Computer Configuration under System\Remote Assistance.

2. Double-tap or double-click Configure Solicited Remote Assistance. Select Disabled, and then tap or click Previous Setting or Next Setting, as appropriate.

3. In the Configure Offer Remote Assistance dialog box, select Disabled, and then tap or click OK.

Working with computer and user script policies

Script policies control the behavior and assignment of computer and user scripts. Four types of scripts can be configured:

- **Computer startup**   Executed during startup
- **Computer shutdown**   Executed prior to shutdown
- **User logon**   Executed when a user logs on
- **User logoff**   Executed when a user logs off

You can write these scripts as command-shell batch scripts, Windows scripts, or Windows PowerShell scripts. Batch scripts use the shell command language. Windows scripts use Windows Script Host (WSH) and are written in a scripting language such as Microsoft Visual Basic Scripting Edition (VBScript) or Microsoft JScript. Windows PowerShell scripts are written in the Windows PowerShell language. Note that policy preferences can in many cases eliminate the need to use computer and user scripts.

Controlling script behavior through policy

Policies that control script behavior are found under the Administrative Templates policies for Computer Configuration under System\Scripts and the Administrative Templates policies for User Configuration under System\Scripts. Through policy, you can control the behavior of startup, shutdown, logon, and logoff scripts. The key policies that you'll use are described in Table 5-4. As you'll observe, there are numerous options for configuring script behavior.

TABLE 5-4 Computer and user script policies

POLICY TYPE	POLICY NAME	DESCRIPTION
Computer	Display Instructions In Shutdown Scripts As They Run	Displays shutdown scripts and their instructions as they execute.
Computer	Display Instructions In Startup Scripts As They Run	Displays startup scripts and their instructions as they execute.

POLICY TYPE	POLICY NAME	DESCRIPTION
Computer	Run Startup Scripts Asynchronously	Enables the system to run startup scripts simultaneously, rather than one at a time.
Computer	Run Windows PowerShell Scripts First At Computer Startup, Shutdown	Determines whether Windows Power-Shell scripts are run before other types of scripts at startup and shutdown.
Computer	Specify Maximum Wait Time For Group Policy Scripts	Sets the maximum time to wait for scripts to finish running. The default value is 600 seconds (10 minutes).
Computer/ User	Run Logon Scripts Synchronously	Ensures that the system waits for logon scripts to finish before displaying the Windows interface.
Computer/ User	Run Windows Power-Shell Scripts First At User Logon, Logoff	Determines whether Windows Power-Shell scripts are run before other types of scripts at logon and logoff.
User	Display Instructions In Logoff Scripts As They Run	Displays logoff scripts and their instructions as they execute.
User	Display Instructions In Logon Scripts As They Run	Displays logon scripts and their instructions as they execute.
User	Run Legacy Logon Scripts Hidden	Hides logon scripts configured through the System Policy Editor in Microsoft Windows NT 4.

Although you can control script behavior in many ways, you'll usually want scripts to behave as follows:

- Windows PowerShell scripts should run first.
- Logon and startup scripts should run simultaneously (in most cases).
- All scripts should be hidden rather than visible.
- The system should wait no more than one minute for a script to complete (in most cases).

To enforce this behavior, follow these steps:

1. Access Group Policy for the computer with which you want to work. Next, access the Administrative Templates policies for Computer Configuration under System\Scripts.

2. Double-tap or double-click Run Windows PowerShell Scripts First At Computer Startup, Shutdown. Select Enabled, and then tap or click OK.

3. Double-tap or double-click Run Windows PowerShell Scripts First At User Logon, Logoff. Select Enabled, and then tap or click OK.

4. Double-tap or double-click Run Logon Scripts Synchronously. Select Disabled, and then tap or click OK.

5. Double-tap or double-click Run Startup Scripts Asynchronously. Select Enabled, and then tap or click OK.

6. Double-tap or double-click Display Instructions In Startup Scripts As They Run. Select Disabled, and then tap or click OK.

7. Double-tap or double-click Display Instructions In Shutdown Scripts As They Run. Select Disabled, and then tap or click OK.

8. Double-tap or double-click Specify Maximum Wait Time For Group Policy Scripts. Select Enabled, and then enter a value of 60 for the wait time in the Seconds box. Tap or click OK.

9. Access the Administrative Templates policies for User Configuration under System\Scripts.

10. Double-tap or double-click Run Legacy Logon Scripts Hidden. Select Enabled, and then tap or click OK.

11. Double-tap or double-click Display Instructions In Logon Scripts As They Run. Select Disabled, and then tap or click OK.

12. Double-tap or double-click Display Instructions In Logoff Scripts As They Run. Select Disabled, and then tap or click OK.

13. Double-tap or double-click Run Windows PowerShell Scripts First At User Logon, Logoff. Select Enabled, and then tap or click OK.

Assigning computer startup and shutdown scripts

Computer startup and shutdown scripts can be assigned as part of Group Policy. In this way, a computer and all its users—or all computers that are members of the site, domain, or OU—execute scripts automatically when they're started or shut down.

To assign computer scripts, follow these steps:

1. For easy management, copy the scripts you want to use to the Scripts\Startup or Scripts\Shutdown folder for the related policy. Scripts are stored in the %SystemRoot%\Sysvol\Sysvol\%UserDnsDomain%\Policies\GUID\Machine folder on domain controllers and %WinDir%\System32\GroupPolicy\Machine on workstations running Windows 8.1.

2. Access the Group Policy console for the resource with which you want to work. Then access policies for Computer Configuration under Windows Settings\Scripts.

3. To work with startup scripts, press and hold or right-click Startup, and then select Properties. To work with shutdown scripts, press and hold or right-click Shutdown, and then select Properties. Next, tap or click Show Files. If you copied the computer scripts to the correct location, you should get the scripts you want to assign.

4. Tap or click Add to assign a script. This opens the Add A Script dialog box. For the Script Name, enter the name of a script you copied to the Scripts\ Startup or the Scripts\Shutdown folder for the related policy. For the Script Parameters, enter any command-line arguments to pass to the command-line script or parameters to pass to the scripting host for a WSH script. Repeat this step to add other scripts.

5. During startup or shutdown, scripts are executed in the order in which they're listed in the Properties dialog box. Select a script name, and then tap or click Up or Down to reposition the script as necessary.

6. If you want to edit the script name or parameters later, select the script in the scripts list, and then tap or click Edit.

7. To delete a script, select the script in the scripts list, and then tap or click Remove.

Assigning user logon and logoff scripts

User scripts can be assigned as part of Group Policy. In this way, all users who access a computer or are members of the site, domain, or OU execute scripts automatically when they log on or log off.

To assign user scripts, complete the following steps:

1. Copy the scripts you want to use to the Scripts\Logon or the Scripts\Logoff folder for the related policy. User scripts are stored in the %SystemRoot%\ Sysvol\Sysvol*%UserDnsDomain%*\Policies\GUID\User folder on domain controllers and under %WinDir%\System32\GroupPolicy\User on workstations running Windows 8.1.

2. Access the Group Policy console for the resource with which you want to work. Then access policies for User Configuration under Windows Settings\Scripts.

3. To work with logon scripts, press and hold or right-click Logon, and then tap or click Properties. To work with logoff scripts, press and hold or right-click Logoff, and then tap or click Properties. Next, tap or click Show Files. If you copied the user scripts to the correct location, you should find the scripts you want to assign.

4. Tap or click Add to assign a script. This opens the Add A Script dialog box. For the Script Name, enter the name of a script you copied to the Scripts\ Logon or the Scripts\Logoff folder for the related policy. For the Script Parameter, enter any command-line arguments to pass to the command-line script or parameters to pass to the scripting host for a WSH script. Repeat this step to add other scripts.

5. During logon or logoff, scripts are executed in the order in which they're listed in the Properties dialog box. Select a script name and tap or click Up or Down to reposition scripts as necessary.

6. If you want to edit the script name or parameters later, select the script in the Scripts list, and then tap or click Edit.

7. To delete a script, select the script in the Scripts list, and then tap or click Remove.

Working with logon and startup policies

Windows 8.1 provides a set of policies to control the logon process, some of which enable you to configure the way programs run at logon. This makes them similar to logon scripts in that you can execute specific tasks at logon. Other policies change the view in the welcome and logon screens. The main logon and startup policies that you'll use are available by using Administrative Templates policies for Computer Configuration and User Configuration under System\Logon and are summarized in Table 5-5.

TABLE 5-5 Logon and startup policies

POLICY TYPE	POLICY NAME	DESCRIPTION
Computer	Always Use Classic Logon	For Windows 7 and earlier, this policy overrides the default simple logon screen and uses the logon screen displayed in previous versions of Windows.
Computer	Allow Users To Select When A Password Is Required When Resuming	Controls whether the user can configure the amount of time after a device's screen turns off before a password is required when waking the device.
Computer	Always Wait For The Network At Computer Startup And Logon	Requires the computer to wait for the network to be fully initialized. At startup, this Group Policy is fully applied rather than applied through a background refresh. At logon, this means the user account cannot be authenticated against cached credentials and must be authenticated against a domain controller.
Computer	Do Not Enumerate Connected Users On Domain-Joined Computers	When a computer is joined to a domain, prevents the Windows Logon user interface from enumerating connected users during logon.
Computer	Enumerate Local Users On Domain-Joined Computers	Enables the Windows Logon user interface to enumerate local users during logon.
Computer	Show First Sign-in Animation	Controls whether Microsoft account users receive an opt-in prompt for services when they log on for the first time. Also controls whether other users encounter the sign-in animation when they log on for the first time.
Computer	Turn Off App Notifications On the Lock Screen	Prevents app notifications from appearing on the lock screen.

POLICY TYPE	POLICY NAME	DESCRIPTION
Computer	Turn On PIN Sign-In	Enables a domain user to sign in by using a PIN.
Computer	Turn Off Picture Password Sign-in	Prevents a domain user from creating and using a picture password for sign-in.
Computer/ User	Do Not Process The Legacy Run List	Disables running legacy run-list applications other than those set through the System Policy Editor in Windows NT 4.
Computer/ User	Do Not Process The Run Once List	Forces the system to ignore customized run-once lists.
Computer/ User	Run These Pro- grams At User Logon	Sets programs that all users should run at logon. Use the full file path (unless the program is in %SystemRoot%).

Setting policy-based startup programs

Although users can configure their startup applications separately, it usually makes more sense to handle this through Group Policy, especially in an enterprise in which the same applications should be started by groups of users. To specify programs that should start at logon, follow these steps:

1. Access Group Policy for the computer with which you want to work. Next, access the Administrative Templates policies for Computer Configuration under System\Logon.

2. Double-tap or double-click Run These Programs At User Logon. Select Enabled.

3. Tap or click Show. In the Show Contents dialog box, specify applications by using their full file or UNC path, such as C:\Program Files (x86)\Internet Explorer\Iexplore.exe or \\DCServ01\Apps\Stats.exe.

4. Close all open dialog boxes.

Disabling run lists through policy

By using Group Policy, you can disable legacy run lists and run-once lists. Legacy run lists are stored in the registry in HKEY_LOCAL_MACHINE\SOFTWARE\Microsoft\ Windows\CurrentVersion\Run and HKEY_CURRENT_USER\Software\Microsoft\ Windows\CurrentVersion\Run.

Run-once lists can be created by administrators to specify programs that should run the next time the system starts but not on subsequent restarts. Run-once lists are stored in the registry under HKEY_LOCAL_MACHINE\SOFTWARE\Microsoft\ Windows\CurrentVersion\RunOnce and HKEY_CURRENT_USER\Software\Microsoft\ Windows\CurrentVersion\RunOnce.

To disable run-once lists, follow these steps:

1. Access Group Policy for the computer with which you want to work. Next, access the Administrative Templates policies for Computer Configuration under System\Logon or the Administrative Templates policies for User Configuration under System\Logon.

2. Double-tap or double-click Do Not Process The Run Once List. Select Enabled, and then tap or click OK.

3. Double-tap or double-click Do Not Process The Legacy Run List. Select Enabled, and then tap or click OK.

CHAPTER 6

Optimizing file security

Whether you are using Windows 8.1 in a domain, a workgroup, or a home-group, few aspects of the operating system are more important than file security and file sharing. File security and file sharing are so interconnected that talking about one without talking about the other is difficult. File security protects important data on your systems by restricting access, and file sharing enables you to share data so that it can be accessed by other users.

File security and sharing options

For computers running Windows 8.1, two factors control file security and sharing options: the disk format and computer settings. The format of the disk deter-mines the degree of file security options available. Disks can be formatted for the FAT file system (FAT16, FAT32, or exFAT), the NTFS file system, or the Resilient File System (ReFS).

> **IMPORTANT**   ReFS is built on the foundations of NTFS and is designed specifi-cally for storage technologies. Because ReFS maintains compatibility with the core features of NTFS, access permissions and share permissions work the same on both ReFS and NTFS volumes. Where NTFS and ReFS diverge is when it comes to extended features, such as compression, encryption, and disk quotas, which are supported by NTFS but not supported by ReFS.

The security options on FAT, NTFS, and ReFS volumes differ greatly:

■ With FAT, you have very limited control over file access. Files can be marked only as read-only, hidden, or system. Although these flags can be set on files and folders, anyone with access to the FAT volume can override or change these settings, which means that there are no safeguards for file access or deletion. Any user can access or delete any file without restriction.

■ With NTFS or ReFS, you can control access to files and folders by using NTFS permissions. NTFS permissions specifically allow or deny access and can be set for individual users and for groups of users. These permission settings give you very granular control over file and folder access. For example, you could specify that users in the Sales Managers group have full control over a folder and its files, but users in the Sales Reps group have no access to the folder whatsoever.

The settings on a computer determine the way in which files can be shared. For Server Message Block (SMB), Windows 8.1 supports two file-sharing models:

- **Standard folder sharing**   Enables you to share the files in any folder on a computer, including those on FAT, NTFS, and ReFS volumes. Two sets of permissions are used to determine who has access to shared folders: access permissions (discussed in the "Controlling access to files and folders with NTFS permissions" section later in this chapter) and share permissions (discussed in the "Sharing files and folders over the network" section in Chapter 7 "Managing file sharing and auditing"). Access permissions and share permissions together enable you to control who has access to shared folders and the level of access assigned. You do not need to move the files you are sharing.

- **Public folder sharing**   Enables you to share files that are in a computer's %SystemDrive%\Users\Public folder. Access permissions on the Public folder determine which users and groups have access to publicly shared files, in addition to what level of access those users and groups have. When you copy or move files to the Public folder, access permissions on the files are changed to match those of the Public folder. Some additional permissions are also added. For more information, see the "Using and configuring public folder sharing" section in Chapter 7.

NOTE   With standard folder sharing, local users don't have automatic access to any data stored on a computer. Local access to files and folders is fully controlled by the security settings on the local disk. If a local disk is formatted with FAT, you can use the read-only, system, or hidden flags to help protect files and folders, but you cannot restrict access. If a local disk is formatted with NTFS or ReFS, you can control access by allowing or denying access to individual users and groups of users.

With public folder sharing, files copied or moved to the Public folder are available to anyone who logs on locally regardless of whether he or she has a standard user account or an administrator user account on the computer. Network access can be granted to the Public folder. Doing so, however, makes the Public folder and its contents open to everyone who can access the computer over the network.

Windows Server 2012 R2 adds new layers of security through compound identities, claims-based access controls, and central access policies. With both Windows 8.1 and Windows Server 2012 R2, you can assign claims-based access controls to file and folder resources on NTFS and ReFS volumes. With Windows Server 2012 R2, users are granted access to files and folder resources, either directly with access permissions and share permissions or indirectly with claims-based access controls and central access policies.

Unlike with early releases of Windows, where only one sharing model could be used at a time, computers running Windows 8.1 can use both sharing models at the same time. The key advantage to standard sharing is that users can share any folder on a computer and don't have to move files or folders from their current location. Public folders, on the other hand, are open drop boxes. When users copy files and folders to public folders (and public folder sharing is enabled), the files and folders are available to other users on the computer and on the network.

File Explorer has several options when you are working with folders. Two key options are:

- **Include In Library**   Creates a link between the folder and its contents in the user's Documents, Music, Pictures, Videos, or another library folder. This lets the user browse and work with the folder's contents as if it were part of the specified library. However, anytime the user works with a file in a library folder, he is actually working with the file in its original location.

- **Share With**   Shares the folder by using standard folder sharing. In a homegroup, users have the option to share the folder with anyone in the homegroup as read-only or read/write. In a workgroup or domain, users have the option of sharing with specific people. In any configuration, users can also select the sharing option Nobody, which effectively removes sharing.

The default sharing configuration for computers depends on whether the computers are members of homegroups, workgroups, or domains. When you set up a homegroup, you specify the types of files to share, and whether to share printers. Computers that are members of the same homegroup can then automatically share printers and files such as pictures, music, videos, and documents.

Sharing folders within a homegroup as read-only or read/write is fairly straightforward. To enable sharing in a homegroup, you complete the following steps:

1. In File Explorer, press and hold or right-click the folder you want to share.
2. Select Share With, and then select Homegroup (View) or Homegroup (View And Edit).

This simple approach to sharing might make homegroups seem appealing to users in your office. However, it also grants very wide access to users' data and is generally inadvisable for the workplace. This is why you should encourage users in a homegroup to share with specific people rather than with everyone. Sharing with specific people is the only technique you can use in workgroups and domains.

To enable sharing with specific people, you complete the following steps:

1. In File Explorer, press and hold or right-click the folder.
2. Select Share With, and then select Specific People. This displays the File Sharing Wizard. By default, the System group is specified as the owner of the share, and the currently logged-on user is granted read/write access.
3. In the File Sharing Wizard, use the options provided to choose the people with whom to share. For example, if you want to include all users with local accounts on the computer, enter **Users**, and then tap or click Add. This is different from sharing with everyone because the Everyone group includes anyone with access permission to the computer, not just those who are domain or local users.

4. The default sharing permission is read-only. To set a permission level for a user or group, tap or click the user or group name, and then select Read or Read/Write.

5. Tap or click Share to share the folder, and then tap or click Done.

To remove sharing, you complete the following steps:

1. In File Explorer, press and hold or right-click the folder.

2. Select Share With, and then select Stop Sharing.

3. In the File Sharing Wizard, select Stop Sharing.

By default, when you create the first standard folder share on a computer, Windows creates the File And Printer Sharing exception in Windows Firewall. This inbound exception makes it possible for other computers on the network to send inbound SMB traffic through Windows Firewall to access the share. To accommodate this, Windows opens the following ports:

- UDP port 137, which is used for NetBIOS name resolution

- UDP port 138, which is used for NetBIOS datagram transmission and reception

- TCP port 139, which is used by the NetBIOS Session service

- Dynamic ports for ICMPv4 and ICMPv6, which are used for echo requests, if applicable

In a nutshell, that is how standard folder sharing works. I'll go into more detail about sharing with specific people in Chapter 7. However, before anyone can share anything, network sharing must be enabled.

Network sharing settings are meant to provide the appropriate level of security for each of the various categories of networks to which a computer can connect. For this reason, Windows maintains a separate network profile for each type of network a computer uses. Generally, most network discovery and sharing settings are disabled by default. You can configure network discovery and sharing settings by following these steps:

1. In Control Panel, under Network And Internet, tap or click Choose Home-group And Sharing Options, and then tap or click the Change Advanced Sharing Settings link.

2. Each available network profile has a separate management panel with con-figuration settings. Use the expand button to display the profile with which you want to work.

3. Network Discovery, an option for the Private, Guest Or Public, and Domain profiles, affects whether a computer can find other computers and devices on the network and whether other computers on the network can find this computer. Turn Network Discovery on or off by selecting the related option.

4. File And Printer Sharing, an option for the Private, Guest Or Public, and Do-main profiles, controls whether a computer can share files and printers. Turn File And Printer Sharing on or off by selecting the related option.

5. In the All Networks profile, Public Folder Sharing controls whether a computer can share files in the Public folders. Turn Public Folder Sharing on or off by selecting an appropriate option.

6. In the All Networks profile, Media Streaming makes it possible for users to share music, videos, and pictures and to access music, videos, and pictures on other computers. Turn Media Streaming on by tapping or clicking the related button, and then configure the Media Streaming options as appropriate. Enabling other users to listen to music, play videos, and view pictures from another computer can adversely affect performance, so you might not want to enable this feature.

7. Windows uses encryption to securely transfer your shared data. By default, the encryption level is set to 128-bit encryption (in most configurations). However, you should be sure that the computers and devices you are sharing with support this level of encryption. Otherwise, select the lower encryption level or upgrade the encryption support on the other devices and computers.

8. In workgroups and homegroups, Password Protected Sharing allows only people with a user account and password on the local computer to access shared resources. Turn Password Protected Sharing on or off by selecting the related option.

9. Tap or click Save Changes to save your settings.

In Group Policy, you can prevent computers from joining homegroups by enabling the Prevent The Computer From Joining A Homegroup policy. This policy is found in the Administrative Templates policies for Computer Configuration under Windows Components\Homegroup.

In Group Policy, you also can restrict the way in which sharing works. The key restrictions on how sharing can be used come from the Prevent Users From Sharing Files Within Their Profile policy. This policy, found in Administrative Templates policies for User Configuration under Windows Components\Network Sharing, controls whether sharing is allowed within folders associated with user profiles, primarily the %SystemDrive%\Users folder. Keep the following in mind when working with the Prevent Users From Sharing Files Within Their Profile setting:

- When this setting is Not Configured, which is the default state, users are allowed to share files within their profile with other users on their network, if a user with administrator privileges on the computer opts in for file sharing. To opt in for file sharing, an administrator has only to share a file within his or her profile.

- When this setting is Enabled, users cannot share files within their profile by using the File Sharing Wizard, and the File Sharing Wizard will not create shares within the %SystemDrive%\Users folder.

- When this setting is Disabled, as might be necessary to override an inherited Enabled setting, users are allowed to share files within their profile with other users on their network, if a user with administrator privileges on the computer opts in for file sharing.

To configure the Prevent Users From Sharing Files Within Their Profile policy in Group Policy, follow these steps:

1. Open a Group Policy Object for editing in the appropriate Group Policy editor. Next, expand Administrative Templates policies for User Configuration under Windows Components\Network Sharing.

2. Double-tap or double-click Prevent Users From Sharing Files Within Their Profile.

3. Select Not Configured, Enabled, or Disabled, and then tap or click OK.

Although it is tempting to use public folder sharing, most organizations—even small businesses—should encourage the use of standard folder sharing for all company files and data. Simply put, standard folder sharing offers more security and better protection. Rather than opening the floodgates to data, standard folder sharing closes them and blocks access appropriately. Increasing security is essential to protecting one of the most valuable assets of any organization—its data.

Share permissions are used only when a user attempts to access a file or folder from a different computer on the network, whereas access permissions are always used whether the user is logged on locally or using a remote system to access the file or folder over the network. When data is accessed remotely, first the share permissions are applied, and then the access permissions are applied.

In many ways, this means that file access permissions and standard folder sharing permissions are like wrappers around your data. File access permissions, the first wrapper, protect your data with regard to local access. If a user logs on to a system locally, file access permissions can allow or deny access to files and folders. File sharing permissions, the second wrapper, are used when you want to enable remote access. If a user accesses data remotely, file sharing permissions allow or deny initial access, but because your data is also wrapped in a file security blanket, the user must successfully pass file access permissions before working with files and folders.

Controlling access to files and folders with NTFS permissions

NTFS permissions, which apply to both NTFS and ReFS volumes, are always evaluated when a file is accessed. NTFS permissions are fairly complex, and to understand their management, you need to understand the following concepts:

- **Basic permissions**   What the basic permissions are and how they are used
- **Claims-based permissions**   What user and device claims are and how they are used
- **Special permissions**   What the special permissions are and how they are used
- **File ownership**   What is meant by file ownership and how file ownership is used
- **Inheritance**   What is meant by inheritance and how inheritance is used
- **Effective permissions**   How to determine the effective permissions on files

Understanding and using basic permissions

In Windows 8.1, the owner of a file or a folder has the right to allow or deny access to that file or folder, as do members of the Administrators group and other authorized users. By allowing a permission, you grant that permission to a user or a group. By denying a permission, you deny that permission to a user or a group. Keep in mind that entries that deny permissions take precedence over entries that allow permissions. As a result, if a user is a member of two groups, and one group is allowed a permission and the other is denied that permission, the user is denied that permission.

By using File Explorer, you can view the currently assigned basic permissions by pressing and holding or right-clicking a file or a folder, tapping or clicking Properties, and then tapping or clicking the Security tab in the Properties dialog box.

As shown in Figure 6-1, the Group Or User Names list shows the users and groups with permissions set for the selected resource. If you select a user or a group, the assigned permissions are shown in the Permissions For list. If permissions are shaded (unavailable), it means they have been inherited from a parent folder. Inheritance is covered in detail in the "Applying permissions through inheritance" section later in this chapter.

FIGURE 6-1 The Security tab shows the currently assigned basic permissions.

Working with and setting basic permissions

All permissions are stored in the file system as part of the access control list (ACL) assigned to a file or a folder. As described in Table 6-1, six basic permissions are used with folders, and five are also used with files. Although some permissions are inherited based on permissions of a parent folder, all permissions are defined explicitly at some level of the file system hierarchy. Permissions are listed in this table in approximate order of their scope, from Full Control, which grants the most permissions, to Read and Write, which grant specific permissions.

TABLE 6-1 Basic file and folder permissions

PERMISSION	DESCRIPTION
Full Control	Grants the user or group full control over the selected file or folder and permits reading, writing, changing, and deleting files and subfolders. A user with Full Control permission for a file or folder can change permissions, delete files in the folder regardless of the permission on the files, and also take ownership of a folder or a file. Selecting this permission also selects all the other permissions.
Modify	Allows the user or group to read, write, change, and delete files. A user with Modify permission can also create files and subfolders, but the user cannot take ownership of files. Selecting this permission selects all the permissions below it.
Read & Execute	Permits viewing and listing files and subfolders in addition to executing files. If applied to a folder, this permission is inherited by all files and subfolders within the folder. Selecting this permission also selects the List Folder Contents and Read permissions.
List Folder Contents (folders only)	Similar to the Read & Execute permission, but available only for folders. Permits viewing and listing files and subfolders, in addition to executing files. Unlike Read & Execute, this permission is inherited by subfolders, but not by files within the folder or subfolders.
Read	Allows the user or group to view and list the contents of a folder. A user with this permission can view file attributes, read permissions, and synchronize files. Read is the only permission needed to run scripts. Read access is required to access a shortcut and its target.
Write	Allows the user or group to create new files and write data to existing files. A user with this permission can also view file attributes, read permissions, and synchronize files. Giving a user permission to write but not delete a file or a folder doesn't prevent the user from deleting the folder's or file's contents.

Equally as important as the basic permissions are the users and groups to which you assign those permissions. If a user or a group whose permissions you want to assign is already selected in the Group Or User Names list on the Security tab, you can modify the assigned permissions by tapping or clicking Edit and then by using the Allow and Deny columns in the Permissions list. Select check boxes in the Allow column to add permissions, or clear check boxes to remove permissions, and then tap or click OK.

To expressly forbid a user or a group from using a permission, select the appropriate check boxes in the Deny column. Because denied permissions have precedence over other permissions, Deny is useful in two specific scenarios:

- If a user is a member of a group that has been granted a permission, but you don't want the user to have the permission and don't want to or can't remove the user from the group, you can override the inherited permission by denying that specific user the right to use the permission.

- If a permission is inherited from a parent folder and you prefer that a user or a group not have the inherited permission, you can override the allowed permission (in most cases) by expressly denying the user or group the use of the permission.

If users or groups whose permissions you want to assign aren't already available in the Group Or User Names list on the Security tab, you can easily add them. To set basic permissions for users or groups not already listed on a file or a folder's Security tab, follow these steps:

1. On the Security tab, tap or click Edit. This displays the Permissions For dialog box.

2. In the Permissions For dialog box, tap or click Add to display the Select Users, Computers, Service Accounts, Or Groups dialog box, as shown in Figure 6-2.

FIGURE 6-2 Use the Select Users, Computers, Service Accounts, Or Groups dialog box to specify users or groups whose permissions you want to configure.

NOTE In a workgroup, this dialog box is titled "Select Users Or Groups." Both dialog boxes serve the same purpose.

TIP Always double-check the value of the From This Location box. In work-groups, computers will always show only local accounts and groups. In domains, this text box is changeable and is set initially to the default (logon) domain of the currently logged-on user. If this isn't the location you want to use for selecting user and group accounts with which to work, tap or click Locations to find a list of locations you can search, including the current domain, trusted domains, and other resources that you can access.

3. Enter the name of a user or a group account. Be sure to reference the user account name rather than the user's full name. When entering multiple names, separate them with semicolons.

4. Tap or click Check Names. If a single match is found for each entry, the dialog box is automatically updated, and the entry is underlined. Otherwise, you'll get an additional dialog box. If no matches are found, you've either entered the name incorrectly or you're working with an incorrect location. Modify the name in the Name Not Found dialog box and try again, or tap or click Locations to select a new location. When multiple matches are found, in the Multiple Names Found dialog box, select the name you want to use, and then tap or click OK. The users and groups are added to the Group Or User Names list.

5. You can now configure permissions for each user and group you added by selecting an account name and then allowing or denying access permissions as appropriate.

Special identities and best practices for assigning permissions

When you work with basic permissions, it's important to understand not only how the permissions are used, but how special identities can be used to help you assign permissions. The special identities you'll encounter the most are Creator Owner and Users, but others are also used occasionally, as described in Table 6-2. Special identities are members of some groups automatically. To configure permissions for a special identity, enter the special identity's name as you would the name of any other user or group.

TABLE 6-2 Special identities used when setting permissions

SPECIAL IDENTITY	DESCRIPTION
Anonymous Logon	Includes any network logons for which credentials are not provided. This special identity is used to enable anonymous access to resources, such as those available on a web server.
Authenticated Users	Includes users and computers who log on with a user name and password; does not include users who log on by using the Guest account, even if the account is assigned a password.

SPECIAL IDENTITY	DESCRIPTION
Creator Owner	The special identity for the account that created a file or a folder. Windows 8.1 uses this group to identify the account that has ultimate authority over the file or folder.
Dialup	Includes any user who accesses the computer through a dial-up connection. This identity is used to distinguish dial-up users from other types of users.
Everyone	Includes all interactive, dial-up, and authenticated users. Although this group includes guests, it does not include anonymous users.
Interactive	Includes any user logged on locally or through a remote desktop connection.
Network	Includes any user who logs on over the network. This identity is used to allow remote users to access a resource and does not include interactive logons that use remote desktop connections.
Users	Includes authenticated users and domain users only. The built-in Users group is preferred over Everyone.

A solid understanding of these special identities can help you more effectively configure permissions on NTFS and ReFS volumes. Additionally, whenever you work with permissions, you should keep the following guidelines in mind:

- **Follow the file system hierarchy** Inheritance plays a big part in how permissions are set. By default, permissions you set on a folder apply to all files and subfolders within that folder. With this in mind, start at the root folder of a local disk or at a user's profile folder (both of which act as top-level folders) when you start configuring permissions.

- **Have a plan** Don't set permissions without a clear plan. If permissions on folders get out of sync, and you are looking for a way to start over so that you have some continuity, you might want to configure the permissions as they should be in a parent folder and then reset the permissions on all subfolders and files in that folder by using the technique discussed in the "Restoring inherited permissions" section later in this chapter.

- **Grant access only as necessary** An important aspect of the file access controls built into NTFS is that permissions must be explicitly assigned. If you don't grant a permission to a user and that user isn't a member of a group that has a permission, the user doesn't have that permission—it's that simple. When assigning permissions, it's especially important to keep this rule in mind because it's tempting just to give users full control rather than the specific permissions they really need. Granting only the specific permissions users need to do their job is known as the *principle of least privilege*.

- **Use groups to manage permissions more efficiently** Whenever possible, you should make users members of appropriate groups, and then assign permissions to those groups rather than to individual users. In this way, you can grant permissions to new users by making them members of the appropriate groups. Then, when a user leaves or goes to another group, you can change the group membership as appropriate. For example, when Sarah joins the sales team, you can add her to the SalesUS and SalesCan groups so that she can access those groups' shared data. If she later leaves the sales team and joins the marketing team, you can remove her from the SalesUS and SalesCan groups and add her to the MarketingUS and MarketingCan groups. This is much more efficient than editing the properties for every folder Sarah needs access to and assigning permissions.

- **Use central access policies to enhance existing access controls** On your domain servers running Windows Server 2012 R2, use central access policies to very precisely define the specific attributes that users and devices must have to access resources.

Assigning special permissions

Windows 8.1 uses special permissions to carefully control the permissions of users and groups. Behind the scenes, whenever you work with basic permissions, Windows 8.1 manages a set of related special permissions that exactly specify the permitted actions. The special permissions that are applied for each of the basic permissions are as follows:

- Read
  - List Folder/Read Data
  - Read Attributes
  - Read Extended Attributes
  - Read Permissions
- Read & Execute or List Folder Contents
  - All special permissions for Read
  - Traverse Folder/Execute File
- Write
  - Create Files/Write Data
  - Create Folders/Append Data
  - Write Attributes
  - Write Extended Attributes
- Modify
  - All special permissions for Read
  - All special permissions for Write
  - Delete

- Full Control
  - All special permissions listed previously
  - Change Permissions
  - Delete Subfolders And Files
  - Take Ownership

Table 6-3 describes how Windows 8.1 uses each special permission.

TABLE 6-3 Special permissions for files and folders

SPECIAL PERMISSION	DESCRIPTION
Change Permissions	Allows you to change basic and special permissions assigned to a file or a folder.
Create Files/Write Data	Create Files allows you to put new files in a folder. Write Data allows you to overwrite existing data in a file (but not add new data to an existing file, which is covered by Append Data).
Create Folders/ Append Data	Create Folders allows you to create subfolders within folders. Append Data allows you to add data to the end of an existing file (but not to overwrite existing data, which is covered by Write Data).
Delete	Allows you to delete a file or a folder. If a folder isn't empty and you don't have Delete permission for one or more of its files or subfolders, you won't be able to delete it unless you have the Delete Subfolders And Files permission.
Delete Subfolders And Files	Allows you to delete the contents of a folder. If you have this permission, you can delete the subfolders and files in a folder even if you don't specifically have Delete permission on the subfolder or the file.
List Folder/Read Data	List Folder lets you view file and folder names. Read Data allows you to view the contents of a file.
Read Attributes	Allows you to read the basic attributes of a file or a folder. These attributes include Read-Only, Hidden, System, and Archive.
Read Extended Attributes	Allows you to view the extended attributes (named data streams) associated with a file.
Read Permissions	Allows you to read all basic and special permissions assigned to a file or a folder.
Take Ownership	Allows you to take ownership of a file or a folder. By default, administrators can always take ownership of a file or a folder and can also grant this permission to others.

SPECIAL PERMISSION	DESCRIPTION
Traverse Folder/ Execute File	Traverse Folder allows direct access to a folder in order to reach subfolders, even if you don't have explicit access to read the data that the folder contains. Execute File allows you to run an executable file.
Write Attributes	Allows you to change the basic attributes of a file or a folder. These attributes include Read-Only, Hidden, System, and Archive.
Write Extended Attributes	Allows you to change the extended attributes (named data streams) associated with a file.

In File Explorer, you can view special permissions for a file or folder by pressing and holding or right-clicking the file or folder with which you want to work, and then tapping or clicking Properties. In the Properties dialog box, select the Security tab, and then tap or click Advanced to display the Advanced Security Settings dialog box, shown in Figure 6-3. In this dialog box, the permissions are presented much as they are on the Security tab. The key differences are that you view individual allow or deny permission sets, whether and from where permissions are inherited, and the resources to which the permissions apply.

FIGURE 6-3 Use the Advanced Security Settings dialog box to configure special permissions.

MORE INFO In Figure 6-3, note that the folder shows the GUID for the owner rather than a user name. With Windows 8.1, this typically is an indicator that the folder or file was created originally by a user running a different operating system on the computer, such as on a computer that is being dual booted.

After you open the Advanced Security Settings dialog box, you can set special permissions for a security principal by completing the following steps:

1. If the user or group already has directly assigned permissions for the file or folder, you can view or modify special permissions by tapping or clicking Edit and then skipping steps 2–5.

2. Tap or click Add to display the Permission Entry For dialog box. Tap or click Select A Principal to display the Select User, Computer, Service Account, Or Group dialog box.

3. Enter the name of a user or a group account. Be sure to reference the user account name rather than the user's full name. Only one name can be entered at a time.

4. Tap or click Check Names. If a single match is found for each entry, the dialog box is automatically updated, and the entry is underlined. Otherwise, you'll get an additional dialog box. If no matches are found, you've either entered the name incorrectly or you're working with an incorrect location. Modify the name in the Name Not Found dialog box and try again, or tap or click Locations to select a new location. When multiple matches are found, in the Multiple Names Found dialog box, select the name you want to use, and then tap or click OK.

5. Tap or click OK. The user and group is added as the Principal and the Permission Entry For dialog box is updated to show this.

6. Only basic permissions are listed by default. Tap or click Show Advanced Permissions to display the special permissions, as shown in Figure 6-4.

FIGURE 6-4 Configure the special permissions that should be allowed or denied.

7. Use the Type list to specify whether you are configuring allowed or denied special permissions, and then select the special permissions that you want to allow or deny. If any permissions are dimmed (unavailable), they are inherited from a parent folder.

NOTE You allow and deny special permissions separately. Therefore, if you want to both allow and deny special permissions, you'll need to configure the allowed permissions and then repeat this procedure starting with step 1 to configure the denied permissions.

8. If the options in the Applies To list are available, choose the appropriate option to ensure that the permissions are properly inherited. The options include the following:

- **This Folder Only** The permissions apply only to the currently selected folder.
- **This Folder, Subfolders And Files** The permissions apply to this folder, any subfolders of this folder, and any files in any of these folders.
- **This Folder And Subfolders** The permissions apply to this folder and any subfolders of this folder. They do not apply to any files in any of these folders.
- **This Folder And Files** The permissions apply to this folder and any files in this folder. They do not apply to any subfolders of this folder.
- **Subfolders And Files Only** The permissions apply to any subfolders of this folder and any files in any of these folders. They do not apply to this folder itself.
- **Subfolders Only** The permissions apply to any subfolders of this folder but not to the folder itself or any files in any of these folders.
- **Files Only** The permissions apply to any files in this folder and any files in subfolders of this folder. They do not apply to this folder itself or to subfolders.

9. When you have finished configuring permissions, tap or click OK.

Assigning claims-based permissions

Claims-based access controls use compound identities to control access to resources. When resources are remotely accessed, claims-based access controls and central access policies rely on Kerberos with armoring for authentication of computer device claims. Kerberos with armoring improves domain security by allowing domain-joined clients and domain controllers to communicate over secure, encrypted channels.

The most basic approach for creating a claim is to define conditions that limit access based on groups to which a user or device can or can't be a member. More advanced approaches use access rules, claims types, and resources properties to carefully define specific criteria that must be met before access is granted.

Put another way, claims define the specific attributes that users and devices must have to access a file or folder. For example, with basic claims based on group membership, you can specify that:

- A user or device can be a member of a group listed in a claim. For example, the device can be a member of the Engineering Computers group.

- A user or device must be a member of each of the groups listed in a claim. For example, the device must be a member of the Engineering Computers and Restricted Access groups.

- A user or device cannot be a member of a group listed in a claim. For example, the device cannot be a member of the Temp Computers group.

- A user or device must not be a member of each group listed in a claim. For example, the device cannot be a member of the Temp Computer or Contract Computers group.

MORE INFO With central access policies, you define central access rules in Active Directory Domain Services (AD DS) and those rules are applied dynamically throughout the enterprise. Central access rules use conditional expressions that require you to determine the resource properties, claim types, and/or security groups required for the policy, in addition to the servers where the policy should be applied.

Before you can define and apply claim conditions to a computer's files and folders, claims-based policy must be enabled. For non–domain-joined computers, you can do this by enabling and configuring the KDC Support For Claims, Compound Authentication And Kerberos Armoring policy in the Administrative Templates policies for Computer Configuration under System\KDC. The policy must be configured to use a specific mode. The available modes are:

- **Supported** Domain controllers support claims, compound identities, and Kerberos armoring. Client computers that don't support Kerberos with armoring can be authenticated.

- **Always Provide Claims** Same as Supported, but domain controllers always return claims for accounts.

- **Fail Unarmored Authentication Requests** Kerberos with armoring is mandatory. Client computers that don't support Kerberos with armoring cannot be authenticated.

For application throughout a domain, claims-based policy should be enabled for all domain controllers in a domain to ensure consistent application. Because of this, you typically enable and configure this policy through the Default Domain Controllers Group Policy Object, or the highest Group Policy Object linked to the domain controllers organizational unit (OU).

REAL WORLD You might have heard that you cannot or should not edit the Default Domain Controllers Group Policy Object. The truth is that this object should only be used to configure a very specific subset of policy.

In Group Policy Management, you'll find the Default Domain Controllers Group Policy Object in the Group Policy Objects container. By default, the Default Domain Controllers Policy GPO has the highest precedence among GPOs linked to the Domain Controllers OU and this is why the GPO has precedence. As a best practice, you should edit the Default Domain Policy GPO only to manage password policy, account lockout policy, and Kerberos policy.

To manage other areas of policy, you should create a new GPO and link it to the domain or an appropriate OU within the domain. That said, several policy settings located under Computer Configuration\Policies\Windows Settings\Security Settings\ Local Policies\Security Options are exceptions to the rule, including:

- Accounts: Rename Administrator Account
- Accounts: Administrator Account Status
- Accounts: Guest Account Status
- Accounts: Rename Guest Account
- Network Security: Force Logoff When Logon Hours Expire
- Network Security: Do Not Store LAN Manager Hash Value On Next Password Change
- Network Access: Allow Anonymous SID/Name Translation

Kerberos Client Support For Claims, Compound Authentication And Kerberos Armoring policy controls whether the Kerberos client running on Windows 8.1 and Windows Server 2012 R2 requests claims and compound authentication. The policy must be enabled for compatible Kerberos clients to request claims and compound authentication for Dynamic Access Control and Kerberos armoring. You'll find this policy in the Administrative Templates policies for Computer Configuration under System\Kerberos.

After you've enabled and configured claims-based policy, you can define claim conditions by completing these steps:

1. In File Explorer, press and hold or right-click the file or folder with which you want to work, and then tap or click Properties. In the Properties dialog box, select the Security tab, and then tap or click Advanced to display the Advanced Security Settings dialog box, shown earlier in Figure 6-3.

2. If the user or group already has directly assigned permissions for the file or folder, you can edit their existing permissions. Here, tap or click the user with which you want to work, tap or click Edit, and then skip steps 3–6.

3. Tap or click Add to display the Permission Entry For dialog box. Tap or click Select A Principal to display the Select User, Computer, Service Account, Or Group dialog box.

4. Enter the name of a user or a group account. Be sure to reference the user account name rather than the user's full name. Only one name can be entered at a time.

5. Tap or click Check Names. If a single match is found for each entry, the dialog box is automatically updated, and the entry is underlined. Otherwise, you'll get an additional dialog box. If no matches are found, you've either entered the name incorrectly or you're working with an incorrect location. Modify the name in the Name Not Found dialog box and try again, or tap or click Locations to select a new location. When multiple matches are found, in the Multiple Names Found dialog box, select the name you want to use, and then tap or click OK.

6. Tap or click OK. The user and group are added as the Principal. Tap or click Add A Condition.

7. Use the options provided to define the condition or conditions that must be met to grant access. With users and groups, set basic claims based on group membership, previously defined claim types, or both. With resource properties, define conditions for property values.

8. When you have finished configuring conditions, tap or click OK.

File ownership and permission assignment

The owner of a file or a folder has the right to allow or deny access to that resource. Although members of the Administrators group and other authorized users also have the right to allow or deny access, the owner has the authority to lock out non-administrator users, and then the only way to regain access to the resource is for an administrator or a member of the Restore Operators group to take ownership of it. This makes the file or folder owner important with respect to what permissions are allowed or denied for a given resource.

The default owner of a file or folder is the person who creates the resource. Ownership can be taken or transferred in several different ways. The current owner of a file or folder can transfer ownership to another user or group. A member of the Administrators group can take ownership of a file or folder or transfer ownership to another user or group—even if administrators are locked out of the resource according to the permissions. Any user with the Take Ownership permission on the file or folder can take ownership, as can any member of the Backup Operators group (or anyone else with the Restore Files And Directories user right, for that matter).

To assign ownership of a file or a folder, complete these steps:

1. In File Explorer, open the file or folder's Properties dialog box by pressing and holding or right-clicking the file or folder and then tapping or clicking Properties.

2. On the Security tab, tap or click Advanced to display the Advanced Security Settings dialog box where the current owner is listed under the file or folder name.

3. Tap or click Change. Use the options in the Select User, Computer, Service Account, Or Group dialog box to select the new owner. If you're taking ownership of a folder, you can take ownership of all subfolders and files within the folder by selecting the Replace Owner On Subcontainers And Objects option (see Figure 6-5).

FIGURE 6-5 Use the Advanced Security Settings dialog box to take ownership of a file or a folder.

4. Tap or click OK twice when you have finished.

Applying permissions through inheritance

In the file and folder hierarchy used by Windows 8.1, the root folder of a local disk and the %UserProfile% folder are the parent folders of all the files and folders they contain by default. Anytime you add a resource, it inherits the permissions of the local disk's root folder or the user's profile folder. You can change this behavior by modifying a folder's inheritance settings so that it no longer inherits permissions from its parent folder. This step creates a new parent folder, and any subfolders or files you add will then inherit the permissions of this folder.

Inheritance essentials

Inheritance is automatic, and inherited permissions are assigned when a file or folder is created. If you do not want a file or folder to have the same permissions as a parent, you have several choices:

- Stop inheriting permissions from the parent folder, and then either convert inherited permissions to explicit permissions or remove all inherited permissions.

- Access the parent folder, and then configure the permissions for the files and folders it contains.

- Try to override an inherited permission by selecting the opposite permission. In most cases, Deny overrides Allow.

Inherited permissions are shaded (unavailable) on the Security tab of a file or folder's Properties dialog box. Also, when you assign new permissions to a folder, the permissions propagate to the subfolders and files contained in that folder and either supplement or replace existing permissions. This propagation lets you grant additional users and groups access to a folder's resources or to further restrict access to a folder's resources independently of a parent folder.

To better understand inheritance, consider the following examples:

- On drive C, you create a folder named Data, and then create a subfolder named CurrentProjects. By default, Data inherits the permissions of the C:\ folder, and these permissions are in turn inherited by the CurrentProjects folder. Any files you add to the C:\, C:\Data, and C:\Data\CurrentProjects folders have the same permissions—those set for or inherited from the C:\ folder.

- On drive C, you create a folder named Docs, and then create a subfolder named Working. You disable inheritance on the Working folder, and then remove the inherited permissions of the parent, C:\. Any files you add to the C:\Docs\Working folder inherit the permissions of the C:\Docs folder and no other.

- On drive C, you create a folder named Backup, and then create a subfolder named Sales. You add permissions to the Sales folder that grant access to members of the Sales group. Any files added to the C:\Backup\Sales folder inherit the permissions of the C:\ folder and also have additional access permissions for members of the Sales group.

REAL WORLD Many new administrators wonder what the advantage of inheritance is and why it is used. Although inheritance occasionally seems like more trouble than it's worth, inheritance enables you to very efficiently manage permissions. Without inheritance, you'd have to configure permissions on every file and folder you create. If you wanted to change permissions later, you'd have to go through all your files and folders again. With inheritance, all new files and folders automatically inherit a set of permissions. If you need to change permissions, you can make the changes in a top-level or parent folder, and the changes can be automatically applied to all subfolders and files in that folder. In this way, a single permission set can be applied to many files and folders without editing the security of individual files and folders.

Viewing inherited permissions

To view the inherited permissions on a file or folder, press and hold or right-click the file or folder in File Explorer, and then tap or click Properties. On the Security tab of the Properties dialog box, tap or click Advanced to display the Advanced Security Settings dialog box, shown earlier in Figure 6-3. The Access column lists the current permissions assigned to the resource. If the permission is inherited, the Inherited From column shows the parent folder. If the permission is inherited by other resources, the Applies To column shows the types of resources that inherit the permission.

Stopping inheritance

When you disable inheritance in a file or folder's security settings, the file or folder stops inheriting permissions from parent folders. You can then elect to either convert inherited permissions to explicit permissions on the file or folder, which would make the permissions editable, or remove all inherited permissions from the file or folder.

If you want a file or folder to stop inheriting permissions from a parent folder, follow these steps:

1. In File Explorer, press and hold or right-click the file or folder, and then tap or click Properties. On the Security tab, tap or click Advanced. This opens the Advanced Security Settings dialog box with the Permissions tab selected by default.

2. On the Permissions tab, you'll find a Disable Inheritance button if inheritance currently is enabled. Tap or click Disable Inheritance.

3. As shown in Figure 6-6, you can now either convert the inherited permissions to explicit permissions or remove all inherited permissions and apply only the permissions that you explicitly set on the folder or file.

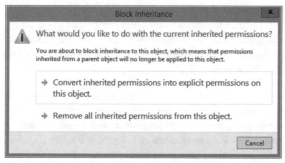

FIGURE 6-6 Copy or remove the inherited permissions.

TIP If you remove the inherited permissions and no other permissions are assigned, everyone but the owner of the resource is denied access. This effectively locks out everyone except the owner of a folder or file. However, administrators still have the right to take ownership of the resource regardless of the permissions. Thus, if an administrator is locked out of a file or a folder and truly needs access, she can take ownership and then have unrestricted access.

Restoring inherited permissions

Over time, the permissions on files and subfolders can become so dramatically different from those of a parent folder that it is nearly impossible to effectively manage access. To make managing file and folder access easier, you might want to take the drastic step of removing all existing permissions on all resources contained in a parent folder and replacing them with permissions inherited from that parent folder. In this way, permissions set on the folder you are working with (the parent folder) replace the permissions set on every file and subfolder contained within this parent folder.

To replace existing permissions with the inherited permissions of a parent folder, follow these steps:

1. In File Explorer, press and hold or right-click the folder, and then tap or click Properties. On the Security tab, tap or click Advanced.

2. On the Permissions tab, select Replace All Child Object Permission Entries With Inheritable Permission Entries From This Object, and then tap or click OK.

3. As shown in Figure 6-7, you receive a prompt explaining that this action will replace all explicitly defined permissions and enable propagation of inheritable permissions. Tap or click Yes.

FIGURE 6-7 Tap or click Yes to confirm that you want to replace the existing permissions.

However, you don't have to completely replace existing permissions to start inheriting permissions from a parent folder. If a file or folder was configured to stop inheriting permissions from a parent folder, you can re-enable inheritance to have the file or folder include the inherited permissions from a parent folder. To do this, follow these steps:

1. In File Explorer, press and hold or right-click the file or folder that should include inherited permissions, and then tap or click Properties. On the Security tab, tap or click Advanced.

2. On the Permissions tab, tap or click Enable Inheritance, and then tap or click OK. Note that the Enable Inheritance button is available only if permission inheritance currently is disabled.

Determining the effective permissions and troubleshooting

NTFS permissions are complex and can be difficult to manage. Sometimes a change—even a very minor one—can have unintended consequences. Users might suddenly find that they are denied access to files they could previously access or that they have access to files to which access should never have been granted. In either scenario, something has gone wrong with permissions. You have a problem, and you need to fix it.

You should start troubleshooting these or other problems with permissions by determining the effective permissions for the files or folders in question. As the name implies, the effective permissions tell you exactly which permissions are in

effect with regard to a particular user or group. The effective permissions are important because they enable you to quickly determine the cumulative set of permissions that apply.

For a user, the effective permissions are based on all the permissions the user has
been granted or denied, no matter whether the permissions are applied explicitly or
obtained from groups of which the user is a member. For example, if JimB is a member of the Users, Sales, Marketing, SpecTeam, and Managers groups, the effective
permissions on a file or a folder are the cumulative set of permissions that JimB has
been explicitly assigned and the permissions assigned to the Users, Sales, Marketing,
SpecTeam, and Managers groups. If JimB is a member of a group that is specifically
denied a permission, JimB will also be denied that permission, even if another group
is allowed that permission. This occurs because deny entries have precedence over
allow entries.

The same is true for user and device claims. If you've configured a claims-based
policy and added a user claim, that user claim can prevent access. Similarly, if there's
a device claim, that device claim can prevent access.

To determine the effective permissions for a user or a group with regard to a file
or folder, complete the following steps:

1. In File Explorer, press and hold or right-click the file or folder with which you
   want to work, and then tap or click Properties. In the Properties dialog box,
   tap or click the Security tab, and then tap or click Advanced.

2. In the Advanced Security Settings dialog box, tap or click the Effective Access
   tab. Use the options provided to determine the effective permissions for users, groups, and devices. Keep the following in mind:

   ■ If you only want to determine access for a particular user or user group,
     tap or click Select A User, enter the name of the user or group, and then
     tap or click OK.

   ■ If you only want to determine access for a particular device or device
     group, tap or click Select A Device, enter the name of the device or the
     device group, and then tap or click OK.

   ■ If you want to determine access for a particular user or user group on a
     particular device or in a device group, specify both a user/user group and
     a device/device group.

3. Tap or click View Effective Access. The effective permissions for the specified
   user or group are displayed by using the complete set of special permissions.
   If a user has full control over the selected resource, he or she will have all the
   permissions, as shown in Figure 6-8. Otherwise, a subset of the permissions
   is selected, and you have to carefully consider whether the user or group has
   the appropriate permissions. Use Table 6-3, earlier in the chapter, to help you
   interpret the permissions.

FIGURE 6-8 Any checked permissions have been granted to the specified user or group.

NOTE You must have appropriate permissions to view the effective permissions of any user or group. It's also important to remember that you cannot determine the effective permissions for implicit groups or special identities, such as Authenticated Users or Everyone. Furthermore, the effective permissions do not take into account those permissions granted to a user because he or she is the Creator Owner.

CHAPTER 7

Managing file sharing and auditing

S haring files enables users to access files from across the network. The most basic way to share files is to create a shared folder and make it accessible to users
through a mapped network drive. Although this standard approach to sharing files
requires a computer that is joined and connected to the enterprise domain, synced
sharing does not. With sync shares, users can use an Internet connection to sync
data to their devices from folders located on enterprise servers. You implement
synced sharing by using Work Folders, a feature that is available when you deploy
servers running Windows Server 2012 R2 or later.

Sharing files and folders over the network

Windows 8.1 supports two file-sharing models: public folder sharing and standard
folder sharing. Either or both models can be used in workgroups and domains, but
standard folder sharing is preferred because it's more secure than public folder
sharing. Standard folder sharing enables you to use a standard set of permissions
to allow or deny initial access to files and folders over a network. Standard folder
sharing settings are enabled or disabled on a per-computer basis. You can turn file
sharing on or off by following these steps:

1. In Control Panel, under the Network And Internet heading, tap or click
   the Choose Homegroup And Sharing Options link, and then tap or click
   Change Advanced Sharing Settings.

2. Each available network profile has a separate management panel with configuration settings. Use the expand button to display the profile with which
   you want to work.

3. To enable file and printer sharing, select Turn On File And Printer Sharing. To
   disable file and printer sharing, select Turn Off File And Printer Sharing. Tap
   or click Apply.

The Server Message Block (SMB) protocol is the primary network file sharing protocol used by computers running Windows. When folders are shared over a network, an SMB client reads and writes to files and requests services from the computer hosting the shared folder. Windows 8.1 and Windows Server 2012 R2 support SMB version 3.0 and include an SMB 3.0–compatible client.

SMB 3.0 brings many enhancements for performance, especially when you use clustered file servers. An out-of-the-box enhancement that doesn't rely on a special configuration is end-to-end encryption of SMB data, which eliminates the need to use IPsec, specialized hardware, or wide area network (WAN) accelerators to protect data from eavesdropping. SMB encryption can be enabled on a per-share basis or for an entire server.

Controlling access to network shares

When a user accesses a file or folder over a network and standard folder sharing is enabled, two levels of permissions are used that together determine the actions a user can perform with regard to a particular shared file or folder. The first level of permissions includes those set on the share itself. These permissions define the maximum level of access. A user or a group can never have more permissions than those granted by the share. The second level of permissions includes those set on the files and folders. These permissions serve to further restrict the permitted actions.

Three share permissions are available:

- **Owner**   Users with this permission have Full Control, Read, and Change permissions, in addition to the further capabilities to change file and folder permissions and take ownership of files and folders. If you have Owner permissions on a shared resource, you have full access to the shared resource.

- **Read/Write**   Users with this permission have Read and Change permissions and the additional capabilities to create files and subfolders, modify files, change attributes on files and subfolders, and delete files and subfolders. If you have Read/Write permissions on a shared resource, you can read, change, and delete data, but you cannot take ownership.

- **Read**   Users with this permission have only Read permission. They can view file and subfolder names, access the subfolders of the share, read file data and attributes, and run program files. If you have Read permission on a shared resource, the most you can do is perform read operations.

Permissions assigned to groups work like this: If a user is a member of a group that is granted share permissions, the user also has those permissions. If a user is a member of multiple groups, the permissions are cumulative. For example, if one group has Read access and another has Read/Write access, the user will have Read/Write access. If one group has Read access and another has Owner access, the user will have Owner access.

You can override this behavior by specifically denying an access permission. Denying permission takes precedence and overrides permissions that have been granted. If you don't want a user or a group to have a permission, configure the share permissions so that the user or group is denied that permission. For example, if a user is a member of a group that has been granted Owner permissions for a share, but the user should have only Read/Write permissions, configure the share to deny Owner permissions to that user.

Creating a shared resource

Folders can be shared both in workgroups and domains. To share the first resource on a computer, you must be a local administrator. Sharing the first resource sets up the computer for sharing other resources and enables other users to share resources they own, or to which they have appropriate access permissions.

You can create shares by using several different tools, including the following:

- **File Explorer**   Use File Explorer when you want to share folders on the computer you are logged on to.
- **Computer Management**   Use Computer Management when you want to share folders on any computer to which you can connect.
- **Net Share**   Use Net Share from the command line when you want to use a script to share folders. Enter **net share /?** at the command prompt for the syntax of the command.
- **SmbShare**   Use the SmbShare module to create and manage shares. Enter **get-help smbshare** at a Windows PowerShell prompt for a list of related cmdlets.

Creating a shared resource is a multipart process. First, you share the folder so that it can be accessed, and then you set the share permissions. Afterward, you should check and modify the file-system permissions as necessary. This section examines sharing a resource and setting its permissions by using File Explorer and Computer Management. For details on working with file system permissions, see the "Controlling access to files and folders with NTFS permissions" section in Chapter 6, "Optimizing file security."

Sharing a resource and setting share permissions in File Explorer

File Explorer supports basic sharing and advanced sharing. With basic sharing, you can share any folder except the root folder of a drive. With advanced sharing, you can share the root folder of a drive and any other folder. The root folders of drives are shared automatically as administrative shares.

To share a folder by using basic sharing, follow these steps:

1. In File Explorer, press and hold or right-click the folder you want to share, select Share With, and then select Specific People. This opens the File Sharing Wizard, shown in Figure 7-1.
2. Enter a name and then tap or click Add, or tap or click the arrow to find a user. In workgroups, computers will always show only local accounts and groups. In domains, you can view local users and groups and also find users in domains.
3. When you tap or click Add, the selected users and groups are added to the Name list. You can then configure permissions for each user and group by

tapping or clicking an account name to display the Permission Level options and then choosing the appropriate permission level. The options for permission levels are Read and Read/Write.

4. Finally, tap or click Share to create the share. After Windows 8.1 creates the share and makes it available for use, note the share name. This is the name by which the shared resource can be accessed. If you want to email a link to the shared resource to someone, tap or click the E-mail link. If you want to copy a link to the shared resource to the Clipboard, tap or click the Copy link. Tap or click Done when you have finished.

FIGURE 7-1 Use the File Sharing Wizard to configure sharing of the selected file or folder.

NOTE Typically, when you create a share, users access the share by using an abbreviated Universal Naming Convention (UNC) path to the share. For example, if you share the C:\Data\Reports\Current folder as Reports on CorPC85, users can access the folder by using the UNC path \\CorPC85\Reports. However, when you share a folder within a user's profile, users access the share by using a path that is relative to the Users folder on the computer. This occurs because Windows configures sharing in relation to where the folder is located in the Users folder. For example, if MollyH shares her Documents folder on CustPC27, the UNC path to the share is \\CustPC27\Users\MollyH\Documents.

To share a folder by using advanced sharing, follow these steps:

1. In File Explorer, press and hold or right-click the folder you want to share, and then tap or click Properties. This opens the folder's Properties dialog box.

2. On the Sharing tab, tap or click Advanced Sharing. In the Advanced Sharing dialog box, select Share This Folder.

3. Windows sets the share name to the folder name by default. Either accept the default share name or enter a different name.

4. Tap or click Permissions. Use the Permissions For dialog box to configure access permissions for the share. Tap or click OK.

5. Tap or click Caching. Use the Offline Settings dialog box to specify whether and how data is cached for offline use. Tap or click OK.

6. Tap or click OK. Click OK again to close the Advanced Sharing dialog box, and then tap or click Close.

Changing or stopping sharing

If you press and hold or right-click a folder that is shared, point to Share With, and then tap or click Stop Sharing, you remove sharing settings and stop sharing the folder. To change sharing permissions, press and hold or right-click the shared folder, point to Share With, and then tap or click Specific People. You can then grant access to additional users and groups, as discussed previously. To remove access for a user or group, select the user or group in the Name list, and then tap or click Remove. When you have finished making changes, tap or click Share to reconfigure sharing options, and then tap or click Done.

When you are using advanced sharing, you can configure sharing by pressing and holding or right-clicking the folder and then tapping or clicking Properties. On the Sharing tab, tap or click Advanced Sharing. You'll then be able to enable or disable alternate shares and specify connection limits for users. You'll also be able to configure permissions and caching.

Sharing a folder and setting share permissions in Computer Management

By using Computer Management, you can share a folder on any computer to which you have administrator access. By connecting remotely to the computer rather than logging on locally, you usually save time because you don't need to access the computer or leave your desk. Follow these steps to use Computer Management to share a folder:

1. Start Computer Management from the Administrative Tools in Control Panel or enter **compmgmt.msc** in the Apps Search box, and then press Enter. By default, Computer Management connects to the local computer, and the root node of the console tree displays the Computer Management (Local) label.

   TIP If you want to use the Create A Shared Folder Wizard to share a folder on a local computer, start the wizard directly and skip steps 1–4. Just enter **shrpubw** at an elevated command prompt, and then tap or click Next when the wizard starts.

2. Press and hold or right-click Computer Management in the console tree, and then tap or click Connect To Another Computer. In the Select Computer dialog box, the Another Computer option is selected by default. Enter the fully qualified domain name of the computer with which you want to work, such as **engpc08.microsoft.com,** where *engpc08* is the computer name and *microsoft.com* is the domain name. If you don't know the computer name and network discovery is enabled, tap or click Browse to search for the computer.

3. Expand System Tools\Shared Folders, and then select Shares to display the shared folders on the system with which you are working, as shown in Figure 7-2.

FIGURE 7-2 All available shared folders on the computer are listed in the Shares node.

4. To start the Create A Shared Folder Wizard, press and hold or right-click Shares, and then tap or click New Share. Tap or click Next to display the Folder Path page.

5. In the Folder Path text box, enter the full path to the folder that you want to share, such as **C:\Data**. If you don't know the full path, tap or click Browse, and then use the Browse For Folder dialog box to find the folder you want to share. The Browse For Folder dialog box also lets you create a new folder that you can then share. Tap or click Next to display the Name, Description, And Settings page.

6. In the Share Name text box, enter a name for the share. Share names must be unique for each system. They can be up to 80 characters in length and can contain spaces.

7. Enter a description of the share's contents in the Share Description text box.

   TIP By default, only files and programs that users specify are available for offline use. Tap or click Change if you want to modify the default offline file settings. You can make all files and programs available for offline use by selecting All Files And Programs That Users Open From The Shared Folder Are Automatically Available Offline, or you can make no files and programs available for offline use by selecting No Files Or Programs From The Shared Folder Are Available Offline. Tap or click OK after making your selection.

8. When you are ready to continue, tap or click Next to display the Shared Folder Permissions page. The available options are as follows:
   - **All Users Have Read-Only Access** Default option. Gives users the right to view files and read data but restricts them from creating, modifying, or deleting files and folders.

- **Administrators Have Full Access; Other Users Have Read-Only Access** Gives administrators full access to the share and gives other users read-only access. Administrators can create, modify, and delete files and folders. On NTFS, this option also gives administrators the right to change permissions and to take ownership of files and folders. Other users can only view files and read data. They can't create, modify, or delete files and folders.
- **Administrators Have Full Access; Other Users Have No Access** Gives only administrators full access to the share.
- **Customize Permissions** Enables you to configure access for specific users and groups, which is usually the best technique to use. To use this option, select Customize Permissions, tap or click Custom, and then set permissions as appropriate for the share.

9. After you set up permissions on the share, tap or click Finish to share the folder. Tap or click Finish again to exit the wizard.

If you later want to stop sharing the folder, you can do this in Computer Management by pressing and holding or right-clicking the shared folder and then tapping or clicking Stop Sharing. When prompted to confirm the action, tap or click Yes.

Creating and managing shared folders in Group Policy

You can share folders by using Group Policy preferences. I recommend this approach only when you can carefully target computers so that only computers that should actually share data are configured with shared folders.

To create a preference item to create, update, replace, or delete shared folders, follow these steps:

1. Open a Group Policy Object for editing in the Group Policy Management Editor. Expand Computer Configuration\Preferences\Windows Settings, and then select Network Shares.

2. Press and hold or right-click the Network Shares node, point to New, and then tap or click Network Share. This opens the New Network Share Properties dialog box.

3. In the New Network Share Properties dialog box, select Create, Update, Replace, or Delete in the Action list.

4. In the Share Name text box, enter a name for the share. Share names must be unique for each system. They can be up to 80 characters in length and can contain spaces.

5. In the Folder Path text box, enter the full path to the folder that you want to share, such as **C:\Data.** If you don't know the full path you want to use but there is an existing folder with the correct path, tap or click the related options button, and then use the Folder Selection dialog box to find the folder like the one you want to share on other computers.

REAL WORLD If you want to use an environment variable in the folder path, press F3 to display a list of system-defined variables. Tap or click the variable you'd like to use, such as LogOnUser. By default, variables are resolved by Group Policy before they are applied to a user's computer. To use the variable as a place-holder that is resolved on the user's computer instead, clear the Resolve Variable check box before you tap or click Select. This inserts a placeholder for the variable to be resolved on the user's computer.

In Group Policy preferences, you can easily distinguish between variables resolved by Group Policy and variables resolved on a user's computer. Variables resolved by Group Policy have the syntax *%VariableName%*, such as %ProgramFiles%. Variables resolved on a user's computer have the syntax *%<VariableName>%*, such as %<ProgramFiles>%.

6. In the Comment text box, enter a description of the share's contents.

7. When you are updating or deleting shares, you can modify or delete all shares of a particular type rather than an individual share. You can do any or all of the following:

   - Update or delete all regular shares (meaning shares that are not hidden, administrative, or special shares) by selecting Update All Regular Shares or Delete All Regular Shares.

   - Update or delete all hidden shares except the administrative shares and special shares (which include drive-letter shares, ADMIN$, FAX$, IPC$, and Print$) by selecting Update All Hidden Non-Administrative Shares or Delete All Hidden Non-Administrative Shares.

   - Update or delete all administrative shares (which include only the drive-letter shares) by selecting Update All Administrative Drive-Letter Shares or Delete All Administrative Drive-Letter Shares.

   NOTE If you want to modify special shares, such as ADMIN$, FAX$, IPC$, and Print$, or other system shares, such as SYSVOL and NETLOGON, you can create a preference item for the share and set the Share Name to the name of the special share.

8. Specify the number of users who can connect to the share. Select Maximum Allowed to enable the maximum number of users allowed by the operating system. Select Allow This Number Of Users to specify a limit.

9. Use the Access-based Enumeration options to specify whether access con-trols should be used to determine whether users can view folders in the share. Select Enable if you want only users with Read permission to be able to view the folders within the share. Select Disable if you want all users to be able to view the folders within the share.

10. Use the options on the Common tab to control how the preference is ap-plied. Because you are enforcing a control, you will usually want to apply the setting every time Group Policy is refreshed. In this case, do not select Apply Once And Do Not Reapply.

11. Tap or click OK. The next time Group Policy is refreshed, the preference item will be applied as appropriate for the Group Policy Object in which you define the preference item.

Using and accessing shared resources

After you share a file or folder, users can connect to it as a network resource or map it to a drive letter on their machines. When a network drive is mapped, users can access it as they do a local drive on their computer.

You can map a network drive to a shared file or folder by completing the following steps:

1. When you open File Explorer, the This PC node should be opened by default. If you have an open File Explorer window and This PC is not the selected node, tap or click the leftmost option button in the address list, and then tap or click This PC.

2. Select the Map Network Drive button on the Computer panel, and then select Map Network Drive. This displays the Map Network Drive dialog box, as shown in Figure 7-3.

FIGURE 7-3 Map the share you want to use to a network drive.

3. Use the Drive list to select a free drive letter to use, and then tap or click the Browse button to the right of the Folder list. In the Browse For Folder dialog box, expand the network folders until you can select the name of the workgroup or the domain with which you want to work. Keep in mind that network discovery must be enabled before you will be able to view shared folders in the Browse For Folder dialog box.

4. When you expand the name of a computer in a workgroup or a domain, you'll view a list of shared folders. Select the shared folder with which you want to work, and then tap or click OK.

5. Select Reconnect At Sign-In if you want Windows 8.1 to connect to the shared folder automatically at the start of each session.

6. Tap or click Finish. If the currently logged-on user doesn't have appropriate access permissions for the share, select Connect Using Different Credentials, and then tap or click Finish. After you tap or click Finish, you can enter the user name and password of the account with which you want to connect to the shared folder. Enter the user name in Domain\Username format, such as **Cpandl\Williams**. Before tapping or clicking OK, select Remember My Credentials if you want the credentials to be saved. Otherwise, you'll need to provide credentials in the future.

When mapping network drives, keep in mind that a computer switches to offline mode in the following scenarios:

- When the server is unavailable
- When on a slow network (as configured in Group Policy)
- When a user selects the Work Offline option in File Explorer
- When the mapped drive is configured to use the Always Offline mode

To enable the Always Offline mode, press and hold or right-click the mapped network drive in File Explorer, and then select Always Available Offline. If necessary, Windows 8.1 will then configure and start the Offline Files service before using the service to copy files and programs that can be cached from the server to the computer with which you are working. Note that if the computer is currently on a slow network, Group Policy settings for slow networks might affect whether files are copied. You can specify how slow links are used with offline files by enabling and configuring the Configure Slow Link Mode policy under Computer Configuration\Administrative Templates\Network\Offline Files.

Always Offline mode is a feature of Windows 8.1 and Windows Server 2012 R2 that only domain-joined computers can use. When the feature is enabled, Windows 8.1 always uses the mapped network drive in offline mode and the caching options configured on the server determine what files and programs are stored on the computer for offline use. By default, only files and programs that users specify are available for offline use and you must modify the shared folder configuration on the server (or via Group Policy) to use a different caching option.

The Offline Files service is responsible for maintaining the offline files cache and synchronizing changes back to the server. By default, the service synchronizes changes in the background every two hours. You can specify how background sync works with offline files by enabling and configuring the Configure Background Sync policy under Computer Configuration\Administrative Templates\Network\Offline Files.

If you later decide that you don't want to map the network drive, open File Explorer and select the This PC node. Under Network Location, press and hold or right-click the network drive icon, and then tap or click Disconnect.

You can access Group Policy and use a preference item to configure the network drives on computers throughout the domain by completing the following steps:

1. Open a Group Policy Object for editing in the Group Policy Management Editor. Expand User Configuration\Preferences\Windows Settings, and then select Drive Maps.

2. Press and hold or right-click the Drive Maps node, point to New, and then tap or click Mapped Drive. This opens the New Drive Properties dialog box.

3. In the New Drive Properties dialog box, select Create, Update, Replace, or Delete in the Action list.

4. In the Location text box, enter the UNC path to the network share, such as **\\CorpServer45\corpdatashare,** or tap or click the related options button to locate a share.

   REAL WORLD If you want to use an environment variable in the share path, click the Location text box and then press F3 to display a list of system-defined variables. Tap or click the variable you'd like to use, such as LogonUser. By default, variables are resolved by Group Policy before they are applied to a user's computer. To use the variable as a placeholder that is resolved on the user's computer instead, clear the Resolve Variable check box before you tap or click Select. This inserts a placeholder for the variable to be resolved on the user's computer.

   In Group Policy preferences, you can easily distinguish between variables resolved by Group Policy and variables resolved on a user's computer. Variables resolved by Group Policy have the syntax *%VariableName%*, such as %ProgramFiles%. Variables resolved on a user's computer have the syntax *%<VariableName>%*, such as %<ProgramFiles>%.

5. Select Reconnect if you want Windows 8.1 to connect to the shared folder automatically at the start of each session.

6. Enter the label for the network drive in the Label As text box.

7. Under Drive Letter, specify how the drive letter should be assigned. To use the first available drive letter starting after a drive letter that you specify, select Use First Available, Starting At, and then specify the starting drive letter. To always use a specific drive letter, choose Use, and then choose the drive letter. Unless you know for sure that a drive letter is available, you'll usually want to use the first available drive letter.

8. Optionally, specify the credentials to use when connecting to the network share.

   - If you want to map a network drive by using credentials other than those of the user, enter the credentials to be used. The password is encrypted and stored as part of the Group Policy Object in the Sysvol on domain controllers.

   - If you want to force a user to enter the required credentials, enter **%<LogonUser>%** in the User Name text box and do not enter anything in the Password and Confirm Password text boxes.

9. Additional options are provided for hiding or showing either the drive you are configuring or all drives. When you show or hide all drives, both network drives and physical drives are affected.

10. Use the options on the Common tab to control how the preference is applied. Because you are enforcing a control, you will usually want to apply the setting every time Group Policy is refreshed. In this case, do not select Apply Once And Do Not Reapply.

11. Tap or click OK. The next time policy is refreshed, the preference item will be applied as appropriate for the Group Policy Object in which you defined the preference item.

Using and accessing shared folders for administration

In Windows 8.1, several special shares are created automatically and are intended for use by administrators or the operating system. Most of the special shares have a dollar sign ($) added to the end of their names, which hides the shares from users. As an administrator, you might occasionally need to create your own hidden shares or work with the standard special shares.

Creating a hidden share is fairly easy. All you need to do is add a dollar sign ($) to the end of the share name. For example, if you want to share the C:\Reports folder but don't want it to be displayed in the standard file share lists, name it Reports$ rather than Reports. Hiding a share doesn't control access to the share, however. Access to shares is controlled by using permissions, regardless of whether a share is visible or hidden.

Which special shares are available on a system depends on the system's configuration. This means that some computers might have more special shares than others. The most commonly found special and administrative shares are listed in Table 7-1.

The best tools to use when you want to work with special or otherwise hidden shares are the Net Share command and Computer Management. To view a list of all shares on the local computer, including special shares for administrators, just enter **net share** at a command prompt. To view a list of all shares available on any computer on the network, complete the following steps:

1. Start Computer Management from the Administrative Tools in Control Panel, or enter **compmgmt.msc** in the Apps Search box, and then press Enter. By default, Computer Management connects to the local computer, and the root node of the console tree has the Computer Management (Local) label.

2. Press and hold or right-click Computer Management in the console tree, and then tap or click Connect To Another Computer. In the Select Computer dialog box, the Another Computer option is selected by default. Enter the host name or the fully qualified domain name of the computer with which you want to work, such as **engpc08** or **engpc08.microsoft.com**, where *engpc08*

is the computer name and *microsoft.com* is the domain name. If you don't know the computer name and network discovery is enabled, tap or click Browse to search for the computer with which you want to work.

3. Expand System Tools and Shared Folders, and then select Shares to display a list of the shares on the system with which you are working.

TABLE 7-1 Special and administrative shares

SHARE NAME	DESCRIPTION
C$, D$, E$, and other local disk shares	A special share to the root of a drive. All local disks, including CD/DVD-ROM drives and their shares, are known as C$, D$, E$, and so on. These shares enable members of the Administrators and Backup Operators groups to connect to the root folder of a local disk and perform administrative tasks. For example, if you map to C$, you are connecting to C:\ and have full access to this local disk.
ADMIN$	An administrative share for accessing the %SystemRoot% folder in which the operating system files reside. This share is meant to be used for remote administration. For administrators working remotely with systems, ADMIN$ provides a convenient shortcut for directly accessing the operating system folder.
IPC$	An administrative share used to support named pipes that programs use for interprocess (or process-to-process) communications. Because named pipes can be redirected over the network to connect to local and remote systems, they also enable remote administration.
PRINT$	Supports printer sharing by providing access to printer drivers. Whenever you share a printer, the system puts the printer drivers in this share so that other computers can access them as needed.

Sometimes when you are managing folders or files, you might not want users to be connected to a shared folder. For example, if you need to move files to a new location, before you move the files, you might want to ensure that no one is using them. One way to determine who is working with shared folders and their related files is to examine user sessions and open files.

Every user who connects to a shared folder creates a user session. To determine who is currently connected, tap or click Sessions under Shared Folders in the console tree. The current users are listed in the right pane. To disconnect a user and end his or her session, press and hold or right-click the session entry in the right pane, tap or click Close Session, and then tap or click OK to confirm the action. To disconnect all user sessions, press and hold or right-click Sessions in the console tree, tap or click Disconnect All Sessions, and then tap or click OK to confirm the action.

Every shared file that is being accessed is listed as an open file. To determine which files are open, tap or click Open Files under Shared Folders in the console tree. The currently open files are listed in the right pane. To close an open file, press and hold or right-click the related entry in the right pane, tap or click Close Open File, and then tap or click OK to confirm the action. To close all open files, press and hold or right-click Open Files in the console tree, tap or click Disconnect All Open Files, and then tap or click OK to confirm the action. Keep in mind that users might lose unsaved changes in files if they are disconnected. Therefore, if possible, notify users before closing files.

Troubleshooting file sharing

You can diagnose and resolve most issues with file sharing by doing the following:

- **Check the connectivity between the computer that is sharing resources and the computer from which the user is trying to access the shared resources**   Both computers must be connected to the network and config-ured with the appropriate TCP/IP settings. Both computers must have firewall configurations that permit inbound and outbound connectivity. The com-puter that is sharing resources must have a File And Printer Sharing excep-tion in Windows Firewall. Windows Firewall supports multiple active profiles, and the active and applicable profile must be configured correctly. If you are using third-party firewall software, inbound connections must be allowed on UDP port 137, UDP port 138, TCP port 139, and all ports for ICMPv4 and (if applicable for echo requests) ICMPv6.

- **Check the connection credentials**   When both computers are members of a domain, the user should connect to the share by using domain credentials. If the user has logged on to his or her computer as a local user rather than a domain user, you want to ensure that the user connects to the share with alternative credentials and that those alternative credentials are for an ap-propriate user account in the appropriate domain.

- **Check the Advanced Sharing settings in the Network And Sharing Center**   To successfully share files on a desktop computer running Windows 8.1, File And Printer Sharing must be enabled for the active (current) network profile and the Prevent Users From Sharing Files Within Their Profiles policy must not be enabled. Computers can be connected to multiple networks simultaneously, and the network type for each active network must be cor-rectly configured in the Network And Sharing Center.

- **Check the network type for the active network**   In the Network And Sharing Center, the network type on both computers must be set appro-priately. If the network type is set to Public, many sharing and connection settings are locked down and restricted.

- **Check share permissions, the underlying NTFS permissions, and the ac-cess flags on files**   The share permissions must be configured to grant the user access. The underlying NTFS permissions must be configured to grant the user access. Access flags on files must be cleared to remove read-only, hidden, or system flags as appropriate.

For deeper troubleshooting, you need to look at the DNS configuration of both computers, in addition to the domain membership of both computers. Ideally, both computers should be on the same network or on networks connected by fast Ethernet connections. Ideally, both computers should be members of the same domain or be in trusted domains.

The Server service is required to share files. On the computer that is sharing files, check to be sure that the Server service is running and is configured correctly. Typically, the Server service should be configured for automatic startup and should run under the LocalSystem account. The Server service depends on a Server SMB driver being available, and you can check this dependency on the Dependencies tab in the Server Properties dialog box.

In Group Policy for the computer that is sharing files, ensure that the user has the Access This Computer From The Network user right. This user right is set by using policies for Computer Configuration under Policies\Windows Settings\Security Settings\Local Policies\User Rights Assignment. By default, all authenticated users have this user right.

In Group Policy, you also can configure Access-Denied Assistance policies to help users determine who to contact if they have trouble accessing files. When you enable and configure Access-Denied Assistance policies, you can customize Access Denied errors with additional help text, links to help pages or documents, and an email address for requesting help.

To enable Access-Denied Assistance for all file types, configure the Enable Access-Denied Assistance On Client For All File Types option as Enabled, and then customize Access-Denied errors by enabling and configuring Customize Message For Access-Denied Errors. These policies are found in the Administrative Templates policies for Computer Configuration under System\Access-Denied Assistance.

Using and configuring public folder sharing

Public folder sharing is designed to enable users to share files and folders from a single location. It enables users to quickly determine everything they've publicly shared with others and organize publicly shared files by type. In this section, I'll examine how public folder sharing works and how public folder sharing can be configured.

Using public folder sharing

With public folder sharing, you copy or move files that you want to share to a computer's %SystemDrive%\Users\Public folder. The Public folder has several subfolders that can be used to help organize public files, including:

- **Public Desktop** A hidden folder used for shared desktop items
- **Public Documents, Public Music, Public Pictures, Public Recorded TV, Public Videos** Folders used for shared document and media files
- **Public Downloads** A folder used for shared downloads

Any content placed in these subfolders is available to all users who log on to the computer (and to all network users, if network access has been granted to the Public folder).

By default, everyone with a user account and password on a computer can access that computer's Public folder. When you copy or move files to the Public folder, access permissions are changed to match those of the Public folder, and some additional permissions are also added.

The default permissions for the Public folder enable local computer users to read, write, change, and delete any public files. In the Public Music, Public Pictures, and Public Videos folders, %ComputerName%\Users is granted Read & Execute and Read permissions.

The default Public folder sharing configuration can be changed in two key ways:

- Allow users with network access to view and open public files but restrict them from changing, creating, or deleting public files. When you configure this option, the implicit group Everyone is granted Read & Execute and Read permissions to public files and Read & Execute, List Folder Contents, and Read permissions on public folders.

- Allow users with network access to view and manage public files. This enables network users to open, change, create, and delete public files. When you configure this option, the implicit group Everyone is granted Full Control permissions to public files and public folders.

Configuring public folder sharing by using these approaches is discussed in the next section.

Configuring public folder sharing

Public folder sharing settings are set on a per-computer basis. The same public folder setting is used for the Public folder and all its subfolders. You can configure public folder sharing by following these steps:

1. In Control Panel, tap or click Choose Homegroup And Sharing Options under Network And Internet. Next, tap or click the Change Advanced Sharing Settings link.

2. Expand All Networks. Under Public Folder Sharing, select the public folder sharing option you want to use. The options available are:

   - **Turn On Sharing So Anyone With Network Access Can Read And Write Files In The Public Folders** Select this option to grant co-owner access to the public folders and all public data to anyone who can access the computer over the network. Windows Firewall settings might prevent external access.

   - **Turn Off Public Folder Sharing** Select this option to turn off network access to the public folders and allow only locally (console) logged-on users access to public data.

3. On private networks, Windows usually manages the connections to other homegroup computers. If you have the same user accounts and passwords on all of your computers, you can have Windows use your account instead to access shared files, shared printers, and the Public folder. Start by expanding the Private network profile. Next, under HomeGroup Connections, select the Use User Accounts And Passwords To Connect To Other Computers option.

4. Tap or click Save Changes to save the changes.

Implementing synced sharing

With sync shares, users can use an Internet or corporate network connection to sync data to their devices from folders located on enterprise servers. You implement synced sharing by using Work Folders. Work Folders is a feature that you can add to servers running Windows Server 2012 R2 or later. Work Folders use a client/server architecture. A Work Folders client is natively integrated into Windows 8.1, and clients for Windows 7, Apple iPad, and other devices are also becoming available.

Understanding work folders

Work Folders make use of the IIS hostable web core. If you deploy roles and features that require a full version of the Web Server (IIS) role, you might find that these roles and features or the Work Folders feature itself don't work together. A conflict can occur because the full version of the Web Server (IIS) role has a Default Web Site that uses port 80 for HTTP communications and port 443 for secure HTTP communications. For example, running Windows Essentials Experience and Work Folders together on the same server requires a special configuration. Typically, you need to change the ports used by Windows Essentials Experience so that they don't conflict with the ports used by Work Folders.

When users access a sync share, a user folder is created as a subfolder of the sync share and this subfolder is where the user's data is stored. The folder naming format for the user-specific folder is set when you create a sync share. The folder can be named by using only the user alias portion of the user's logon name or the full logon name in *alias@domain* format. The format you choose primarily depends on the level of compatibility required. Using the full logon name eliminates potential conflicts when users from different domains have identical user aliases, but this format is not compatible with redirected folders.

To maintain compatibility with redirected folders, you should configure the sync folder to use aliases. However, in enterprises with multiple domains, the drawback to this approach is that conflicts could exist between identical user aliases in different domains. Although the automatically configured permissions for a user folder would prevent johng from the cpandl.com domain from accessing a user folder created for johng from the adatum.com domain, the conflict would cause problems. If there was an existing folder for johng from the cpandl.com domain, the server would not be able to create a user folder for johng from the adatum.com domain.

With Work Folders, you have several important options during initial setup. You can:

- Select Encrypt Work Folders to encrypt files in Work Folders on client devices.

- Select Automatically Lock Screen And Require A Password to ensure the screens on client devices lock automatically and require an access password.

Encryption is implemented by using the Encrypting File System (EFS). EFS encrypts files with an enterprise encryption key rather than an encryption key generated by the client device. The enterprise encryption key is specific to the enterprise ID of the user (which by default is the primary SMTP address of the user). Having an enterprise encryption key that is separate from a client's standard encryption key is important to ensure encrypted personal files and encrypted work files are managed separately.

When files are encrypted, administrators can use a selective wipe to remove enterprise files from a client device. The selective wipe simply removes the enterprise encryption key and thus renders the work files unreadable, but it does not affect any encrypted personal files. Because the work files remain encrypted, there's no need to actually delete the work files from the client device. That said, you could run Disk Optimizer on the drive where the work files were stored. During optimization, Disk Optimizer should then overwrite the sectors where the work files were stored. Selective wipe only works when you've enabled the encryption option on Work Folders.

Although encryption is one way to protect enterprise data, another way to protect enterprise data is to configure client devices to lock screens and require a password for access. The exact policy enforced requires:

- A minimum password length of 6 characters
- A maximum password retry of 10
- A screen that automatically locks in 15 minutes or less

If you enforce the use of automatic lock screens and passwords, any device that doesn't support these requirements is prevented from connecting to the Work Folder.

By default, sync shares are not available in the same way as standard file shares. Because of this, users can only access sync shares by using the Work Folders client. If you want to make sync shares available to users as standard file shares, you must enable SMB access. After you enable SMB access, users can access files stored in Work Folders by using syncing and by mapping network drives.

REAL WORLD When a user makes changes to files in Work Folders, the changes might not be immediately apparent to others using the same Work Folders. For example, if a user deletes a file from a Work Folder by using SMB, other users accessing the Work Folder might still perceive the file as available. This inconsistency can occur because by default clients only poll the sync server every 10 minutes for SMB changes. A sync server also uses a Work Folders client to check periodically for changes users have made by using SMB; the default polling interval is 5 minutes. When the server identifies changes, the server relays the changes the next time a client syncs. Following this, you can determine that it could take up to 15 minutes for a change made using SMB to fully propagate. You can specify how frequently the server checks for changes made locally on the server or through SMB by using the Set-SyncServerSetting cmdlet with the -MinimumChangeDetectionMins parameter. However, because the server must check the change information for each file stored in the sync share, you need to be careful that you don't configure a server to try to detect changes too frequently. A server that checks for changes too frequently can become overloaded. Remember, change detection uses more resources as the number of files stored in the sync share increases.

To enable detailed logging of Work Folders, you can enable and configure the Audit Object Access policy setting for a Group Policy Object (GPO) processed by the server. You'll find this setting in the Administrative Templates for Computer Configuration under Windows Settings\Security Settings\Local Policies\Audit Policy. After you enable Audit Object Access, add an audit entry for the specific folders you want to audit. In File Explorer, press and hold or right-click a folder you want to audit, and then select Properties. In the Properties dialog box, on the Security tab, select Advanced. In the Advanced Security Settings dialog box, use the options on the Auditing tab to configure auditing.

You deploy Work Folders in the enterprise by performing these procedures:

1. Add the Work Folders role to servers that you want to host sync shares.
2. Use Group Policy to enable discovery of Work Folders.
3. Create sync shares on your sync servers and, optionally, enable SMB access to sync shares.
4. Configure clients to access Work Folders.

As detailed in the "Configuring policy for Work Folders" section in Chapter 5, "Configuring user and computer policies," you must add the Work Folders role to servers that you want to host sync shares, and then use Group Policy to enable discovery of Work Folders. Afterward, you can create sync shares, enable SMB access, and configure clients as discussed in this section.

Creating sync shares and enabling SMB access

You create a sync share to identify a local folder on a sync server that will be synchronized and accessible to domain users via the Work Folders client. Because sync shares are mapped to local paths on sync servers, I recommend that you create any folders that you want to use before creating sync shares. This will make it easier to select the exact folders with which you want to work.

To create a sync share, complete the following steps:

1. In Server Manager, select File And Storage Services, and then select Work Folders.
2. On the Work Folders panel, select Tasks, and then select New Sync Share. This opens the New Sync Share Wizard. If the Before You Begin page is displayed, select Next.

3. On the Select The Server And Path page, shown in Figure 7-4, select the server with which you want to work. Keep in mind that only servers that have the Work Folders role installed are available for selection.

FIGURE 7-4 Specify the server and folder to use.

4. When configuring sync shares, you have several options. You can:
   - Add syncing to an existing file share by choosing the Select By File Share option and then selecting the file share that should also be synced.
   - Add syncing to an existing local folder by choosing Enter A Local Path, selecting Browse, and then using the Select Folder dialog box to locate and choose the folder to sync.
   - Add syncing to a new local folder by choosing Enter A Local Path and then entering the path to use.

5. When you are ready to continue, tap or click Next. If you specified a new folder location, you are prompted to confirm whether you want to create this folder. Select OK to create the folder and continue.

6. On the Specify The Structure For User Folders page, choose a folder-naming format for the subfolders where user data is stored. To use only the user alias portion of the user's logon name for naming user folders, choose User Alias. To use the full logon name for naming user folders, choose User Alias@ Domain.

7. By default, all folders and files stored under the user folder are synced automatically. If you'd prefer that only a specific folder is synced, select the Sync Only The Following Subfolder check box, and then enter the name of the folder, such as Documents. Select Next to continue.

8. On the Enter The Sync Share Name page, enter a share name and description before selecting Next to continue.

9. On the Grant Sync Access To Groups page, shown in Figure 7-5, use the options provided to specify the users and groups that should be able to access the sync share. To add a user or group, select Add and then use the Select User Or Group dialog box to specify the user or group that should have access to the sync share.

SECURITY ALERT Any users and groups you specify will be granted permissions on the base folder, which allows the users and groups to create folders and access files in their folders. Specifically, Creator/Owner is granted Full Control on subfolders and files only. The users and groups are granted List Folder/Read Data, Create Folders/Append Data, Traverse Folder/Execute File, and Read/Write attributes on the base folder. Local System is granted Full Control of the base folder, subfolders, and files. Administrator is granted Read permission on the base folder.

FIGURE 7-5 Specify the users and groups that should have access to the sync share.

10. By default, inherited permissions are disabled and users have exclusive access to their user folders. Because of this, only the user who stores a file has access to this file on the share. If the base folder for the share has permissions that you want to be applied to user folders, such as those that would grant administrators access to user folders, clear the Disable Inherited Permissions And Grant Users Exclusive Access To Their Files check box. When you are ready to continue, select Next.

11. On the Specify Device Policies page, you have two options. You can select Encrypt Work Folders to encrypt files in Work Folders on client devices. You can select Automatically Lock Screen And Require A Password to ensure the screens on client devices lock automatically and require a password for access.

12. Select Next to continue, and then confirm your selections. Select Create to create the sync share. If the wizard is unable to create the sync share, you'll get an error and will need to note the error and take appropriate corrective action. A common error you might get occurs when the server hosts both Work Folders (which use the hostable web core) and the full Web Server (IIS) role. Before you can create sync shares, you'll need to modify the ports used so they do not conflict, or install Work Folders on a server that doesn't have the full Web Server (IIS) role.

If you did not select an existing file share during setup and want to enable the sync share for SMB access, open File Explorer. In File Explorer, press and hold or right-click the folder, select Share With, and then select Specific People. Finally, configure file sharing as discussed earlier in this chapter.

Accessing Work Folders on clients

Users with a domain user account can access Work Folders from a client device over the Internet or over the corporate network. You can configure Work Folder access for a user by completing the following steps:

1. In Control Panel, select System And Security, and then select Work Folders. On the Manage Work Folders page, select Set Up Work Folders.

2. On the Enter Your Work Email Address page, enter the user email address, such as johng@cpandl.com, and then select Next. If the client device is joined to the domain, you will not be prompted for the user's credentials. Otherwise, you are prompted for the user's credentials. After the user enters her credentials, you can select Remember My Credentials to store the user's credentials for future use, and then select OK to continue.

3. On the Introducing Work Folders page, note where the work files for the user will be stored. By default, work files are stored in a user profile subfolder called Work Folders. For example, the work files for JohnG would be stored under %SystemDrive%\Users\JohnG\WorkFolders. To store work files in another location, select Change, and then use the options provided to specify a new save location for work files. When you are ready to continue, select Next.

4. On the Security Policies page, review the security policies that will be applied, and then have the user select the I Accept These Policies On My PC check box. You will not be able to continue if you do not select this check box.

5. Select Set Up Work Folders to create Work Folders on the client device.

After you configure Work Folders for initial use on a client device, the user can access Work Folders in File Explorer. When a user opens File Explorer, the This PC node should be opened by default. If so, the user just needs to double-tap or double-click Work Folders to view work files. If a user has an open File Explorer window and This PC is not the selected node, she just needs to tap or click the leftmost option button in the address list, and then tap or click This PC.

As the user works with files, the changes the user makes trigger sync actions with the server. If the user doesn't change any files locally for an extended period of time, the client connects to the server every 10 minutes to determine whether there are changes to sync.

Auditing file and folder access

Although access permissions help protect data, they don't indicate who was trying to access files and folders inappropriately or who's been deleting important files, either accidentally or intentionally. To track who accessed files and folders and what they did, you must configure auditing for file and folder access. You can track file and folder access by enabling auditing, specifying which files and folders to audit, and then monitoring the security logs.

Enabling auditing for files and folders

You configure auditing policies by using Group Policy or local security policy. Use Group Policy when you want to set auditing policies throughout the enterprise. Use local security policy when you want to set auditing policies on a specific computer, keeping in mind that local policy can be overridden by Group Policy.

To enable auditing of files and folders, do one of the following:

- To configure local policy for a specific computer, start the Local Security Policy tool. If you've enabled Show Administrative Tools as a Start setting, you'll find a related tile on the Start screen. Another way to do this is by pressing the Windows key, typing **secpol.msc**, and then pressing Enter. In Local Security Policy, expand Local Policies, and then select Audit Policy.

- To configure enterprise policy, open a Group Policy Object for editing in the Group Policy Management Editor. Next, under Computer Configuration, expand Policies\Windows Settings\Security Settings\Local Policies, and then select Audit Policy.

Next, double-tap or double-click Audit Object Access. This displays the Audit Object Access Properties dialog box. Under Audit These Attempts, select the Success check box to log successful access attempts, the Failure check box to log failed access attempts, or both check boxes, and then tap or click OK. This enables auditing, but it doesn't specify which files and folders should be audited.

Configuring and tracking auditing

After you've enabled Audit Object Access, you can control whether and how folder and file usage is tracked by setting the level of auditing for individual folders and files. Keep in mind that auditing is available only on NTFS volumes and that inheritance rules apply to auditing of files and folders. This enables you, for example, to audit access to every file or folder on a volume by specifying that you want to audit the root folder of the volume.

You specify files and folders to audit by completing the following steps:

1. In File Explorer, press and hold or right-click the file or folder to be audited, and then tap or click Properties.

2. In the Properties dialog box, tap or click the Security tab, and then tap or click Advanced.

3. In the Advanced Security Settings dialog box, tap or click Continue on the Auditing tab. This displays an editable version of the Auditing tab, shown in Figure 7-6.

FIGURE 7-6 Review the current auditing settings and make new selections.

4. Tap or click Add to display the Auditing Entry For dialog box. Tap or click Select A Principal to display the Select User, Computer, Service Account, Or Group dialog box.

5. Enter the name of a user or a group account. Be sure to reference the user account name rather than the user's full name. Only one name can be entered at a time.

6. Tap or click Check Names. If a single match is found, the dialog box is automatically updated, and the entry is underlined. Otherwise, you'll get an additional dialog box. If no matches are found, you've either entered the name incorrectly or you're working with an incorrect location. Modify the name in the Name Not Found dialog box and try again, or tap or click Locations to select a new location. When multiple matches are found, in the Multiple Names Found dialog box, select the name you want to use, and then tap or click OK.

7. Tap or click OK. The user and group are added, and the Principal in the Auditing Entry For dialog box is updated to show this. Only basic permissions are listed by default. Tap or click Show Advanced Permissions to display the special permissions, as shown in Figure 7-7.

FIGURE 7-7 Specify the actions to audit for the designated user, group, or computer.

8. Use the Applies To list to specify how the auditing entry is to be applied. The options include the following:

- **This Folder Only**   The auditing entries apply only to the currently selected folder.

- **This Folder, Subfolders And Files**   The auditing entries apply to this folder, any subfolders of this folder, and any files in any of these folders.

- **This Folder And Subfolders**   The auditing entries apply to this folder and any subfolders of this folder. They do not apply to any files in any of these folders.

- **This Folder And Files**   The auditing entries apply to this folder and any files in this folder. They do not apply to any subfolders of this folder.

- **Subfolders And Files Only**   The auditing entries apply to any subfolders of this folder and any files in any of these folders. They do not apply to this folder itself.

- **Subfolders Only**   The auditing entries apply to any subfolders of this folder, but not to the folder itself or any files in any of these folders.

- **Files Only**   The auditing entries apply to any files in this folder and any files in subfolders of this folder. They do not apply to this folder itself or to subfolders.

9. Use the Type list to specify whether you are configuring auditing for successful access, failed access, or both, and then specify which actions should be audited. The events you can audit are the same as the special permissions listed in Tables 6-1 and 6-3 in Chapter 6.

10. If you are working with a folder and want to replace the auditing entries on all child objects of this folder (and not on the folder itself), select Only Apply These Settings To Objects And/Or Containers Within This Container.

    REAL WORLD The Apply To option lets you specify the locations *where* you want the auditing settings to apply. The Only Apply These Settings To Objects And/Or Containers Within This Container option controls *how* auditing settings are applied. When this option is selected, auditing settings on the parent object replace settings on child objects. When this option is cleared, auditing settings on the parent are merged with existing settings on child objects.

11. If you're using claims-based policies and want to limit the scope of the auditing entry, you can add claims-based conditions to the auditing entry. For example, if all corporate computers are members of the Domain Computers group, you might want to closely audit access by devices that aren't members of this group.

12. When you have finished configuring auditing, tap or click OK. Repeat this process to audit other users, groups, or computers.

Often you'll want to track only failed actions. This way, you know if someone was trying to perform an action and failed. Keep in mind that a failed attempt doesn't always mean that someone is trying to break into a file or folder. A user just might have double-tapped or double-clicked a folder or file to which he or she doesn't have access. In addition, some types of actions can cause multiple failed attempts to be logged even when the user performed the action only once. Regardless, you should always check multiple failed attempts because of the possibility that someone is attempting to break into a computer.

Any time files and folders that you've configured for auditing are accessed, the action is written to the system's security log, which you can open in Event Viewer. Successful actions, such as successful file reads, cause successful events to be recorded. Failed actions, such as failed file deletions, cause failed events to be recorded. To configure advanced audit policy, open a Group Policy Object for editing in the Group Policy Management Editor. Next, expand Windows Settings\Security Settings\Advanced Audit Policy Configuration, and then expand Audit Policies. You'll then have separate nodes for configuring policies related to:

- Account Logon
- Account Management
- Detailed Tracking
- DS Access
- Logon/Logoff
- Object Access
- Policy Change

- Privilege Use
- System
- Global Object Access Auditing

In the left pane, select a category you'd like to audit, such as Account Logon, to view the available subcategories in the right pane. Next, double-tap or double-click the subcategory you want to configure, such as Audit Credential Validation. In the related properties dialog box, select Configure The Following Audit Events. Next, select Success, Failure, or both to indicate the related events to track, and then tap or click OK. This enables auditing for that subcategory.

Maintaining data access and availability

M aintaining data access and availability is a key part of user and system administration. Beyond standard file and folder management, the main tasks you'll perform frequently include configuring File Explorer options, managing offline file settings, working with disk quotas, and managing branch caching. File Explorer options control the available file and folder management features, in addition to the available file types. Offline file settings control the availability of files and folders when users are working offline. Quotas help limit the amount of disk space available to users. Branch caching stores downloaded documents and files locally for faster retrieval.

Configuring File Explorer options

When you think about it, most of your time working with a computer is spent managing files and folders. You create files and folders to store and organize information. You move the files and folders from one location to another. You set file and folder properties, and perform other related tasks. Because you spend so much time working with files and folders, a few simple management techniques can go a long way toward saving you time and effort.

Customizing File Explorer

File Explorer is the tool of choice for working with files and folders. Unfortunately, its default settings are configured for the widest cross-spectrum of users and not experienced users or administrators. For example, as an administrator, you often want to view hidden items and file extensions, but, by default, File Explorer doesn't display hidden file types or file extensions.

With Windows 8.1, related options can be quickly enabled in the View panel. In File Explorer, tap or click View to open the View panel. Next, select Hidden Items to display hidden items (but not protected operating system files), and then select File Name Extensions to display file name extensions. To override other settings, complete the following steps:

1. In the View panel in File Explorer, tap or click Options. This displays the Folder Options dialog box with the General tab selected.

2. As shown in Figure 8-1, select the View tab to display the advanced settings for File Explorer.

FIGURE 8-1 Set options for File Explorer by using the Folder Options dialog box.

3. You can now customize File Explorer settings. Options available include:

   - **Always Show Icons, Never Thumbnails** By default, File Explorer shows large thumbnail images of the actual content for pictures and other types of files. For folders that have many pictures, this option can be annoying because File Explorer has to render the thumbnail representation of each image. To disable thumbnails except when you select the Thumbnails option on the View menu, select this option.

   - **Display File Icon On Thumbnails** By default, File Explorer adds file icons to the thumbnails it displays. To display thumbnails without file icons, clear this option.

   - **Display File Size Information In Folder Tips** By default, when you point to a folder name or folder icon, File Explorer displays a tooltip showing the folder's creation date and time, the size of the folder, and a partial list of files. To display less information (only the creation date and time), clear this option.

- **Display The Full Path In The Title Bar**   By default, when you press Alt+Tab and then hold down the Alt key, Windows opens the flip view, which shows a preview of all open windows without requiring you to click the taskbar. In this view, you can cycle through the open windows by pressing the Tab key or by using your mouse. By default, Windows displays the folder name for a File Explorer window. Select this option to display the file path for File Explorer windows instead.

- **Hidden Files And Folders**   By default, File Explorer does not display hidden files, folders, or drives. To display hidden files, folders, and drives, select Show Hidden Files, Folders, And Drives. (The Hidden Items option on the View menu can also be used to manage this option.)

- **Hide Empty Drives**   By default, File Explorer does not display information about empty drives in the This PC window. To display information about empty drives, clear this option.

- **Hide Extensions For Known File Types**   By default, File Explorer does not display file extensions for known file types. To display file extensions for all file types, clear this option. (The File Name Extensions option on the View menu can also be used to manage this option.)

- **Hide Folder Merge Conflicts**   By default, File Explorer does not display information about merge conflicts for folders. To display information about merge conflicts, clear this option.

- **Hide Protected Operating System Files**   By default, File Explorer does not display operating system files. To display operating system files, clear this option.

- **Launch Folder Windows In A Separate Process**   By default, Windows runs all instances of File Explorer in the same process. This saves memory and generally speeds up the process of opening new windows, but it also means that all instances of File Explorer are dependent on each other. If one instance crashes, they all crash, and if one instance is in a pending or wait state, all instances could become locked. To modify this behavior and have Windows start a new process for each instance of File Explorer, select this option.

- **Restore Previous Folder Windows At Logon**   File Explorer can track folders that users have open when they log off and reopen the folders the next time they log on. By default, this feature is disabled. To enable this feature, select this option.

- **Show Drive Letters**   By default, File Explorer displays drive letters as part of the information on the Locations bar. Clear this option if you don't want to view drive letters.

- **Show Encrypted Or Compressed NTFS Files In Color**   By default, File Explorer lists encrypted files and compressed files by using different colors than the colors used for standard files. Encrypted files are displayed with green text, and compressed files are displayed with blue text. Clear this option if you don't want to use different colors.

- **Show Pop-Up Description For Folder And Desktop Items** By default, File Explorer shows tooltips with additional information about a file or folder when you point to the file or folder. Clear this option if you don't want to view tooltips.

- **Show Preview Handlers In Preview Pane** By default, when the Preview pane is visible, File Explorer displays previews of selected files and folders. Clear this option if you don't want to view previews.

- **Show Status Bar** By default, File Explorer displays a status bar. If you want to hide the status bar, clear this option.

- **Use Check Boxes To Select Items** By default, File Explorer enables you to select files, folders, and other items by using only the standard selection techniques, such as click, Shift+click, and Ctrl+click. Select this option if you want File Explorer to display check boxes to select multiple files and folders.

- **Use Sharing Wizard** By default, File Explorer uses the File Sharing Wizard for configuring file sharing, as discussed in Chapter 7, "Managing file sharing and auditing." If you prefer to use only the advanced file sharing options, clear this option. When you try to share files, you need to tap or click Advanced Sharing on the Sharing tab so that you can configure permissions, caching, and connections settings separately.

- **When Typing Into List View** By default, when you are working with the list view and press a letter key, File Explorer selects the first file or folder with that letter at the start of its name. If you would rather have File Explorer enter the text that you type into the Search box, select the Automatically Type Into The Search Box option.

Configuring advanced File Explorer options

Both users and administrators spend a lot of time working with File Explorer or one of the related views, such as This PC. As an administrator, you'll often want to do more with File Explorer. You might want to perform one of the following tasks:

- Deploy computers that have certain File Explorer features blocked out. For example, you might want to block users' access to the Hardware tab, preventing them from viewing or changing hardware on a computer.

- Hide or restrict access to local disks. For example, you might want to prevent users from accessing the CD/DVD-burning features on the computers that you deploy.

These and other advanced configuration options for computers are discussed in this section.

Setting Group Policy for File Explorer and folder views

As with many other Windows 8.1 features, you can use Group Policy to control the options available in File Explorer. Because many of these options extend to folder views and settings, they are useful to examine. Table 8-1 provides an overview of policies that you might want to implement and how these policies are used when they are enabled. These Administrative Templates policies for User Configuration are located in Windows Components\File Explorer.

TABLE 8-1 Policies for File Explorer

POLICY NAME	POLICY DESCRIPTION
Allow Only Per User Or Approved Shell Extensions	Shell extensions extend the feature set available in File Explorer. This setting permits a computer to run only shell extensions that have been approved by an administrator or that don't affect other users on that computer. Approved shell extensions must have a registry entry in HKEY_LOCAL_MACHINE\SOFTWARE\Microsoft\Windows\CurrentVersion\Shell Extensions\Approved.
Display Confirmation Dialog When Deleting Files	Displays a confirmation dialog box whenever you delete files or move files to the Recycle Bin.
Hide The Manage Item On The File Explorer Context Menu	Removes the Manage item from the shortcut menu in File Explorer views and the Start screen. This shortcut menu option group is used to open Computer Management.
Hide These Specified Drives In My Computer	In File Explorer views, hides icons representing selected hard drives. Users can still gain access to drives through other methods.
Location Where All Default Library Definition Files For Users/Machines Reside	Can be used to control where default library definition files reside.
Prevent Access To Drives From My Computer	Prevents users from accessing files on selected drives in File Explorer views. Users also can't use the Run or Map Network Drive command to access files on these drives.
Remove "Map Network Drive" And "Disconnect Network Drive"	Prevents users from mapping or disconnecting network drives by using File Explorer. This doesn't prevent the use of other techniques, such as the command prompt.
Remove CD Burning Features	Removes CD creation and modification features from File Explorer. Users are not prevented from using other CD-burning programs.
Remove DFS Tab	Removes the DFS tab from File Explorer and File Explorer–based windows, preventing users from using the tab to view or change Distributed File System (DFS) settings. Note that the DFS tab is available only when DFS is configured in the workgroup or domain.

POLICY NAME	POLICY DESCRIPTION
Remove File Explorer's Default Context Menu	Prevents users from pressing and holding or right-clicking and displaying shortcut menus on the desktop and in File Explorer.
Remove File Menu From File Explorer	Removes the File menu from File Explorer views but doesn't prevent users from using other means to perform tasks that are available on this menu.
Remove Hardware Tab	Removes the Hardware tab from all dialog boxes, preventing users from using the tab to view, change, or troubleshoot hardware devices.
Remove Security Tab	Removes the Security tab from the Properties dialog boxes for files, folders, shortcuts, and drives. This prevents users from changing or viewing the related file and folder permissions.
Start File Explorer With Ribbon Minimized	Controls whether File Explorer displays the full or minimized ribbon. Options are available for when File Explorer is first opened or for all new windows.
Turn Off Caching Of Thumbnail Pictures	Disables the caching of thumbnail views.
Turn Off The Display Of Thumbnails And Only Display Icons	Disables the creation and display of thumbnails when users access local computer folders. This can reduce wait times and make accessing a folder the first time faster for users, although users might need to view media files to distinguish between them.
Turn Off The Display Of Thumbnails And Only Display Icons On Network Folders	Disables the creation and display of thumbnails when users access network folders. This can reduce wait times and make accessing a folder the first time faster for users, although users might need to view media files to distinguish between them.
Turn Off Windows Libraries Features That Rely On Indexed File Data	Disables all Arrangement views except By Folder, and all Search filter suggestions other than Date Modified and Size. Also disables the view of file content snippets in Content mode and excludes libraries from Start searches.

As detailed in Table 8-1, many File Explorer policies control the availability of options such as menu items and tabs in dialog boxes. To configure these options for all users of a computer, follow these steps:

1. Open a Group Policy Object for editing in the Group Policy Management Editor. The related Administrative Templates policies for User Configuration are located in Windows Components\File Explorer.

2. Double-tap or double-click the policy you want to configure. This displays a properties dialog box. Select one of the following options:

- **Not Configured** Specifies that no changes will be made to the registry for this policy

- **Enabled** Enables the policy and updates the registry

- **Disabled** Disables the policy and updates the registry

3. Tap or click OK.

NOTE You'll find detailed coverage of some of these policies in later sections of this chapter. In particular, be sure to read the next section, "Managing drive access in File Explorer," which covers hiding or preventing access to drives in File Explorer.

Managing drive access in File Explorer

You might want to block access to files on certain drives or even hide certain drives on a system. You manage this through Group Policy. The policies you use are Hide These Specified Drives In My Computer and Prevent Access To Drives From My Computer.

Hiding drives prevents users from accessing the drives in File Explorer views, but it doesn't prevent users from using other techniques to access the drives. In contrast, blocking access to drives prevents users from accessing any files on the drives and ensures that these files cannot be accessed by using File Explorer or the Run or Map Network Drive command. It doesn't, however, hide drive icons or the folder structure in File Explorer.

To hide selected drives or to prevent access to files on selected drives, follow these steps:

1. Open a Group Policy Object for editing in the Group Policy Management Editor. The related Administrative Templates policies for User Configuration are located in Windows Components\File Explorer.

2. To hide drives, double-tap or double-click Hide These Specified Drives In My Computer, and then select Enabled. Next, specify which drives you are hiding, and then tap or click OK. Key options are the following:

- Select Restrict All Drives to restrict access only to all internal hard drives and floppy disk drives.

- Select Restrict A And B Drives Only to restrict access only to floppy disk drives.

- Select Restrict A, B And C Drives Only to restrict access only to floppy disk drives and drive C.

- Select Restrict C Drive Only to restrict access only to drive C.

- Select Restrict D Drive Only to restrict access only to drive D.

- Select Do Not Restrict Drives to remove additional restrictions that would otherwise apply.

3. To block access to files on specific drives, double-tap or double-click Prevent Access To Drives From My Computer, and then select Enabled. Next, select the drives to which you want to restrict access, and then tap or click OK.

NOTE The List Folder Contents permission controls whether a user can view files in a folder. If you want to ensure that users cannot view the names of folders on drives, you should also hide the drives. This is the easiest way to hide all the folders on a drive from view.

Managing offline files

Configuring offline files is a multistep process that begins with appropriate settings in Group Policy, continues with configuring specific offline folders, and ends with setting user options for working offline. Although users who work offline primarily use laptops that they take home or to other locations, all users can benefit from offline file configurations. Configuring Group Policy for offline files is discussed in Chapter 5, "Configuring user and computer policies." This section provides more details about offline files and provides specific steps for configuring them.

Understanding offline files

Offline files enable users to store network files on their computers so that the files are available when the users are not connected to the network or a network outage occurs. After offline files are configured, Windows 8.1 automatically uses them whenever network files are not available. This enables users to continue working on network files without interruption. When the connection to the network is reestablished, Windows 8.1 synchronizes the files on the user's computer with the files in the network folder.

The way that changes are applied depends on how they were made. If multiple users make changes to a particular offline file, they can use conflict resolution features to save their version of the file over the existing version, keep the existing version, or save both versions on the network. If a user deletes an offline file, the file is also deleted on the network, except if someone has modified the file on the network so that it has a more recent date and time stamp. In this exceptional case, the file is deleted from the user's computer, but not from the network. If users change an offline file that someone else deletes from the network, they can choose to save their version to the network or delete it from their computer.

Windows 8.1 provides several features that affect the way that offline files are used, including:

- **Change-only syncing** Windows 8.1 provides faster synchronization by syncing only the changed blocks of files. Only the changed blocks are written back to the server during synchronization.

- **Unavailable file and folder ghosting** When part of the contents of a folder is made available offline, Windows 8.1 creates ghosted entries of other files and folders to preserve the online context. When you are not connected to a remote location, you'll find ghost entries for online items, in addition to entries for offline items.

- **Offloaded Data Transfer**   When data is being copied or moved within or between compatible storage arrays, this transparent and automatically enabled feature of Windows Server 2012 R2 offloads the file transfer to the storage devices, bypassing the host computers. As an example, if a user copies or moves a folder from a shared folder from one file server to another and those servers use compatible storage arrays (or the same storage array), the data would be transferred directly, bypassing the host servers.

- **Synchronization on costed networks**   By default, offline files are not synchronized in the background on cellular and other networks that might charge fees when roaming or near or over data plan usage. Adjust the threshold for slow-link mode by using Configure Slow-Link Mode, and configure background syncing by using Enable File Synchronization On Costed Networks. The related Administrative Templates policies for Computer Configuration are located under Network\Offline Files.

- **Caching of redirected folders**   By default, special folders that are redirected to network shares are available offline automatically. If you don't want redirected special folders to be available offline, you can exclude specific or all folders from being cached offline by using Do Not Automatically Make Specific Redirected Folders Available Offline. The related Administrative Templates policy for User Configuration is located under System\Folder Redirection.

Both users and administrators have control over when offline files are synchronized. Automatic synchronization can be triggered by user logon and logoff and by computers entering the sleep or hibernate modes. The exact settings for automatic synchronization depend on Group Policy and user settings. For details on configuring offline files through Group Policy, see the "Configuring Offline File policies" section in Chapter 5.

Users can initiate a sync of an entire network folder, a specific folder and its contents, or a specific file by pressing and holding or right-clicking the resource in File Explorer, selecting Sync, and then selecting Sync Selected Offline Files.

You also can manually control synchronization through Sync Center. You can open Sync Center in several ways:

- In Control Panel, tap or click View By, and then select either Large Icons or Small Icons. Next, tap or click Sync Center.

- In the Settings Search box, type **Sync Center,** and then press Enter.

Making files or folders available offline

Shared network folders can be made available for use offline. By default, all subfolders and files within the shared folders are also available offline. If necessary, you can change the availability of individual files and subfolders. Keep in mind that new files added to a shared folder that is designated for offline use are not automatically distributed to users working offline. The offline folder must be synchronized to obtain the updates.

You can configure offline files by using File Explorer or the Computer Management console. Because Computer Management enables you to work with and manage offline files on any of your network computers, it's usually the best tool to use. Making files or folders available offline is a three-step process. First you share folders, then you make those folders available for offline use, and finally, you have the users specify the files and folders they want to use offline.

Step 1: Share folders

In the Computer Management console, you make a folder available for sharing by completing the following steps:

1. Press and hold or right-click Computer Management in the console tree, and then tap or click Connect To Another Computer. Use the Select Computer dialog box to choose the computer with which you want to work.

2. In the console tree, expand System Tools and Shared Folders, and then select Shares. The current shares on the system are displayed in the Details pane.

3. Press and hold or right-click Shares, and then tap or click New Share. This starts the Create A Shared Folder Wizard, which can be used to share folders, as discussed in Chapter 7 in the "Sharing a folder and setting share permissions in Computer Management" section.

Step 2: Make folders available for offline use

In the Computer Management console, you make a shared folder available for offline use by completing these steps:

1. Press and hold or right-click Computer Management in the console tree, and then tap or click Connect To Another Computer. Use the Select Computer dialog box to choose the computer with which you want to work.

2. In the console tree, expand System Tools and Shared Folders, and then select Shares.

3. Double-tap or double-click the share you want to configure for offline use. On the General tab, tap or click Offline Settings.

4. In the Offline Settings dialog box, shown in Figure 8-2, select one of the following options:

   - **Only The Files And Programs That Users Specify Are Available Offline**   Use this setting when you want users to specify any files that they want to work with offline. This is the default option and is the best choice when multiple users want to modify the same files within a folder. After they are configured for manual caching, files are automatically downloaded and made available for offline use. If an older version of a document was cached previously, the older version is deleted. When a file is used online, the server version always reflects that the file is in use. With this option, you can also enable BranchCache. This makes it possible for computers in a branch office to cache files that are downloaded from a shared folder, and then securely share the files to other computers in the branch office.

- **All Files And Programs That Users Open From The Shared Folder Are Automatically Available Offline**   Use this setting for folders containing user data and programs. Opened files and program executables are automatically downloaded and made available for offline use. If an older version of a document was cached previously, the older version is deleted from the local cache. When a file is used online, the server version always reflects that the file is in use. Prompts are displayed if version conflicts occur.

FIGURE 8-2 Configure caching options for offline files in the Offline Settings dialog box.

With this option, you can also select Optimize For Performance to enable expanded caching of programs. Expanded caching enables programs that are shared over the network to be cached so that they can be run locally, which improves performance.

5. Tap or click OK twice.

Step 3: Specify the offline files and folders to use

After you've created the shares and configured offline use of those shares as appropriate, you can specify the files and folders to use offline by following these steps:

1. Map a network drive to a shared file or folder, as discussed in Chapter 7 in the "Using and accessing shared resources" section.

2. In File Explorer, tap or click the location path selection button, and then tap or click This PC. This opens the This PC window.

3. Create the offline file cache by doing one of the following:

   - To copy the contents of a shared folder to the user's computer and make it available for offline use, under Network Location, press and hold or right-click the shared location, and then tap or click Always Available Offline.

   - To copy only a selected folder (and its contents) or a selected file to the user's computer and make it available offline, use the This PC console to locate a specific file or folder on the network share, and then press and hold or right-click the file or folder and tap or click Always Available Offline.

Designating files and folders for offline use creates a local cache of the contents of the files and folders on the user's computer. It also establishes a sync partnership between the local computer and the sharing computer or extends an existing sync partnership to incorporate the additional shared files and folders. Sync partnerships can be managed by using Sync Center, as discussed in the next section, "Managing offline file synchronization."

You are considered to be working offline whenever your computer is not connected to the LAN. You know you are working offline when you find a red X over Network Drives in the This PC window or over the Network icon in the notification area of the taskbar. When you work offline, you can work with network files in the same way in which you work with files when you are connected to the network. You have the same permissions when you work offline. Therefore, if you have only read access to a file when you're connected to the network, you will still be able only to read the file, not modify it, when you're working offline.

Managing offline file synchronization

Synchronizing the offline files cache keeps the files up to date on the client computer and merges any changes the user has made back to the shared folder. The way Windows syncs depends on whether the computer is on a fast link, a slow link, or a costed network.

Sync Center, shown in Figure 8-3, simplifies the management of cached offline files and folders. In Sync Center, a sync partnership is established for every shared folder that has locally cached contents. Each sync partnership has a set of properties that enables you to control whether and how syncing occurs.

You can open Sync Center from Control Panel. In Control Panel, tap or click View By, and then select either Large Icons or Small Icons. Next, tap or click Sync Center. After you display Sync Center, you can easily check for synchronization problems, start or stop syncing, and configure syncing.

In Sync Center, the View Sync Partnerships page is selected by default. On this page, you can manually synchronize offline files by pressing and holding or right-clicking the Offline Files entry and then selecting Sync Offline Files.

FIGURE 8-3 Use Sync Center to view and manage synchronization.

Group Policy settings control how offline file synchronization works. Generally, offline files are automatically synchronized when a user reconnects to the network after being disconnected from the network or electing to work offline. You can also configure synchronization so that it occurs at one of the following times:

- At a specific, scheduled time
- When the user logs on
- When the computer is idle
- When the user locks or unlocks Windows

Scheduling syncing

You can create and manage scheduled synchronization by following these steps:

1. In Sync Center, press and hold or right-click the sync partnership with which you want to work, and then tap or click Schedule For Offline Files.

2. If you've previously scheduled synchronization for this resource, you can do the following:

   - **Create a new schedule** Tap or click Create A New Sync Schedule, and then follow the remaining steps in this procedure.

   - **View or edit an existing schedule** Tap or click View Or Edit An Existing Sync Schedule, tap or click the schedule to change, tap or click Next, and then follow the remaining steps in this procedure.

   - **Delete an existing schedule** Tap or click Delete An Existing Sync Schedule, tap or click the schedule to delete, and then tap or click Delete. Tap or click OK, and then skip the remaining steps in this procedure.

3. Review the items you are configuring and clear the check boxes for any items you don't want to configure. Tap or click Next, and then tap or click At A Scheduled Time.

4. The Start On and At options are configured so that scheduled syncing will start immediately, as shown in Figure 8-4. If you want to start scheduled syncing on a different date and time, use the options provided to change the start date and time.

FIGURE 8-4 Create a sync schedule.

5. The Repeat Every option sets the sync interval. The default interval is once every day. You can set the repeat interval to a value in minutes, hours, days, weeks, or months. Because only changes are synced, you might want to sync more frequently than you would with early Windows operating systems. For example, with important files, you might want to sync every three to four hours.

6. If you want to configure when syncing starts or stops, tap or click More Options. By default, sync starts only if the computer is awake and not in sleep or hibernate state. You also can configure syncing to:

   - Start only if the computer has been idle for at least *N* minutes, where *N* is a value you provide.
   - Start only if the computer is running on external power (as opposed to battery).
   - Stop sync if the computer wakes up from being idle.
   - Stop the sync if the computer is no longer running on external power.

7. When you are ready to continue, tap or click Next. Enter a descriptive name for the scheduled synchronization, and then tap or click Save Schedule.

Syncing on an event or action

You can create and manage synchronization based on events or actions by following these steps:

1. In Sync Center, tap or click the sync partnership with which you want to work, and then tap or click Schedule.

2. If you've previously scheduled synchronization for this resource, you can do the following:

   ■ **Create a new schedule**   Tap or click Create A New Sync Schedule, and then follow the remaining steps in this procedure.

   ■ **View or edit an existing schedule**   Tap or click View Or Edit An Existing Sync Schedule, tap or click the schedule to change, tap or click Next, and then follow the remaining steps in this procedure.

   ■ **Delete an existing schedule**   Tap or click Delete An Existing Sync Schedule, tap or click the schedule to delete, and then tap or click Delete. Tap or click OK, and then skip the remaining steps.

3. Review the items you are configuring, clear the check boxes for any items you don't want to configure, and then tap or click Next. Tap or click When An Event Occurs.

4. As shown in Figure 8-5, use the check boxes provided to specify the events and actions that start automatic syncing. You can start synchronization:

   ■ When a user logs on to the computer.

   ■ When the computer has been idle for at least *N* minutes, where *N* is a value you provide.

   ■ When a user locks the computer.

   ■ When a user unlocks the computer.

FIGURE 8-5 Sync based on events and actions.

5. When you are ready to continue, tap or click Next. Enter a descriptive name for the scheduled sync, and then tap or click Save Schedule.

Resolving synchronization conflicts and errors

Synchronization results provide details, errors, and warnings. To view current sync results, open Sync Center, and then tap or click View Sync Results. You can review sync details to determine when syncing was started, stopped, or completed. You can review errors and warnings to determine whether there are problems with the synchronization configuration.

Synchronization conflicts occur if a user makes changes to an offline file that is updated online by another user. You can view and resolve synchronization conflicts by following these steps:

1. In Sync Center, tap or click View Sync Conflicts. The main pane specifies whether there are any conflicts, as shown in Figure 8-6.

FIGURE 8-6 Conflicts are listed according to document name, file type, time, partnership, and conflict type.

2. To display the Resolve Conflict dialog box, double-tap or double-click a conflict you want to resolve.

3. You can now do the following:

   - Tap or click the version you want to keep. If you want to keep the local version and overwrite the network version, tap or click the version listed as On This Computer. If you want to keep the network version and overwrite the local version, tap or click the version listed as being on the shared network location.

   - Tap or click Keep Both Versions to write the local version to the shared network location with a new file name. Generally, the new file name will be the same as the old file name, but with a numeric suffix indicating the version increment. If you are at all unsure about which version of a file to keep, keep both versions, and then compare the two versions carefully for changes that should be merged or discarded.

Configuring disk usage limits for offline files

In Sync Center, you can control how much space is used and available for offline files. By default, the maximum amount of space that can be used and is available for offline files is a percentage of the size of the disk on which user profiles are stored on the computer. To configure disk usage limits for offline files, follow these steps:

1. In Sync Center, tap or click Manage Offline Files. This opens the Offline Files dialog box.

2. On the Disk Usage tab, you'll find the amount of space used by all offline files and related temporary files, as shown in Figure 8-7. Temporary files are created as users work with offline files on the computer.

FIGURE 8-7 Configure disk limits for offline files.

3. Note the limit for all offline files and related temporary files. This is specified as a limit in megabytes (MB) or gigabytes (GB), in addition to a percentage of the size of the disk on which user profiles are stored on the computer.

4. Tap or click Change Limits. In the Offline Files Disk Usage Limits dialog box, use the options provided to set the limit for all offline files and related temporary files, and then tap or click OK.

5. To delete temporary files that are not in use, tap or click Delete Temporary Files. Deleting temporary files does not affect the copies of the network files stored locally.

6. Tap or click OK.

Managing encryption for offline files

To enhance security, you can specify whether offline files are encrypted. If you encrypt offline files, only the files stored on your computer are encrypted and not the files on the network. Users do not need to decrypt the encrypted files before working with them. Decryption is performed automatically by the operating system. To encrypt offline files, follow these steps:

1. In Sync Center, tap or click Manage Offline Files. This opens the Offline Files dialog box.

2. On the Encryption tab, note whether the offline files are or are not encrypted. If offline files are not encrypted, tap or click Encrypt to encrypt all offline files, and then tap or click OK.

If you want to disable encryption later, repeat this procedure but tap or click Unencrypt.

Making offline files unavailable

As an administrator, you can specify files that should not be available for offline use. Typically, you'll do this when a shared folder contains specific files that users shouldn't manipulate. To make a file unavailable for offline use, you should set a specific exclusion policy, as described in the "Configuring Offline File policies" section of Chapter 5.

In the Computer Management console, you make a shared folder unavailable for offline use by completing these steps:

1. Press and hold or right-click Computer Management in the console tree, and then tap or click Connect To Another Computer. Use the Select Computer dialog box to choose the computer with which you want to work.

2. In the console tree, expand System Tools and Shared Folders, and then select Shares.

3. Double-tap or double-click the share you want to configure for offline use. On the General tab, tap or click Offline Settings.

4. In the Offline Settings dialog box, select No Files Or Programs From The Shared Folder Are Available Offline.

5. Tap or click OK.

To completely disable the use of offline files on a client computer, complete these steps:

1. In Sync Center, tap or click Manage Offline Files. This opens the Offline Files dialog box.

2. On the General tab, tap or click Disable Offline Files, and then tap or click OK.

If you want to enable offline files later, repeat this procedure, but tap or click Enable Offline Files.

Configuring disk quotas

The following sections discuss how to use and manage disk quotas. Disk quotas enable you to manage disk space usage and are configured on a per-volume basis. Only NTFS file system volumes can have quotas. The first step in configuring quotas is to enable disk quota policies, as described in the "Configuring disk quota policies" section of Chapter 5. After you configure the necessary policies, you can set up quotas for specific volumes on a system.

Using disk quotas

Administrators use disk quotas to manage disk space usage for critical volumes, such as those that provide corporate or user data shares. When you enable disk quotas, you set a disk quota limit and a disk quota warning level. The disk quota limit sets the maximum space that can be used (which prevents users from writing additional information to a volume), logs events when a user exceeds the limit, or both. You use the disk quota warning to warn users and to log warning events when users approach their disk quota limits.

> **REAL WORLD** Although most administrators configure quotas that are enforced, you can set disk quotas that are not enforced. You might wonder why you would do this. Sometimes you might want to track disk space usage on a per-user basis and know when users have exceeded some predefined limit. Instead of denying the users additional disk space, however, you can track the overage by recording an event in the application log.

Disk quotas apply only to standard users, not to administrators. Administrators can't be denied disk space even if they exceed enforced disk quota limits. Disk quota limits and warnings can be set in kilobytes (KB), megabytes (MB), gigabytes (GB), terabytes (TB), petabytes (PB), and exabytes (EB). In a typical environment, you'll use megabytes or gigabytes. For example, on a corporate data share that is used by members of a department, you might limit disk space usage to between 20 and 100 GB. For a user data share, you might set the level much lower, such as 5 to 20 GB, restricting the user from creating large amounts of personal data. Often, you'll set the disk quota warning as a percentage of the disk quota limit. For example, you could set the warning at 90 to 95 percent of the disk quota limit.

Because disk quotas are tracked on a per-volume, per-user basis, disk space used by one user does not affect the disk quotas for other users. Thus, if one user exceeds his limit, any restrictions applied to this user don't apply to other users. For example, if a user exceeds a 5-GB disk quota limit and the volume is configured to prevent writing over this limit, the user can no longer write data to the volume. He can, however, remove files and folders from the volume to free up disk space, move files and folders to a compressed area on the volume, or elect to compress files. Moving files to a different location on the volume doesn't affect the quota restriction. The amount of file space is the same unless the user moves uncompressed files and folders to a folder with compression. In any case, the restriction on a single user does not affect other users' ability to write to the volume (as long as the volume has free space).

You can enable disk quotas on local volumes and on remote volumes. To manage disk quotas on local volumes, you work with the local disk itself. To manage disk quotas on remote volumes, you must share the root directory for the volume and then set the disk quota on the volume. Keep in mind that when you enable disk quotas on a local volume, operating system and application program files are not included in the volume usage for the user who installed those files. Generally, system files are owned by the TrustedInstaller account, and program files are owned by the System account.

Only members of the Domain Administrators group or the local system Administrators group can configure disk quotas. Through local Group Policy, you can enable disk quotas for an individual computer. Through site, domain, or organizational unit (OU) policies, you can enable disk quotas for groups of users and computers. Keeping track of disk quotas does cause some overhead on computers, which is a function of the number of disk quotas being enforced, the total size of volumes and their data, and the number of users to which the disk quotas apply.

Although disk quotas appear to be tracked on a per-user basis, behind the scenes, Windows 8.1 manages disk quotas according to security identifiers (SIDs). Because disk quotas are tracked by SIDs, you can safely modify user names without affecting the disk quota configuration. Tracking by SIDs causes some additional overhead when you view disk quota statistics for users because Windows 8.1 must correlate SIDs to user account names so that the account names can be displayed in dialog boxes. This requires contacting the local user manager service or the domain controller as necessary. After names are looked up, they are cached to a local file so that they are available immediately the next time they are needed. The query cache is updated infrequently, so if you notice a discrepancy between what is displayed and what is configured, you need to refresh the information. Usually, this is done by selecting Refresh or pressing F5 in the current window.

Enabling disk quotas on NTFS volumes

Disk quotas are set on a per-volume basis. Because only NTFS volumes can have disk quotas, you cannot configure disk quotas on FAT or ReFS volumes. The best way to configure disk quotas is through Group Policy, as discussed in Chapter 5. After the appropriate policies are configured, you can create disk quota entries to manage per-user and per-group quotas.

If you'd rather configure quotas on each computer, you can enable disk quotas on an NTFS volume by following these steps:

1. Start Computer Management. You are connected to the local computer by default. If you want to configure disk quotas on a remote computer, press and hold or right-click Computer Management in the console tree, and then tap or click Connect To Another Computer. In the Select Computer dialog box, select the computer with which you want to work.

2. In the console tree, expand Storage, and then select Disk Management. The volumes configured on the selected computer are displayed in the details pane.

3. By using the Volume List or Graphical view, press and hold or right-click the volume with which you want to work, and then tap or click Properties.

4. Tap or click the Quota tab, as shown in Figure 8-8. Select the Enable Quota Management check box.

FIGURE 8-8 After you enable quota management, you can configure a quota limit and quota warning for all users on this computer.

5. To set a default disk quota limit that is applied to each user on this computer, select Limit Disk Space To, and then use the options provided to set a limit. Next, set the default warning limit by using Set Warning Level To. The disk quota warning limit should usually be 90 to 95 percent of the disk quota limit.

   TIP Although the default quota limit and warning apply to all users, you can use the Quota Entries dialog box to override the default and configure different levels for individual users. If you create many unique quota entries and don't want to re-create them on a volume with similar characteristics and usage, you can export the quota entries and import them on a different volume.

6. To enforce the disk quota limit and prevent users from going over the limit, select the Deny Disk Space To Users Exceeding Quota Limit check box. Keep in mind that this creates a physical limitation for users, but not for administrators.

7. To configure logging when users exceed a warning limit or the quota limit, use the Log Event check boxes.

8. If the quota system isn't currently enabled, you'll get a prompt asking you to enable the quota system. Tap or click OK so that Windows 8.1 can rescan the volume and update disk usage statistics. Actions can be taken against users who exceed the current limit or warning levels. These include preventing users from writing to the volume, notifying users the next time they access the volume, and logging applicable events in the application log.

Viewing disk quota entries

Disk space usage is tracked on a per-user basis. When disk quotas are enabled, each user storing data on a volume has an entry in the disk quota file. This entry is updated periodically to show the current disk space used, the applicable quota limit, the applicable warning level, and the percentage of allowable space being used. As an administrator, you can modify disk quota entries to set different limits and warning levels for particular users. You can also create disk quota entries for users who have not yet saved data on a volume. By creating entries, you ensure that when a user does make use of a volume, she has an appropriate limit and warning level.

To view the current disk quota entries for a volume, follow these steps:

1. Start Computer Management. You are connected to the local computer by default. If you want to view disk quotas on a remote computer, press and hold or right-click Computer Management in the console tree, and then tap or click Connect To Another Computer. In the Select Computer dialog box, select the computer with which you want to work.

2. In the console tree, expand Storage, and then select Disk Management. The volumes configured on the selected computer are displayed in the Details pane.

3. By using the Volume List or Graphical view, press and hold or right-click the volume with which you want to work, and then tap or click Properties.

4. On the Quota tab, tap or click Quota Entries. This displays the Quota Entries For dialog box.

    Disk quota entries show current disk space usage on a particular volume in addition to applicable quota limits and warning levels. The status is meant to quickly depict whether a user has gone over the limit. A status of OK means the user is working within the quota boundaries. Any other status usually means that the user has reached the warning level or the quota limit.

Creating disk quota entries

You can create disk quota entries for users who have not yet saved data on a volume in addition to users who have already saved data on a volume. This enables you to set custom limits and warning levels for any user as necessary. Usually, you'll use this feature when one user frequently stores more information than others do. For example, a graphic designer might have much larger storage needs than a customer-support person does. The good news about custom quota entries is that you can export them to other volumes, which enables you to quickly apply the same set of rules to multiple volumes.

To create a quota entry on a volume, follow these steps:

1. In Computer Management, expand Storage, and then select Disk Management. By using the Volume List or Graphical view, press and hold or right-click the volume with which you want to work, and then tap or click Properties.

2. On the Quota tab, tap or click Quota Entries. Current quota entries for all users are listed. To refresh the listing, tap or click Refresh on the View menu.

3. If the user doesn't have an existing entry on the volume, create one by tapping or clicking New Quota Entry on the Quota menu. This opens the Select Users dialog box.

4. In the Select Users dialog box, type the name of a user in the Enter The Object Names To Select box, and then tap or click Check Names. If multiple matches are found, select the account you want, and then tap or click OK. If no matches are found, update the name you entered and try again. Repeat this step as necessary, and then tap or click OK.

5. After you've selected a name, the Add New Quota Entry dialog box is displayed. You have several options. You can remove all quota restrictions for this user by selecting Do Not Limit Disk Usage. In addition, you can set a specific limit and warning level by selecting Limit Disk Space To and then entering the appropriate values.

6. Tap or click OK to close the Add New Quota Entry dialog box.

Updating and customizing disk quota entries

You can modify and customize disk quota entries for individual users at any time by following these steps:

1. In Computer Management, expand Storage, and then select Disk Management. By using the Volume List or Graphical view, press and hold or right-click the volume with which you want to work, and then tap or click Properties.

2. On the Quota tab, tap or click Quota Entries. Current quota entries for all users are listed. To refresh the list, tap or click Refresh on the View menu.

3. Double-tap or double-click the quota entry for the user. This displays the Quota Settings For dialog box, which is similar to the dialog box shown previously in Figure 8-8.

4. To remove all quota restrictions for this user, select Do Not Limit Disk Usage.

5. To modify the current limit and warning level, select Limit Disk Space To, and then enter the appropriate values.

6. Tap or click OK.

Deleting disk quota entries

When you've created disk quota entries on a volume and a user no longer needs to use the volume, you can delete the associated disk quota entry. When you delete a disk quota entry, all files owned by the user on the volume are collected and displayed in a dialog box so that you can permanently delete the files, take ownership of the files, or move the files to a folder on a different volume.

To delete a disk quota entry for a user and manage the remaining files on the volume, follow these steps:

1. In Computer Management, expand Storage, and then select Disk Management. By using the Volume List or Graphical view, press and hold or right-click the volume with which you want to work, and then tap or click Properties.

2. On the Quota tab, tap or click Quota Entries. Current quota entries for all users are listed. To refresh the listing, press F5 or tap or click Refresh on the View menu.

3. Select the disk quota entry that you want to delete, and then press Delete or select Delete Quota Entry from the Quota menu. You can select multiple entries by using the Shift key or Ctrl key.

4. When prompted to confirm the action, tap or click Yes. This displays the Disk Quota dialog box with a list of files owned by the selected user or users.

5. Use the List Files Owned By list to display files for the user whose quota entry you are deleting. You must then specify how to handle the files for the user. You can handle each file separately by selecting a file and then choosing an appropriate option. Select multiple files by using the Shift key or Ctrl key. The following options are available:

   - **Show Folders Only** Changes the view to show only folders in which the user has files. In this way, you can delete, move, or take ownership of all the user's files in a particular folder.

   - **Show Files Only** Shows all files that the user owns according to the folder in which they were created.

   - **Permanently Delete Files** Select the files to delete, and then tap or click Delete. When prompted to confirm the action, tap or click Yes.

   - **Take Ownership Of Files** Select the files of which you want to take ownership, and then tap or click Take Ownership.

   - **Move Files To** Select the files that you want to move, and then, in the boxes provided, enter the path to a folder on a different volume. If you don't know the path that you want to use, tap or click Browse to display the Browse For Folder dialog box. After you find the folder, tap or click Move.

6. Tap or click Close when you have finished managing the files. If you've handled all user files appropriately, the disk quota entries are deleted.

Exporting and importing disk quota settings

Rather than re-create custom disk quota entries on individual volumes, you can export the settings from a source volume and import them to another volume. Both volumes must be formatted by using NTFS. To export and then import disk quota entries, perform the following steps:

1. Start Computer Management. You are connected to the local computer by default. If you want to work with disk quotas on a remote computer, press and hold or right-click Computer Management in the console tree, and then tap or click Connect To Another Computer. In the Select Computer dialog box, select the computer with which you want to work.

2. In the console tree, expand Storage, and then select Disk Management. The volumes configured on the selected computer are displayed in the details pane.

3. By using the Volume List or Graphical view, press and hold or right-click the source volume, and then tap or click Properties.

4. On the Quota tab, tap or click Quota Entries. This displays the Quota Entries For dialog box.

5. On the Quota menu, tap or click Export. This displays the Export Quota Settings dialog box. Choose the location in which to save the file containing the quota settings. Specify a name for the file in the File Name box, and then tap or click Save.

> **TIP** If you save the settings file to a mapped drive on the target volume, you'll have an easier time importing the settings. Quota files are usually fairly small, so you don't need to worry about disk space usage.

6. From the Quota menu, choose Close to close the Quota Entries dialog box. Tap or click OK to close the Properties dialog box.

7. In the console tree, press and hold or right-click Computer Management. On the shortcut menu, tap or click Connect To Another Computer. In the Select Computer dialog box, select the computer containing the target volume on which you want to use the exported settings.

8. Expand Storage, and then select Disk Management. By using the Volume List or Graphical view, press and hold or right-click the target volume, and then tap or click Properties.

9. Tap or click the Quota tab, ensure that Enable Quota Management is selected, and then tap or click Quota Entries. This displays the Quota Entries dialog box for the target volume.

10. On the Quota menu, tap or click Import. In the Import Quota Settings dialog box, select the quota settings file that you saved previously. Tap or click Open.

11. If the volume had previous quota entries, you can replace or keep existing entries. When prompted about a conflict, tap or click Yes to replace an existing entry, or tap or click No to keep the existing entry. The option to replace or keep existing entries can be applied to all entries on the volume by selecting Do This For All Quota Entries prior to tapping or clicking Yes or No.

Disabling disk quotas

You can disable quotas for individual users or all users on a volume. When you disable quotas for a particular user, that user is no longer subject to the quota restrictions, but disk quotas are still tracked for other users. When you disable quotas on a volume, quota tracking and management are completely removed. To disable quotas for a particular user, follow the technique outlined in the "Updating and customizing disk quota entries" section earlier in this chapter.

To disable quota tracking and management on a volume, follow these steps:

1. Start Computer Management. You are connected to the local computer by default. If you want to disable disk quotas on a remote computer, press and hold or right-click Computer Management in the console tree, and then tap or click Connect To Another Computer. In the Select Computer dialog box, select the computer with which you want to work.

2. In the console tree, expand Storage, and then select Disk Management. The volumes configured on the selected computer are displayed in the details pane.

3. By using the Volume List or Graphical view, press and hold or right-click the volume, and then tap or click Properties.

4. On the Quota tab, clear the Enable Quota Management check box. Tap or click OK. When prompted to confirm, tap or click OK.

Using branch caching

Windows BranchCache is a file-caching feature that works in conjunction with Background Intelligent Transfer Service (BITS). By using Group Policy, administrators can enable branch caching so that computers can retrieve documents and other types of files from a local cache rather than retrieving files from servers over the network.

Branch caching works with files transferred by using HTTP and Server Message Block (SMB). This means that files transferred from both intranet web servers and internal file servers are cached. Caching can dramatically improve response times and reduce transfer times for documents, webpages, and multimedia content.

BranchCache uses a client-server architecture and is tightly integrated into Windows File and Storage Services. Two versions of BranchCache are available:

-   Branch caching version 1 was released originally with Windows 7 and Windows Server 2008 Release 2 (and made available to Windows Vista with BITS 4.0 installed).

-   Branch caching version 2 was released with Windows 8 and Windows Server 2012.

The two versions work in different ways and use incompatible caching approaches. Version 1 uses a traditional caching approach. With Version 2, BranchCache takes advantage of data deduplication techniques to optimize data transfers over the wide area network (WAN) to branch offices. Because of this, BranchCache version 2 uses variable-size chunking and compression to achieve greater efficiencies when transferring files. Cached files aren't stored as data streams and instead are replaced with stubs that point to data blocks within a common cache store. Chunking files ensures that compatible client computers download only one instance of duplicate content and that BranchCache stores only one instance of duplicate content. Chunking files also makes it possible to transfer only the part of a file that has changed rather than an entire file. It is also important to note that if the shared folder is on a volume that has already been deduplicated, BranchCache can use the already chunked files and there is no need to reprocess the files for transfer.

Generally speaking, LAN boundaries determine how the feature works after it is implemented. If a LAN is connected to the central office over a network on which the round-trip network latency is more than 80 milliseconds, clients on that LAN will use the local cache when it is available. Note also that multiple LANs connected together over a fast network can also use a single local cache.

When you enable branch caching, the first time that a file is accessed from an intranet website or file server over the network, Windows transfers the file from the originating server and caches the file locally within the remote office. When the same user or a different user at the remote office accesses the file later, Windows looks for the file in the local cache. If it finds the file, Windows queries the originating server to determine if the file has changed since it was cached. If the file has not changed, Windows retrieves the file from the local cache, eliminating the need to transfer the file over the WAN. If the file has changed, Windows retrieves the file from the originating server and updates the copy of the file in the cache.

With version 2, cached data is stored encrypted by default to enhance security, and hosted cache on Windows servers is maintained with Extensible Storage Engine (ESE) database technology. Using an ESE database enables a hosted cache server to store terabytes of data and serve many clients efficiently. Additionally, administrators can preload content onto hosted cache servers before the content is requested. Preloading ensures the content is available for quick access from local cache. If you preload content from media, such as an external drive or DVD, you eliminate the need to transfer the content over the network.

You can configure branch caching in one of two modes:

- **Distributed cache**   In this mode, the user's desktop computer running a compatible version of Windows hosts a distributed file cache. A server running at the remote office is not needed because each local computer caches and sends out files.

- **Hosted cache**   In this mode, compatible file servers located in the remote office host the local file cache. The servers cache files and send them to clients located in the remote office.

NOTE   Although BranchCache version 2 enables you to scale the caching solution across multiple servers, BranchCache version 1 enables only one hosted cache server in a remote office.

Obviously, there are advantages and disadvantages to both caching modes. With the distributed cache mode, you do not need to install servers before you can enable branch caching, but users' desktops have to maintain the cache and distribute files, which requires processing power and could adversely affect performance. With the host cache mode, you must install servers before you can enable branch caching, but after the servers are up and running, all the processing and overhead for maintaining the cache is handled by the servers, and this is a significant advantage over the distributed cache mode.

Keep the following in mind:

- Branch caching doesn't prevent users from saving files locally—it works with read requests, such as when a user requests a file from a file server.
- Branch caching works seamlessly with encryption and secure transfer technologies, such as SMB Signing and SMB Encryption.
- By default, network files are cached in the remote office only when the round-trip network latency is more than 80 milliseconds.

You install and configure BranchCache by doing the following:

- Install a BranchCache-enabled file server by adding the BranchCache For Network Files role service to the file server.
- Install a BranchCache-enabled content server (such as a web server or BITS-based applications server) by adding the BranchCache feature to the server.
- Install a hosted cache server by adding the BranchCache feature to the server in the branch office.
- Install a BranchCache-enabled client by enabling BranchCache and a Branch-Cache mode (either distributed or hosted) on the client.

You can enable and configure branch caching by completing the following steps:

1. Open a Group Policy Object for editing in the appropriate Group Policy editor. The related Administrative Templates policies for Computer Configuration are located in Network\BranchCache.

2. Double-tap or double-click Turn On BranchCache. In the Properties dialog box, select Enabled, and then tap or click OK.

3. Do one of the following:

   - To enable distributed branch caching, double-tap or double-click Set BranchCache Distributed Cache Mode. In the Properties dialog box, select Enabled, and then tap or click OK.
   - To enable hosted branch caching to support BranchCache version 1 clients, double-tap or double-click Set BranchCache Hosted Cache Mode. In the Properties dialog box, select Enabled, enter the host name of the BranchCache version 1 caching server, and then tap or click OK.
   - To enable hosted branch caching to support BranchCache version 2 clients, double-tap or double-click Configure Hosted Cache Servers. In the Properties dialog box, select Enabled and then select Show. Use the Show Contents dialog box to enter the fully qualified host name or IP address of each version 2 caching server for the office location to which the Group Policy Object will be applied. Tap or click OK twice.

NOTE If you enable the Configure Hosted Cache Server policy, Windows 8.1 clients will ignore the settings of the Set BranchCache Hosted Cache Mode policy.

REAL WORLD In a mixed environment, the different caching approaches of version 1 and version 2 of BranchCache can result in caching inefficiencies and compatibility problems. If you want Windows 8.1 clients to use version 1 rather than version 2, you can do this by enabling the Configure Client BranchCache Version Support policy and setting the related version option to Windows Vista With BITS 4.0 Installed, Windows 7, or Windows Server 2008 R2.

4. If you want to specify the network latency required to trigger caching, double-tap or double-click Configure BranchCache For Network Files. In the Properties dialog box, select Enabled. Enter the round-trip network latency above which network files must be cached. This value is specified in milliseconds. If you enter 0, files will always be cached.

5. If you enabled hosted branch caching, double-tap or double-click Set Percentage Of Disk Space Usage For Client Computer Cache. In the Properties dialog box, select Enabled. Enter the percentage of total disk space that client computers should dedicate to BranchCache, and then tap or click OK. By default, the maximum cache size is 5 percent of the total disk space.

With BranchCache version 2, it is also possible for compatible clients to search Active Directory for hosted cache servers associated with their current Active Directory site and automatically configure themselves for hosted cache mode if applicable. To do this, use the Enable Automatic Hosted Cache Discovery By Service Connection Point policy.

CHAPTER 9

Configuring and troubleshooting TCP/IP networking

This chapter focuses on managing network and wireless connections, which are used to communicate on a network. For networking to work properly, you must install networking components and configure network communications by using Dynamic Host Configuration Protocol (DHCP), Domain Name System (DNS), and Windows Internet Naming Service (WINS). DHCP is used for dynamic configuration of networking and IP address settings. Both DNS and WINS provide name resolution services. DNS is the preferred service, and WINS is maintained for backward compatibility with earlier releases of the Windows operating system.

Navigating Windows 8.1 networking features

The networking features in Windows 8.1 include:

- **Network Explorer**   Provides a central console for browsing computers and devices on the network
- **Network And Sharing Center**   Provides a central console for viewing and managing a computer's networking and sharing configurations
- **Network Diagnostics**   Provides automated diagnostics to help resolve networking problems

Before looking at how these networking tools are used, I'll discuss the Windows 8.1 features on which these tools rely: network discovery, which controls the ability to view other computers and devices, and network awareness, which reports changes in network connectivity and configuration.

Understanding network discovery and network categories

The network discovery settings of the computer with which you are working determine the computers and devices you can browse or view in Windows 8.1 networking tools. Network discovery settings work in conjunction with a computer's Windows Firewall settings to block or allow the following:

- Discovery of network computers and devices
- Discovery of your computer by others

Network discovery settings are meant to provide the appropriate level of security for each type of network to which a computer can connect. Three categories of networks are defined:

- **Domain network** Intended as a designation for a network in which computers are connected to a corporate domain to which they belong
- **Private network** Intended as a designation for a network in which computers are being used in a workgroup or homegroup and are not connected directly to the public Internet
- **Public network** Intended as a designation for a network in a public place, such as a coffee shop or airport, rather than an internal network

NOTE By default, network discovery and file sharing are not enabled, but they can be enabled on domain, work, and home networks. By using the Network window or Change Advanced Sharing Settings option in Network And Sharing Center, you can enable network discovery and file sharing. This step reduces restrictions and permits computers on the network to discover other computers and devices on that network and share files. However, by default, network discovery and file sharing are blocked on a public network. This enhances security by preventing computers on the public network from discovering other computers and devices on that network. When network discovery and file sharing are disabled, files and printers that you have shared from the computer cannot be accessed from the network. Additionally, some programs might not be able to access the network.

Because a computer saves settings separately for each category of network, you can specify different settings for blocking and allowing network traffic for each category. The first time you connect your computer to a network, Windows 8.1 attempts to determine whether you are at home, at work, or in a public location. The selection sets the network category. If you change your network connection or connect to a new network, Windows 8.1 will try to determine the category for that network. If Windows 8.1 is unable to determine the network category, it uses the public network category. If you join a computer to a domain, the network to which the computer is connected changes to a domain network.

Based on the network category, Windows 8.1 configures settings that either turn network discovery on or off. The On (enabled) state means that this computer can discover other computers and devices on the network and that other computers on the network can discover this computer. The Off (disabled) state means that this computer cannot discover other computers and devices on the network and that other computers on the network cannot discover this computer.

Sometimes Windows 8.1 assigns the public network category when a computer actually is in a private network and part of a workgroup (or prior to joining a homegroup). Typically, this problem occurs because the TCP/IP settings are improperly configured. However, even when the TCP/IP settings and the computer are properly configured, you might also experience this problem.

For networking to work properly, you will need to change the network category. Otherwise, the computer might not connect to and work with other resources on the network. Why? Windows Firewall and Windows Firewall With Advanced Security both use the network category to determine how to secure the computer. Computers have separate Windows Firewall profiles for each network category, and the strictest firewall profile is the Public profile.

One way to resolve this problem is to use the HomeGroup Troubleshooter to change the network category from Public to Private. To make this change, follow these steps:

1. In Control Panel, under Network And Internet, select Choose HomeGroup And Sharing Options. Tap or click Start The HomeGroup Troubleshooter.

2. When the troubleshooter starts, tap or click Next.

3. On the Troubleshoot Network Problems page, you should receive a message stating that some networking problems are HomeGroup-related. Choose Skip This Step.

4. The troubleshooter should detect that the network location is incorrectly set. When prompted to change the network location to private, select Apply This Fix.

5. If you are trying to create or join a homegroup, follow the prompts. Otherwise, tap or click Cancel to exit the troubleshooter.

REAL WORLD Sometimes a computer with the network category set as public will have problems joining a domain. Although the computer's TCP/IP settings can be the source of the problem, so can the firewall profile being applied. Because the Public firewall profile is the strictest by default, the settings could block connections required to join the domain. You can work around this by temporarily disabling Windows Firewall or by following the steps in the previous procedure to force Windows to change the network category from public to private.

Working with Network Explorer

Network Explorer displays a list of discovered computers and devices on the network. You can access Network Explorer in several ways:

- On the Start screen, tap or click File Explorer. In File Explorer, tap or click the location path selection button, and then tap or click Network.

- In Control Panel, tap or click Network And Internet. Under the Network And Sharing Center heading, tap or click View Network Computers And Devices.

NOTE In File Explorer, the Address Path has four interface elements: a Location Indicator icon, a Location Path Selection list button, Location Path entries, and a Previous Locations button. Be sure to tap or click the Location Path Selection list button and not the Location Indicator icon.

The network discovery settings for the computer determine which computers and devices are listed in Network Explorer. If network discovery is enabled, you'll find other computers on the network, as shown in Figure 9-1. If network discovery is blocked, you'll receive a message about this in the notification area of Network Explorer. Tapping or clicking this warning message and then selecting Turn On Network Discovery enables network discovery and opens the appropriate Windows Firewall ports so that network discovery is allowed. If no other changes have been made with regard to network discovery, the computer will be in the discovery-only state. You need to configure sharing of printers, files, and media manually, as discussed in Chapter 7, "Managing file sharing and auditing."

FIGURE 9-1 Use Network Explorer to allow network discovery and to browse resources as permitted by the current configuration.

If you have appropriate permissions, you can browse any computer or device listed in Network Explorer. Double-tap or double-click the icon for the computer to access its shared resources. Double-tap or double-click the icon for a device to access its management interface or browse its resources.

Network Explorer's toolbar provides several options:

- **Network And Sharing Center** When you want to view network status or manage network settings, tap or click Network And Sharing Center. See the next section, "Working with Network And Sharing Center," for more information.

- **Add Devices And Printers** Starts the Add A Device Wizard. Use the wizard to add a local, network, wireless, or Bluetooth printer in addition to wireless devices that were detected but not configured.

- **Search Active Directory** Opens the Find dialog box, which you can use to search for users, contacts, groups, computers, printers, shared folders, and more in Active Directory Domain Services (domain only).

Working with Network And Sharing Center

Network And Sharing Center, as shown in Figure 9-2, provides the current network status in addition to an overview of the current network configuration. In Control Panel, you can access Network And Sharing Center by tapping or clicking View Network Status And Tasks under the Network And Internet heading.

FIGURE 9-2 Use Network And Sharing Center to view the network status and details.

Network And Sharing Center lists the currently active networks by name and provides an overview of the networks. Network names are listed in bold. The value below the network name shows the category of the current network as Domain Network, Private Network, or Public Network. The Access Type specifies whether and how the computer is connected to its current network. Values for the Access Type are No Network Access, No Internet Access, or Internet. If you tap or click the name of a network connection, you can display the related status dialog box.

Tapping or clicking Change Adapter Settings displays the Network Connections page, which you can use to manage network connections. To configure sharing, tap or click Change Advanced Sharing Settings. You'll then find options for configuring the computer's sharing and network discovery settings for each network profile. To manage a profile, expand the profile's view panel by tapping or clicking the Expand button (showing a down arrow), tap or click the setting with which you want to work, and then tap or click Save Changes. To turn on or off network discovery, tap or click Turn On Network Discovery or Turn Off Network Discovery as appropriate, and then tap or click Save Changes.

From Network And Sharing Center, you can attempt to diagnose a networking problem. To do this, tap or click Troubleshoot Problems, tap or click a troubleshooter to run, such as Incoming Connections or Network Adapter, and then follow the prompts. Windows Network Diagnostics attempts to identify the network problem and provide a possible solution.

Installing networking components

If you want to install networking on a computer, you must install TCP/IP network-ing and a network adapter. Windows 8.1 uses TCP/IP as the default LAN and WAN protocol. Networking components are typically installed during Windows 8.1 installation. You can also install TCP/IP networking through the network connection Properties dialog box.

Working with TCP/IP and the Dual TCP/IP stack

The TCP and IP protocols enable computers to communicate across various net-works and the Internet by using network adapters, such as network interface cards, USB-attachable network adapters, PC Card network adapters, or built-in adapters on the motherboard. Windows 8.1 has a dual IP-layer architecture in which both Internet Protocol version 4 (IPv4) and Internet Protocol version 6 (IPv6) are imple-mented and share common Transport and Frame layers.

IPv4 and IPv6 are used in very different ways. IPv4 has 32-bit addresses and is the primary version of IP used on most networks, including the Internet. IPv6 has 128-bit addresses and is the next generation of IP.

IPv4's 32-bit addresses are commonly expressed as four separate decimal values, such as 127.0.0.1 or 192.168.1.20. The four decimal values are referred to as *octets* because each represents 8 bits of the 32-bit number. With standard unicast IPv4 addresses, a variable part of the IP address represents the network ID and an-other variable part represents the host ID. There is no correlation between a host's IPv4 address and the internal machine (MAC) address used by the host's network adapter.

IPv6's 128-bit addresses are divided into eight 16-bit blocks delimited by colons. Each 16-bit block is expressed in hexadecimal form. With standard unicast IPv6 ad-dresses, the first 64 bits represent the network ID and the last 64 bits represent the network interface. Here is an example of an IPv6 address:

FEC0:0:0:02BC:FF:BECB:FE4F:961D

Because many IPv6 address blocks are set to 0, a contiguous set of 0 blocks can be expressed as "::", a notation referred to as the *double-colon notation.* By using double-colon notation, the two 0 blocks in the previous address are compressed as follows:

FEC0::02BC:FF:BECB:FE4F:961D

If three or more 0 blocks are included, they would be compressed in the same way. For example, FFE8:0:0:0:0:0:0:1 becomes FFE8::1.

When networking hardware is detected during installation of the operating system, both IPv4 and IPv6 are enabled by default, and there is no need to install a separate component to enable support for IPv6. The modified IP architecture is referred to as the *Dual TCP/IP stack*. Table 9-1 summarizes the key TCP/IP features implemented in the Dual TCP/IP stack. Table 9-2 summarizes the key features that are specific to IPv6.

TABLE 9-1 Key TCP/IP features in the Dual TCP/IP stack

FEATURES SUPPORTED	DESCRIPTION
Automatic Black Hole Router Detection	Prevents TCP connections from terminating because of intermediate routers silently discarding large TCP segments, retransmissions, or error messages.
Automatic Dead Gateway Retry	Ensures that an unreachable gateway is checked periodically to determine whether it has become available.
Compound TCP	Optimizes TCP transfers for the sending host by increasing the amount of data sent in a connection while ensuring that other TCP connections are not affected.
Extended Selective Acknowledgments	Extends the way Selective Acknowledgments (SACKs) are used, enabling a receiver to indicate up to four noncontiguous blocks of received data and to acknowledge duplicate packets. This helps the receiver determine when it has retransmitted a segment unnecessarily and adjust its behavior to prevent future retransmissions.
Modified Fast Recovery Algorithm	Provides faster throughput by altering the way in which a sender can increase the sending rate if multiple segments in a window of data are lost and the sender receives an acknowledgment stating that only part of the data has been successfully received.
Neighbor Unreachability Detection for IPv4	Determines when neighboring nodes and routers are no longer reachable and reports the condition.
Network Diagnostics Framework	Provides an extensible framework that helps users recover from and troubleshoot problems with network connections.
Receive Window Auto Tuning	Optimizes TCP transfers for the host receiving data by automatically managing the size of the memory buffer (the receive window) to use for storing incoming data based on the current network conditions.
Routing Compartments	Prevents unwanted forwarding of traffic between interfaces by associating an interface or a set of interfaces with a logon session that has its own routing tables.
SACK-Based Loss Recovery	Makes it possible to use SACK information to perform loss recovery when duplicate acknowledgments have been received and to recover more quickly when multiple segments are not received at the destination.

FEATURES SUPPORTED	DESCRIPTION
Spurious Retransmission Timeout Detection	Provides correction for sudden, temporary increases in retransmission timeouts and prevents unnecessary retransmission of segments.
TCP Extended Statistics	Helps determine whether a performance bottleneck for a connection is the sending application, the receiving application, or the network.
Windows Filtering Platform	Provides application programming interfaces (APIs) for extending the TCP/IP filtering architecture so that it can support additional features.

TABLE 9-2 Key Dual TCP/IP stack features for IPv6

FEATURE SUPPORTED	DESCRIPTION
DHCPv6-Capable DHCP Client	Extends the DHCP client to support IPv6, and enables stateful address autoconfiguration with a DHCPv6 server.
IP Security	Enables use of Internet Key Exchange (IKE) and data encryption for IPv6.
IPv6 over Point-to-Point Protocol (PPPv6)	Allows native IPv6 traffic to be sent over PPP-based connections, which in turn enables remote access clients to connect with an IPv6-based Internet service provider (ISP) through dial-up or PPP over Ethernet (PPPoE)–based connections.
Link-Local Multicast Name Resolution (LLMNR)	Allows IPv6 hosts on a single subnet without a DNS server to resolve each other's names.
Multicast Listener Discovery version 2 (MLDv2)	Provides support for source-specific multicast traffic and is equivalent to Internet Group Management Protocol version 3 (IGMPv3) for IPv4.
Random Interface IDs	Prevents scanning of IPv6 addresses based on the known company IDs of network adapter manufacturers. By default, Windows 8.1 generates random interface IDs for nontemporary, autoconfigured IPv6 addresses, including public and link-local addresses.
Symmetric Network Address Translators	Maps the internal (private) address and port number to different external (public) addresses and ports, depending on the external destination address.

The DNS client for Windows 8.1 has a number of enhancements that improve name resolution on IPv4 and IPv6 networks. These new features include:

- **Adaptive query timeout**   With adaptive query timeout, the DNS client adapts the timeout interval based on the time required for previous queries. Thus, instead of waiting 1,000 milliseconds (ms) before timing out a query, Windows adjusts the timeout based on past performance for the network, resulting in timeouts between 25ms and 1,000ms.

- **Query coalescing**   With query coalescing, the DNS client combines multiple DNS queries for the same name. This results in only one query and optimizes performance.

- **Parallel queries**   With parallel queries, the DNS client issues IPv4 and IPv6 queries for A and AAAA records in parallel when both IP interfaces are enabled, which streamlines the query process and improves performance. Link-local multicast name resolution (LLMNR) and NetBIOS queries also are issued in parallel for IPv4 and IPv6.

- **Persistent cache**   With a persistent cache, the DNS client maintains the DNS cache across changes that occur on the same network. For example, the DNS client now persists the cache after address change notifications and when the computer is resuming from the sleep or standby state.

Installing network adapters

Network adapters are hardware devices that are used to communicate on networks. You can install and configure network adapters by completing the following steps:

1. Follow the manufacturer's instructions. For example, you might need to use the software provided by the manufacturer to modify the Interrupt setting or the Port setting of the adapter.

2. If you are installing an internal network interface card (NIC), shut down the computer, unplug it, and install the adapter card in the appropriate slot on the computer. When you've finished, plug in and start the computer.

3. Windows 8.1 should detect the new adapter during startup. If you have a separate driver disc for the adapter, you should insert it now. Otherwise, you might be prompted to insert a driver disc.

4. If Windows 8.1 doesn't detect the adapter automatically, follow the installation instructions in Chapter 8, "Managing hardware devices and drivers" of *Windows 8.1 Administration Pocket Consultant: Essentials & Configuration* by William R. Stanek (Microsoft Press, 2013).

5. If networking services aren't installed on the system, install them as described in the next section.

Installing networking services and TCP/IP

If you're installing TCP/IP after installing Windows 8.1, log on to the computer by using an account with administrator privileges, and then follow these steps:

1. In Control Panel, tap or click Network And Internet, and then tap or click Network And Sharing Center.

2. In Network And Sharing Center, under View Your Active Networks, tap or click the link for the network connection.

   TIP If the network connection you want to work with isn't active, tap or click Connect To A Network. In Network Connections, press and hold or right-click the connection you want to work with, and then tap or click Properties.

3. In the Status dialog box, tap or click Properties. This displays a Properties dialog box for the connection with the Networking tab selected, as shown in Figure 9-3.

FIGURE 9-3 Use the Properties dialog box for a connection to install and configure TCP/IP.

4. If Internet Protocol Version 6 (TCP/IPv6), Internet Protocol Version 4 (TCP/IPv4), or both aren't shown in the list of installed components, you need to install them. Tap or click Install, tap or click Protocol, and then tap or click Add. In the Select Network Protocol dialog box, select the protocol to install, and then tap or click OK. To install both TCP/IPv6 and TCP/IPv4, repeat this step.

5. In the Properties dialog box for the network connection, make sure that the following are selected, as appropriate: Internet Protocol Version 6 (TCP/IPv6), Internet Protocol Version 4 (TCP/IPv4), or both. Tap or click OK.

6. As necessary, follow the instructions in the next section for configuring network connections for the computer.

Configuring network connections

A network connection is created automatically if a computer has a network adapter and is connected to a network. If a computer has multiple network adapters and is connected to a network, a network connection is created for each adapter. If no network connection is available, you should connect the computer to the network or create a different type of connection, as explained in the "Managing network connections" section later in this chapter.

Computers use IP addresses to communicate over TCP/IP. Windows 8.1 provides the following ways to configure IP addressing:

- **Manually**   IP addresses that are assigned manually are called *static IP addresses*. Static IP addresses are fixed and don't change unless you change them. You usually assign static IP addresses to Windows servers. When you do this, you need to configure additional information to help the server navigate the network.

- **Dynamically**   A DHCP server (if one is installed on the network) assigns dynamic IP addresses at startup, and the addresses might change over time. Dynamic IP addressing is the default configuration.

- **Alternatively** (IPv4 only)   When a computer is configured to use DHCPv4 and a DHCPv4 server is not available, Windows 8.1 assigns an alternate private IP address automatically. By default, the alternate IPv4 address is in the range 169.254.0.1 to 169.254.255.254, with a subnet mask of 255.255.0.0. You can also specify a user-configured alternate IPv4 address, which is particularly useful for laptop users.

Configuring static IP addresses

When you assign a static IP address, you need to provide the computer with the IP address you want to use, the subnet mask for this IP address, and, if necessary, the default gateway to use for internetwork communications and the IP addresses of DNS servers for name resolution. An IP address is a numeric identifier for a computer. IP addressing schemes vary according to how your network is configured, but they're typically assigned based on a particular network segment.

IPv6 addresses and IPv4 addresses are very different, as discussed in the "Working with TCP/IP and the Dual TCP/IP stack" section earlier in this chapter. In IPv6, the first 64 bits represent the network ID, and the remaining 64 bits represent the network interface. In IPv4, a variable number of the initial bits represent the network ID, and the rest of the bits represent the host ID. For example, if you're working with IPv4 and a computer on the network segment 10.0.10.0 with a subnet mask of 255.255.255.0, the first three octets identify the network. The network's unique ID is 10.0.10.0. The address range you have available for computer hosts is 10.0.10.1 to 10.0.10.254. In this range, the address 10.0.10.255 is reserved for network broadcasts.

If you're on a private network (meaning a network that is indirectly connected to the Internet), you should use private IPv4 addresses. Private network IPv4 addresses are summarized in Table 9-3.

TABLE 9-3 Private IPv4 network addressing

PRIVATE NETWORK ID	SUBNET MASK	USABLE IP ADDRESS RANGE	BROADCAST ADDRESS
10.0.0.0	255.0.0.0	10.0.0.0–10.255.255.254	10.255.255.255
172.16.0.0	255.240.0.0	172.16.0.0–172.31.255.254	172.31.255.255
192.168.0.0	255.255.0.0	192.168.0.0–192.168.255.254	192.168.255.255

All other IPv4 network addresses are public and must be leased or purchased. If the network is connected directly to the Internet and you've obtained a range of IPv4 addresses from your ISP, you can use the IPv4 addresses you've been assigned.

Using the Ping command to check an address

Before you assign a static IP address, you should make sure that the address isn't already in use or reserved for use with DHCP. You can use the Ping command to find out whether an address is in use. Open a command prompt and enter **ping**, followed by the IP address you want to check.

To test the IPv4 address 10.0.10.12, you would use the following command:

```
ping 10.0.10.12
```

To test the IPv6 address FEC0::02BC:FF:BECB:FE4F:961D, you would use the following command:

```
ping FEC0::02BC:FF:BECB:FE4F:961D
```

If you receive a successful reply from the ping test, the IP address is in use and you should try another one. If the request times out for all four ping attempts, the IP address isn't active on the network at this time and probably isn't in use. However, a firewall could be blocking your ping request. Your company's network administrator should also be able to confirm whether an IP address is in use.

Configuring a static IPv4 or IPv6 address

One LAN connection is available for each network adapter installed. These connections are created automatically. To configure static IP addresses for a particular connection, complete the following steps:

1. In Control Panel, tap or click Network And Internet, and then tap or click Network And Sharing Center.
2. In Network And Sharing Center, under View Your Active Networks, tap or click the link for the network connection.
3. In the Status dialog box for the network connection, tap or click Properties. This displays the Properties dialog box for the network connection.
4. Double-tap or double-click Internet Protocol Version 6 (TCP/IPv6) or Internet Protocol Version 4 (TCP/IPv4), depending on the type of IP address you are configuring.

5. For an IPv6 address, do the following:

   ■ Tap or click Use The Following IPv6 Address, and then enter the IPv6 address in the IPv6 Address text box. The IPv6 address you assign to the computer must not be used anywhere else on the network.

   ■ The Subnet Prefix Length ensures that the computer communicates over the network properly. Windows 8.1 should insert a default value for the subnet prefix in the Subnet Prefix Length text box. If the network doesn't use variable-length subnetting, the default value should suffice. If the network does use variable-length subnets, you need to change this value as appropriate for your network.

6. For an IPv4 address, do the following:

   ■ Tap or click Use The Following IP Address, and then enter the IPv4 address in the IP Address text box. The IPv4 address you assign to the computer must not be used anywhere else on the network.

   ■ The Subnet Mask ensures that the computer communicates over the network properly. Windows 8.1 should insert a default value for the subnet mask into the Subnet Mask text box. If the network doesn't use variable-length subnetting, the default value should suffice, but if it does use variable-length subnets, you need to change this value as appropriate for your network.

7. If the computer needs to access other TCP/IP networks, the Internet, or other subnets, you must specify a default gateway. Enter the IP address for the network's default router in the Default Gateway text box.

8. DNS is needed for domain name resolution. Enter a preferred address and an alternate DNS server address in the text boxes provided.

9. When you've finished, tap or click OK twice, and then tap or click Close. Repeat this process for other network adapters and IP protocols you want to configure.

10. With IPv4 addressing, configure WINS as necessary, following the technique outlined in the "Configuring WINS resolution" section later in this chapter.

Configuring dynamic IP addresses and alternate IP addressing

Although static IP addresses can be used with workstations, most workstations use dynamic IP addressing, alternate IP addressing, or both. You configure dynamic and alternate addressing by completing the following steps:

1. In Control Panel, tap or click Network And Internet, and then tap or click Network And Sharing Center.

2. In Network And Sharing Center, under View Your Active Networks, tap or click the link for the network connection.

3. In the Status dialog box for the network connection, tap or click Properties. This displays the Properties dialog box for the network connection.

NOTE In the Status dialog box for the network connection, one LAN connection is shown for each network adapter installed. These connections are created automatically. If you don't find a LAN connection for an installed adapter, check the driver for the adapter. It might be installed incorrectly.

4. Double-tap or double-click Internet Protocol Version 6 (TCP/IPv6) or Internet Protocol Version 4 (TCP/IPv4), depending on the type of IP address you are configuring.

5. Select Obtain An IPv6 Address Automatically or Obtain An IP Address Automatically, as appropriate for the type of IP address you are configuring. If you want, select Obtain DNS Server Address Automatically or Use The Following DNS Server Addresses, and then enter a preferred and alternate DNS server address in the text boxes provided.

6. When you use dynamic IPv4 addressing with desktop computers, you should configure an automatic alternate address. To use this configuration, on the Alternate Configuration tab, be sure that Automatic Private IP Address is selected. Tap or click OK twice, tap or click Close, and then skip the remaining steps.

7. When you use dynamic IPv4 addressing with mobile computers, you usually want to configure the alternate address manually. To use this configuration, on the Alternate Configuration tab, select User Configured. Then, in the IP Address text box, enter the IP address you want to use. The IP address that you assign to the computer should be a private IP address, as shown earlier in Table 9-3, and it must not be in use anywhere else when the settings are applied.

8. With dynamic IPv4 addressing, complete the alternate configuration by entering a subnet mask, default gateway, and DNS and WINS settings. When you've finished, tap or click OK twice, and then tap or click Close.

NOTE You'll find more detailed information on configuring laptops in the "Configuring networking for mobile devices" section in Chapter 10, "Managing mobile networking and remote access."

Configuring multiple gateways

To provide fault tolerance in case of a router outage, you can configure computers running Windows 8.1 so that they use multiple default gateways. When multiple gateways are assigned, Windows 8.1 uses the gateway metric to determine which gateway is used and at what time. The gateway metric indicates the routing cost of using a gateway. The gateway with the lowest routing cost, or metric, is used first. If the computer can't communicate with this gateway, Windows 8.1 tries to use the gateway with the next lowest metric.

The best way to configure multiple gateways depends on the configuration of your network. If computers use DHCP, you probably want to configure the additional gateways through settings on the DHCP server. If computers use static IP addresses, or you want to set gateways specifically, assign them by completing the following steps:

1. In Control Panel, tap or click Network And Internet, and then tap or click Network And Sharing Center.

2. In Network And Sharing Center, under View Your Active Networks, tap or click the link for the network connection.

3. In the Status dialog box for the network connection, tap or click Properties. This displays the Properties dialog box for the network connection.

4. Double-tap or double-click Internet Protocol Version 6 (TCP/IPv6) or Internet Protocol Version 4 (TCP/IPv4), depending on the type of IP address you are configuring.

5. Tap or click Advanced to open the Advanced TCP/IP Settings dialog box, as shown in Figure 9-4.

FIGURE 9-4 Use the Advanced TCP/IP Settings dialog box to configure multiple IP addresses and gateways (for IPv4 on the left, and IPv6 on the right).

6. The Default Gateways area shows the current gateways that have been manually configured (if any). You can enter additional default gateways as necessary. Tap or click Add, and then enter the gateway address in the Gateway text box.

7. By default, Windows 8.1 automatically assigns a metric to the gateway. You can also assign the metric manually. To do this, clear the Automatic Metric check box, and then enter a metric in the text box provided.

8. Tap or click Add, and then repeat steps 6 and 7 for each gateway you want to add.

9. Tap or click OK three times, and then tap or click Close.

Configuring DNS resolution

DNS is a host name resolution service that you can use to determine the IP address of a computer from its host name. This enables users to work with host names, such as *http://www.msn.com* or *http://www.microsoft.com,* rather than an IP address, such as 192.168.5.102 or 192.168.12.68. DNS is the primary name service for Windows 8.1 and the Internet.

As with gateways, the best way to configure DNS depends on the configuration of your network. If computers use DHCP, you'll probably want to configure DNS through settings on the DHCP server. If computers use static IP addresses, or you want to specifically configure DNS for an individual user or system, you should configure DNS manually.

Basic DNS settings

You can configure basic DNS settings by completing the following steps:

1. In Control Panel, tap or click Network And Internet, and then tap or click Network And Sharing Center.

2. In Network And Sharing Center, under View Your Active Networks, tap or click the link for the network connection.

3. In the Status dialog box for the network connection, tap or click Properties. This displays the Properties dialog box for the network connection.

4. Double-tap or double-click Internet Protocol Version 6 (TCP/IPv6) or Internet Protocol Version 4 (TCP/IPv4), depending on the type of IP address for which you are configuring DNS.

5. If the computer is using DHCP and you want DHCP to specify the DNS server address, select Obtain DNS Server Address Automatically. Otherwise, select Use The Following DNS Server Addresses, and then enter a primary and an alternate DNS server address in the text boxes provided.

6. Tap or click OK twice, and then tap or click Close.

Advanced DNS settings

You configure advanced DNS settings by using the DNS tab of the Advanced TCP/IP Settings dialog box, as shown in Figure 9-5. You use the options on the DNS tab as follows:

- **DNS Server Addresses, In Order Of Use**   Use this area to specify the IP address of each DNS server that is used for domain name resolution. Tap or click Add if you want to add a server IP address to the list. Tap or click Remove to remove a selected server address from the list. Tap or click Edit to edit the selected entry. You can specify multiple servers for DNS resolution. Their priority is determined by the order. If the first server isn't available to respond to a host name resolution request, the next DNS server in the list is accessed, and so on. To change the position of a server in the list, select it, and then use the up arrow or down arrow button.

FIGURE 9-5 Use the DNS tab of the Advanced TCP/IP Settings dialog box to configure advanced DNS settings (for IPv4 on the left, and IPv6 on the right).

- **Append Primary And Connection Specific DNS Suffixes**   This option is typically selected by default. Use this option to resolve unqualified computer names in the primary domain. For example, if the computer name Gandolf is used, and the parent domain is microsoft.com, the computer name would resolve to gandolf.microsoft.com. If the fully qualified computer name doesn't exist in the parent domain, the query fails. The parent domain used is the one set in the System Properties dialog box on the Computer Name tab. (To check the settings, tap or click System And Security in Control Panel, and then tap or click System.)

- **Append Parent Suffixes Of The Primary DNS Suffix**   This option is selected by default. Use this option to resolve unqualified computer names by using the parent/child domain hierarchy. If a query fails in the immediate parent domain, the suffix for the parent of the parent domain is used to try to resolve the query. This process continues until the top of the DNS domain hierarchy is reached. For example, if the computer name Gandolf is used in the dev.microsoft.com domain, DNS would attempt to resolve the computer name to gandolf.dev.microsoft.com. If this didn't work, DNS would attempt to resolve the computer name to gandolf.microsoft.com.

- **Append These DNS Suffixes (In Order)**   Select this option to specify DNS suffixes to use for name resolution rather than resolving names through the parent domain. Tap or click Add if you want to add a domain suffix to the list. Tap or click Remove to remove a selected domain suffix from the list. Tap or click Edit to edit the selected entry. You can specify multiple domain suffixes, which are used in order. If the first suffix doesn't resolve properly, DNS attempts to use the next suffix in the list. If this fails, the next suffix is used, and so on. To change the order of the domain suffixes, select the suffix, and then use the up arrow or down arrow button to change its position.

- **DNS Suffix For This Connection** This option sets a specific DNS suffix for the connection that overrides DNS names already configured for this connection. However, you'll usually set the DNS domain name by tapping or clicking System And Security in Control Panel, tapping or clicking System, and then tapping or clicking Change Settings. In the System Properties dialog box, tap or click Change on the Computer Name tab, and then tap or click More. You can now enter the primary DNS suffix for the computer in the text box provided. Tap or click OK three times to save your changes.

- **Register This Connection's Addresses In DNS** Use this option if you want all IP addresses for this connection to be registered in DNS under the computer's fully qualified domain name. This option is selected by default.

  Dynamic DNS updates are used in conjunction with DHCP to enable a client to update its A (Host Address) record if its IP address changes and to enable the DHCP server to update the PTR (Pointer) record for the client on the DNS server. DHCP servers can also be configured to update both the A and PTR records on the client's behalf. Dynamic DNS updates are supported only by BIND 5.1 or later DNS servers, in addition to all current versions of Windows Server.

- **Use This Connection's DNS Suffix In DNS Registration** Select this option if you want all IP addresses for this connection to be registered in DNS under the parent domain.

Configuring WINS resolution

WINS is a name-resolution service that resolves computer names to IPv4 addresses. Using WINS, the computer name PC18, for example, could be resolved to an IP address that enables computers on a Microsoft network to find one another and transfer information. WINS is needed to support applications that use NetBIOS over TCP/IP, such as Microsoft Exchange Server 2003, the .NET command-line utilities, and network browsing for users in environments prior to Windows Vista and Windows Server 2008. If you don't have NetBIOS applications on the network or infrastructure prior to Windows Vista or Windows Server 2008, you don't need to use WINS.

You can also configure Windows 8.1–based computers to use the local file LMHOSTS to resolve NetBIOS computer names. However, LMHOSTS is consulted only if standard name resolution methods fail. In a properly configured network, these files are rarely used. Thus, the preferred method of NetBIOS computer-name resolution is WINS in conjunction with a WINS server.

As with gateways and DNS, the best way to configure WINS depends on the configuration of your network. If computers use DHCP, you'll probably want to configure WINS through settings on the DHCP server. If computers use static IPv4 addresses, or you want to configure WINS specifically for an individual user or system, you should configure WINS manually.

You can manually configure WINS by completing the following steps:

1. Open the Advanced TCP/IP Settings dialog box, and then tap or click the WINS tab. You'll find the WINS Addresses, In Order Of Use area, as shown in Figure 9-6.

FIGURE 9-6 In IPv4, use the WINS tab of the Advanced TCP/IP Settings dialog box to configure WINS resolution for NetBIOS computer names.

2. In the WINS Addresses, In Order Of Use area, specify the IPv4 address of each WINS server that is used for NetBIOS name resolution. Tap or click Add if you want to add a server IPv4 address to the list. Tap or click Remove to remove a selected server from the list. Tap or click Edit to edit the selected entry.

3. You can specify multiple servers, which are used in order, for WINS resolution. If the first server isn't available to respond to a NetBIOS name resolution request, the next WINS server in the list is accessed, and so on. To change the position of a server in the list, select it, and then use the up arrow or down arrow button.

4. To enable LMHOSTS lookups, select the Enable LMHOSTS Lookup check box. If you want the computer to use an existing LMHOSTS file defined somewhere on the network, retrieve this file by tapping or clicking Import LMHOSTS. You generally will use LMHOSTS only when other name resolution methods fail.

5. WINS name resolution requires NetBIOS Over TCP/IP services. Select one of the following options to configure WINS name resolution by using NetBIOS:

   ■ If you use DHCP and dynamic addressing, you can get the NetBIOS setting from the DHCP server. Select Default: Use NetBIOS Setting From The DHCP Server.

   ■ If you use a static IP address or the DHCP server does not provide NetBIOS settings, select Enable NetBIOS Over TCP/IP.

   ■ If WINS and NetBIOS are not used on the network, select Disable NetBIOS Over TCP/IP. This eliminates the NetBIOS broadcasts that would otherwise be sent by the computer.

6. Tap or click OK three times, and then tap or click Close. As necessary, repeat this process for other network adapters.

TIP LMHOSTS files are maintained locally on a computer-by-computer basis, which can eventually make them unreliable. Rather than relying on LMHOSTS, be sure that your DNS and WINS servers are configured properly and are accessible to the network for centralized administration of name resolution services.

Managing network connections

Network connections enable computers to access resources on the network and the Internet. One network connection is created automatically for each network adapter installed on a computer. This section examines techniques that you can use to manage these connections.

Enabling and disabling network connections

Network connections are created and enabled automatically. If you want to disable a connection so that it cannot be used, complete the following steps:

1. In Control Panel, tap or click Network And Internet, and then tap or click Network And Sharing Center.

2. In Network And Sharing Center, in the left pane, tap or click Change Adapter Settings.

3. In Network Connections, press and hold or right-click the connection, and then tap or click Disable.

4. Later, if you want to enable the connection, press and hold or right-click the connection, and then tap or click Enable.

If you want to disconnect from a network or start another connection, complete the following steps:

1. In Control Panel, tap or click Network And Internet, and then tap or click Network And Sharing Center.

2. In Network And Sharing Center, in the left pane, tap or click Change Adapter Settings.

3. In Network Connections, press and hold or right-click the connection, and then tap or click Disconnect. Typically, only remote access connections have a Disconnect option.

4. Later, if you want to activate the connection, press and hold or right-click the connection in Network Connections, and then tap or click Connect.

Checking the status, speed, and activity for network connections

To check the status of a network connection, follow these steps:

1. In Control Panel, tap or click Network And Internet, and then tap or click Network And Sharing Center.

2. In Network And Sharing Center, under View Your Active Networks, tap or click the link for the network connection.

3. This displays the Status dialog box for the network connection. If the connection is disabled or the media is unplugged, you won't be able to access this dialog box. Enable the connection or connect the network cable to resolve the problem, and then try to display the Status dialog box again.

The General tab of the Status dialog box for the network connection, as shown in Figure 9-7, provides useful information about the following:

- **IPv4 Connectivity**   The current IPv4 connection state and type. The status typically appears as Local when you are connected to an internal network, Internet when a computer can access the Internet, or No Internet Access when not connected to a network.

- **IPv6 Connectivity**   The current IPv6 connection state and type. The status typically appears as Local when you are connected to an internal network, Internet when a computer can access the Internet, or No Internet Access when not connected to a network.

- **Media State**   The state of the media. Because the Status dialog box is available only when the connection is enabled, this usually appears as Enabled.

- **Duration**   The amount of time the connection has been established. If the duration is fairly short, the user either recently connected to the network or the connection was recently reset.

- **Speed**   The speed of the connection. This should read 10.0 Mbps for 10–megabits-per-second (Mbps) connections, 100.0 Mbps for 100-Mbps connections, and 1.0 Gbps for 1–gigabit-per-second (Gbps) connections. An incorrect setting can affect the computer's performance.

- **Bytes**   The number of bytes sent and the number received by the connection. As the computer sends or receives packets, you'll notice the computer icons indicate the flow of traffic.

FIGURE 9-7 The General tab of the Status dialog box for the selected network connection provides access to summary information regarding connections, properties, and support.

Viewing network configuration information

In Windows 8.1, you can view the current configuration for network adapters in several ways. To view configuration settings by using the Status dialog box, follow these steps:

1. In Control Panel, tap or click Network And Internet, and then tap or click Network And Sharing Center.

2. In Network And Sharing Center, in the left pane, tap or click Change Adapter Settings.

3. In Network Connections, double-tap or double-click the connection. This displays the Status dialog box for the network connection. If the connection is disabled or the media is unplugged, you won't be able to access this dialog box. Enable the connection or connect the network cable to resolve the problem, and then try to display the Status dialog box again.

4. Tap or click Details to view detailed information about the IP address configuration, including the following:

   - **Physical Address**   The machine or media access control (MAC) address of the network adapter. This address is unique for each network adapter.
   - **IPv4 Address**   The IPv4 address assigned for IPv4 networking.
   - **IPv4 Subnet Mask**   The subnet mask used for IPv4 networking.
   - **IPv4 Default Gateway**   The IPv4 address of the default gateway used for IPv4 networking.
   - **IPv4 DNS Servers**   The IP addresses for DNS servers used with IPv4 networking.

- **IPv4 WINS Server**   The IP addresses of the WINS server used with IPv4 networking.

- **IPv4 DHCP Server**   The IP address of the DHCPv4 server from which the current lease was obtained (DHCPv4 only).

- **Lease Obtained**   A date and time stamp for when the DHCPv4 lease was obtained (DHCPv4 only).

- **Lease Expires**   A date and time stamp for when the DHCPv4 lease expires (DHCPv4 only).

You can also use the Ipconfig command to view advanced configuration settings by following these steps:

1. Open a command prompt. One way to do this is to enter **cmd** in the Apps Search box, and then press Enter.

2. At the command line, enter **ipconfig /all** to receive detailed configuration information for all network adapters configured on the computer.

NOTE The command prompt is started in standard user mode. This is not an elevated command prompt.

Renaming network connections

Windows 8.1 initially assigns default names for network connections. In Network Connections, you can rename a connection by pressing and holding or right-clicking the connection, tapping or clicking Rename, and then entering a new connection name. If a computer has multiple network connections, proper naming can help you and others better understand the uses of a particular connection. Access Network Connections by tapping or clicking Change Adapter Settings in Network And Sharing Center.

Troubleshooting and testing network settings

Windows 8.1 includes many tools for troubleshooting and testing TCP/IP connectivity. The following sections look at automated diagnostics, basic tests that you should perform whenever you install or modify a computer's network settings, and techniques for resolving difficult networking problems involving DHCP and DNS. The final section shows you how to perform detailed network diagnostics testing.

Diagnosing and resolving network connection problems

Occasionally, network cables can become unplugged or the network adapter might experience a problem that temporarily prevents it from working. After you plug the cable back in or solve the adapter problem, the connection should automatically reconnect. You can diagnose network connection problems by pressing and holding or right-clicking the Network notification icon on the taskbar and tapping or clicking Troubleshoot Problems.

Windows Network Diagnostics then tries to identify the problem. Another way to start Windows Network Diagnostics is to press and hold or right-click the connection in Network Connections, and then tap or click Diagnose.

As shown in Figure 9-8, a list of possible solutions is provided if identifiable con-figuration problems are detected. Some solutions provide automated fixes that can be executed by tapping or clicking the solution. Other solutions require manual fixes, such as resetting a network router or a broadband modem. If your actions don't fix the problem, refer to other appropriate parts of this troubleshooting section.

FIGURE 9-8 Resolve the problem by making a selection or performing a required action.

Diagnosing and resolving Internet connection problems

Because services, protocols, and configuration settings have so many interdepen-dencies, troubleshooting network problems can be difficult. Fortunately, Windows 8.1 includes a powerful network diagnostics tool for pinpointing problems that relate to the following:

- General network connectivity problems
- Internet service settings for email, newsgroups, and proxies
- Settings for modems, network clients, and network adapters
- DNS, DHCP, and WINS configuration
- Default gateways and IP addresses

In Network And Sharing Center, you can diagnose connection problems by tap-ping or clicking Troubleshoot Problems, and then tapping or clicking a troubleshooter to run, such as Network Adapter, Incoming Connections, or Internet Connection.

The troubleshooter then tries to identify the problem. If identifiable configura-tion problems exist, a list of possible solutions is provided. Some solutions provide automated fixes that can be executed by tapping or clicking the solution. Other solutions require manual fixes, such as resetting a network router or a broadband modem. If your actions don't fix the problem, refer to other appropriate parts of this troubleshooting section.

Performing basic network tests

Whenever you install a new computer or make configuration changes to a computer's network settings, you should test the configuration. The most basic TCP/IP test is to use the Ping command to test the computer's connection to the network. To use it, enter **ping** *<host>* at the command prompt, where *<host>* is either the computer name or the IP address of the host computer you're trying to reach.

With Windows 8.1, you can use the Ping command in the following ways to test the configuration:

- **Try to ping IP addresses**   If the computer is configured correctly and the host you're trying to reach is accessible to the network, Ping should receive a reply, if pinging is allowed by the computer's firewall. If Ping can't reach the host or is blocked by a firewall, Ping times out.

- **On domains that use WINS, try to ping NetBIOS computer names**   If NetBIOS computer names are resolved correctly by Ping, the NetBIOS facilities, such as WINS, are correctly configured for the computer.

- **On domains that use DNS, try to ping DNS host names**   If fully qualified DNS host names are resolved correctly by Ping, DNS name resolution is configured properly.

You might also want to test network browsing for the computer. If the computer is a member of a Windows 8.1 domain and computer browsing is enabled throughout the domain, log on to the computer and then use File Explorer or Network Explorer to browse other computers in the domain. Afterward, log on to a different computer in the domain and try to browse the computer you just configured. These tests tell you whether DNS resolution is being handled properly in the local environment. If you can't browse, check the configuration of the DNS services and protocols.

> **REAL WORLD**   Access to network resources in Network Explorer is dependent on the Computer Browser service and the network discovery settings. The Computer Browser service is responsible for maintaining a list of computers on a network. If the service is stopped or isn't working properly, a computer won't view available resources in Network Explorer. You can check the status of the Computer Browser service in Computer Management. Expand Services And Applications, and then select Services in the left pane. The status of the Computer Browser service should be Started. If the status is blank, the service isn't running and should be started.

In some cases, the Computer Browser service might be running as usual, but there might not be an updated list of resources in Network Explorer. This can happen because the service performs periodic updates of the resource list rather than checking continuously for updates. If a resource you want to use isn't listed, you can wait for it to become available (which should take less than 15 minutes in most cases), or you can connect to the resource directly by using the Universal Naming Convention (UNC) name or IP address of the resource, as discussed in the "Using and accessing shared resources" section in Chapter 7.

In some cases, discovering and sharing might be set to block network discovery. You need to enable network discovery to resolve this by following these steps:

1. In Control Panel, tap or click View Network Status And Tasks under the Network And Internet heading.

2. In Network And Sharing Center, in the left pane, tap or click Change Advanced Sharing Settings.

3. You'll then view options for configuring the computer's sharing and network discovery settings for each network profile. Manage the settings for each profile, as appropriate. For example, if network discovery is disabled for a profile and should be enabled, tap or click the related Turn On Network Discovery option.

4. Tap or click Save Changes.

Resolving IP addressing problems

The current IP address settings of a computer can be obtained as described in the "Viewing network configuration information" section earlier in this chapter. If a computer is having problems accessing network resources or communicating with other computers, an IP addressing problem might exist. Take a close look at the IP address currently assigned, in addition to other IP address settings, and use the following pointers to help in your troubleshooting:

- If the IPv4 address currently assigned to the computer is in the range 169.254.0.1 to 169.254.255.254, the computer is using Automatic Private IP Addressing (APIPA). An automatic private IP address is assigned to a computer when it is configured to use DHCP, and its DHCP client cannot reach a DHCP server. When using APIPA, Windows 8.1 will periodically check for a DHCP server to become available. If a computer doesn't eventually obtain a dynamic IP address, this usually means the network connection has a problem. Check the network cable and, if necessary, trace the cable back to the switch or hub to which it is connected. You also should check the status of the DHCP server to verify that it's running.

- If the IPv4 address and the subnet mask of the computer are currently set as 0.0.0.0, the network is either disconnected or someone attempted to use a static IP address that duplicated another IP address already in use on the network. In this case, you should access Network Connections and determine the state of the connection. If the connection is disabled or disconnected, this status should be shown. Press and hold or right-click the connection, and then tap or click Enable or Repair. If the connection is already enabled, you need to modify the IP address settings for the connection.

- If the IP address is dynamically assigned, check to be sure that another computer on the network isn't using the same IP address. You can do this by disconnecting the network cable for the computer that you are troubleshooting and then pinging the IP address in question from another computer. If you receive a response from the Ping command, you know that another computer is using the IP address. This computer probably has an improper static IP address or a reservation that isn't set up properly.

- If the IP address appears to be set correctly, check the network mask, gateway, DNS, and WINS settings by comparing the network settings of the computer you are troubleshooting with those of a computer that is known to have a good network configuration. One of the biggest problem areas is the network mask. When subnetting is used, the network mask for one area of the network might be very similar to that of another area. For example, the network mask in one IPv4 area might be 255.255.255.240, and it might be 255.255.255.248 in another IPv4 area.

Releasing and renewing DHCP settings

DHCP servers can assign many network configuration settings automatically. These include IP addresses, default gateways, primary and secondary DNS servers, primary and secondary WINS servers, and more. When computers use dynamic addressing, they are assigned a lease on a specific IP address. This lease is good for a specific time period and must be renewed periodically. When the lease needs to be renewed, the computer contacts the DHCP server that provided the lease. If the server is available, the lease is renewed and a new lease period is granted. You can also renew leases manually on individual computers or by using the DHCP server itself.

Problems can occur during the lease assignment and renewal process that prevent network communications. If the server isn't available and cannot be reached before a lease expires, the IP address can become invalid. If this happens, the computer might use the alternate IP address configuration to set an alternate address, which in most cases has settings that are inappropriate and prevent proper communications. To resolve this problem, you need to release and then renew the DHCP lease.

Another type of problem occurs when users move around to various offices and subnets within an organization. In being moved from location to location, their computers might obtain DHCP settings from the wrong server. When the users return to their offices, the computers might seem sluggish or perform incorrectly due to the settings assigned by the DHCP server at another location. If this happens, you need to release and then renew the DHCP lease.

You can release and renew DHCP leases by completing the following tasks:

1. In Network And Sharing Center, in the left pane, tap or click Change Adapter Settings.

2. In Network Connections, press and hold or right-click the connection with which you want to work, and then tap or click Diagnose.

3. After Windows Network Diagnostics tries to identify the problem, a list of possible solutions is provided. If the computer has one or more dynamically assigned IP addresses, one of the solutions should be Automatically Get New IP Settings. Tap or click this option.

You can also follow these steps to use the Ipconfig command to release and renew settings:

1. Open an elevated command prompt. One way to do this is to enter **cmd** in the Apps Search box, press and hold or right-click Command Prompt on the Apps screen, and then tap or click Run As Administrator.

2. To release the current settings for all network adapters, enter **ipconfig /release** at the command line. Then renew the lease by entering **ipconfig /renew**.

3. To only renew a DHCP lease for all network adapters, enter **ipconfig /renew** at the command line.

4. You can check the updated settings by entering **ipconfig /all** at the command line.

REAL WORLD If you don't release the old DHCP settings before trying to renew the DHCP settings, the computer will try to renew the settings on the network to which it was last connected. If the computer is on a new network, the computer might not be able to establish a connection to the server or device that assigned the DHCP settings previously.

If a computer has multiple network adapters and you want to work with only one or a subset of the adapters, you can do this by specifying all or part of the connection name after the ipconfig /renew or ipconfig /release command. Use the asterisk as a wildcard character to match any characters in a connection's name. For example, if you want to renew the lease for all connections with names starting with Loc, you can enter the command ipconfig /renew Loc*. If you want to release the settings for all connections containing the word Network, you can enter the command ipconfig /release *Network*.

Registering and flushing DNS

The DNS resolver cache maintains a history of DNS lookups that have been performed when a user accesses network resources by using TCP/IP. This cache contains forward lookups, which provide host-name-to-IP-address resolution, and reverse lookups, which provide IP-address-to-host-name resolution. After a DNS entry is stored in the resolver cache for a particular DNS host, the local computer no longer has to query external servers for DNS information on that host. This enables the computer to resolve DNS requests locally, which provides a quicker response.

The period of time in which entries are stored in the resolver cache depends on the Time to Live (TTL) value assigned to the record by the originating server. To view current records and find the remaining TTL value for each record, in an elevated command prompt, enter **ipconfig /displaydns**. These values are given as the number of seconds that a particular record can remain in the cache before it expires. These values are continually being counted down by the local computer. When the TTL value reaches 0, the record expires and is removed from the resolver cache.

Occasionally, you'll find that the resolver cache needs to be cleared to remove old entries and enable computers to check for updated DNS entries before the usual expiration and purging process takes place. Typically, this happens because server

IP addresses have changed, and the current entries in the resolver cache point to the old addresses rather than the new ones. Sometimes the resolver cache itself can become out of sync, particularly when DHCP has been misconfigured.

REAL WORLD   Skilled administrators know that several weeks in advance of the actual change, they should start to decrease the TTL values for DNS records that are going to be changed. Typically, this means reducing the TTL from a number of days (or weeks) to a number of hours, which allows for quicker propagation of the changes to computers that have cached the related DNS records. After the change is complete, administrators should restore the original TTL value to reduce renewal requests.

In most cases, you can resolve problems with the DNS resolver cache by flushing the cache or reregistering DNS. When you flush the resolver cache, all DNS entries are cleared out of the cache and new entries are not created until the next time the computer performs a DNS lookup on a particular host or IP address. When you reregister DNS, Windows 8.1 attempts to refresh all current DHCP leases and then performs a lookup on each DNS entry in the resolver cache. By looking up each host or IP address again, the computer renews and reregisters the entries in the resolver cache. You'll generally want to flush the cache completely and enable the computer to perform lookups as needed. Reregister DNS only when you suspect that there are problems with DHCP and the DNS resolver cache.

You can use the Ipconfig command to flush and reregister entries in the DNS resolver cache by following these steps:

1. Open an elevated command prompt. One way to do this is to enter **cmd** in the Apps Search box, press and hold or right-click Command Prompt on the Apps screen, and then tap or click Run As Administrator.

2. To clear out the resolver cache, enter **ipconfig /flushdns** at the command line.

3. To renew DHCP leases and reregister DNS entries, enter **ipconfig /registerdns** at the command line.

4. When the tasks are complete, you can check your work by entering **ipconfig /displaydns** at the command line.

Managing mobile networking and remote access

Users often want to connect to their organization's network from an off-site computer. To do so, they need a dial-up, broadband, virtual private network (VPN), or DirectAccess connection. Dial-up networking enables users to connect off-site computers to their organization's network by using a modem and a standard telephone line. Broadband enables users to connect off-site computers to their organization's network by using high-speed Digital Subscriber Line (DSL) routers or cable modems. VPN and DirectAccess use encryption to provide secure connectivity over an existing connection, which can be a local area, dial-up, or broadband connection. Increasingly, wireless connections are also being used. With a wireless connection, computers establish connections by using a network adapter that has an antenna that enables it to communicate with similar wireless devices.

Configuring networking for mobile devices

Most mobile devices need more than one network configuration: one for the office, one for home, and maybe another for when the user is traveling. At the office, the mobile device uses settings that are assigned by a DHCP server on the corporate network. At home, the mobile device uses different network settings to communicate on the home network and access a shared printer and a broadband Internet device. In some cases, a mobile device might need a configuration that makes a Wi-Fi connection when the user is away from his or her desk, and a configuration that uses DHCP when the mobile device is physically connected to the network, or vice versa. When a system uses DHCP to obtain its primary network settings, you can configure alternate network settings for those times when a DHCP server isn't available, such as when the user is traveling or at home. Systems can use alternate configurations either automatically or through user interaction. When in meeting rooms or elsewhere on the go, mobile device users are also likely to need to connect to networked projectors, a task for which the Connect To A Network Projector Wizard provides an easy solution.

Working with mobility settings

Windows Mobility Center, shown in Figure 10-1, provides a single location for managing important settings for mobile devices and includes a series of control tiles that provide quick access to the commonly used settings. On a mobile device, you can access Windows Mobility Center by pressing and holding or right-clicking the Power icon in the taskbar's notification area and then tapping or clicking Windows Mobility Center. In Control Panel, you can open Mobility Center by selecting Adjust Commonly Used Mobility Settings under the Hardware And Sound heading.

FIGURE 10-1 Manage important settings for mobile devices.

The control tiles of Windows Mobility Center enable you to adjust mobility settings by using options such as sliders to adjust the display's brightness, a selection list to change the power plan, and a toggle button to turn presentation settings on or off. Although the set of control tiles available depends on the type of mobile device and the manufacturer, the following are the most common control tiles:

- **Battery Status** Shows the status of the mobile device's battery. You can use the selection list provided to change from one power plan to another. If you've created any custom power plans, these are also available. Tap or click the related icon to open the Power Options page in Control Panel.

- **Brightness**   Enables you to manage the brightness setting for the display. If brightness is configurable on the mobile device, use the slider to adjust the brightness. Tap or click the related icon to open the Power Options page in Control Panel. Note that the Power icon in the notifications area of the taskbar has similar options. Note that the Settings panel also has a Brightness control.

- **External Display**   Enables you to connect to a secondary display device, which might be necessary to give a presentation. Tap or click Connect Display to access a secondary display device connected through a cable. Tap or click the related icon to open the Screen Resolution page in Control Panel.

- **Presentation Settings**   Enables you to turn presentation mode on or off. In presentation mode, the mobile device's display and hard disk do not enter sleep mode when the computer is inactive. Tap or click Turn On to enter presentation mode. Tap or click the related icon to open the Presentation Settings dialog box.

- **Sync Center**   Enables you to view the status of file synchronization and initiate syncing. Tap or click Sync to start a new sync by using Sync Center. Tap or click the related icon to open the Sync Center page in Control Panel.

- **Volume**   Enables you to manage the current volume setting. If volume is configurable on your mobile device, use the slider to adjust the volume. Select Mute to mute the sound. Tap or click the related icon to open the Sound dialog box. Note that the Volume icon in the notifications area of the taskbar has similar options.

NOTE Some mobile device manufacturers customize Windows Mobility Center by adding their own control tiles to extend these common options. For example, some HP mobile devices include the HP Wireless Assistant control tile, which you can use to configure wireless networking settings for the integrated wireless device.

Travelling users will want to know how to turn off networking quickly. There are several ways to do this but the easiest is to turn on Airplane Mode. When Airplane Mode is on, all networking is temporarily disabled. When you later turn Airplane Mode off, all networking is re-enabled. To turn on Airplane Mode, open the Networks pane by tapping or clicking the Network icon in the notification area of the task bar. Enable Airplane Mode by tapping or clicking the related option. Airplane Mode should then be set to On.

You also can turn Airplane Mode on by following these steps:

1. Slide in from the right side of the screen, or press Windows key + I.

2. Tap or click the icon for the current network.

3. Tap or click the Airplane Mode toggle switch, which should be set to On.

If you repeat either procedure, the next time you tap or click the Airplane Mode toggle, the mode should be set to Off.

Configuring dynamic IP addresses

DHCP gives you centralized control over IP addresses and TCP/IP default settings. If a network has a DHCP server, you can assign a dynamic IP address to any of the network adapter cards on a computer. Afterward, you rely on the DHCP server to supply the basic information necessary for TCP/IP networking. To enable dynamic IP addressing for both IPv4 and IPv6, separate DHCP services must be set up for both IPv4 and IPv6.

To configure dynamic IP addresses, complete these steps:

1. In Control Panel, tap or click View Network Status And Tasks under the Network And Internet heading.

2. In the left pane in Network And Sharing Center, tap or click Change Adapter Settings.

3. Network Connections displays a list of all network connections configured for use on the computer. Press and hold or right-click the connection you want to configure, and then tap or click Properties.

4. Double-tap or double-click Internet Protocol Version 4 (TCP/IPv4), or select Internet Protocol Version 4 (TCP/IPv4), and then tap or click Properties. This displays the Internet Protocol Version 4 (TCP/IPv4) Properties dialog box, as shown in Figure 10-2.

FIGURE 10-2 To use DHCP, configure the computer to obtain an IP address automatically.

5. Select Obtain An IP Address Automatically. You can also select Obtain DNS Server Address Automatically, or select Use The Following DNS Server Addresses, and then enter preferred and alternate Domain Name System (DNS) server addresses in the text boxes provided.

6. Tap or click OK.

7. If your organization or network uses IPv6, double-tap or double-click Internet Protocol Version 6 (TCP/IPv6). Select Obtain An IPv6 Address Automatically. You can also select Obtain DNS Server Address Automatically, or select Use The Following DNS Server Addresses, and then enter preferred and alternate DNS server addresses. Tap or click OK.

8. Configure alternate private IP addressing as necessary (as discussed in the next section).

Configuring alternate private IP addresses

Only IPv4 connections have alternate configurations. When you use DHCP with an IPv4 connection, an automatic private IP address is assigned when the DHCP server can't be reached during startup or when the current IP address lease expires. The automatic private IP address is in the range 169.254.0.1 to 169.254.255.254, with a subnet mask of 255.255.0.0. Because the automatic private IP address configuration does not include default gateway, DNS, or WINS server settings, a computer using the alternate IP addressing is isolated on a separate network segment in the Automatic Private IP Addressing (APIPA) range.

If you want to ensure that a computer uses specific IP address and network configuration settings when a DHCP server is not available, you need to specify an alternate configuration. One of the key reasons for using an alternate configuration is to accommodate mobile device users who take their computers home from work. In this way, the user's mobile device can be configured to use a dynamically assigned IP address at work and an alternate IP address configuration at home. Before you get started, you might want to ask users for their home networking settings, including the IP address, gateway, and DNS server addresses required by their Internet service provider (ISP).

To configure alternate private IP addresses, complete the following steps:

1. In Control Panel, tap or click View Network Status And Tasks under the Network And Internet heading.

2. In the left pane in Network And Sharing Center, tap or click Change Adapter Settings.

3. Network Connections displays a list of all network connections configured for use on the computer. Press and hold or right-click the connection you want to configure, and then tap or click Properties.

4. Double-tap or double-click Internet Protocol Version 4 (TCP/IPv4) to open the Internet Protocol Version 4 (TCP/IPv4) Properties dialog box. You can also select Internet Protocol Version 4 (TCP/IPv4), and then tap or click Properties.

5. If you have already configured the adapter to obtain an IP address automatically, you should be able to tap or click the Alternate Configuration tab, as shown in Figure 10-3.

FIGURE 10-3 Use the Alternate Configuration tab to configure private IP addresses for the computer.

6. On the Alternate Configuration tab, select the User Configured option. Then, in the IP Address text box, enter the IP address you want to use. The IP address you assign to the computer should be a private IP address, and it must not be in use anywhere else at the time the settings are applied. Private IP addresses are typically in the range 10.0.0.1 to 10.255.255.254, 172.16.0.1 to 172.31.255.254, or 192.168.0.1 to 192.168.255.254 (excluding IP addresses reserved for network IDs and broadcasts).

7. The subnet mask ensures that the computer communicates over the network properly. Windows 8.1 should insert a default value into the box for the subnet mask. If the network doesn't use subnets, the default value should suffice. However, if the network does use subnets, you need to change this value as appropriate for the target network.

8. If the computer needs to access other TCP/IP networks, the Internet, or other subnets, you must specify a default gateway. Enter the IP address of the network's default router in the Default Gateway box.

9. DNS servers are needed for domain name resolution. Enter a preferred and an alternate DNS server address in the boxes provided.

10. If WINS is used on the network for compatibility with previous versions of Windows, configure a preferred and an alternate WINS server by using the boxes provided.

11. When you've finished, tap or click OK twice, and then tap or click Close.

Connecting to networked projectors

Many meeting rooms and conference centers have networked projectors that are used for making presentations. To use this type of projector, you must connect your computer to the LAN, and then access the projector over the network by using the Connect To A Network Projector Wizard. This wizard walks you through the steps of finding projectors on a network and establishing a connection.

Before a mobile device can use the wizard, you must add the Network Projection feature. To do this, follow these steps:

1. In Control Panel, tap or click Programs, and then tap or click Turn Windows Features On Or Off under the Programs And Features heading.

2. In the Windows Features dialog box, tap or click the Network Projection check box, and then tap or click OK.

When you install the Network Projection feature, the Connect To A Network Projector utility is added to the Apps screen under the Windows Accessories heading. The utility also should be available on the Start screen. Before giving a presentation, users might want to configure the following standard settings for presentations:

- Turn Off The Screen Saver
- Set The Volume
- Show A Specific Background Or Background Image

These settings are configured in the Presentation Settings dialog box. When working with Mobility Center, you can open this dialog box by tapping or clicking the Network Projector icon on the Presentation Settings tile.

You can use the Connect To A Network Projector Wizard by following these steps:

1. Tap or click Connect To A Network Projector on the Start screen or the Apps screen.

2. If you haven't previously attempted to connect to a network projector and Windows Firewall is active, tap or click Allow The Network Projector To Communicate With My Computer. This enables the network projector to communicate with the computer through Windows Firewall.

3. If you want to select from projectors found on the local network, tap or click Search For A Projector. The wizard searches for projectors on the network and returns its results along with a list of any projectors you've recently used. Tap or click the projector you want to use, provide the access password for the projector if necessary, and then tap or click Next.

4. If you know the network address of the projector, tap or click Enter The Projector Network Address. On the Enter The Network Address Of A Network Projector page, enter the network address of the projector, such as *http://intranet.cpandl.local/projectors/confb-proj1*. Enter any required access password, and then tap or click Connect.

5. After you've established a connection to the projector, tap or click Finish to exit the wizard and begin using the projector.

Understanding mobile networking and remote access

Although the underlying technologies are fundamentally different, direct-dial, broadband, VPN, and DirectAccess connections all make it possible for users to access your organization's network remotely. With a typical direct-dial network configuration, off-site users use their computer's modem and a standard telephone line to connect to a modem pool located at the office. A Windows server managing the modem pool and running Routing And Remote Access authenticates the logon ID and password and authorizes the user to connect to the internal network. The user can then access network resources just as she does when working on site.

Figure 10-4 shows a direct-dial connection that uses a modem pool. Analog modems use dedicated telephone lines to connect users to the internal network at speeds up to 33.6 kilobits per second (Kbps) per line. Digital modems use channels of a T1 line to connect users to the internal network at speeds up to 56 Kbps per line. In a standard configuration, you might have 8, 12, or 16 modems configured in the pool, each with its own line (or channel). Typically, the modem pool has a lead number that users can call. This number connects to the first modem in the pool. When the lead number is busy, the line rolls over to the next number, which connects to the next modem in the pool, and so on, enabling users to dial a single number to gain access to all modems in the pool.

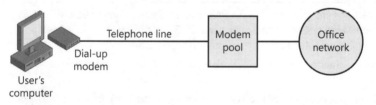

FIGURE 10-4 Use a dial-up connection to access an office network through a modem pool.

Unlike direct-dial connections, which can be made directly to the office network, broadband connections are made through an ISP's network. The user's DSL router, cable modem, or cellular modem establishes a connection to the ISP, which in turn connects the user to the public Internet. To connect to the office network, a broadband user must establish a VPN or DirectAccess connection between his computer and the office network. Figure 10-5 shows how VPN and DirectAccess work when the user has either a telephone line and DSL router or a cable and a cable modem.

A VPN is an extension of a private network across the public Internet. After a user is connected, it appears to her that she is directly connected to the office network, and she can access network resources just as she does when working on site. These seamless connections are possible because a virtual tunnel is established between the user's computer and the office network, where the VPN technology takes care of routing information over the public Internet. One of two VPN technologies is typically used: Point-to-Point Tunneling Protocol (PPTP) or Layer 2 Tunneling Protocol (L2TP).

FIGURE 10-5 Use a virtual tunnel to access an office network.

Both L2TP and PPTP offer encryption and protection from attacks, but only L2TP uses Internet Protocol security (IPsec) for advanced encryption, making it the more secure of the two technologies. Unfortunately, L2TP is more difficult to configure. When you use L2TP, you need to use Microsoft Certificate Services or a third-party certificate server to issue individual certificates for each system that will connect to the network by using L2TP.

In addition to using a VPN with a broadband connection, you can use a VPN with a dial-up connection. In this configuration, users go through their ISP to establish a connection to the public Internet and then establish a private connection to the office network. When this configuration becomes standard procedure for dial-up users, your organization won't need dedicated private lines like those reserved for a modem pool.

Another virtual tunneling option is DirectAccess. Although fundamentally different from VPN, the basic idea is the same—a DirectAccess connection is an extension of a private network across the public Internet. After a user is connected (which happens automatically after the feature is enabled), it appears to him that he is directly connected to the office network, and he can access network resources just as he does when working on site. These seamless connections are possible because a virtual tunnel is established between the user's computer and the office network, where the DirectAccess technology takes care of routing information over the public Internet.

For Windows Server 2012 R2, DirectAccess and Routing And Remote Access Service (RRAS) are combined into the Remote Access server role, and the new implementation works differently than the original implementation for Windows Server 2008 R2. With the new implementation, DirectAccess remains a client/server technology that relies on IPv6 and IPsec, but it no longer requires public key infrastructure (PKI). Although Windows Server 2008 R2 DirectAccess uses two IPsec tunnels to establish connectivity to the corporate network, Windows Server 2012 R2 DirectAccess uses a single IPsec tunnel by default (because the standard implementation doesn't rely on certificate-based authentication). However, for two-factor authentication, such as with smart cards and Network Access Protection (NAP) integration, you'll need to deploy DirectAccess by using two IPsec tunnels.

Windows Server 2012 R2 DirectAccess supports multiple domains and has built-in support for network load balancing. Although DirectAccess clients communicate by using IPv6 while connected remotely, the RemoteAccess server includes a built-in protocol translation (NAT64) and a name resolution gateway (DNS64) that can convert IPv6 communications from DirectAccess clients to IPv4 for internal servers. This makes it possible for DirectAccess clients to access IPv4-only intranet computers, but doesn't allow IPv4-only intranet computers to initiate connections to DirectAccess clients. The reason for this is that network address translation is unidirectional and meant for communications initiated by DirectAccess clients.

Client computers must run the Enterprise edition of Windows 7 or later. Server computers must run Windows Server 2008 Release 2 or later. To use DirectAccess, you must set up and configure IPv6 for use by both client and server computers throughout the enterprise, including DNSv6 and DHCPv6 as appropriate.

In the Administrative Templates policies for Computer Configuration under Network\Network Connections, you can use the Route All Traffic Through The Internal Network policy to control how DirectAccess works. By default, when a user is connected to a workplace, the user's computer accesses Internet resources directly rather than going through the workplace network. If you enable the routing policy, the user's computer accesses the Internet through the workplace network.

Obviously, both configuration approaches have advantages and disadvantages. If you don't route Internet traffic through the internal network, you reduce the workload and traffic levels on the workplace's connection to the Internet, but you lose the additional security and safeguards that might be in place to protect the internal network. If you route Internet traffic through the internal network, you increase the workload and traffic levels on the workplace's connection to the Internet, and possibly dramatically increase latency and response times when the user works with Internet resources. However, you also ensure that any additional security and safeguards in place to protect the internal network are enforced.

Creating connections for remote access

As discussed previously, you can create both dial-up and broadband connections for remote access. If you want additional security, you can also configure these connections to use VPN. After it is enabled, DirectAccess is seamless for the user, and the user needs only to establish a connection to the Internet to access the workplace network.

Windows 8.1 provides a wizard for creating these connections. In most cases, you'll want to access this wizard through Network And Sharing Center. In Network And Sharing Center, tap or click Set Up A New Connection Or Network. You can then create a dial-up, broadband, or VPN connection.

REAL WORLD   Consider whether Group Policy can help you reduce your workload. If you want to use the same connection settings on multiple computers, you can create dial-up and VPN connections by using Group Policy preferences. You also can import the settings into Group Policy. Either way, the connections are then available to all computers affected by the Group Policy Object. You can use this technique to deploy new connection configurations, update existing configurations when you need to make changes, and delete existing configurations and replace them with new ones.

Creating a dial-up connection

Windows 8.1 provides two options for making dial-up connections. You can create a dial-up connection to an ISP or a dial-up connection to a workplace. Although the connections are created by using slightly different techniques, the settings for the connection options are the same, with the following exceptions:

- A dial-up connection to an ISP does not use the Client For Microsoft Networks component, and it redials by default if the line is dropped.

- A dial-up connection to a workplace does use the Client For Microsoft Networks component, and it does not redial by default if the line is dropped.

The networking component Client For Microsoft Networks enables Windows 8.1 systems to communicate in a Windows domain or workgroup. Because most workplaces use Windows domains or workgroups and some ISPs don't, the component is configured for workplace environments and not for ISPs.

Creating dial-up connections is a two-part process. Before you create a dial-up connection, you should check the current phone and modem options, which specify dialing rules. After the dialing rules are configured, you can create the dial-up connection.

Working with dialing rules and locations

Dialing rules are used with modems to determine how phone lines are accessed, the caller's area code, and what additional features should be used when dialing connections. Sets of dialing rules are saved as dialing locations in the Phone And Modem tool.

VIEWING AND SETTING THE DEFAULT DIALING LOCATION

To view and set the default dialing location, follow these steps:

1. In Control Panel, select either Large Icons or Small Icons in the View By drop-down list.

2. Tap or click Phone And Modem. The first time you start this tool, you'll get the Location Information dialog box, as shown in Figure 10-6.

FIGURE 10-6 The first time you use the Phone And Modem tool, you must configure the initial location.

3. Answer the following questions to configure the default location, which is named (My Location):

   - **What Country/Region Are You In Now?**   Select the country or region you are in, such as United States.

   - **What Area Code (Or City Code) Are You In Now?**   Enter the appropriate area or city code, such as **212**.

   - **If You Need To Specify A Carrier Code, What Is It?**   You can specify the telephone carrier to use when dialing and establishing connections by entering its carrier code. A carrier code might be necessary if you are making long-distance or international calls.

   - **If You Dial A Number To Access An Outside Line, What Is It?**   Enter the number you need, if any, to access an outside line. An access number might be necessary to bypass a switch panel within a company or when dialing from a hotel.

4. In The Phone System At This Location Uses option, select Tone Dialing or Pulse Dialing. Most areas of the United States and Canada use tone dialing.

5. After you configure an initial location and tap or click OK, you'll get the Phone And Modem dialog box, as shown in Figure 10-7.

   From this point on, you no longer need to set up an initial location.

   Locations configured for the computer are shown by name and area code in the Locations list. The location from which you are currently dialing is selected and highlighted in bold.

FIGURE 10-7 Check dialing rules to ensure that they are configured properly.

6. Initially, the default location is set as My Location. By selecting a different lo-
    cation, you can make it the current or default location. I recommend editing
    the default location (My Location) to rename it so that the name includes the
    city or office location. To view the configuration of a selected location, tap
    or click Edit. To rename the location, enter a new value in the Location Name
    text box on the General tab, and then tap or click OK.

NOTE Of all the available dialing rules, the area code is the one that you'll work with
most often. During installation of the operating system, a default location might have
been created with the area code specified by the person who set up the computer. In
many cases, the default area code is not the one that the user needs to use when dialing another location from home.

CREATING DIALING LOCATIONS

You can create dialing locations to set unique rules for each area code from which
the user makes dial-up connections. To create a dialing location, follow these steps:

1. In Control Panel, select either Large Icons or Small Icons in the View By
    drop-down list.

2. Tap or click Phone And Modem. In the Phone And Modem dialog box,
    on the Dialing Rules tab, tap or click New. This displays the New Location
    dialog box.

3. The New Location dialog box has three tabs:

- **General** Sets the location name, country/region, and area code. On this tab, you can also set access numbers for outside lines for local or long-distance calls, disable call waiting, and specify whether tone or pulse dialing is used. Be sure to use an appropriate location name. Typically, this is the name of the city or metropolitan area from which the user is dialing.

- **Area Code Rules** Sets rules that determine how phone numbers are dialed from the location's area code to other area codes and within the location's area code. These rules are useful when multiple area codes that are not long distance are included in the same location. They are also useful when calls within the area code might be local or long distance based on phone number prefixes.

- **Calling Card** Sets a calling card to use when dialing from this location. Calling card information for major carriers is provided, and you can also create calling card records.

4. When you have finished creating the location, check that the default location in the Phone And Modem dialog box is correct. You might need to select a different entry. Tap or click OK.

DELETING DIALING LOCATIONS

To delete a dialing location, follow these steps:

1. In Control Panel, select either Large Icons or Small Icons in the View By drop-down list. Tap or click Phone And Modem.

2. In the Phone And Modem dialog box, select the location you want to permanently remove, and then tap or click Delete. If prompted to confirm the action, tap or click Yes.

3. Select the dialing location that you want to use as the default, and then tap or click OK.

Creating a dial-up Internet connection to an ISP

You can create dial-up connections in the following ways:

- If users are dialing up through an ISP that has point of presence (POP) locations throughout the United States and the world, you'll usually want to configure dialing rules and connections for specific locations. For example, you could create a dial-up location called Seattle and a dial-up connection called Connect To ISP In Seattle. In this configuration, you would specify the area code for Seattle, in addition to any special dialing rules, and then configure the connection to use the ISP's access numbers for Seattle. You would also need to show users how to change their current locations for when they travel from place to place.

- If users are dialing an 800 number or long distance to access the office modem pool or a special out-of-area access number for an ISP, you'll usually want to configure separate connections rather than separate locations. Here, you would create a connection that dials long distance to establish the connection, and a connection that is used when the user is in the local area. You would then need only one dialing location.

To create a dial-up Internet connection, follow these steps:

1. Before you create a dial-up connection, you should check the current phone and modem options, as discussed in the "Working with dialing rules and locations" section earlier in this chapter.

   NOTE If you use dialing rules with a connection and then set area and country codes, you are enabling the connection to be used for long-distance calls, which sometimes can be very expensive. If this isn't what you want, you might want to reconsider those selections.

2. In Network And Sharing Center, tap or click Set Up A New Connection Or Network. This starts the Set Up A Connection Or Network Wizard.

3. Select Connect To The Internet, and then tap or click Next. If the computer is already connected to the Internet, tap or click Set Up A New Connection Anyway. If you have an existing dial-up connection, you can reconfigure that connection or create a new connection. Typically, you'll want to create a new connection, so tap or click No, Create A New Connection.

4. Select Dial-Up. In the Dial-Up Phone Number text box, specify the phone number to dial for this connection.

5. Set account information for the connection. Enter the user name in the text box provided, and then enter the password. Although you can specify that the password is remembered by selecting Remember This Password, doing so is a poor security practice because it enables anyone with access to the computer to use the connection.

6. In the Connection Name text box, enter the name for the connection, such as Service Provider. Keep in mind that the name should be short (50 or fewer characters), but descriptive.

7. If you want the connection to be available to all users of the computer, select Allow Other People To Use This Connection. This option is useful when you plan to assign the connection through Group Policy and have not provided user logon information.

8. Tap or click Connect to create the dial-up connection and begin establishing a connection. Next, if you don't want to establish a connection now, tap or click Skip to bypass connection activation. Tap or click Close. To test the connection settings, follow the steps outlined in the "Establishing connections" section later in this chapter.

REAL WORLD Most organizations use digital phone systems, which don't allow you to make an analog connection to an outside line. If this is the case at your office, you need to access an analog line before you can test the connection. Some digital phones can be equipped with digital-to-analog converters that you can use for testing dial-up connections. You might find these converters used with conference phones or fax machines, or you might find that conference phones or fax machines are already connected to analog phone lines.

Creating a dial-up connection to a workplace

Creating a dial-up connection to a workplace is similar to creating a dial-up connection to the Internet. You create a dial-up connection to a workplace by following these steps:

1. In Network And Sharing Center, tap or click Set Up A New Connection Or Network. This starts the Set Up A Connection Or Network Wizard.

2. Select Connect To A Workplace, and then tap or click Next. If you have a connection already, you can reconfigure that connection or create a new connection. Typically, you'll want to create a new connection, so tap or click No, Create A New Connection.

3. On the How Do You Want To Connect page, tap or click Dial Directly.

4. Specify the phone number to dial for this connection by using the Telephone Number text box. In the Destination Name text box, enter the name for the connection, such as Corporate Office or Seattle Office. Keep in mind that the name should be short (50 or fewer characters), but descriptive.

5. If you want to use a smart card for the connection, select Use A Smart Card.

6. If you want the connection to be available to all users of the computer, select Allow Other People To Use This Connection. This option is best when you plan to assign the connection through Group Policy and have not provided user logon information.

7. If you don't want to test the connection now, select Don't Connect Now. In most cases, you'll want to use this option to bypass the connection activation. Otherwise, the connection might fail because you are setting up a connection for an alternate location, such as the user's home Internet connection, and these settings won't work through the organization's network.

8. Tap or click Next. Set account information for the connection. Enter the user name in the text box provided, and then enter the password.

   SECURITY ALERT Although you can specify that the password is remembered by selecting Remember This Password, this is a poor security practice because it enables anyone with access to the computer to use the connection.

9. If you are connecting to a domain, you can specify the logon domain in the Domain text box.

10. If you previously specified that you didn't want to connect now, tap or click Create to create the connection. Otherwise, tap or click Connect to create the connection and connect to it. Tap or click Close.

In Group Policy, you can create, edit, and remove dial-up connections by using network options preferences. To configure network options preferences, follow these steps:

1. Open a Group Policy Object for editing in the Group Policy Management Editor. To configure preferences for computers, expand Computer Configuration\Preferences\Control Panel Settings, and then select Network Options. To configure preferences for users, expand User Configuration\Preferences\ Control Panel Settings, and then select Network Options.

2. Press and hold or right-click the Network Options node, point to New, and then tap or click Dial-Up Connection. This opens the New Dial-Up Properties dialog box.

3. In the Action list, select Create, Update, or Replace, as appropriate.

4. If you want the connection to be available to all users of the computer, select All Users Connection. Otherwise, select User Connection to apply the connection only to the user for whom the policy is being processed.

5. Enter a connection name and connection phone number.

6. Use the options on the Common tab to control how the preference is applied. Often, you'll want to apply a policy only once. If so, select Apply Once And Do Not Reapply.

7. Tap or click OK. The next time Group Policy is refreshed, the preference item will be applied as appropriate for the Group Policy Object in which you defined the preference item.

Creating a broadband connection to the Internet

In many respects, broadband connections are much easier to configure than dial-up connections. When you work with broadband, you don't need to set up dial-up rules or locations. You don't need to worry about calling cards, ISP access numbers, or redialing preferences, and this makes broadband much easier to work with.

Most broadband providers give users a router or a modem that users will need to connect to the service provider. Each user must also have a network adapter on his or her computer that is connected to a DSL router or cable modem. In this configuration, the necessary connection is established over a LAN rather than a specific broadband connection. Therefore, it is the network connection that must be properly configured to gain access to the Internet. You won't need to create a broadband connection.

You can, however, create a specific broadband connection if needed. In some cases, you need to do this to set specific configuration options, such as secure authentication, required by an ISP, or you might want to use this technique to set the user name and password required by the broadband provider.

You create a broadband connection to the Internet by following these steps:

1. In Network And Sharing Center, tap or click Set Up A New Connection Or Network. This starts the Set Up A Connection Or Network Wizard.

2. Select Connect To The Internet, and then tap or click Next. If the computer is already connected to the Internet, tap or click Set Up A New Connection Anyway. If you have another usable connection already, you can reconfigure that connection for use or create new connection. Typically, you'll want to create a new connection, so tap or click Set Up A New Connection Anyway. Tap or click No, Create A New Connection, and then tap or click Next.

3. On the How Do You Want To Connect page, tap or click Broadband (PPPoE) to create a broadband connection to the Internet.

4. Do the following, and then tap or click Next:

   ■ Set account information for the connection. Enter the user name in the text box provided, and then enter the password.

   ■ In the Connection Name text box, enter the name for the connection, such as Seattle Office Secure Broadband. Keep in mind that the name should be short (50 or fewer characters), but descriptive.

   ■ If you want the connection to be available to all users of the computer, select Allow Other People To Use This Connection. This option is best when you plan to assign the connection through Group Policy and have not provided user logon information.

5. Tap or click Connect to create the connection and connect to it. In most cases, the connection will fail because you are setting up a connection for an alternate location, such as a remote office, and these settings won't work through the organization's network. As a result, you'll have an option to tap or click Skip to bypass connection activation. Tap or click Close.

TIP With a broadband connection, you need a DSL router or cable modem to test the connection. Be sure to configure any special settings required by the ISP, as detailed in the "Configuring connection properties" section later in this chapter.

Creating a VPN connection

VPNs are used to establish secure communications channels over an existing dial-up or broadband connection. You must know the IP address or fully qualified domain name of the remote access server to which you are connecting. If the necessary connection is available and you know the host information, you can create the connection by following these steps:

1. In Network And Sharing Center, tap or click Set Up A New Connection Or Network. This starts the Set Up A Connection Or Network Wizard.

2. To create a VPN connection, select Connect To A Workplace, and then tap or click Next.

3. If you have an existing dial-up connection, select No, Create A New Connection, and then tap or click Next.

4. Tap or click Use My Internet Connection (VPN).

5. Users will need to establish a connection to the Internet—via dial-up or broadband—before attempting to use the VPN. Select an existing connection to use, and then tap or click Next.

6. Enter the IPv4 or IPv6 address or fully qualified domain name of the computer to which you are connecting, such as 157.54.0.1 or external.microsoft.com. In most cases, this address is for the remote access server configured for the office network.

7. Enter a name for the connection in the Destination Name text box. If the computer is configured to use a smart card for authentication, select Use A Smart Card.

8. If you want the connection to be available to all users of the computer, select Allow Other People To Use This Connection. This option is best when you plan to assign the connection through Group Policy and have not provided user logon information.

9. Tap or click Create.

In Group Policy, you can create, edit, and remove VPN connections by using network options preferences. To configure network options preferences, follow these steps:

1. In the Group Policy Management Editor, open a Group Policy Object for editing. To configure preferences for computers, expand Computer Configuration\Preferences\Control Panel Settings, and then select Network Options. To configure preferences for users, expand User Configuration\Preferences\Control Panel Settings, and then select Network Options.

2. Press and hold or right-click the Network Options node, point to New, and then tap or click VPN Connection. This opens the New VPN Properties dialog box.

3. In the Action list, select Create, Update, or Replace, as appropriate.

4. If you want the connection to be available to all users of the computer, select All Users Connection. Otherwise, select User Connection to apply the connection only to the user for whom the policy is being processed.

5. Enter a connection name and connection IP address. Alternatively, select Use DNS Name, and then enter the fully qualified domain name to use.

6. On the Security tab, select Advanced. Use the Data Encryption list to specify whether and how encryption should be used. In most cases, you'll want to require encryption. Under Logon Security, specify the security options to use.

7. Use the options on the Common tab to control how the preference is applied. Often, you'll want to apply a policy only once. If so, select Apply Once And Do Not Reapply.

8. Tap or click OK. The next time Group Policy is refreshed, the preference item will be applied as appropriate for the Group Policy Object in which you defined the preference item.

Joining a device to a workplace

You can join a device to a workplace to have the device become a known device. After the device is joined to a workplace, the device can access workplace resources and applications. You can join a Windows device to a workplace by following these steps:

1. Log on to the device by using a Microsoft account.

2. Open PC Settings. One way to do this is by pressing the Windows key + I, and then clicking Change PC Settings.

3. Under PC Settings\Network, select Workplace.

4. When prompted for credentials, log on by using a domain account, such as tedb@pocket-consultant.com. After you enter your password and select OK, you should get a message stating "This device has joined your workplace network."

For a workplace join to work, the Windows device must trust the SSL certificate that was used to configure the Device Registration Service (DRS). DRS is a role service that you must configure as part of the initial setup of the Active Directory Federation role. DRS provisions devices in Active Directory Domain Services and creates a certificate on the device that represents the device identity.

Devices that are not based on Windows can also join workplaces. For example, you can join an iOS device to a workplace by following these steps:

1. The iOS device doesn't trust the certificate used to configure the Device Registration Service (DRS), so you will need to install the certificate.

2. Open Safari and enter the URL for the DRS Over-The-Air Profile endpoint, such as *https://corpservices.pocket-consultant.com/enrserver/otaprofile*.

3. Log on to the page by using a domain account, such as *tedb@pocket-consultant.com*.

4. The first time you access apps by using an iOS device, you will be prompted to install a profile. On the Install Profile screen, select Install.

5. If you need to enter a PIN to unlock the device, enter the PIN when prompted.

6. When the profile installation is complete, you'll encounter the Profile Installed screen. Select Done.

Configuring connection properties

Whether you are working with dial-up, broadband, or VPN connections, you'll often need to set additional properties after creating a connection. The key properties that you will work with are examined in this section.

NOTE As you work with connection properties, keep in mind that VPN connections use existing connections and that the configuration of each connection is separate. With VPN, the primary connection is established first by using the settings assigned to that connection, and then the VPN connection is attempted by using the VPN connection settings. With this in mind, you should configure the primary connection first, and then configure the options for VPN. You should change this approach only when you are troubleshooting problems with VPN. In this case, you should start with the VPN configuration and work your way back to the settings for the primary connection.

Configuring automatic or manual connections

Windows 8.1 can be configured to establish dial-up, broadband, or VPN connections automatically when users access programs, such as a web browser, that need to connect to the Internet. The ways in which automatic connections work depend on settings in the Internet Options tool. The dial-up options include the following:

- **Never Dial A Connection**   Users must manually establish a connection.
- **Dial Whenever A Network Connection Is Not Present**   The connection is established automatically when it's needed, but only when the network connection isn't working.
- **Always Dial My Default Connection**   The default connection is always established when an Internet connection is needed (even if other connections are already established).

TIP The way you configure automatic connections really depends on the way your organization works. Contrary to what some administrators think, mobile device users are usually less frustrated when their computers are set to never dial a connection. Users might not have access to a dial-up connection when they are out of the office, for example, and having the computer attempt to dial a connection when a user is meeting with customers or giving a presentation can be disruptive. On the other hand, if you are configuring dial-up networking for users with desktops at a remote or home office, they'll probably want to use automatic connections.

To configure computers to connect manually, follow these steps:

1. In Control Panel, tap or click Network And Internet. In Network And Internet, tap or click Internet Options. In the Internet Properties dialog box, tap or click the Connections tab, as shown in Figure 10-8.
2. Select Never Dial A Connection, and then tap or click OK.

FIGURE 10-8 Configure manual or automatic connections by using the Connections tab.

You can configure automatic connections by following these steps:

1. In Control Panel, tap or click Network And Internet. In Network And Internet, tap or click Internet Options. In the Internet Properties dialog box, tap or click the Connections tab.

2. Select Dial Whenever A Network Connection Is Not Present to establish a connection automatically if a network connection isn't working. Select Always Dial My Default Connection to always attempt to establish a connection.

3. The Dial-Up And Virtual Private Network Settings list shows the dial-up, broadband, and VPN connections that are currently configured. Select the connection you want to use by default when establishing a connection, and then tap or click Set Default.

4. Tap or click OK.

Configuring proxy settings for mobile connections

As with connections themselves, proxy server settings can be set manually or automatically. With manual configuration, you need to configure each proxy server property step by step. With automatic configuration, the computer attempts to detect proxy server settings and then configure the appropriate options, or the computer reads a configuration script to use in configuring the proxy.

> **NOTE** Proxy settings can be configured for multiple systems through Group Policy. If you elect not to configure proxy settings through Group Policy, you can configure them on a per-connection basis, as discussed in this section.

Configuration scripts can be stored in a file on the local computer or at an Internet address. Using configuration scripts can save a lot of time, especially when you consider that each connection you create is configured separately. Further, because VPN connections are established on top of an existing setting, the proxy settings for the VPN can be different from those set in the original connection.

To use automatic proxy configuration for a connection, complete the following steps:

1. In Control Panel, tap or click Network And Internet. In Network And Internet, tap or click Internet Options. In the Internet Properties dialog box, tap or click the Connections tab.

2. In the Dial-Up And Virtual Private Network Settings list, select the dial-up connection that you want to configure, and then tap or click Settings. This displays a Settings dialog box similar to the one shown in Figure 10-9.

FIGURE 10-9 Proxy settings can be automatically configured through detection or scripts.

3. To attempt to detect proxy settings automatically when establishing the connection, select Automatically Detect Settings.

4. To use a configuration script, select Use Automatic Configuration Script, and then enter the file path or URL for the script. With file paths, you can use environment variables, such as %UserProfile%\PROXY.VBS. With URLs, be sure to use the computer URL, such as *http://proxy.microsoft.com/proxy.vbs*.

5. To ensure that only automatic settings are used, clear the Use A Proxy Server For This Connection check box.

6. Tap or click OK twice.

To use manual proxy configuration, complete the following steps:

1. In Control Panel, tap or click Network And Internet. In Network And Internet, tap or click Internet Options. In the Internet Properties dialog box, tap or click the Connections tab.

2. In the Dial-Up And Virtual Private Network Settings list, select the dial-up connection you want to configure, and then tap or click Settings.

3. Clear the Automatically Detect Settings and Use Automatic Configuration Script check boxes if they are selected.

4. Select Use A Proxy Server For This Connection. The Bypass Proxy Server For Local Addresses check box is not selected by default. In most cases, however, you won't want to use a proxy for requests made to servers on the same network segment, so you'll also want to select Bypass Proxy Server For Local Addresses. It is important to note that if Bypass Proxy Server For Local Addresses is not selected, users might need additional permissions to access intranet servers through your proxy servers.

5. Tap or click Advanced to display the Proxy Settings dialog box, as shown in Figure 10-10.

FIGURE 10-10 You can use the same proxy for all services, or you can configure multiple proxies.

6. By using the text boxes in the Servers area, set the IP address for proxies. You'll find the following two columns of text boxes:

   ■ **Proxy Address To Use** Sets the IP address of the related proxy server or servers. Enter the IP address for each service. If multiple proxies are configured for a particular service, enter the IP address for each proxy server in the order in which you want the web client to attempt to use them. Each address must be separated by a semicolon. If a proxy isn't configured for a service, do not fill in the related text box.

- **Port** Sets the port number on which the proxy server responds to requests. Most proxies respond to port 80 for all requests. That said, the standard ports are port 80 for Hypertext Transfer Protocol (HTTP), port 443 for Secure Sockets Layer (SSL; listed as Secure), port 21 for File Transfer Protocol (FTP), and port 1081 for Socks. Check with your organization's web administrator for the proper settings.

7. The Use The Same Proxy Server For All Protocols check box enables you to use the same IP address and port settings for the HTTP, SSL, FTP, and Socks services. You have the following options:

   - If your organization has one proxy server that handles all requests, select the Use The Same Proxy Server For All Protocols check box. Enter the IP address that you want to use, and the port number on which the server responds.

   - If you want to use a unique proxy server or servers for each type of service, clear the Use The Same Proxy Server For All Protocols check box, and then enter the necessary IP addresses and port numbers in the text boxes provided.

8. If your network has multiple segments or specific servers that shouldn't use proxies, enter the appropriate IP addresses or IP address ranges in the Exceptions list. Multiple entries must be separated by a semicolon. The asterisk (*) character can be used as a wildcard character to specify an address range of 0 through 255, such as 192.*.*.*, 192.168.*.*, or 192.168.10.*.

9. Tap or click OK three times.

Configuring connection logon information

Each connection that you create has separate settings for logon information. You can set a user name, password, and domain by performing the following steps:

1. In Control Panel, tap or click Network And Internet. In Network And Internet, tap or click Internet Options. In the Internet Properties dialog box, tap or click the Connections tab.

2. In the Dial-Up And Virtual Private Network Settings list, select the connection you want to configure, and then tap or click Settings.

3. Enter the user name and password for the connection in the User Name and Password text boxes.

4. If a domain name is required, enter the domain name in the Domain text box.

5. Tap or click OK twice.

Setting a connection to use the appropriate logon information isn't the last step in ensuring a proper configuration. You should also set options that specify whether users are prompted for logon information or a phone number. If a logon domain is required to establish a connection, you should ensure that the logon domain is passed with the other logon information. By default, the domain name is not included.

To configure additional options, follow these steps:

1. In Control Panel, tap or click Network And Internet. In Network And Internet, tap or click Internet Options. In the Internet Properties dialog box, tap or click the Connections tab.

2. In the Dial-Up And Virtual Private Network Settings list, select the connection you want to configure, and then tap or click Settings.

3. In the Settings dialog box, tap or click Properties.

4. In the Properties dialog box, tap or click the Options tab. You can now configure the following options:

   - To display status messages while connecting, select Display Progress While Connecting.

   - To ensure that users are prompted for logon information if necessary, select Prompt For Name And Password, Certificate, Etc.

   - To ensure that the logon domain is included when requested, select Include Windows Logon Domain.

   - To prompt for a phone number when needed, select Prompt For Phone Number.

5. Tap or click OK three times.

Configuring automatic disconnection

For dial-up connections, you can specify whether Windows 8.1 disconnects the phone line when the connection hasn't been actively used for a specified amount of time and when the connection might no longer be needed. To configure disconnect options, follow these steps:

1. In Control Panel, tap or click Network And Internet. In Network And Internet, tap or click Internet Options. In the Internet Properties dialog box, tap or click the Connections tab.

2. In the Dial-Up And Virtual Private Network Settings list, select the connection you want to configure, and then tap or click Settings.

3. In the Settings dialog box, tap or click Properties. In the Properties dialog box, tap or click the Options tab. Use the Idle Time Before Hanging Up option to specify whether Windows 8.1 disconnects the phone line when the connection hasn't been actively used for a specified time. The available values are Never, 1 Minute, 5 Minutes, 10 Minutes, 20 Minutes (the default), 30 Minutes, 1 Hour, 2 Hours, 4 Hours, 8 Hours, and 24 Hours.

4. Tap or click OK to return to the Settings dialog box. In the Settings dialog box, tap or click Advanced on the Dial-Up Connection Settings panel. Select or clear Disconnect When Connection May No Longer Be Needed to specify whether Windows 8.1 disconnects when a user quits all Internet programs that would otherwise use the connection.

5. Tap or click OK three times.

> **TIP** If users complain about getting disconnected during dial-up sessions, the Disconnect settings might be the problem. Talk with the users about how they use the Internet and then determine whether you should change the settings to better meet their needs. Another reason for disconnection is if the Idle Time Before Hanging Up option is used. However, you typically want an idle connection to be disconnected at some point.

Setting a connection to use dialing rules

Dial-up connections can be configured with or without dialing rules. If you don't use dialing rules with a connection, the seven-digit phone number assigned to the connection is dialed at all times. When you assign dialing rules, the current dialing location determines whether the connection is attempted as a local or long-distance phone call.

To view or set the dialing rules for a connection, follow these steps:

1. In Control Panel, tap or click Network And Internet. In Network And Internet, tap or click Internet Options. In the Internet Properties dialog box, tap or click the Connections tab.

2. In the Dial-Up And Virtual Private Network Settings list, select the dial-up connection that you want to configure, and then tap or click Settings.

3. In the Dial-Up Connection Settings dialog box, tap or click Properties. This displays the Dial-Up Connection Properties dialog box.

4. To ensure that the connection uses the appropriate dialing rules, on the General tab, select Use Dialing Rules, and then enter an area code and select a country/region code.

5. If you don't want to use dialing rules, clear the Use Dialing Rules check box.

6. Tap or click OK three times.

Configuring primary and alternate phone numbers

With dial-up connections, you can configure two types of phone numbers: the primary number to dial whenever a connection is attempted, and alternate phone numbers to try if a primary number fails. To configure phone numbers, follow these steps:

1. In Control Panel, tap or click Network And Internet. In Network And Internet, tap or click Internet Options. In the Internet Properties dialog box, tap or click the Connections tab.

2. In the Dial-Up And Virtual Private Network Settings list, select the dial-up connection that you want to configure, and then tap or click Settings.

3. In the Dial-Up Connection Settings dialog box, tap or click Properties. This displays the Dial-Up Connection Properties dialog box.

4. The primary phone number is listed in the Phone Number text box. Enter a new number as necessary.

5. Tap or click Alternates. This displays the Alternate Phone Numbers dialog box. You can now manage primary and alternate phone numbers by using the following techniques:

   - To add a phone number, tap or click Add to open the Add Alternate Phone Number dialog box. Next, enter the seven-digit alternate local number in the Phone Number text box. You can use a dash if you want to, as in 555-1234. If you want to set dialing rules, select Use Dialing Rules, and then enter an area code and select a country/region code. Tap or click OK.

   - To change the order in which numbers are dialed, select a number, and then use the up or down arrow icon to change its position in the Phone Numbers list. The top number in the list becomes the primary number.

   - To edit a phone number, select the number in the Phone Numbers list, and then tap or click Edit. Next, use the Edit Alternate Phone Number dialog box to change the number.

   - To remove a number, select the number in the Phone Numbers list, and then tap or click Delete.

6. If you want to use alternate numbers automatically, select If A Number Fails, Try The Next Number. You can also have Windows 8.1 move a number to the top of the list (making it the primary number) if Windows 8.1 is able to dial it successfully after a previous number fails. To do this, select Move Successful Numbers To Top Of The List.

7. Tap or click OK four times.

Configuring identity validation

Proper identity validation is essential to maintaining the integrity of your network. When users dial in to the office, you should ensure that identities are validated securely if at all possible. This isn't the default setting for standard dial-up connections, however. With most connections, the user's logon information can be passed in cleartext over the connection. If you don't allow unencrypted passwords to be used, this forces Windows 8.1 to attempt to pass logon information by using a secure technique, such as Challenge Handshake Authentication Protocol (CHAP) or MS-CHAP Version 2 rather than cleartext. You can also configure connections to use Extensible Authentication Protocol.

With dial-up and broadband connections, you can use any of these options. With VPN, you can use only the secure techniques. When you require a secured password, you can also automatically pass the Windows logon name, password, and domain specified in the configuration. Passing the Windows logon information automatically is useful when users connect to the office and must be authenticated in the Windows domain. With both secure validation techniques, you can require data encryption and force Windows 8.1 to disconnect if encryption cannot be used. Data encryption is automatically used with Windows Authentication for both secured passwords and smart cards.

To configure identity validation, follow these steps:

1. In Control Panel, tap or click Network And Internet. In Network And Internet, tap or click Internet Options. In the Internet Properties dialog box, tap or click the Connections tab.

2. In the Dial-Up And Virtual Private Network Settings list, select the connection you want to configure, and then tap or click Settings.

3. In the Settings dialog box, tap or click Properties.

4. In the Properties dialog box, tap or click the Security tab. With VPNs, you can specify the connection protocol to use or use automatic detection. If you require secure passwords, you can also set automatic logon and require data encryption. Both options are useful when logging on to a Windows domain. The settings must be supported, however; if they aren't, users won't be able to validate their logons and connections won't be completed.

   If you use smart cards, you should also require data encryption. Data encryption is essential to ensuring the integrity and security of the data passed between the originating computer and the authenticating computer. If you select Require Encryption and the connection is not secured with encryption, the client computer will drop the connection.

5. Specify the allowed authentication protocols, and then tap or click OK.

Configuring networking protocols and components

The way in which networking protocols and components are configured depends on the type of connection. As shown in Table 10-1, dial-up connections can use either Point-to-Point Protocol (PPP) or Serial Line Internet Protocol (SLIP) as the connection protocol. Broadband connections use Point-to-Point Protocol over Ethernet (PPPoE). Most VPN connections use either PPTP or L2TP. Newer VPN connections, however, can use Secure Sockets Tunneling Protocol (SSTP) or IKEv2. With IKEv2, connections can use machine certificates during authentication.

TABLE 10-1 Connection protocol availability by connection type

CONNECTION TYPE	CONNECTION PROTOCOL	DESCRIPTION
Dial-up	PPP	Used to establish connections to Windows servers over dial-up.
Dial-up	SLIP	Used to establish connections to UNIX servers over dial-up; available if you've installed third-party software.
Broadband	PPPoE	Used to establish a point-to-point broadband connection over Ethernet.
VPN	Automatic	Used to detect automatically which VPN protocol is available and establish a virtual tunnel by using that protocol.
VPN	PPTP VPN	Sets the PPTP for a VPN. PPTP is an extension of PPP.
VPN	L2TP IPsec VPN	Sets the L2TP for a VPN. L2TP uses IPsec to enhance security.
VPN	IKEv2	Sets the IKE Version 2 for a VPN. IKEv2 uses IPsec tunnel mode to enhance security.
VPN	SSTP	Sets the SSTP for a VPN. SSTP transports PPP or L2TP traffic through an SSL channel.
DirectAccess	IPv6 over IPsec	Used to establish a secure tunnel to a workplace over an existing connection.

Three network components are used with mobile networking: Transmission Control Protocol/Internet Protocol (TCP/IP), File And Printer Sharing For Microsoft Networks, and Client For Microsoft Networks. As Table 10-2 shows, the way these components are configured by default depends on the type of connection that was created originally. You can change these settings to suit your needs. If necessary, you can also install additional networking components.

TABLE 10-2 Default component configuration by connection type

DIAL-UP COMPONENT	DESCRIPTION	BROAD-BAND	STANDARD DIAL-UP	DIAL-UP TO OFFICE	VPN
Transmission Control Protocol/ Internet Protocol (TCP/IP)	TCP/IPv4 and TCP/IPv6 are required for network communications. By default, DHCP is used with connections unless overridden in the property settings.	Yes	Yes	Yes	Yes
File And Printer Sharing For Microsoft Networks	Enables the sharing of printers and files over the network connection; allows for mapping printers and drives.	No	No	No	Yes
Client For Microsoft Networks	Enables Windows Authentication in Windows domains; enables the computer to act as the domain client.	No	No	Yes	Yes

To view or change the networking options for a connection, follow these steps:

1. In Control Panel, tap or click Network And Internet. In Network And Internet, tap or click Internet Options. In the Internet Properties dialog box, tap or click the Connections tab.

2. In the Dial-Up And Virtual Private Network Settings list, select the connection that you want to configure, and then tap or click Settings.

3. In the Settings dialog box, tap or click Properties.

4. In the Properties dialog box, tap or click the Networking tab. You can now do the following:

   ■ Enable network components by selecting the related check box in the This Connection Uses The Following Items list.

   ■ Disable network components by clearing the related check box in the This Connection Uses The Following Items list.

   TIP If any of the network components shown in Table 10-2 are not available and are necessary for the connection, you can install them by tapping or clicking Install on the Networking tab. Afterward, select the component type, tap or click Add, and then select the component to use in the list provided.

5. By default, connections use DHCP to configure network settings, including the IP address, subnet mask, default gateway, DNS servers, and WINS servers. If you want to assign a static IP address or override other default settings, select Internet Protocol Version 4 (TCP/IPv4) or Internet Protocol Version 6 (TCP/IPv6), and then tap or click Properties. This displays a Properties dialog box that can be configured as discussed earlier in the chapter.

6. Tap or click OK three times.

Enabling and disabling Windows Firewall for network connections

With dial-up, broadband, and VPN connections, you might want to give the computer added protection against attacks by using Windows Firewall. This built-in firewall protects Windows 8.1 systems by restricting the types of information that can be communicated. By enforcing the appropriate restrictions, you reduce the possibility that malicious individuals can break into a system—and reducing security risks is extremely important when users are accessing the organization's network from outside your protective firewalls and proxy servers.

Windows Firewall is enabled by default for all connections and can be enabled or disabled for each type of network to which a user connects. To enable or disable Windows Firewall on a per-connection basis, follow these steps:

1. In Control Panel, tap or click System And Security.

2. Tap or click Windows Firewall. In the left pane of the Windows Firewall page, tap or click Turn Windows Firewall On Or Off.

3. Windows Firewall settings for each network type to which a user can connect are listed on the Customize Settings page. Select Turn On Windows Firewall or Turn Off Windows Firewall for each network type as appropriate.

4. Tap or click OK when you have finished.

Establishing connections

As discussed in the "Configuring automatic or manual connections" section earlier in this chapter, dial-up, broadband, and VPN connections can be established manually or automatically. The manual method lets users choose when to connect. The automatic method connects when users start a program, such as a web browser, that requires network access.

Establishing a dial-up connection

Dial-up connections use a telephone line to establish a connection between two modems. To establish a dial-up connection, follow these steps:

1. Tap or click the Network notification icon on the taskbar; or slide in from the right side of the screen, tap Settings, and then tap the Network icon.

2. On the Networks panel, tap or click the dial-up connection that you want to use, and then tap or click Connect.

3. Confirm that the user name is correct. If the password for the account was previously entered and saved, you can use the cached password without having to reenter it. Otherwise, if you need to enter a password or change the password, enter the password for the account.

4. To use the user name and password whenever you attempt to establish this connection, select Save This User Name And Password For The Following Users, and then select Me Only.

> *TIP* To use the user name and password when any user attempts to establish this connection, select Save This User Name And Password For The Following Users, and then select Anyone Who Uses This Computer. Don't use this option if you plan to distribute this connection through Group Policy, because you don't want to give out your connection password.

5. The Dial drop-down list shows the number that will be dialed. The primary number is selected by default. To choose an alternate number, tap or click the drop-down list, and then select the number you want to use.

6. Tap or click Dial. When the modem connects to the ISP or office network, the connection speed is displayed. The connection speed is negotiated on a per-call basis and depends on the maximum speed of the calling modem and the modem being called, the compression algorithms available, and the quality of the connection.

You can view the connection properties by pressing and holding or right-clicking the dial-up connection on the Networks panel and then selecting View Connection Properties. If you have problems connecting with a dial-up connection, use these tips to help you troubleshoot:

- **Problem:** The modem dials and reaches the other modem but cannot connect. It continues to make connection noises until you cancel the operation.

  Resolution: The phone lines are usually the source of the problem. Static or noise on the line can cause connection failures. Check the connections between the modem and the wall. Check with the phone company to find out if they can test the line and resolve the problem.

- **Problem:** The modem dials and seems to connect, but then the service provider or office network connection is dropped unexpectedly. The connection doesn't seem to complete successfully.

  Resolution: Check your networking protocols and components, as discussed in the "Configuring networking protocols and components" section earlier in this chapter. If these settings seem to be okay, determine whether you are passing Windows logon and domain information, because this might be required. See the "Configuring connection logon information" section earlier in this chapter for more details.

- **Problem:** The user cannot access resources in the Windows domain.

  Resolution: The Client For Microsoft Networks component might be required to access resources on the office network. Enable this component and ensure that the domain information is being passed as necessary.

- **Problem:** The user can never get through. The modem seems to be dialing the number incorrectly. You can hear it dialing too many or too few numbers.

  Resolution: Check the dialing rules for the connection, in addition to the currently selected dialing location. Be sure that these are configured properly for the user's current location.

- **Problem:** A No Dial Tone message is displayed, but the modem is installed correctly and seems to be okay.

  Resolution: Check the phone cord and ensure that it is connected properly. Some modems have two line jacks, one labeled Phone/In and one labeled Line/Out. The phone cord from the wall jack should be plugged into the Line/Out jack. Some phone jacks are configured for data only, indicating a plug for a high-speed line rather than a phone or modem. Try a different jack.

- **Problem:** The computer freezes when the user tries to use the modem.

  Resolution: This is most likely caused by a device conflict. For configuring and troubleshooting devices, follow the techniques discussed in Chapter 8, "Managing hardware devices and drivers" in *Windows 8.1 Administration Pocket Consultant: Essentials & Configuration* by William R. Stanek (Microsoft Press, 2013).

- **Problem:** Some services freeze or don't work.

  Resolution: Check the proxy and firewall settings. These settings can restrict the services that are available.

Establishing a broadband connection

Broadband connections are established by using a cable modem and a cable line or a DSL router and a telephone line. To establish a broadband connection, follow these steps:

1. Tap or click the Network notification icon on the taskbar; or slide in from the right side of the screen, tap Settings, and then tap the Network icon.

2. On the Networks panel, tap or click the broadband connection that you want to use, and then tap or click Connect.

3. If the user name and password for the connection haven't been set previously, enter the user name and password when prompted, and then tap or click OK.

You can view the connection properties by pressing and holding or right-clicking the broadband connection on the Networks panel and then selecting View Connection Properties.

Windows 8.1 caches the credentials for broadband connections and uses the credentials each time you connect. To clear the cached credentials so that you can provide new credentials, press and hold or right-click the broadband connection on the Networks panel, and then select Clear Cached Credentials.

If you have problems connecting with broadband, use these tips to help you troubleshoot:

- **Problem:** You cannot connect. The connection doesn't seem to work at all.

  Resolution: Check your network connections. Be sure that the lines connecting the DSL router or cable modem and the computer are plugged in properly.

- **Problem:** The connection is dropped unexpectedly. The connection doesn't seem to complete successfully.

  Resolution: Check your networking protocols and components as discussed in the section "Configuring networking protocols and components." If these settings seem to be okay, determine whether you are passing Windows logon and domain information, because this might be required. See the "Configuring connection logon information" section earlier in this chapter for more details.

- **Problem:** Some services freeze or don't work.

  Resolution: Check the proxy and firewall settings. These settings can restrict the services that are available.

- **Problem:** You cannot access resources in the Windows domain.

  Resolution: The Client For Microsoft Networks component might be required to access resources on the office network. Enable this component and ensure that the domain information is being passed as necessary.

Establishing a VPN connection

A VPN connection is made over an existing network connection, dial-up connection, or broadband connection. VPN connections are displayed separately from dial-up, broadband, and LAN connections. To establish a VPN connection, follow these steps:

1. Tap or click the Network notification icon on the taskbar; or slide in from the right side of the screen, tap Settings, and then tap the Network icon.

2. On the Networks panel, tap or click the VPN connection that you want to use, and then tap or click Connect.

3. If the connection is configured to dial another type of connection first, Windows 8.1 tries to establish this connection before attempting the VPN connection. If prompted to establish this connection, tap or click Yes, and then dial the connection, as discussed in the "Establishing a dial-up connection" section earlier in this chapter.

4. After the necessary connection is established, you'll get the Connect dialog box. After you confirm that the user name is correct and enter the password for the network account (if it doesn't already appear), tap or click Connect.

You can view the connection properties by pressing and holding or right-clicking the VPN connection on the Networks panel and then selecting View Connection Properties. If you have problems establishing the connection, use these tips to help you troubleshoot:

- **Problem:** You cannot connect. The connection doesn't seem to work at all.

  Resolution: Check your network connections. Be sure that the lines connecting the DSL router or cable modem and the computer are plugged in properly. For a dial-up connection, make sure that the phone line is connected to the modem.

- **Problem:** You get an error message regarding the host name.

  Resolution: The host name might be incorrectly specified. Check the settings to be sure that the host name is fully expressed, such as external01.microsoft.com rather than just external01. DNS resolutions might not be working properly, either. If this is the case, enter the IP address for the host rather than the host name.

- **Problem:** You get an error message regarding a bad IP address.

  Resolution: Check or reenter the IP address. If the IP address is correct, TCP/IP networking might be improperly configured. Check your networking protocols and components, as discussed in the "Configuring networking protocols and components" section earlier in this chapter. You might need to set a default gateway and a static IP address for the connection.

- **Problem:** A message stating that the protocol isn't supported is displayed, and the connection doesn't seem to complete successfully.

  Resolution: Set the protocol to automatic rather than to a specific setting of PPTP, L2TP, SSTP, or IKEv2. Check the secure logon settings. They might be set to require a secure password instead of a smart card, or vice versa. If these settings seem to be okay, determine whether you are passing Windows logon and domain information, because this might be required. See the "Configuring connection logon information" section earlier in this chapter for more details.

- **Problem:** You cannot map network drives or access printers.

  Resolution: The File And Printer Sharing For Microsoft Networks component is required to map drives and printers. Enable this component, as discussed in the "Configuring networking protocols and components" section earlier in this chapter.

- **Problem:** Some services freeze or don't work.

  Resolution: Check the proxy and firewall settings. These settings can restrict the services that are available.

Connecting to a workplace

After you join a device to a workplace, you can connect to the workplace and access applications. To connect to a workplace by using a Windows device, follow these steps:

1. Log on to the device by using a Microsoft account.

2. In Internet Explorer, enter the URL for the app you want to use, such as *https://corpservices.pocket-consultant.com/claimapp*.

3. The first time you access the workplace, you will need to log on. Log on to the app by using a domain account, such as tedb@pocket-consultant.com.

To connect to a workplace by using an iOS device, follow these steps:

1. In Safari, enter the URL for the app you want to use, such as *https://corpservices pocket-consultant.com/claimapp*.

2. The first time you access the workplace, you will need to log on. Log on to the app by using a domain account, such as tedb@pocket-consultant.com.

The browser will maintain the credentials in its credentials cache and you will only need to log on again if the credentials are removed or changed.

Wireless networking

To make it easier for users to take their mobile devices with them to meetings and to other locations in the office, many organizations have wireless networks. Wireless networks can be deployed and used in many different configurations. This section examines the most common configurations.

Wireless network devices and technologies

When you are working with wireless networks, the most common terms you'll run across are *wireless network adapter* and *wireless access point*. Wireless adapters include PC cards for laptops, Peripheral Component Interconnect (PCI) cards for desktops, and USB devices (which can be used with laptops or desktops). However, most of today's mobile devices have the wireless adapter built in. A wireless adapter uses a built-in antenna to communicate with an access point. Typically, an access point is directly connected to the organization's physical network and might also function as a network switch or hub itself, meaning it has physical ports that enable direct cable connections in addition to wireless connections. Other names for access points include wireless base stations and wireless gateways.

The most widely used wireless network adapters and access points are based on the IEEE 802.11 specification. Wireless devices that are based on this specification can be Wi-Fi certified to show that they have been thoroughly tested for performance and compatibility. Table 10-3 compares the features of the current wireless technologies based on IEEE 802.11, including 802.11ac, which is newly supported in Windows 8.1. As shown in the table, each standard has its benefits and drawbacks. It should be noted that 802.11a is not included in the table, because the standard has largely been supplanted by 802.11b, 802.11g, and other more current standards.

TABLE 10-3 Wireless networking technologies

	WIRELESS STANDARD			
FEATURES	802.11B	802.11G	802.11N	802.11AC
Speed	Up to 11 Mbps	Up to 54 Mbps	Up to 540 Mbps	Up to 1.35 Gbps
Transmission frequency	2.4 GHz	2.4 GHz	2.4 GHz, 5 GHz, or both	5 GHz
Effective indoor range	Approximately 100 to 150 feet	Approximately 100 to 150 feet	Approximately 200 to 300 feet	Approximately 200 to 300 feet
Compatibility	Can interoperate with 802.11g devices (at 11 Mbps); 802.11g wireless adapters can operate with 802.11b access points (at 11 Mbps)	Can operate with 802.11b devices (at 11 Mbps)	Can operate with 802.11b devices (at 11 Mbps) and 802.11g devices (at 54 Mbps)	Backward compatible with 802.11n and 802.11a devices

Newer 802.11 transmission specifications include 802.11n and 802.11ac. 802.11n offers speeds up to 540 megabits per second (Mbps) and can interoperate with devices that use 802.11b and 802.11g. 802.11ac offers speeds up to 1.3 gigabits per second (Gbps) and can interoperate with devices that use 802.11n and 802.11a. To achieve high transmission speeds, 802.11n and 802.11ac can use multiple receivers and multiple transmitters. Each transmitter can transmit one or more streams of data. The more streams of data that a device can use across all transmitters and receivers, the higher the throughput. However, many standard 802.11n and 802.11ac devices with multiple transmitters and receivers combine strong, weak, and reflected signals into one data stream to maximize the range. 802.11ac can be more

reliable over longer distances that other technologies because the technology provides directional signal transmission and reception. Thus, unlike other standards, which use omnidirectional signals that are transmitted indiscriminately in every possible direction, 802.11ac transmitters can determine the relative direction of a receiver and strengthen the signal in that direction.

For added security, IEEE has defined the 802.11i standard. Unlike the 802.11b, 802.11g, 802.11n, and 802.11ac standards, the 802.11i standard isn't about transmission speeds and frequencies. 802.11i is a security standard that you can add to the existing standards. More specifically, it adds security functionality to the radio specifications of 802.11a, 802.11b, 802.11g, and 802.11n. This means that 802.11a network adapters and access points can include the 802.11i security functionality, as can 802.11b, 802.11g, and 802.11n wireless products.

NOTE Keep in mind that some computers (particularly mobile devices) contain integrated chip sets that support multiple wireless networking technologies. Wi-Fi Protected Access 2 (WPA2) is the approved Wi-Fi Alliance implementation of 802.11i. WPA2 implements all mandatory elements of the 802.11i standard.

REAL WORLD Take a close look at compatibility issues before you deploy wireless devices that aren't based on IEEE 802.11. Increasingly, you'll notice devices that achieve high speeds. Some of these devices achieve speed boosts through compression and other similar techniques while staying within the guidelines of the IEEE 802.11 specification. Others might use network technologies that are proprietary, requiring you to use that company's wireless adapters and access points to achieve the transmission improvements. For more information on wireless standards and certified devices, go to *www.wi-fi.org*.

Wireless security

Securing a wireless network is very different from securing a wired network. With a wired network, a cable is used to connect a computer to the network. A user must use a cable to be physically connected to the network and must have access to one of your internal switches or hubs. If an unauthorized person connects a machine to the network, it is fairly easy to determine this and trace the physical cable to the intruder's computer.

When you install wireless networking, anyone within range of one of your wireless access points has access to your network. Not only can they intercept the wireless signals that are being broadcast, they can also try to crack into the network. The bad news is that it is difficult to locate the intruder because there's no physical wire to trace. The really bad news is that if intruders can gain access to a wireless access point, they are usually inside your organization's firewall. To protect the network, you should configure its firewall, if one is available, and configure the wireless devices to encode all wireless transmissions.

The most basic wireless encryption scheme is Wired Equivalent Privacy (WEP). With WEP, you encrypt data by using 40-bit, 128-bit, 152-bit, or higher private key encryption. With WEP, all data is encrypted by using a symmetric key derived from the WEP key or password before it is transmitted, and any computer that wants to read the data must be able to decrypt it by using the key. In a typical wired environment, the shared key encryption alone is sufficient to safeguard your data. In a wireless environment with high traffic volume, it is possible that someone could successfully break the shared key, and because the shared key doesn't change automatically over time, the intruder would then have access to your organization's internal network.

Because WEP provides only the most basic security, its use is strongly discouraged except in cases in which no alternative exists. The preferred alternatives to WEP are Wi-Fi Protected Access (WPA) and WPA2. WPA was adopted by the Wi-Fi Alliance as an interim standard prior to the ratification of 802.11i. WPA2 is based on the official 802.11i standard and is fully backward compatible with WPA.

WPA and WPA2 are able to rotate keys for added security and to change the way in which keys are derived. By changing the encryption keys over time and ensuring that they aren't derived in one specific way, WPA and WPA2 can improve security significantly over WEP. WPA-compatible and WPA2-compatible devices can operate in enterprise mode or in a personal, home/small office configuration, as explained in the following points:

- Enterprise mode provides authentication by using IEEE 802.1X and EAP. In the enterprise mode, wireless devices have two sets of keys: session keys and group keys. Session keys are unique to each association between an access point and a wireless client. They are used to create a private virtual port between the access point and the client. Group keys are shared among all clients connected to the same access point. Both sets of keys are generated dynamically and are rotated to help safeguard the integrity of keys over time.

- Personal mode provides authentication via a preshared key or password. In a personal, home/small office configuration, WPA uses a preshared encryption key rather than a changing encryption key. Here, the user enters a master key (the group key) into the access point and then configures all the other wireless devices to use this master key. A wireless device uses the master key as a starting point to generate the session key mathematically. It then regularly changes the session key so that the same session key is never used twice. Because the key rotation is automatic, key management is handled in the background.

- WPA and WPA2 are fully compatible with 802.11a, 802.11b, 802.11g, and 802.11n. Many wireless devices that shipped before WPA and WPA2 became available can be made fully compatible with WPA and WPA2 through a software upgrade. With WPA, no additional modifications are necessary. The same is not necessarily true with WPA2, because some wireless devices might require processor or other hardware upgrades to be able to perform the computationally intensive Advanced Encryption Standard (AES) encryption.

When working with WPA and WPA2, keep the following in mind:

- All products that are Wi-Fi certified for WPA2 are interoperable with products that are Wi-Fi certified for WPA.
- Both WPA and WPA2 have personal and enterprise modes of operation.
- Both WPA and WPA2 use 802.1X and EAP for authentication.
- WPA provides strong data encryption via Temporal Key Integrity Protocol (TKIP).
- WPA2 provides enhanced data encryption via AES, which makes it possible for WPA2 to meet the Federal Information Processing Standard (FIPS) 140-2 requirement of some government agencies.

NOTE Both WPA and WPA2 offer a high level of security to help ensure that private data remains private and that access to wireless networks is restricted to authorized users. Only WPA2 provides strong encryption through AES, which is a requirement for some corporate and government users.

Another advanced wireless security technology is Robust Security Network (RSN), which is supported by 802.11i-compatible devices. RSN enables wireless devices to negotiate their authentication and encryption algorithms dynamically. This means that the authentication and encryption algorithms used by RSN-compatible devices can be changed. New authentication techniques and algorithms can be added to address security issues. RSN is based on EAP and AES.

Installing and configuring a wireless adapter

Other than mobile devices with built-in wireless adapters, the two main types of wireless adapters you'll use are PC cards for laptops and PCI cards for desktops. These adapters are the easiest to configure—and I've found them to be the most reliable. The other type of wireless adapter that you might encounter is a device that connects to a laptop or desktop computer with a USB cable. When using USB wireless devices, keep in mind that there are several USB specifications, including USB 2.0 and USB 3.0, the faster, newer specification. A wireless device that complies with USB 3.0 must be connected to a USB 3.0 port to function properly and at the speeds you expect.

As part of the installation process, most installation software will help you configure the wireless device. In the process, you might need to specify the name of the wireless network to which you want to connect and the mode in which the wireless device will run. Wireless adapters can run in one of two operating modes:

- **Ad hoc** In ad hoc mode, you configure the wireless adapter to connect directly to other computers with wireless adapters.
- **Infrastructure** In infrastructure mode, you configure the wireless adapter for use on a wireless network. In this configuration, the adapter expects to connect to an access point rather than to another computer directly.

After you specify the adapter mode, you might need to specify the encryption key that will be used. If your organization uses WEP security, in most cases you will have to enter the required encryption key, which is usually referred to as the *network key*. With WPA/WPA2 security, you most often use a certificate or a smart card to supply the required encryption key.

Working with wireless networks and wireless connections

After you've completed the installation of the device, you should be able to connect over the wireless network. Much like a wired network card, which has an Ethernet connection, a wireless network card has a Wi-Fi connection that is in turn connected to a specific network that is designated as a public network, private network, or domain network. If a computer has both a wired and a wireless connection, it might have two active connections: one to a wired network and one to a wireless network.

Wi-Fi connections provide the following additional details about the network and the connection:

- The name of the wireless network in parentheses after the connection type designator
- The current signal strength (signal strength of one bar is poor; signal strength of five bars is excellent)
- A Disconnect link for disconnecting the wireless connection

To view the settings for a wireless connection, complete these steps:

1. In Control Panel, tap or click View Network Status And Tasks under the Network And Internet heading.
2. In the left pane in Network And Sharing Center, tap or click Change Adapter Settings.
3. Network Connections displays a list of all network connections configured for use on the computer. Press and hold or right-click the wireless connection with which you want to work, and then tap or click Properties.
4. You'll get a dialog box similar to the one shown in Figure 10-11. You can use the Wi-Fi Status dialog box to check the status of the connection and to maintain the connection, in much the same way as you can for other types of connections. The duration and speed of the connection is also displayed.

FIGURE 10-11 Determine the status and signal strength of a wireless network connection.

As with Ethernet connections, Wi-Fi connections have configurable properties. This means that every discussion about configuring network connection properties also applies to Wi-Fi connections. You can do the following:

- Install and uninstall networking features for clients, services, and protocols. In the Wi-Fi Status dialog box, tap or click Wireless Properties, and then tap or click Install or Uninstall as appropriate.

- Set TCP/IPv6 and TCP/IPv4 settings for DHCP, static IP, and dynamic IP addressing. In the Wi-Fi Status dialog box, tap or click Properties, and then double-tap or double-click Internet Protocol Version 6 (TCP/IPv6) or Internet Protocol Version 4 (TCP/IPv4).

- Disable or diagnose wireless connections. In the Wi-Fi Status dialog box, tap or click Disable or Diagnose as appropriate.

If you have problems establishing a wireless connection and automated diagnostics can't resolve the problem, use these tips to help you troubleshoot:

- **Problem:** Limited or no connectivity to the wireless network.

  Resolution: Check the signal strength. If the signal strength is low (poor), you need to move closer to the access point or redirect your antenna. For a built-in antenna, you might need to change the position of the mobile device relative to the access point. The problem could also be that the network did not connect and configure network addressing properly. To check the connection state, tap or click the connection link in Network And Sharing Center, and then review the connection status in the Status dialog box. If the media state is not set to Enabled, tap or click Diagnose to try to resolve the problem by using automatic network diagnostics.

- **Problem:** Not connected or unable to connect to the wireless network.

   Resolution: If you are out of the broadcast area, your computer will not be able to connect to the wireless network. Tap or click the Network notification icon on the taskbar. The computer will display the Networks sidebar, where you can determine whether networks are available and in range. You also can verify that Airplane Mode is turned off. No connections are possible when Airplane Mode is enabled. To connect to a Wi-Fi network, tap or click a connection, and then tap or click Connect. If you are unable to connect to the network or don't find the network in the list, try moving closer to the access point or changing the position of your antenna or computer relative to the access point. The computer also might not be configured properly for establishing a wireless connection on this network.

TIP   You'll have better connection speeds—up to the maximum possible with the wireless technology you are using—when you have a stronger signal. If the signal strength is weak, the connection speed might be reduced considerably. To improve the signal strength, try moving the adapter's antenna (if one is available) or try changing the position of the computer relative to the access point.

Connecting to wireless networks

Any wireless access point broadcasting within range should be available to a computer with a wireless adapter. By default, Windows 8.1 automatically determines the appropriate settings. If a connection requires a password or other credentials, you are prompted for the credentials when you try to connect to the wireless network. You can also preconfigure wireless connections for users. This enables you to configure different authentication, encryption, and communication options as necessary.

   You can preconfigure a connection for a wireless network by completing the following steps:

1. In Network And Sharing Center, tap or click Set Up A New Connection Or Network. This starts the Set Up A Connection Or Network Wizard.

2. Select Manually Connect To A Wireless Network, and then tap or click Next. You now need to enter information about the wireless network to which you want to connect. Your network administrator should have this information.

3. In the Network Name box, enter the network name (also referred to as the network's secure identifier, or service set identifier [SSID]).

4. Use the Security Type list to select the type of security being used. The encryption type is then filled in automatically for you.

5. With WEP and WPA-Personal, you must enter the required security key or password phrase in the Security Key box. For example, a WEP key typically is one of the following:

   - 5 case-sensitive characters
   - 13 case-sensitive characters
   - 10 hexadecimal, case-insensitive characters
   - 26 hexadecimal, case-insensitive characters

6. By default, the connection is started automatically whenever the user logs on. If you also want the computer to connect to the network regardless of whether the network can be reached—for example, when the computer is out of range of the wireless base—select Connect Even If The Network Is Not Broadcasting. If you don't select this option, the connection is listed on the Networks panel only when the network is within range and broadcasting its SSID.

7. Tap or click Next, and then tap or click Close.

Typically, when you are within the broadcast range of a wireless network, you won't need to preconfigure a connection and can instead connect directly, letting Windows determine the correct settings. To connect to a wireless network, complete the following steps:

1. Tap or click the Network notification icon on the taskbar; or slide in from the right side of the screen, tap Settings, and then tap the Network icon.

2. On the Networks panel, under the Wi-Fi heading, available wireless networks are listed by name, status, and signal strength.

3. You can now connect to or disconnect from a wireless network:

    ■ To connect to a wireless network, select the network, and then tap or click Connect.

    ■ To disconnect from a wireless network, select the network, and then tap or click Disconnect.

Managing and troubleshooting wireless networking

You can manage wireless networks by using the Network panel. If you press and hold or right-click a wireless connection, you have additional management options:

■ **Show Estimated Data Usage**   Shows the estimated amount of data transferred over the connection. Tap or click Reset to reset the data usage counter.

■ **Set As Metered Connection**   Specifies that the connection is metered, so that Windows 8.1 applies rules and policies for metered connections.

■ **Set As Non-Metered Connection**   Specifies that the connection is not metered, so that Windows 8.1 no longer applies rules and policies for metered connections.

■ **Forget This Network**   Removes a saved connection from the list of available connections. This is useful if a manually created connection is no longer needed.

■ **Turn Sharing On Or Off**   Enables you to specify whether you want to turn on sharing between computers and connect to devices on this network.

■ **View Connection Properties**   Opens the Properties dialog box for the connection with the Security tab selected. This provides a quick way to view or modify the security settings.

Windows 8.1 includes many tools for troubleshooting and testing network connectivity. The "Troubleshooting and testing network settings" section in Chapter 9, "Configuring and troubleshooting TCP/IP networking," discusses techniques for diagnosing and resolving network issues. On wireless networks, you'll encounter similar issues. In addition to reviewing those troubleshooting techniques, you'll also want to do the following:

- Review the security configuration for the wireless network and check that the settings are correct. Reenter the security key or passphrase.

- Ensure that the wireless device is positioned correctly and within range of the wireless access point. You might want to try moving the computer closer to the access point.

- Ensure that there is no interference from other devices that use the same transmission range or from other devices that create magnetic fields. You might want to move or turn off devices that could be causing interference.

Index

Symbols and Numbers

About the author

William Stanek (*www.williamstanek.com*) is the award-winning author and series editor of the bestselling Pocket Consultant series. William is one of the world's leading technology experts and has more than 20 years of hands-on experience with advanced programming and development. Over the years, his practical advice has helped millions of programmers, developers, and network engineers all over the world. Dubbed "A Face Behind the Future" in 1998 by *The Olympian*, William has been helping to shape the future of the written word for more than two decades. William's 150th book was published in 2013, and more than 7.5 million people have read his many works. William's current books include *Windows Server 2012 Inside Out,* and the *Pocket Consultants* for Exchange Server 2013, Windows Server 2012 R2, and Windows 8.1.

William has been involved in the commercial Internet community since 1991. His core business and technology experience comes from more than 11 years of military service. He has substantial experience in developing server technology, encryption, and Internet solutions. He has written many technical white papers and training courses on a wide variety of topics. He frequently serves as a subject matter expert and consultant.

William has an MS with distinction in information systems, and a BS in computer science, magna cum laude. He is proud to have served in the Persian Gulf War as a combat crew member on an electronic warfare aircraft. He flew on numerous combat missions into Iraq and was awarded nine medals for his wartime service, including one of the United States of America's highest flying honors, the Air Force Distinguished Flying Cross. Currently, he resides in the Pacific Northwest with his wife and children.

William recently rediscovered his love of the great outdoors. When he's not writing, he can be found hiking, biking, backpacking, traveling, or trekking in search of adventure with his family!

Find William on Twitter at WilliamStanek and on Facebook at *www.facebook.com/William.Stanek.Author.* Please visit *www.Pocket-Consultant.com* to find links to stay in touch with William.

Now that you've read the book...

Tell us what you think!

Was it useful?
Did it teach you what you wanted to learn?
Was there room for improvement?

Let us know at http://aka.ms/tellpress

Your feedback goes directly to the staff at Microsoft Press,
and we read every one of your responses. Thanks in advance!